Texts in Philosophy
Volume 26

Karl Popper

A Centenary Assessment

Volume III

Science

Texts in Philosophy Series Editors
Vincent F. Hendriks   vincent@hum.ku.dk
John Symons   jsymons@utep.edu
Dov Gabbay   dov.gabbay@kcl.ac.uk

Karl Popper

A Centenary Assessment

Volume III

Science

Edited by

Ian Jarvie

Karl Milford

and

David Miller

This edition is a reprint of the Ashgate edition of 2006.

ISBN 978-1-84890-192-6

College Publications
Scientific Director: Dov Gabbay
Managing Director: Jane Spurr

http://www.collegepublications.co.uk

Original cover design by Laraine Welch

Printed by Lightning Source, Milton Keynes, UK

Contents

C   Biology

D   Social Sciences

List of Tables

Preface

For five warm summer days (3-7 July 2002), more than 300 people from more than 50 countries attended KARL POPPER 2002, a congress held in Vienna to commemorate the 100th anniversary of Popper's birth (28 July 1902). The principal activity at the meetings held in the main building of the University of Vienna, his alma mater, was, in keeping with Popper's outlook, critical engagement with his intellectual achievement in the many fields to which he contributed. Besides the investigation, development, and critical assessment of Popper's ideas, participants were able to enjoy a walking tour of Vienna sites relevant to Popper's early career, a recital of his organ fugue at the church of St Michael in Heiligenstadt, an exhibition at the Palais Palffy of his life and work, the unveiling of a bronze bust in the *Arkadenhof* in the University main building, and the opening ceremony at the City Hall (*Rathaus*) at which the Honorary President of the Congress, Professor Dr Hans Albert, gave the Inaugural Address. There was also an excursion after the congress to the University at Klagenfurt, where Popper's working library is housed.

The three volumes are a selection from more than 200 invited lectures and contributed papers presented at Vienna. The cull was made as follows. Chairs of sessions and members of the programme committee made an initial selection based upon what they had heard and read. Contributions planned for publication elsewhere were excluded. Every selected paper was sent to two referees. Authors made their final revisions in the light of the referees' reports. We are grateful to those who shortened their papers on request.

The present volume is devoted to papers on the various sciences to which Popper contributed (logic, physics, biology, the social sciences). Volume I contains papers on Popper's life and influence, and on democracy and the open society. Volume II contains papers on his metaphysics and epistemology.

The notes on the contributors and editors have been revised for this edition. The text of the volume is otherwise identical with that of the Ashgate edition of 2006, except for the correction of a few typographical and linguistic errors, some amendments to the index, and some inconsequential formatting changes.

KARL POPPER 2002 was more than six years in the planning. Many were involved in its organization, but it would not have taken place without the heroic efforts of Heidi König in Vienna. The editors should like to thank, in addition, the speakers, chairs, and referees, and Mrs Melitta Mew and the Karl Popper Charitable Trust. All royalties earned by these three volumes will go to the Trust.

Ian Jarvie
Karl Milford
David Miller

Notes on the Contributors

(*revised 2016*)

Manuel Bächtold, was awarded a Diploma in Physics by the Swiss Federal Institute of Technology, Lausanne, and a PhD in Philosophy by the University of Paris I. He works currently as Maître de conférences - membre du LIRDEF, équipe ERES at the University of Montpellier. Book: *Linterprétation de la mécanique quantique, une approche pragmatiste*. Paris: Hermann, 2009. E-mail: `manuel.bachtold@fde.univ-montp2.fr`

Daniela M. Bailer-Jones † led a project at the University of Heidelberg on Causality, Cognition, and the Constitution of Natural Phenomena. At the University of Cambridge she completed an MPhil in physics in 1993 and a PhD in philosophy of science in 1997, and she worked or did research at the Universities of Paderborn, Bonn, and Pittsburgh. She died in 2006.

Lawrence A. Boland teaches economics and methodology at Simon Fraser University. He has published seven books on economic methodology — the most recent are *The Foundations of Economic Methodology: Popperian Perspectives*, Routledge 2003, and *Model Building in Economics: Its Purposes and Limitations*, Cambridge 2014. The other five can be downloaded at `www.sfu.ca/~boland/`. E-mail: `boland@sfu.ca`

Boudewijn de Bruin is Professor in the Faculties of Economics and Business, and of Philosophy, University of Groningen. He obtained his PhD from the Institute for Logic, Language, and Computation in Amsterdam with a dissertation on the logic of game-theoretic explanations. Research interests are Wittgensteins philosophy of mathematics, philosophy of the social sciences, social ontology, logic, and epistemology. His current projects include ethics and stereotyping. Book: *Ethics and the Global Financial Crisis: Why Incompetence is Worse than Greed*, Cambridge 2015. E-mail: `B.P.de.Bruin@rug.nl`

Josep Corcó graduated in Philosophy (1989) and obtained his PhD (1995) at the University of Navarre (Pamplona) with a dissertation about Karl Popper's cosmovision. Since 1997 he has taught philosophy at Universitat Internacional de Catalunya (Barcelona). His current research is focused on the relationship between science and society. E-mail: `jcorco@uic.es`

Maria Luisa Dalla Chiara is Emerita Professor of Philosophy of Science at the University of Florence. She is a Past President of the International Quantum Structure Association and of the Società Italiana di Logica e Filosofia delle Scienze. Her recent research mainly concerns philosophy of physics, quantum logic, and quantum computation. E-mail: `dallachiara@unifi.it`

Melis Erdur received her undergraduate degrees in philosophy and mathematics, her master's degree in philosophy, from Bogazici University, Istanbul, and her PhD from New York University. In 2014-2015 she was a postdoctoral fellow at the Edmond J. Safra Center for Ethics at the University of Tel Aviv. Her main areas of interest are epistemology and meta-ethics. E-mail: `meliser@post.tau.ac.il`

Michael Esfeld is Professor of Epistemology and Philosophy of Science at the University of Lausanne. His main area of research is the metaphysics of science, in particular the philosophy of physics. In 2008 he received the Cogito award for the dialogue between human and natural sciences, and in 2012 the Research Award of the Alexander von Humboldt Foundation. Since 2010, he has been a Fellow of Leopoldina, the National Academy of Germany. E-mail: `Michael-Andreas.Esfeld@unil.ch`

Mathias Frisch is Associate Professor of Philosophy at the University of Maryland, College Park. His book *Inconsistency, Asymmetry, and Non-Locality*, Oxford 2005, examines philosophical issues in classical electrodynamics, including the source of the temporal asymmetry of wave and radiation phenomena. E-mail: `mfrisch@umd.edu`

Steve Fuller is Auguste Comte Professor of Social Epistemology at the University of Warwick. His recent books include *Science: The Art of Living*, Acumen and McGill–Queens University Press, 2010; *Humanity 2.0: What It Means to Be Human in the Past, Present and Future*, Palgrave Macmillan, 2011; *Preparing for Life in Humanity 2.0*, Palgrave Macmillan, 2012; *The Proactionary Imperative: A Foundation for Transhumanism* (with Veronika Lipinska), Palgrave Macmillan, 2014; *Knowledge: The Philosophical Quest in History*, Routledge 2015. E-mail: `S.W.Fuller@warwick.ac.uk`

Roberto Giuntini is Professor of Logic and Philosophy of Science in the Faculty of Education at the University of Cagliari. His main research publications are in quantum theory and quantum logic. E-mail: `giuntini@unica.it`

Eduard Glas is Associate Professor of Mathematics and Philosophy of Mathematics at Delft University of Technology. E-mail: `e.glas@tudelft.nl`

Evelyn Gröbl-Steinbach (Schuster) is Professor of Social Philosophy and Political Theory at the Johannes Kepler University in Linz. She was vice-president of the Austrian Society for Philosophy from 1998 to 2000. She is working on neo-pragmatism, critical theory, critical rationalism, and ethics. She has published many papers on the philosophy of Habermas. E-mail: `evelyn.schuster@jku.at`

Maurice Lagueux is Associate Professor of Philosophy at the University of Montreal. His research interests are economic methodology, the philosophy of history, and the philosophy of architecture. He has published papers in journals such as *Journal of Economic Methodology, Economics and Philo-*

sophy, Theory and Decision, and *Philosophy of the Social Sciences.* E-mail: maurice.lagueux@umontreal.ca

Allan Megill is Professor of History at the University of Virginia. He has co-edited (with John Nelson and Donald McCloskey) *The Rhetoric of the Human Sciences,* University of Wisconsin Press 1987, has edited *Rethinking Objectivity,* Duke 1994, and has written *Prophets of Extremity,* California 1985, *Karl Marx: The Burden of Reason,* Rowman & Littlefield 2002, and *Historical Knowledge: Historical Error,* University of Chicago Press 2007. E-mail: megill@virginia.edu

David Miller. See NOTES ON THE EDITORS on p. xv below.

Thomas Mormann studied mathematics, linguistics, and philosophy and obtained a PhD in mathematics. He has written numerous articles on philosophy of science, philosophy of Logical Empiricism, and neo-Kantianism. He has edited *Scheinprobleme in der Philosophie und andere metaphysikkritische Schriften,* Meiner 2005, a volume of Carnap's early unpublished antimetaphysical writings. E-mail: ylxmomot@sf.ehu.es

Peter Munz † was born in Germany, and educated in Italy. A historian of the early middle ages, he studied philosophy under both Popper and Wittgenstein. Emeritus Professor of History, Victoria University, Wellington. Author of numerous books on medieval history, the philosophy of history, philosophy of religion, and modern philosophy. He died in 2006.

Andrés Rivadulla is Professor of Philosophy of Science at the Universidad Complutense, Madrid. He has published four books in Spanish on general philosophy of science, the philosophy of probability, and the history and philosophy of physics, which constitute his research fields. He has also contributed to international collective works and journals, such as *The British Journal for the Philosophy of Science, Erkenntnis,* and *Synthese.* E-mail: arivadulla@filos.ucm.es

Jacob Rosenthal graduated with a diploma in mathematics from the University of Würzburg. He obtained a PhD in philosophy from the University of Konstanz with a thesis on objective interpretations of probability statements. He is currently at the University of Konstanz, where he teaches philosophy of science and ethics. Book: *Handlung, Rationalität und Determinismus. Überarbeitete Habilitationsschrift, erscheint in der Reihe Ideen und Argumente,* De Gruyter 2015. E-mail: Jacob.Rosenthal@uni-konstanz.de

Peter Schroeder-Heister is Professor of Logic and Philosophy of Language at the University of Tübingen, holding a joint appointment in philosophy and computer science. His main area of interest is general proof theory and its application to questions of meaning, validity, consequence, and computation. He is interested also in the history of these fields, in particular in the development of Gentzen-type systems. E-mail: psh@informatik.uni-tuebingen.de

Renan Springer de Freitas is Associate Professor of Sociology at the Federal University of Minas Gerais (Belo Horizonte). He has published *Sociology of Knowledge, Pragmatism and Evolutionary Thought* (in Portuguese), EDUSC 2003, as well as articles on this subject in *Philosophy of the Social Sciences*, one of which has been translated into Japanese. E-mail: `springer@netuno.lcc.ufmg.br`

Joanna Swann is a philosopher of education with a particular interest in learning and method. Recent publications include *Learning, Teaching and Education Research in the 21st Century: An Evolutionary Analysis of the Role of Teachers* (Continuum 2012). She retired in 2012 from her position as Principal Lecturer in Education Studies at the University of Brighton. E-mail: `joannaswann@yahoo.co.uk`

Shijun Tong is Professor of Philosophy at East China Normal University (ECNU), and Vice-President of the Shanghai Academy of Social Sciences (SASS). Among his numerous works are *Western Philosophy at the Times of Marx and Engels* (in Chinese, co-authored, 1994, Shanghai) and (in English) *Dialectics of Modernization: Habermas and the Chinese Discourse of Modernization*, Wild Peony (Sydney) 2000. He is also the Chinese translator of Jürgen Habermas's *Faktizität und Geltung*, Beijing 2003. E-mail: `tongsj@yahoo.com`

Kei Yoshida is Assistant Professor at the Faculty of Social Sciences, Waseda University, Tokyo. He specializes in the philosophy of science and the philosophy of the social sciences. He is the author of *Rationality and Cultural Interpretivism: A Critical Assessment of Failed Solutions*, Lexington Books 2014. E-mail: `kei.yoshida@gmail.com`

Notes on the Editors

(*revised 2016*)

Ian Jarvie (editor in chief) is Distinguished Research Professor in Philosophy (Emeritus) at York University, Toronto, and Managing Editor of the journal *Philosophy of the Social Sciences*. His books include *The Revolution in Anthropology*, Routledge 1964; *Philosophy of the Film*, Routledge 1987; and *The Republic of Science*, Rodopi 2001. E-mail: `jarvie@yorku.ca`

Karl Milford is Associate Professor of Economics at the University of Vienna. He has written extensively on the epistemological views of Carl Menger, for example in *Zu den Lösungsversuchen des Induktions und Abgrenzungsproblems bei Carl Menger*, Verlag der Österreichischen Akademie der Wissenschaften 1989. E-mail: `karl.milford@univie.ac.at`

David Miller is Emeritus Reader in Philosophy at the University of Warwick, where he taught logic (and some other things) from 1969 until 2007. He is the editor of *Popper Selections*, Princeton 1985, and author of *Critical Rationalism. A Restatement and Defence*, Open Court 1994, and of *Out of Error. Further Essays on Critical Rationalism*, Ashgate 2006. Web site: `http://www.warwick.ac.uk/go/dwmiller`; E-mail: `dwmiller57@yahoo.com`

PART 4
Science

A: Mathematics and Logic

Truthlikeness for Theories on Countable Languages*

Thomas Mormann

1 Introduction

With only slight oversimplification one may assert that the various theories of truthlikeness are governed by a single guiding metaphor: Truth, or better, the true theory W, is conceptualized as being located in a logical space of theories in such a way that the difference between W and a false theory F is a sort of distance between W and F: the larger the distance $d(W, F)$ the more F differs from the whole truth. Indeed Popper, who is considered as one of the founding fathers of a theory of truthlikeness or verisimilitude, seems to have been captivated by the above mentioned spatial metaphor when in *Conjectures and Refutations* he asked the question (1963, Chapter 10, § x):

> Is it not dangerously misleading to talk as if Tarskian truth were located some-where in a kind of metrical or at least topological space so that we can sensibly say of two theories — say an earlier theory t_1 and a later theory t_2, that t_2 has superseded t_1, or progressed beyond t_1, by approaching more closely to the truth than t_1?
>
> I do not think that this kind of talk is at all misleading. On the contrary, I believe that we simply cannot do without something like this idea of a better or worse approximation to truth.

In order to overcome a merely metaphorical conception of 'distance from the truth', one has to show that for a given logical space of theories one

*I should like to thank two anonymous referees for their very helpful and conscientious comments.

can define a non-trivial metric structure. Or, at least, one has to show that
for general reasons such a metrical structure exists. Popper addressed this
problem properly only for finite logical spaces for propositional theories (cp.
Popper 1976, § 2). In this contribution I should like to argue that Popper was
more right than he might have imagined. Theories on countable languages may
indeed be conceptualized as being located in a metrical space. This thesis is
to be understood literally, not metaphorically. More precisely, I propose to
construct for theories that can be formulated in a countable language L a
logical space $T(L)$ endowed with an appropriate metric that satisfies most of
the structural requirements that have been proposed for such a metric in the
literature. This metric is objective in the sense that it does not depend on
'intuitive' choices but is determined by structural facts, at least to a large
extent. The point at which a conventional choice has to be made can be
determined quite precisely, namely when it comes to the choice of a metric
that is compatible with the 'objective' ordered topological structure.

The outline of the paper is as follows: In the next section we recall the
rudiments of topology, order theory, and metric spaces we need in the following
sections. In particular we state a fundamental theorem of Urysohn–Carruth,
which asserts that under mild restrictions every ordered metrical space can
be assumed to have a metric that is compatible with the order structure. This
theorem will be crucial for the main result of this paper. In § 3 we characterize
the theories $T(L)$ of a language L as the class of deductively closed sets of
the Lindenbaum algebra LINDA(L) of logically equivalent propositions. This
sets the stage for the topological representation of LINDA(L) carried out
in § 4. In § 5 the logical space $T(L)$ of theories, conceived of as a Vietoris
space of closed subsets of the Stone space $ST(L)$ is constructed. Thereby the
Urysohn–Carruth metrization theorem can be used to show that this space
can be endowed with a metric that is adequate for the purposes of truth
approximation. In § 6 some relations between the account of truthlikeness
advocated in this paper and Poincaré's conventionalist stance in geometry
are pointed out.

2   Topology, metric, and order

In this section the basic notions of topology, theory of metric spaces and order structures are recalled that will be needed in the following. This section
can offer only a very brief and incomplete survey. For a more thorough introduction to the topics mentioned in this section the reader is recommended to
consult the literature (Davey & Priestley 1990, James 1999, Nachbin 1965,
Nagata 1985, Niiniluoto 1987, §§ 1.1 and 1.2). Let us start with topology.

Definition 2.1 Let X be a set. A topological structure $\mathcal{O}(X)$ on X is given
by a subset $\mathcal{O}(X) \subseteq \mathcal{P}(X)$ of the power set $\mathcal{P}(X)$ of X that is assumed to
satisfy the following properties:

(i) $\emptyset$ and X belong to $\mathcal{O}(X)$.

(ii)   If A_i is an arbitrary collection of subsets of X belonging to $\mathcal{O}(X)$, then the set-theoretical union $\bigcup A_i$ also is an element of $\mathcal{O}(X)$.

(iii)   If A and B belong to $\mathcal{O}(X)$, then the intersection $A \cap B$ belongs to $\mathcal{O}(X)$.

The elements of $\mathcal{O}(X)$ are called *open sets*. An open set U that contains some element α is called an (open) neighbourhood of α. The set-theoretical complements of open sets are called *closed* sets.[1] The set of closed sets of a topological space $\langle X, \mathcal{O}(X) \rangle$ is denoted by $\mathcal{C}(X)$. Closed sets obey the dual conditions to those of Definition 2.1. Obviously, a topological structure on X is defined by $\mathcal{C}(X)$ as well as by $\mathcal{O}(X)$.

Definition 2.2 Let $\langle X, \mathcal{O}(X) \rangle$ be a topological space. A *base* of the topology $\mathcal{O}(X)$ is a subset B of $\mathcal{O}(X)$ closed under finite intersections, such that any open set is a union of elements of B. A *subbase* of $\mathcal{O}(X)$ is a subset S of $\mathcal{O}(X)$ such that any element of $\mathcal{O}(X)$ is the union of finite intersections of elements of S. Dually, a *closed base* is a subset $D \subseteq \mathcal{C}(X)$ that is closed under finite unions such that any element of $\mathcal{C}(X)$ is an intersection of elements of D. A topological space $\langle X, \mathcal{O}(X) \rangle$ is *second countable* if & only if it has a *countable* base. If $\langle X, \mathcal{O}(X) \rangle$ is a topological space the Cartesian product $X \times X$ is endowed with the topology that has $\{U \times V \mid U, V \in \mathcal{O}(X)\}$ as a base. This topology is called the *product topology* on $X \times X$.

Denote the set of real numbers by $\mathbf{R}$. The standard topology of $\mathbf{R}$ is the topology having as a base the set of open rational intervals $(x, z) := \{y \mid x < y < z\}$. Correspondingly, the class of closed intervals provides a closed base for this topology. With respect to this topology, $\mathbf{R}$ is second countable. More generally, let $\langle X, d \rangle$ be a metrical space, that is, a set X endowed with a real valued function $d : X \times X \longmapsto \mathbf{R}$ satisfying the following axioms:

(1) $d(x, y) \quad \geq \quad 0$

(2) $d(x, y) = 0 \quad \Longleftrightarrow \quad x = y$

(3) $d(x, y) \quad = \quad d(y, x)$

(4) $d(x, z) \quad \leq \quad d(x, y) + d(y, z).$

The metrical space X is rendered a topological space by defining an open base B as follows: $B := \{y \mid d(x, y) < 1/n$ for some $x \in X$ and $n \in \mathbf{N}\}$. In the following, all metric spaces are assumed to be endowed with this topology. There may be different metrics defined on X defining the same topology. Hence, the topological structure of a metrical space does not uniquely determine its metrical structure.

---

[1]One should note that a set may be open and closed. This is only linguistically a paradox. For instance, for every topological space $\langle X, \mathcal{O}(X) \rangle$ the sets $\emptyset$ and X are open and closed. An open and closed set is often called *clopen*.

Definition 2.3 Let $\langle X, \mathcal{O}(X)\rangle$ be a topological space.

(i) X is *Hausdorff* if & only if distinct points α and β have disjoint open neighbourhoods U and V, respectively, that is, U and V are disjoint with $\alpha \in U$ and $\beta \in V$.

(ii) X is *normal* if & only if for disjoint closed sets A and B there are disjoint open sets U and V with $A \subseteq U$ and $B \subseteq V$.

(iii) X is *compact* if & only if every family of open sets A_i such that $X = \bigcup A_i$ has a finite subfamily $A_1, \ldots, A_n$ such that $X = A_1 \cup \cdots \cup A_n$.

The set of real numbers $\mathbf{R}$ endowed with the standard topology is a non-compact normal Hausdorff space. The closed unit interval $[0, 1]$ is a compact Hausdorff space.[2] More generally, metrical spaces are Hausdorff spaces, but they need not be compact. A topological space is *metrizable* if and only if its topology is induced by a metric. That is to say, it has a base defined by some metric. With respect to metrizability we need the following fundamental theorem (cp. Nagata 1985, pp. 253f.):

Theorem 2.4 (Urysohn) A second countable compact Hausdorff space is metrizable.

A refined version of this theorem lies at the heart of the theory of truth approximation to be formulated in this paper. More precisely, it will be shown that the logical space $T(L)$ of theories of a countable language L is a topological space to which a refined version of Theorem 2.4 applies. This refinement concerns logical order. Theories are naturally ordered with respect to logical strength, and somehow or other one has to deal with it. Generally speaking, the interplay between topological, metrical, and order structures turns out to be essential for a working theory of truth approximation. The following definition is useful to fix the relation between topological, metrical, and order structures (cp. Gierz et al. 1980, p. 272):

Definition 2.5 A (partial) order relation on a set X is a binary relation that is reflexive, antisymmetric, and transitive.

(i) A set X endowed with a partial order $\leq$ is called a *poset*.

(ii) A topological space X is a *pospace* (partially ordered space) if and only if X is a poset *and* the order relation $\leq$ is a *closed* set with respect to the product topology on $X \times X$; that is, the set $\{\langle x, y\rangle \mid x, y \in X$ and $x \leq y\}$ is closed in $X \times X$.

Next let us assume that the pospace X is also endowed with a metrical structure d in the sense that the topological structure is induced by a metric d. Then, it is natural to ask how the order structure is related to the metrical structure. Somehow the order structure should respect the metric structure and vice versa. The following definition formulates a reasonable connection between metric and order structure:

---

[2]As is well-known, a compact Hausdorff space is normal.

Definition 2.6 Let X be a poset endowed with a metric d. The metric d is *radially convex* if $x \leq y \leq z$ implies $d(x, y) + d(y, z) = d(x, z)$.

For instance, the standard metric on the real line $\mathbf{R}$ is radially convex. For $n \geq 2$, one may define an order on $\mathbf{R}^n$ by $x \leq z$: if & only if $x_i \leq z_i$ where $x = (x_i)$ and $z = (z_i)$ for each i. With respect to this order the standard Euclidean metric of $\mathbf{R}^n$ is no longer radially convex. A radially convex metric on $\mathbf{R}^n$ is defined by $d(x, y) = \sum |x_i - y_i|/2^i$ for each $x, y \in \mathbf{R}^n$. This metric is equivalent to the standard metric in the sense that it induces the same topology on $\mathbf{R}^n$. Hence, it is natural to ask if each metrical pospace admits a radially convex metric equivalent to the original metric. For compact pospaces, this question is answered in the affirmative by the following theorem of Carruth (1968, p. 229):

Theorem 2.7 (Urysohn–Carruth metrization theorem) A compact pospace X with a metric d has an equivalent metric d^* that is *radially convex*.

The aim of this paper is to show that the logical space $T(L)$ of theories of a countable language L is indeed a compact metric pospace, and therefore may be assumed to have a radially convex metric. As far as I know, the notion of a radially convex metric does not appear in the literature dealing with matters of truth approximation, but related notions have been discussed by several authors. In (1984) Miller develops a pseudo-metrical[3] theory of Boolean algebras $\mathfrak{B}$ that is based on the following two axioms for a real-valued function $d : \mathfrak{B} \times \mathfrak{B} \longmapsto \mathbf{R}$ (ibidem, p. 99):

(0) $$d(x, y) + d(y, z) \geq d(x, z)$$
(1) $$d(x, y) \geq d(zx, zy) + d(x + z, x + y)$$

The inequality (0) is just the familiar 'triangle inequality' for distance functions. The meaning of (1) is more intricate. (1) may be interpreted as the essential link between the lattice structure and the metrical structure. As is shown by Miller, (0) and (1) imply that d is indeed a radially convex pseudo-metric which satisfies some further special properties. On the other hand, it seems that one cannot show that radial convexity entails (1). The relation between Miller's account and the one developed in this paper may roughly described as follows: Miller *assumes* that the Boolean algebra $\mathfrak{B}$ is endowed with a real-valued function d satisfying (0) and (1). Then he shows that this function is a radially convex pseudo-metric. In this paper it is shown that any countable Boolean algebra can be endowed with a radially convex metric. Hence, we show that for countable Boolean algebras Miller's assumption can be partially satisfied.

---

[3] In contrast to a metrical distance function, for a pseudo-metric it may happen that for two distinct elements x and y one has $d(x, y) = 0$. Actually, Miller's account is somewhat more general in that d need not be real-valued, but this is of no concern for the present paper.

3   Theories as deductively closed sets of the Lindenbaum algebra

In this section we begin to build up the logical space of theories formulated in a countable propositional language L. Then the true theory W may be thought to be located in such a way that the 'truthlikeness' of a theory can be conceived as 'distance from the truth'. In order to keep the technical apparatus as lean as possible let us concentrate on theories $F, G, \ldots$ (among them the true theory W) that can be formulated in a classical propositional language L having a countable alphabet. That is to say, the logic of L is classical bivalent logic, L has the usual logical constants $\wedge, \vee, \neg$, and so on, and at most countably many propositional constants $p_1, p_2, \ldots, p_n, \ldots$.[4] The first thing to note is that under these assumptions the class of (finite) well-formed formulas of L is still countable, since finite strings can be coded by natural numbers.[5]

If we want to deal with the logical relations of theories and propositions we need not work with the propositions, that is, the well-formed formulas of L. Rather, we can restrict our attention to the equivalence classes of *logically equivalent* propositions. In other words, we can replace the algebra of well-formed formulas of L by the Lindenbaum algebra LINDA(L):

Definition and Lemma 3.1 Let L be a propositional language of classical logic. Two formulas a and b are said to be logically equivalent if and only if $a \leftrightarrow b$ is a tautology of propositional logic. The set of equivalence classes $[a]$ is denoted by LINDA(L) and is called the Lindenbaum algebra of L. LINDA(L) is a Boolean algebra whose operations are defined by the operations of L:

$$[a] \wedge [b] := [a \wedge b], [a] \vee [b] := [a \vee b], \neg[a] := [\neg a].$$

The order relation $\leq$ of LINDA as a Boolean algebra is just the order of logical consequence. That is to say $[a] \leq [b] := [a] \Rightarrow [b]$. The unit of LINDA(L) is denoted by 1 and the bottom element by 0. For typographical reasons we write in the following 'a' instead of '$[a]$'.

LINDA(L) may be characterized as the algebraic structure that determines the logical relations between propositions, and, as we shall see in a moment, also the logical relations between theories formulated in the language L. Following Tarski, a theory is defined as a set of propositions of L closed under logical consequence. In the language of algebraic logic this can be expressed as follows:

Definition 3.2 Let LINDA(L) be the Lindenbaum algebra of a countable language L. A *theory* F on L is a subset of L that is closed with respect to

---

[4]It may be shown (not in this paper) that the restriction to propositional logic is not necessary. Virtually the same argument goes through for a countable first-order language. Even the assumption of classical logic can be dropped in favour of more general logics that have a well-behaved Lindenbaum algebra. Finally, even the first-order assumption may be weakened, if one is prepared to give up the strict correspondence between the syntactic and the semantic level. The only non-negotiable assumption for the argument of this paper is that the language is countable. In this paper I am content to treat the simplest case, to wit, classical propositional logic with countably many propositional constants.

[5]For a detailed proof see, for example, Dunn & Hardegree (2001), p. 139.

logical consequence. Hence, algebraically, theories are characterized as *filters* of the Boolean lattice LINDA(L), that is, as subsets of LINDA(L) satisfying the following two conditions:

(i) F is upward closed: $a \leq b$ and $a \in F$ implies $b \in F$.

(ii)   If $a, b \in F$, then $a \wedge b \in F$.

The set of theories of L is denoted by $T(L)$. For later use, the following special class of filters will turn out to be important.

(iii) F is a prime filter if & only if $a \vee b \in F$ implies $a \in F$ or $b \in F$.

One may distinguish at least the following three other kinds of theories (or filters):

(iv)$_1$ The theory F is a finitely axiomatizable theory if & only if $F = \{a \mid b \leq a\}$ for some $b \in F$. Such a theory is called the principal filter generated by b.

(iv)$_2$ The theory F is a complete theory if & only if for all $a \in$ LINDA(L) either $a \in F$ or $\neg a \in F$. A complete theory is also called an ultrafilter.[6]

(iv)$_3$ The theory F is consistent if & only if $F \neq$ LINDA(L). The Boolean algebra LINDA(L) is called the trivial filter or the trivial theory on L.

At first glance, it is not at all obvious that complete theories exist. Indeed, the existence of sufficiently many ultrafilters, that is, complete theories, presupposes the validity of the axiom of choice or some similar principle (see Davey & Priestley 1990, Chapter 9). The axiom of choice is assumed throughout the rest of this paper without further mention. Then the true theory W in the sense of Popper may be conceptualized as a distinguished ultrafilter, that is, as a distinguished complete theory W for which either $a \in W$ or $\neg a \in W$ for all $a \in$ LINDA(L).

There is a natural map $r :$ LINDA(L) $\longmapsto T(L)$ defined by $r(a) := \{b \mid a \leq b\}$. In order to render this map order-preserving one defines an order relation $\leq$ on $T(L)$ by $F \leq G := G \subseteq F$. Here, $\subseteq$ is the standard set-theoretical order defined on $T(L)$ due to the fact that filters are subsets of LINDA(L). As is well known, $T(L)$ endowed with this order $\leq$ is not just an ordered structure but is a complete co-Heyting algebra $\langle T(L), \leq \rangle$ (Tarski 1935, Johnstone 1982).[7] Since $r :$ LINDA(L) $\longmapsto T(L)$ is order-preserving, one may consider the order relation $\leq$ on $T(L)$ as a natural generalization of the logical order of propositions of LINDA(L).

For $\langle T(L), \leq \rangle$ one can define a theory of truthlikeness, or, more generally, a qualitative (order-theoretical) theory of theory comparison that is essent-

---

[6]Obviously, the notion of a filter can be defined for general lattices. For Boolean algebras the notions of ultrafilter and prime filter coincide. This does not hold for more general lattices: if LINDA(L) is not Boolean, ultrafilters are prime filters, but the reverse does not hold.

[7]These authors consider the set-theoretical order $\subseteq$ on $T(L)$ that is opposite to the 'logical' order $\leq$. Hence for them, the structure of $T(L)$ is that of a Heyting algebra.

ially equivalent to the 'naive approach' of Kuipers (2002). This can be seen as follows: recall that the intersection $\bigcap F_i$ of an arbitrary family of filters is again a filter. More precisely, it is the supremum of the F_i with respect to the order relation $\leq$. Hence, for any subset $S \subseteq \mathrm{LINDA}(L)$ there is a maximal filter F with $F \leq S$, to wit, the set-theoretical intersection of all filters including S. Hence, for any filter F its quasi-complement $F^{\#}$ is defined by $F^{\#} := \bigcap\{F_i \mid \mathbf{C}F \subseteq F_i\}$, $\mathbf{C}F$ being the set-theoretical complement of F. Moreover, for two filters F and G there is a unique largest filter $F \vee G$ included in both, to wit, the intersection of all filters that include F and G. Hence one may define:

Definition 3.3 Let U, V, and R be theories on L. Then U is at least as close to the target theory R as V is ($U \leq_R V$) if and only if

$$(U \cap R^{\#}) \cup (U^{\#} \cap R) \subseteq (V \cap R^{\#}) \cup (V^{\#} \cap R)$$

This definition corresponds to Kuipers's 'naive approach'. The only difference is that $T(L)$ is not a Boolean algebra of sets but only a complete co-Heyting algebra. This means essentially that the quasi-complement $V^{\#}$ of V satisfies only some weaker versions of the familiar laws of a Boolean complement:

(3.4) $(U \wedge U^{\#})^{\#} = 1$ $U^{\#\#} \leq U$ $U^{\#} = U^{\#\#\#}$

Since Definition 3.3 depends only on the logical structure, one may call it an objective qualitative measure of similarity. Or, in the case the target theory R is the true theory W, the relation $\leq_W$ defines an objective logical measure of truthlikeness.[8] The shortcomings of this 'naive account' are well-known and need not be rehearsed here (cp. Miller 1984, Kuipers 2000, Chapter 10). As an important flaw of Definition 3.3 I take the fact that according to it most theories are not comparable. As will be shown, this shortcoming can be repaired. Any theory of truthlikeness that intends to improve on the naive approach by rendering more theories comparable should preserve the naive account as far as possible; that is, assuming that one has a metric d measuring the distances between theories these distances should be compatible with the logical order relations between theories established by the naive account. In the following it will be shown that this can be achieved by radially convex metrics.

4 The Stone Representation Theorem

In order to endow the set of theories $T(L)$ of L with an appropriate metric, that is, with a metric that respects the existing logical order structure, in this section we are going to construct a faithful topological representation of $T(L)$ as the co-Heyting algebra of closed sets of a topological space. The

---

[8] It should be noted that for Kuipers, though not for Popper or Miller, the true theory W is not an ultrafilter.

underlying set of the topological space to be constructed is the set $ST(L) :=$ $\{F_p \mid Fp$ is a proper prime filter of $\text{LINDA}(L)\}$. The topology on $ST(L)$ is defined by the lattice $\mathcal{C}(ST(L)))$ of closed sets as follows: For every filter $V \in T(L)$ define the range $r(V) \subseteq ST(L)$ by $r(V) := \{F_p \mid V \subseteq F_p\}$. The proof that $\langle r(V), V \in T(L) \rangle$ defines a topology on $ST(L)$ is a routine exercise. More precisely we get:

Theorem 4.1 Let L be a countable language with classical logic. The topological space $\langle ST(L), \mathcal{O}(ST(L)) \rangle$ is a second countable, compact Hausdorff space, and the finitely axiomatizable theories a are represented by the clopen subsets $r(a)$ of $ST(L)$.

Proof: This theorem is nothing but a specialization of the famous Stone Representation Theorem (cp. Halmos 1963, Johnstone 1982) to the case of countable Boolean algebras.

Invoking Theorem 2.4 we get:

Corollary 4.2 The topological space $\langle ST(L), \mathcal{O}(ST(L)) \rangle$ is metrizable.

Let us pause for a moment and take stock of what we have achieved so far. We have shown that by intrinsic logical means, that is, without introducing further primitives, the space of prime theories may be endowed with a metric that is compatible with the underlying topological structure of that space. This metric is in no way unique. Moreover, it is logically rather useless, since evidently all prime theories are logically incompatible. What we should like to have, however, is a metric not only for the rather inaccessible prime theories, but for all theories. This metric should be compatible with the logical relations existing between theories. In the next section, these desiderata are shown to be satisfiable. In order to understand why and how this can be done, it is useful to consider in some more detail the proof of Urysohn's metrization theorem.

The basic idea of the proof is to metrize a given topological space X by showing that it can be embedded in a certain metric space in such a way that this embedding induces a metrical structure on X. Denote by I the closed unit interval $[0, 1]$ endowed with the standard topology. The embedding space just mentioned is the so-called Hilbert cube $I^{\mathbf{N}}$ defined as follows:

Definition 4.3 Let $I := [0, 1]$ be the closed unit interval endowed with the standard metric, that is, $d(x, y) := |x - y|$. Denote the countable product of I with itself by $I^{\mathbf{N}}$. The space $I^{\mathbf{N}}$ is called the *Hilbert cube*. The elements of $I^{\mathbf{N}}$ are countable sequences x of real numbers with $0 \leq x_i \leq 1$. A metric d on $I^{\mathbf{N}}$ is defined by $d(x, y) := \sum d(x_i, y_i)/2^i$. The topology defined by d renders $I^{\mathbf{N}}$ a second countable, compact Hausdorff space.

The embedding of X into $I^{\mathbf{N}}$ is done is the following way: one constructs countably many continuous functions ('Urysohn functions') $f_n : X \longmapsto I$, $n \in \mathbf{N}$, which separate the points of X, in the sense that for distinct points α

and β there is always a function f_n with $f_n(\alpha) \neq f_n(\beta)$. The product function $f = (f_n)_{n \in \mathbf{N}}$ defines an embedding $e : X \longmapsto I^{\mathbf{N}}$ by $e(x) := (f_n(x))_{n \in \mathbf{N}}$. Then the metric structure of the Hilbert cube $I^{\mathbf{N}}$ may then be pulled back by e to X rendering it a metric space:

The metric structure of $ST(L)$ allows us to measure the distance between the points of $ST(L)$, that is, prime theories. This is not very useful in itself, since prime theories are rather elusive entities. What we are interested in, however, is measuring the distances between general theories in such a way that their order relations are respected.

To cope with this task, first note that $I^{\mathbf{N}}$ is not just a metric space but even a pospace with respect to the order relation $\leq$ defined by $x \leq y : x_i \leq y_i$ for all $i \in \mathbf{N}$. Secondly, the metric of Definition 4.3 is radially convex with respect to this order relation. Moreover, it satisfies the condition $d(x,z) \geq d(x \wedge y, y \wedge z) + d(x \vee y, y \vee z)$. In the next section it will be shown that the space of theories $T(L)$ is still a second countable compact Hausdorff space. Hence it can be embedded into the Hilbert cube. Moreover, due to the Urysohn–Carruth metrization theorem this can be done in such a way that the space of theories inherits the radially convex metric of $I^{\mathbf{N}}$.

5 The logical space of theories as a Vietoris space

The final step for constructing a metric suitable for truth approximation is to endow the set of theories, that is, the set $\mathcal{C}(ST(L))$ of closed sets of $ST(L)$ with an appropriate metric, that is, with a metric that respects the existing topology and the order structure on $\mathcal{C}(ST(L))$. Recall that $\mathcal{C}(ST(L))$ can be conceived as an order structure $\langle \mathcal{C}(ST(L)), \leq \rangle$ where $\leq$ is the opposite order to set-theoretical inclusion $\subseteq$.[9] In order to apply the Urysohn–Carruth metrization Theorem 2.4 one has to show that $\langle \mathcal{C}(ST(L)), \leq \rangle$ is a pospace. That is to say, it has to be endowed with a topology, and this topology has to be compatible with the order relation $\leq$ in the sense that the graph of $\leq$ is closed with respect to the product topology of $\mathcal{C}(ST(L)) \times \mathcal{C}(ST(L))$ (see Definition 2.5 (ii)). The recipe for endowing $\mathcal{C}(ST(L))$ with a topological structure may be traced back to Vietoris and Hausdorff in the twenties of the last century. It goes like this.

Theorem 5.1 Assume $\langle X, \mathcal{O}(X) \rangle$ to be a second countable compact Hausdorff space. Denote the set of closed subsets of X by $\mathcal{C}(X)$, and define a set of subsets of $\mathcal{C}(X)$ by

$$t(U) \quad := \quad \{F \mid F \in \mathcal{C}(X) \text{ and } F \subseteq U\}$$
$$m(U) \quad := \quad \{F \mid F \in \mathcal{C}(X) \text{ and } F \cap U \neq \emptyset\}$$

where U ranges over all open subsets of X. Then $\{t(U) \mid U \in \mathcal{O}(X)\} \cup \{m(U) \mid U \in \mathcal{O}(X)\}$ defines a subbase of a second countable compact Hausdorff

---

[9]We rely on the opposite order so as to have the map LINDA $\mapsto$ ST(LINDA) an order preserving map instead of a order reversing one.

topology on $\mathcal{C}(X)$. The set $\mathcal{C}(X)$ endowed with this topology is called the *Vietoris* space of $\langle \mathcal{C}(X), \mathcal{O}(\mathcal{C}(X)) \rangle$ of X.

With respect to the natural order of set-theoretical inclusion $\subseteq$ of closed subsets of X the Vietoris space $\mathcal{C}(X)$ can be conceived as an order structure. Using the following elementary reformulation of the concept of a pospace (cp. Gierz et al. 1980, p. 273) one can show that it is indeed a pospace:

Theorem 5.2 Let $\langle X, \leq \rangle$ be a poset with topology $\mathcal{O}(X)$. X is a pospace if & only if whenever $a, b \in X$ and NOT $(a \leq b)$, there exist open sets $U, V \in O(X)$ with $a \in U$ and $b \in V$ such that if $x \in U$ and $y \in V$, then NOT $(x \leq y)$.

Theorem 5.3 Let X be a compact Hausdorff space. Then the Vietoris space $\mathcal{C}(X)$ of closed subsets of X is a pospace.
  Proof: Assume $a, b \in \mathcal{C}(X)$ and NOT $(a \leq b)$. Hence there are $\alpha \in a$ and $\beta \in b$. Since X is normal, the closed sets $\{\alpha\}$ and b have disjoint open neighbourhoods $V(\alpha)$ and $R(b)$. Let $R(a)$ be an open set containing a. Note that $a \in m(V(\alpha))$. Hence $R(a) \cap m(V(a))$ is an open neighbourhood of a. More precisely, $t(R(a)) \cap m(V(\alpha))$ and $R(b)$ are open neighbourhoods of a and b such that for all $x \in t(R(a)) \cap m(V(\alpha))$ and $y \in t(R(b))$ we have NOT $(x \leq y)$. The reason is simply that the elements y of $R(b)$ do not contain the point α while the elements x of $t(R(a)) \cap m(V(\alpha))$ are open neighbourhoods of α by definition. Hence, $\mathcal{C}(X)$ is a pospace.

Thanks to Theorem 5.3, we may apply the Urysohn–Carruth metrization theorem (2.4) to the space of theories $\langle \mathcal{C}(ST(L)), \leq \rangle$ obtaining a radially convex metric d on $\mathcal{C}(ST(L))$. Putting things together we finally have reached the main theorem of this paper:

Theorem 5.4 Let L be a countable language. Then the logical space $T(L)$ of theories on L can be conceived of as the Vietoris space $\mathcal{C}(ST(L))$ of closed sets of $ST(L)$.[10] Then $T(L)$ is a *pospace* that can be endowed with a radially convex metric.

This metric can be used for truth approximation, or, more generally, for a metrical theory of theory comparison. It is, as it should be, in line with the underlying topological structure, and at least partially with the relevant logical structure, to wit the order structure $\leq$. For the time being, I do not know if it satisfies the further condition Miller (1984) set up for a good metric of truthlikeness In order to understand how this deficit may be overcome it is useful to dwell in some more detail upon Carruth's proof of his metrization theorem. It mimics exactly the proof of the classical theorem of Urysohn according to which a second countable compact Hausdorff space X is metrizable

---

[10]In a somewhat different manner, Brink, Pretorius, & Vermeulen (1992) use the order structure of the Vietoris space to define an order-theoretical notion of truth approximation. The main difference to the present paper is that they do not consider the possibility of endowing T(L) with a (radially convex) metrical structure.

since there is an embedding $e : X \longmapsto I^{\mathbf{N}}$. Explicitly, X is rendered a metric space by restricting the standard metric of $I^{\mathbf{N}}$ to $e(X)$ and then pulling it back to X itself. The essential point is that thanks to technical results of Nachbin (1965) Carruth proves that the embedding function e is *order-preserving*, that is, for $a, b \in X$ and $a \leq b$ one has $e(a) \leq e(b)$. What he does *not* prove is that in the case of the Vietoris space $\mathcal{C}(X)$ is that the embedding e is also a lattice homomorphism. He does not prove that the embedding e satisfies also $e(a \wedge b) = e(a) \wedge e(b)$, and $e(a \vee b) = e(a) \vee e(b)$. If this could be done one could immediately derive Miller's requirement $d(a,b) \geq d(c \wedge a, c \wedge b) + d(c \vee a, c \vee b)$. As is easily checked, this is true for the standard metric of the Hilbert cube, and could be pulled back to $\mathcal{C}(X)$. Hence, if the embedding $e : \mathcal{C}(X) \longmapsto I^{\mathbf{N}}$ can be proved to be a lattice homomorphism one may pull back the 'good' metric of $I^{\mathbf{N}}$ to a 'good' metric on $\mathcal{C}(X)$.

6 Geometric conventionalism and logical spaces

The radially convex metric d constructed for the logical space of theories $T(L)$ in no way is unique. The construction of the order-preserving embedding $e : T(L) \longmapsto I^{\mathbf{N}}$ by the Urysohn–Carruth proof is highly non-constructive and involves several choices. This does not mean that d is arbitrary: recall that it has to respect the topological *and* the order structure. This ensures that the trivial metric (for example) is excluded. More precisely one may say that for the construction of d the ordered topological structure of $T(L)$ has to be taken as a priori, since it flows directly from the language L and its logic. On the other hand, moving from the ordered topological structure to the metric structure of $T(L)$ involves a conventional choice. This should not be considered as a flaw. Quite the contrary. It is very plausible that questions of truthlikeness and theory approximation do not totally depend on 'objective' facts but are also a matter of pragmatically motivated decisions (Miller 1994, Chapter 10, §4).

It may be useful to compare the problem of a priori and conventional structural strata of the logical space $T(L)$ with the corresponding problem of physical space. As is well known, a hundred years ago Poincaré subscribed to a sort of partial conventionalism with respect to the structure of physical space. According to him, the underlying topological structure of space was a priori while the metrical structure was conventional. $T(L)$, the results of this paper suggest an analogous result: there is an underlying objective topological structure defined by logic alone. On the other hand, there is some choice in constructing a metric for $T(L)$ via its embedding in the Hilbert cube $I^{\mathbf{N}}$. This may be considered as a conventional component in matters of truthlikeness.

Bibliography

Brink, C., Pretorius, J. P. G., & Vermeulen, J. J. C. (1992). 'Verisimilitude via Vietoris'. *Journal of Logic and Computation* **2**, pp. 709-718.

Carruth, J. H. (1968). 'A Note on Partially Ordered Compacta'. *Pacific Journal of Mathematics* **24**, pp. 229-231.

Davey, B. A. & Priestley, H. (1990). *Introduction to Lattices and Order*. Cambridge: Cambridge University Press.

Dunn, J. M. & Hardegree, G. M. (2001). *Algebraic Methods in Philosophical Logic*. Oxford: Oxford University Press.

Gierz, G., Hofmann, K. H., Keimel, K., Lawson, J. D., Mislove, M., & Scott, D. S. (1980). *A Compendium of Continuous Lattices*. Berlin & Heidelberg: Springer.

Halmos, P. (1963). *Lectures on Boolean Algebras*. New York: van Nostrand.

James, I. M. (1999). *Topologies and Uniformities*. Berlin: Springer.

Johnstone, P. (1982). *Stone Spaces*. Cambridge: Cambridge University Press.

Kuipers, T. A. F. (2000). *From Instrumentalism to Constructive Realism, On Some Relations between Confirmation, Empirical Progress, and Truth Approximation*. Dordrecht: Kluwer Academic Publishers.

Miller, D. W. (1984). 'A Geometry of Logic'. In H. J. Skala, S. Termini, & E. Trillas, editors (1984), pp. 91-104. *Aspects of Vagueness*. Dordrecht: D. Reidel Publishing Company.

——— (1994). *Critical Rationalism: A Restatement and Defence*. Chicago & La Salle IL: Open Court Publishing Company.

Nachbin, L. (1965). *Topology and Order*. New York: Van Nostrand.

Nagata, J. (1985). *Modern General Topology*. Amsterdam: North-Holland Publishing Company.

Niiniluoto, I. (1987). *Truthlikeness*. Dordrecht: D. Reidel Publishing Company.

Popper, K. R. (1963). *Conjectures and Refutations*. London: Routledge and Kegan Paul. 5th edition 1989. London: Routledge.

——— (1976). 'A Note on Verisimilitude'. *The British Journal for the Philosophy of Science* **27**, pp. 147-159.

Tarski, A. (1935). 'Grundzüge des Systemenkalküls, Erster Teil'. *Fundamenta Mathematicae* **25**, pp. 503-526. English translation in Chapter XII of A. Tarski (1956). *Logic, Semantics, Metamathematics*. Oxford: Clarendon Press. 2nd edition 1983. Indianapolis IN: Hackett.

42

Popper's
Structuralist Theory of Logic[*]

Peter Schroeder-Heister

In what follows I take a fresh look at Popper's papers on the foundations of (deductive) logic published between 1947 and 1949 (referred to as P1–P6). In my study of 1984 (Schroeder-Heister 1984b) I gave a detailed analysis of these papers including the objections raised and points made within the logic community. These objections and, in particular, the fact that Tarski refused to take a look at them[1] eventually led Popper to abandon his project of 'new foundations for logic' (title of P2) which he had started 'with much enthusiasm' (Popper 1974, p. 1095).

In Schroeder-Heister (1984b) I argued that Popper's theory can be given a coherent sense when it is read as an attempt to delineate logical from extra-logical signs, a point whose significance Popper had stressed himself, in particular in his reply to Lejewski in the Schilpp volume (Lejewski 1974; Popper 1974). I now think that the logicality aspect, though important, is not the whole story and definitely not the central point of Popper's theory.[2] Rather I shall argue that Popper puts forward a structuralist approach according to which logic is a metalinguistic theory of consequence, in terms of which logical operations are characterized. I borrow the term 'structuralist' from Koslow's monograph (1992), where such an approach is developed in much detail. Popper's view will be reconstructed against the background of Koslow's work, which represents a mature account allowing me to evaluate the merits of Popper's ideas.

By a 'structuralist theory of logic' Koslow denotes an approach that characterizes logical systems axiomatically in terms of 'implication relations'. An implication relation corresponds to a finite consequence operation in Tarski's sense, which can also be described by Gentzen-style structural rules.[3] Logical

---

[*]I should like to thank the two anonymous referees of this paper for their careful reading of the manuscript and for many helpful comments and suggestions.

[1]Letter to the author of 9 July 1982.

[2]In letters to the author of 10 July and 19 August 1982, after taking notice of the logicality interpretation, Popper actually claimed that somehow laying the foundations of logic might be possible after all, in addition to the task of delineating logical signs.

[3]However, the designation 'structuralist' has nothing to do with 'structural rules', but rather with the fact that 'structures' in the model-theoretic sense are defined.

compounds are then characterized as objects satisfying certain constraints stated in terms of implication relations. For example, a conjunction C of A and B satisfies the conditions that

(i) C implies both A and B, and

(ii) C is the weakest object (weakest with respect to the given implication relation) such that (i) is fulfilled; that is, for any C', if C' implies both A and B, then C' implies C.

Koslow develops a structuralist theory in the precise metamathematical sense, which does not specify the domain of objects in any sense beyond the axioms given. Even if the domain is supposed to be a language, the structural axioms do not tell what a conjunction of A and B looks like (if there is one at all). Rather, if a language or any other domain of objects equipped with an implication relation is given, the structuralist approach may be used to *single out* logical compounds by checking their *implicational properties*. It does not postulate axioms and inference rules for a formal object language. Whether and how implication structures are realized as object languages, is left entirely open. In particular, nothing is being said about the particular inferential format used in such a realization (for example, whether it takes the form of a Hilbert-style or a Gentzen-style system).

I claim that Popper's approach, though often formulated by him in a misleading way and (by far) lacking the precision of Koslow's, is exactly of this kind. I shall try to present it as a coherent theory without going into all details of his line of argument. I also confine myself to propositional logic, as this eases my presentation and entirely suffices to give an idea of Popper's basic aims. The details of the first-order case are even less consistent and more problematic than those of the propositional one. For further issues, I refer to my 1984 paper (Schroeder-Heister 1984b). Often the details of Popper's presentation are a stumbling block to an overall understanding of his view. It is the *global* picture that makes his theory interesting, not so much the individual steps of his exposition. If one wanted to build further on his ideas, one would anyway take a better developed theory such as Koslow's as a starting point.

My paper is divided as follows. In the first section I give a brief sketch of Koslow's theory. Section 2 deals with Popper's inferential definitions, delineating them from Koslow's characterizations. In section 3, I argue that and why Popper's approach cannot be turned into a semantics and therefore is not a justification of a logical system. The concluding remarks (section 4) point to the fact that the structuralist reading of Popper's theory is well in line with his general philosophical views. The appendices illuminate other interesting aspects of Popper's work, for instance his axiomatization of structural rules and his usage of multiple succedent consequence.

1 Koslow's structuralist theory of logic

I give a brief outline of Koslow's theory as far as it is relevant for the reconstruction of Popper's approach, restating it in my terminology and notation, which in some cases is more explicit than Koslow's, and in many respects more 'formalistic'. As indicated, Koslow (1992) characterizes logical systems as structures in the metamathematical (model-theoretic) sense rather than as syntactically specified systems with axioms and inference rules. The domains of his structures are sets of objects for which a (finite) consequence relation is available. Koslow himself speaks of 'implication relations'. I shall speak of 'deducibility relations', keeping 'implication' from now on for the propositional connective (which may occur both in the metalanguage and in the object languages considered). The reader should bear in mind that 'deducibility' is here considered an abstract term that is not bound to the concept of deduction in formal languages.

A *deducibility structure* $\langle \mathcal{D}, \vdash \rangle$ consists of a non-empty domain $\mathcal{D}$ and a relation '$\vdash$' between finite subsets and elements of $\mathcal{D}$, called a *deducibility relation*, which satisfies the following conditions:

$$\Gamma \cup \{A\} \vdash A$$
$$\Gamma \vdash A \,\&\, \Delta \cup \{A\} \vdash B \,\Rightarrow\, \Gamma \cup \Delta \vdash B,$$

where capital Greek letters stand for subsets of $\mathcal{D}$ and capital Latin letters for elements of $\mathcal{D}$, and where $\&$ and $\Rightarrow$ are metalinguistic conjunction and implication, with $\&$ binding stronger than $\Rightarrow$. I use the common abbreviations, leaving out the set brackets to the left of $\vdash$, and writing $\Gamma, A \vdash B$ for $\Gamma \cup \{A\} \vdash B$ and $\Gamma, \Delta \vdash A$ for $\Gamma \cup \Delta \vdash A$.

Given a deducibility structure $\langle \mathcal{D}, \vdash \rangle$, an n-place logical operation H over $\langle \mathcal{D}, \vdash \rangle$ is a function that associates with any n-tuple of objects a (possibly empty) set of objects, which are all interdeducible, more formally,

$$H : \mathcal{D}^n \longrightarrow \mathcal{P}(\mathcal{D})$$

such that $A \dashv\vdash B$ holds for all $A, B \in H(A_1, \ldots, A_n)$. Furthermore, it is assumed that H is invariant with respect to interdeducibility, that is to say that $H(A_1, \ldots, A_i, \ldots, A_n) = H(A_1, \ldots, A_i', \ldots, A_n)$, if $A_i \dashv\vdash A_i'$, and $H(A_1, \ldots, A_n)$ is closed under interdeducibility, that is, $A \in H(A_1, \ldots, A_n)$ is implied by $A \dashv\vdash B$ and $B \in H(A_1, \ldots, A_n)$. Since a logical operation is unique up to interdeducibility, the set $H(A_1, \ldots, A_n)$ may be identified with any of its elements, if it is non-empty.

Let $\langle s_1, \ldots, s_m \rangle$ be a signature, that is, an m-tuple of non-negative integers (corresponding to the arities of logical operations considered). A *logic structure* of signature $\langle s_1, \ldots, s_m \rangle$ is then given as $\langle \mathcal{D}, \vdash, H_1, \ldots, H_m \rangle$ such that

(i) $\langle \mathcal{D}, \vdash \rangle$ is a deducibility structure

(ii)   Each H_i ($1 \leq i \leq m$) is an s_i-place logical operation over $\langle \mathcal{D}, \vdash \rangle$.

An *inferential characterization* of an n-place logical operation H is a (met-alinguistic) formula $\mathfrak{A}(A, A_1, \ldots, A_n)$ with at most $n + 1$ variables such that

(1.3) $\qquad\qquad A \in H(A_1, \ldots, A_n) \quad \Leftrightarrow \quad \mathfrak{A}(A, A_1, \ldots, A_n).$

This means in particular that the first argument of $\mathfrak{A}$ is uniquely determined up to interdeducibility, that is, for any $A \in H(A_1, \ldots, A_n)$, the *uniqueness condition*

(1.4) $\qquad\qquad (\forall B)(B \dashv\vdash A \quad \Leftrightarrow \quad \mathfrak{A}(B, A_1, \ldots, A_n))$

is satisfied, which is equivalent to

$$\mathfrak{A}(B, A_1, \ldots, A_n) \ \& \ \mathfrak{A}(B', A_1, \ldots, A_n) \ \Rightarrow \ B \dashv\vdash B'$$

plus

$$\mathfrak{A}(B, A_1, \ldots, A_n) \ \& \ B \dashv\vdash B' \ \Rightarrow \ \mathfrak{A}(B', A_1, \ldots, A_n).$$

If there is an inferential characterization $\mathfrak{A}$ of H, H is said to be *inferentially characterized*. Conversely, if an $\mathfrak{A}$ is given such that (1.2) holds, then (1.1) defines a logical operation H such that $\mathfrak{A}$ is an inferential characterization of H. A logic structure $\langle \mathcal{D}, \vdash, H_1, \ldots, H_m \rangle$ is called *inferentially characterized*, if with each logical operation H_i an inferential characterization $\mathfrak{A}_i$ is associated. In what follows, I shall always assume that logic structures are inferentially characterized.

So far, the syntactic form of $\mathfrak{A}$ has been left unspecified. If nothing else is said, I assume that $\mathfrak{A}$ is built up from deducibility '$\vdash$' as the only predicate by using first-order logical constants.

It is characteristic of the structuralist approach that, even if the domain $\mathcal{D}$ consists of syntactically specified expressions of some object language rather than arbitrary objects, the results of logical operations need not have a standard form. If $\mathcal{D}$ contains for every A_1 and A_2 a conjunction A of A_1 and A_2, then A need not have a form like $A_1 \wedge A_2$. However, if $H_\wedge$ is the logical operation of conjunction, and if conjunctions of two expressions always exist, then $\mathcal{D}$ can easily be extended by introducing $A_1 \wedge A_2$ as a standard expression for a conjunction of A_1 and A_2 by just adding $A_1 \wedge A_2$ to $H_\wedge(A_1, A_2)$. It is obvious that this extension is conservative. In this way, any logical operation H available in a language can be represented explicitly by a logical constant in a conservative extension, provided the following *existence condition* is satisfied for H:

(1.5) $\qquad\qquad (\forall A_1, \ldots, A_n)(\exists A)\mathfrak{A}(A, A_1, \ldots, A_n).$

This condition is not necessarily fulfilled. It is easy to construct deducibility structures where, for example, disjunctions do not always exist (see Koslow 1992, p. 118).

In Koslow's theory inferential characterizations $\mathfrak{A}(A, A_1, \ldots, A_n)$ have a specific syntactic form. They provide inferential conditions corresponding to elimination rules in natural deduction and then require A to be the weakest object satisfying these conditions. Formally, the inferential characterizations for the four standard operations of intuitionistic logic (conjunction, disjunction, implication, and negation) can be stated as follows.

$$\mathfrak{A}_\wedge(A, A_1, A_2) \quad :\Leftrightarrow \quad A \vdash A_1 \ \& \ A \vdash A_2 \qquad\qquad \text{elimination}$$
$$\& \ (\forall B)(B \vdash A_1 \ \& \ B \vdash A_2 \ \Rightarrow \ B \vdash A) \qquad \text{minimality}$$
('A is a conjunction of A_1 and A_2')

$$\mathfrak{A}_\vee(A, A_1, A_2) \quad :\Leftrightarrow \quad (\forall C)(A_1 \vdash C \ \& \ A_2 \vdash C \ \Rightarrow \ A \vdash C) \qquad \text{elimination}$$
$$\& \ (\forall B)((\forall C)(A_1 \vdash C \ \& \ A_2 \vdash C \ \Rightarrow \ B \vdash C)$$
$$\Rightarrow \ B \vdash A) \qquad\qquad\qquad \text{minimality}$$
('A is a disjunction of A_1 and A_2')

$$\mathfrak{A}_\rightarrow(A, A_1, A_2) \quad :\Leftrightarrow \quad A, A_1 \vdash A_2 \qquad\qquad\qquad\quad \text{elimination}$$
$$\& \ (\forall B)(B, A_1 \vdash A_2 \ \Rightarrow \ B \vdash A) \qquad \text{minimality}$$
('A is an implication between A_1 and A_2')

$$\mathfrak{A}_\neg(A, A_1) \quad\quad :\Leftrightarrow \quad (\forall C)(A, A_1 \vdash C) \qquad\qquad\qquad \text{elimination}$$
$$\& \ (\forall B)((\forall C)(B, A_1 \vdash C) \ \Rightarrow \ B \vdash A) \quad \text{minimality}$$
('A is a negation of A_1')

As I am only illustrating the method of inferential characterizations, I do not consider here parametric versions, which also take into account additional assumptions ('contexts'), which may be present in deducibility statements. For example, with such parameters, the elimination condition in $\mathfrak{A}_\vee$ should be

$$(\forall \Gamma)(\forall C)(\Gamma, A_1 \vdash C \ \& \ \Gamma, A_2 \vdash C \Rightarrow \Gamma, A \vdash C).$$

It can easily be seen that $\mathfrak{A}_\wedge, \mathfrak{A}_\vee, \mathfrak{A}_\rightarrow, \mathfrak{A}_\neg$ are in fact inferential characterizations of corresponding operations $H_\wedge, H_\vee, H_\rightarrow$ and $H_\neg$, respectively, as the uniqueness condition (1.2) is fulfilled. This is due to the minimality requirements (see Koslow 1992, pp. 81ff.)

Inferentially characterized logical operations in Koslow's sense have the following two remarkable properties: They are (i) stable and (ii) distinct (see Koslow 1992, p. 10).

Ad (i): Suppose H is inferentially characterized by $\mathfrak{A}$ with respect to some deducibility structure $\langle \mathcal{D}, \vdash \rangle$. Let $\langle \mathcal{D}', \vdash' \rangle$ be a deducibility structure extending $\langle \mathcal{D}, \vdash \rangle$, that is, $\mathcal{D} \subseteq \mathcal{D}'$ and $\vdash \ \subseteq \ \vdash'$. Let $\mathfrak{A}'$ result from $\mathfrak{A}$ by replacing $\vdash$ with $\vdash'$ throughout. Then H is called *stable* with respect to $\langle \mathcal{D}', \vdash' \rangle$ if

$$(\forall A, A_1, \ldots, A_n \in \mathcal{D})(\mathfrak{A}(A, A_1, \ldots, A_n) \ \Leftrightarrow \ \mathfrak{A}'(A, A_1, \ldots, A_n)),$$

that is, objects that are conjunctions, disjunctions, implications, and nega-
tions in $\langle \mathcal{D}, \vdash \rangle$ remain conjunctions, disjunctions, implications, and negations,
when $\langle \mathcal{D}, \vdash \rangle$ is extended to $\langle \mathcal{D}', \vdash' \rangle$. The following can easily be shown:
suppose that $\langle \mathcal{D}', \vdash' \rangle$ is a conservative extension $\langle \mathcal{D}, \vdash \rangle$, that is, $\mathcal{D} \subseteq \mathcal{D}'$,
$\vdash \subseteq \vdash'$, and

$$(\forall \Delta \subseteq \mathcal{D})(\forall A \in \mathcal{D})(\Delta \vdash' A \;\Rightarrow\; \Delta \vdash A).$$

Then H is stable with respect to $\langle \mathcal{D}', \vdash' \rangle$. In short, *inferentially characterized logical operations are stable with respect to conservative extensions* (see
Koslow 1992, pp. 10, 31). This holds for inferential characterizations of logical
operations in general. It does not depend on their specific syntactic form, in
particular not on the minimality conditions.

Ad (ii): *Distinctness* of inferentially characterized logical operations H_1 and
H_2 of arities n and $n+m$, respectively, over $\langle \mathcal{D}, \vdash \rangle$ simply means that they
are different, that is, that there are $A_1, \ldots, A_{n+m} \in \mathcal{D}$ such that

$$H_1(A_1, \ldots, A_n) \neq H_2(A_1, \ldots, A_{n+m}).$$

Whether H_1 and H_2 are distinct, depends on their inferential characterizations. Koslow shows that the standard logical operations $H_\wedge, H_\vee, H_\rightarrow$ and
$H_\neg$ are pairwise distinct *if the underlying deducibility structure $\langle \mathcal{D}, \vdash \rangle$ is
non-trivial*, that is, if not every B is deducible from every Δ (Koslow 1992,
pp. 10, 151-153).

An approach developed by the author (Schroeder-Heister 1984a) is similar
to Koslow's in certain respects. It characterizes logical constants as expressing
the *common content* of systems of conditions. This essentially means that
from logical compounds exactly those sentences should be derivable that can
be derived from the premises of their introduction rules. This again means
that elimination rules are taken as a basis, and the compounds are weakest
sentences having the power of major premises of elimination rules.[4] This idea
was developed in the syntactic setting of a calculus of rules of higher levels, not
in a metalinguistic structuralist theory like Koslow's. However, it could easily
be used to extend Koslow's structuralist approach by generalized elimination
principles for arbitrary logical operations.

2 Popper's theory

Popper develops a structuralist theory of logic based on deducibility structures
(§ 2.1) and inferential characterizations of logical constants (§ 2.2), whose internal form is less restricted than Koslow's (§ 2.3).

---

[4]The *major premise* of an elimination rule is the formula from which a logical operator
is eliminated. If, for instance, a step of $\rightarrow$-elimination (*modus ponens*) leads from $A \rightarrow B$
and A to B, then $A \rightarrow B$ is its major premise and A its minor premise. See Prawitz (1965)
for this terminology.

2.1 Popper's deducibility structures

Popper bases the structures he investigates on the principles

$$\Gamma, A \vdash A$$
$$(\Gamma \vdash B_1 \& \cdots \& \Gamma \vdash B_n) \Rightarrow (B_1, \ldots, B_n \vdash C \Rightarrow \Gamma \vdash C)$$

called 'reflexivity' and 'generalized transitivity', respectively (see P1, p. 278; P2, pp. 198-200). He uses the symbols '/' and '//' for what are here denoted by '$\vdash$' and '$\dashv\vdash$'. Normally he does not regard antecedents (= left-hand sides) of deducibility statements as sets, but has explicit rules for permutation and contraction, a point that can be disregarded here. Principles like reflexivity and generalized transitivity are called 'absolutely valid', because they do not refer to logical connectives in some object language. They are independent of the distinction between logical and extra-logical signs (P1, p. 279). These principles are the same as those given by Hertz (1923) as the basis of his system. Hertz was the first to formulate what Gentzen (1935) later called 'structural rules'. Gentzen immediately built on Hertz when developing his sequent calculus (see Schroeder-Heister 2002). It is not clear how well acquainted Popper was with Gentzen's work, when he wrote his papers.[5] At that time (the late 1940s), Gentzen systems did not yet belong to the basic inventory of logic. In any case it is remarkable that Popper realized the significance of structural principles as the basis of logical reasoning. Even twelve years after Gentzen's thesis this was not a commonplace.

It is obvious that reflexivity and generalized transitivity are equivalent to the principles governing deducibility structures in the sense of § 1. So it may be said that, like Koslow, Popper starts with deducibility structures $\langle \mathcal{D}, \vdash \rangle$, in terms of which logical operations are explained. Popper even tries to axiomatize '$\vdash$' in such a way that reflexivity and generalized transitivity become derivable, as discussed in Appendix 1. Popper also occasionally considers deducibility statements whose succedent (= right-hand side) may contain more than one formula, or even none at all — see Appendix 2.

At this point a remark about the principles governing deducibility relations as compared with structural rules in Gentzen's sense is appropriate. Formally, the *principle*

$$\Gamma \vdash A \& \Delta \cup \{A\} \vdash B \Rightarrow \Gamma \cup \Delta \vdash B$$

is to be distinguished from the *rule* of Cut

$$\frac{\Gamma \vdash A \quad \Delta, A \vdash B}{\Gamma, \Delta \vdash B}$$

---

[5] Both Hertz and Gentzen are only very briefly mentioned at a few places in Popper's papers. One might even suspect that it was Bernays who drew his attention to Hertz and Gentzen, when his papers had been essentially completed. That his 'main intention was to simplify logic by developing what has been called by others "natural deduction" ' (Popper 1974, p. 1096) appears to be a later re-interpretation, which is only partially true, because, as will be seen, it is not the development of a particular object-linguistic deduction system or form of deduction that Popper is aiming at.

in sequent-style systems. The latter one uses '$\vdash$' as an object-linguistic operator, whereas both Koslow's and Popper's theories are entirely metalinguistic,
without any preference for a particular object-linguistic style of reasoning.
Nevertheless the close relationship between structural rules and principles for
deducibility or consequence is obvious, and one might use sequent-style rules
as representations of deducibility principles, and vice versa, keeping their
fundamental distinctness in mind.[6]

2.2 Inferential definitions

Popper now proceeds by presenting what he calls 'inferential definitions' of
logical constants. The inferential definitions for conjunction $\wedge$, disjunction $\vee$,
implication $\rightarrow$ and classical negation $\sim$ run as follows:[7]

(2.1) $\quad A \dashv\vdash A_1 \wedge A_2 \quad \Leftrightarrow \quad (\forall C)(A \vdash C \Leftrightarrow A_1, A_2 \vdash C)$

(2.2) $\quad A \dashv\vdash A_1 \vee A_2 \quad \Leftrightarrow \quad (\forall C)(A \vdash C \Leftrightarrow A_1 \vdash C \ \& \ A_2 \vdash C)$

(2.3) $\quad A \dashv\vdash A_1 \rightarrow A_2 \quad \Leftrightarrow \quad (\forall C)(C \vdash A \Leftrightarrow C, A_1 \vdash A_2)$

(2.4) $\quad A \dashv\vdash \sim A_1 \quad\quad \Leftrightarrow \quad (\forall C, D)(A, C \vdash A_1 \Rightarrow A, C \vdash D \ \& \ C \vdash A_1).$

So the general form of an inferential definition for an n-place connective
$J(A_1, \ldots, A_n)$ is

(2.5) $\quad\quad A \dashv\vdash J(A_1, \ldots, A_n) \quad \Leftrightarrow \quad \mathfrak{A}_J(A, A_1, \ldots, A_n),$

where $\mathfrak{A}_J$ is an expression in the metalanguage with no more than $n+1$ open
places. It is obvious that (2.5) brings Popper's inferential definitions already
close to the way inferential characterizations were introduced in § 1.

Although Popper's terminology is quite unfortunate, calling (2.1)–(2.4) *explicit definitions* of logical constants (P2, p. 218), he makes it clear at many
places that he does not want to define particular expressions of some object
language. Instead he insists that he wants a purely metalinguistic characterization of the logical operations independently of whether they exist syntactically. The following quotations, in which the emphasis is Popper's own, are
from P2, p. 208, ibidem, P3, p. 564, P2, p. 207, and P3, p. 562.

> ...we say that $a \wedge b$ is *a* conjunction of a and b, rather than that
> it is *the* conjunction of a and b.

> ...what we have defined is not so much the conjunction of a and
> b but the precise *logical force* (or the logical import) of any state-
> ment c that is equal in force to a conjunction of a and b.

---

[6] Actually, at many places, Popper calls principles such as generalized transitivity 'rules'
(see P3, p. 565, and P2, *passim*). In a footnote on Gentzen (P4, p. 52), he emphasizes that
the *metalinguistic* character of his own theory distinguishes it from Gentzen's.

[7] Again I use my terminology and omit, as Popper himself does, parametric context
formulas. The examples are from P2, p. 218.

... we do not define, e.g., conjunction, but rather the logical force of conjunction.

We do not even assume that the language we are discussing — the language to which our statements $a, b, c, \ldots$ belong — possesses a special sign for linking statements into conjunctions.

Our theory is completely metalinguistic.

This suggests that rather than read the logical constants $\wedge$, $\vee$, $\rightarrow$, $\sim$ in (2.1)–(2.4) as particular term-forming operators, one should interpret $A \dashv\vdash A_1 \wedge A_2$, $A \dashv\vdash A_1 \vee A_2$, $A \dashv\vdash A_1 \rightarrow A_2$, $A \dashv\vdash \sim A_1$ in Koslow's sense as expressing the availability of a set of terms A of equal logical force. One would then write

$$
\begin{aligned}
A \in H_\wedge(A_1, A_2) &\quad \text{for} \quad A \dashv\vdash A_1 \wedge A_2, \\
A \in H_\vee(A_1, A_2) &\quad \text{for} \quad A \dashv\vdash A_1 \vee A_2, \\
A \in H_\rightarrow(A_1, A_2) &\quad \text{for} \quad A \dashv\vdash A_1 \rightarrow A_2, \\
A \in H_\sim(A_1) &\quad \text{for} \quad A \dashv\vdash \sim A_1,
\end{aligned}
$$

and in general

$$
A \in H_J(A_1, \ldots, A_n) \quad \text{for} \quad A \dashv\vdash J(A_1, \ldots, A_n).
$$

Thus one arrives at inferential definitions whose general (outer) form

$$
(2.6) \qquad A \in H_J(A_1, \ldots, A_n) \quad \Leftrightarrow \quad \mathfrak{A}_J(A, A_1, \ldots, A_n)
$$

corresponds exactly to (1.1) of § 1. Only the internal form of the inferential characterizations $\mathfrak{A}_J$ is different (see below § 2.3).[8]

That Popper intended something of this kind is clear from passages such as the following (P2, p. 214, Popper's emphasis), where he describes an implication-like expression (written by Popper as $a > b$) as

a *variable name* of any statement which stands in a certain logical relationship to the two statements a and b.

He even reads (2.1) as 'A is a conjunction of A_1 and A_2 iff ...', and so on (see P2, p. 206). This makes it clear that using compounds such as $A_1 \wedge A_2$, $A_1 \rightarrow A_2$, and so on, as syntactically specified terms is prone to misunderstandings. Unfortunately, Popper often uses them in that way, for example by substituting $A_1 \wedge A_2$ for A in (2.1) to obtain certain inference rules (see P3, p. 565).

The reaction from the reviewers of Popper's papers was only natural: as a fundamental objection, they saw hidden existence assumptions in inferential

---

[8]For the sake of terminological precision it should be pointed out that for Popper an inferential definition is an expression of the form (2.5), whereas an inferential characterization in my (or Koslow's) sense is just its right hand side (that is, an $\mathfrak{A}$). Therefore I say that Popper's inferential definitions *make use of* or *provide* inferential characterizations.

definitions,[9] which is, of course, true, if conjunctions and other combinations are considered terms of a particular form. There are far too many misleading formulations by Popper which support this reading.[10]

Koslow's set notation (2.6) avoids all these problems. However, when rephrasing (2.5) as (2.6), it must be explicitly demanded, as it is demanded in the presentation of Koslow's theory (see (1.2)), that $\mathfrak{A}(A, A_1, \ldots, A_n)$ characterize A up to interdeducibility. This uniqueness condition is built into the left hand side of Popper's inferential definitions.

Thus my proposal is to read Popper's inferential definitions (2.5) as providing inferential characterizations of logical operations in the sense of § 1, for which both (1.1) and (1.2) hold. In other words, Popper defines logic structures $\langle \mathcal{D}, \vdash, H_1, \ldots, H_m \rangle$, where $H_1, \ldots, H_m$ are logical operations inferentially characterized by certain $\mathfrak{A}_1, \ldots, \mathfrak{A}_m$. This is a neat view of Popper's aim with a maximum of support in his papers.

2.3 The internal form of Popper's inferential characterizations and the logicality problem

The basic contrast to Koslow is that Popper imposes no specific restriction on the form of an $\mathfrak{A}(A, A_1, \ldots, A_n)$ except that it guarantees the uniqueness of A. As the different patterns of the right hand sides of (2.1)–(2.4) indicate, $\mathfrak{A}$ may take various distinct forms. For example, (2.1) and (2.2) can be read as saying that conjunction and disjunction are *strongest* elements of the domain (with respect to $\vdash$) such that the standard introduction rules for them are valid, (2.3) says that an implication is a *weakest* element such that the elimination rule (*modus ponens*) holds, and (2.4) says that the rule of *self-affirmation*

$$\frac{\begin{array}{c}[\sim A_1]\\A_1\end{array}}{A_1}$$

(a variant of the classical *reductio* rule) as well as the *contradiction* rule

$$\frac{A_1 \quad \sim A_1}{C}$$

are valid without maximality or minimality requirement. Only (2.3) corresponds to Koslow's idea (elimination principle plus minimality condition). An

---

[9]Most clearly Kleene (1947/1948) and Hasenjaeger (1949). Other reviews were by Curry (1948/1949) and McKinsey (1948) (all not very favourable). For more details see Schroeder-Heister (1984b).

[10]There is a single place, in P3, p. 569, where Popper claims that existence postulates have to be 'added' when applying the results to some specific object language, which means that existence of operators is not presupposed. However, this is not enough to prevent readers from seeing implicit existence assumptions in his using terms such as $A \wedge B$, $A \vee B$, and so on.

alternative definition for classical negation is given by

$$(2.7) \qquad A \dashv\vdash \sim A_1 \quad \Leftrightarrow \quad (\forall C)(A, A_1 \vdash C \,\&\, (A, C \vdash A_1 \Rightarrow C \vdash A_1))$$

(P1, p. 282; P2, p. 220, note), which is a variant of (2.4). A further definition of classical negation uses deducibility statements with multiple succedents, which essentially is a characterization by using the *excluded middle* (see Appendix 2).

As an inferential definition for intuitionistic negation, Popper proposes

$$(2.8) \qquad A \dashv\vdash \neg A_1 \quad \Leftrightarrow \quad (\forall C)(A, A_1 \vdash C \,\&\, (A_1, C \vdash A \Rightarrow C \vdash A)),$$

which is obtained from (2.7) by interchanging A and A_1 in the right conjunct (see P1, p. 282, note, and P2, p. 220, note). This corresponds to the fact that instead of classical self-affirmation only its intuitionistic counterpart

$$\frac{\begin{array}{c}[A_1]\\ \neg A_1\end{array}}{\neg A_1}$$

(*'self-denial'* — a variant of the intuitionistic *reductio* rule) is expected to hold. The right hand side of (2.8) is equivalent to $\mathfrak{A}_\neg(A, A_1)$ as defined by Koslow (see § 1).[11]

This all indicates that the form of $\mathfrak{A}$ is not restricted in any particular way.[12] This is confirmed also by the fact that Popper deals with classical negation extensively, which is not possible in frameworks with $\mathfrak{A}$ having Koslow's restricted form, which naturally leads to intuitionistic logic. Therefore, in Popper, $\mathfrak{A}$ is just a metalinguistic logical formula with '$\vdash$' as the only extra-logical constant.

It is important to see that the uniqueness restriction is not as innocent as it perhaps seems to be at first glance. It excludes certain characterizations of well-known operations, which one would normally consider logical. Take the negation $\neg_w$ (in the following called *weak negation*), which in natural deduction is characterized by the self-denial rule

$$\frac{\begin{array}{c}[A_1]\\ \neg_w A_1\end{array}}{\neg_w A_1}$$

---

[11] In fact, Popper himself (P5, p. 111) considers a version corresponding to Koslow's.

[12] Perhaps except that it starts with a universal quantifier; see P3, p. 564. There Popper states the general form of inferential definitions as

$$a \dashv\vdash \text{the definiendum} \Leftrightarrow (\text{for every} \dots : \ (\dots))$$

But even here this universal quantifier is not considered a matter of principle, but just a description of the particular forms of inferential definitions given in the sequel to this remark. — In P6, he explicitly discusses the possibility of characterizing logical compounds as strongest or weakest statements for which certain introduction or elimination rules, respectively, hold. Apart from the fact that he considers these options as two alternatives and not opting, as Koslow does, for one of them, it is clear from the context that he does not insist on such a form.

alone (without the contradiction rule), and whose inferential characterization is

$$\mathfrak{A}_w(A, A_1) :\Leftrightarrow (\forall C)(A_1, C \vdash A \Rightarrow C \vdash A).$$

That the uniqueness requirement is not fulfilled for $\mathfrak{A}_w(A, A_1)$ can be seen as follows: suppose $\mathfrak{A}_\neg(A, A_1)$ is now the inferential characterization of intuitionistic negation in Popper's sense (the right side of (2.8)), that is,

$$\mathfrak{A}_\neg(A, A_1) :\Leftrightarrow (\forall C)(A, A_1 \vdash C \ \& \ (A_1, C \vdash A \Rightarrow C \vdash A)).$$

Suppose $\mathfrak{A}_t(A, A_1)$ is defined as

$$\mathfrak{A}_t(A, A_1) :\Leftrightarrow (\forall C)(C \vdash A),$$

which is the inferential characterization of a unary trivial truth operation. Obviously, both $\mathfrak{A}_\neg$ and $\mathfrak{A}_t$ satisfy uniqueness. Furthermore, it is clear that

$$\mathfrak{A}_\neg(A, A_1) \ \Rightarrow \ \mathfrak{A}_w(A, A_1)$$

as well as

$$\mathfrak{A}_t(A, A_1) \ \Rightarrow \ \mathfrak{A}_w(A, A_1).$$

Therefore, if for some A_1 in the given deducibility structure there are both an intuitionistic negation $\neg A_1$ and a truth operator $t A_1$ available, then both $\mathfrak{A}_w(\neg A_1, A_1)$ and $\mathfrak{A}_w(t A_1, A_1)$ hold. This means that, if $\mathfrak{A}_w$ is in fact an inferential characterization, for which uniqueness holds,

$$\neg A_1 \dashv\vdash t A_1$$

is valid, which trivializes the deducibility structure. Since deducibility structures, which, for some A_1, contain both $\neg A_1$ and $t A_1$, can easily be constructed, $\mathfrak{A}_w$ is not an inferential characterization. In fact, there is no inferential characterization for $\neg_w$, if the language considered is non-trivial. If everything is deducible in the language, then, of course, every $\mathfrak{A}$ is an inferential characterization.[13]

Observations such as these motivated me, in Schroeder-Heister (1984b), to interpret Popper's theory as a theory of logicality. According to this idea, an n-ary operation J is counted as logical if an inferential characterization

---

[13]This is an adaptation of an argument given by Popper for Johansson's minimal negation $\neg_j$ (see P5, p. 117, and Schroeder-Heister 1984b, pp. 101ff.). I chose $\neg_w$ rather than the slightly stronger (and more common) $\neg_j$, as for $\neg_w$ a formula $\mathfrak{A}_w(A, A_1)$ can be given that at least looks like an inferential characterization, whereas for minimal negation, which in natural deduction is characterized by the intuitionistic *reductio* rule

$$\frac{\overset{[A_1]}{C} \quad \overset{[A_1]}{\neg_j C}}{\neg_j A_1},$$

not even that is possible.

$\mathfrak{A}_J(A, A_1, \ldots, A_n)$ in Popper's sense is available for it. Weak negation would then not be logical, whereas classical negation would be so, and so on. This interpretation has strong support from some remarks in Popper's papers (for example, P1, p. 286) and in particular from later remarks in the Schilpp volume (Popper 1974, p. 1096). I even argued that one might consider those inferential characterizations $\mathfrak{A}$ as fundamental that contain only the metalinguistic operators of implication ($\Rightarrow$), conjunction (&), and universal quantification ($\forall$), as they suffice to formulate virtually all inferential characterizations. On that view, positive logic with implication, conjunction, and universal quantification would lie at the heart of deductive reasoning, representing some sort of basic logic, in terms of which other operations can be characterized. I still think this view can be upheld. However, it runs short of what Popper really intended. According to my reading now, Popper's message is that logical operations can be structurally characterized up to interdeducibility in terms of deducibility, using first-order metalinguistic means only. That this might at the same time indicate how to tackle the logicality problem, should be regarded only as an (important) side aspect.

3 Structuralist theory versus semantics

The title of his main philosophical paper on deduction: 'New Foundations for Logic' (P2), may suggest that Popper is aiming at a *justification* of the logical laws. Nothing is further from the truth. His structuralist theory, as I have reconstructed it, is a tool for metalinguistically *describing* logical theories, but never for *justifying* them. A justification would have to develop some sort of semantics of the logical operations and then determine which inferences or consequences are valid, and which are not valid, with respect to this semantics. The aim of the structuralist approach is to deal with a domain $\mathcal{D}$, for which a deducibility relation '$\vdash$' is given, and to characterize the operations available in $\langle \mathcal{D}, \vdash \rangle$. There is no *normative* task involved, which sometimes there is in semantics, as a semantics can distinguish between good and bad inferences and therefore between the right and wrong logic. The structuralist approach can distinguish only between candidates and non-candidates for logical operations. So Popper's talking of 'foundations' cannot be understood as justificationist.

Why is Popper's theory not suitable as a semantics? One might argue that an inferential characterization $\mathfrak{A}_J(A, A_1, \ldots, A_n)$ of some constant J could be used to introduce it explicitly into the language considered, provided there is some A such that $\mathfrak{A}_J(A, A_1, \ldots, A_n)$ holds, which might then be called $J(A_1, \ldots, A_n)$. However, this is not what Popper aims at.

A strong indication for this is the fact that Popper does not consider conservativeness a criterion for selecting certain inferential characterizations, and for preferring them to others. Normally, in a semantic theory, when introducing a new constant J, the new laws should not affect what can be formulated with the 'old' vocabulary, that is the vocabulary without J. For example, if I have a theory containing J_1 and I introduce J_2, then the new laws involving J_2 should not enable me to derive new laws for J_1 alone. In this sense, the theory for J_2 and J_1 together should be a *conservative extension* of the theory for J_1 alone.

Now in his inferential definitions, Popper explicitly deals with the situation where conservativeness does not hold. He does not consider this to be problematic but rather an interesting case to be discussed, in particular with respect to the relationship between different sorts of negations, such as intuitionistic and classical ones. The general phenomenon is the following. Given two inferential definitions $\mathfrak{A}_1(A, A_1, \ldots, A_n)$ and $\mathfrak{A}_2(A, A_1, \ldots, A_n)$, suppose that

$$(3.1) \qquad \mathfrak{A}_1(A, A_1, \ldots, A_n) \quad \Rightarrow \quad \mathfrak{A}_2(A, A_1, \ldots, A_n).$$

Then, owing to the uniqueness requirement, the operations characterized by $\mathfrak{A}_1$ and $\mathfrak{A}_2$ cannot be distinguished. For if both $\mathfrak{A}_1(A, A_1, \ldots, A_n)$ and $\mathfrak{A}_2(B, A_1, \ldots, A_n)$ hold, then, by (3.1), $\mathfrak{A}_2(A, A_1, \ldots, A_n)$ must hold too, which, by uniqueness, gives $A \dashv\vdash B$, which again yields $\mathfrak{A}_1(B, A_1, \ldots, A_n)$.

This means that, if an inferentially characterized operation is (seemingly) stronger than another one, in the sense that it satisfies the laws of the weaker one, then these operations cannot be distinguished; that is, the laws of the 'stronger' one hold also for the 'weaker' one, which violates conservativeness. The prominent example, which is considered by Popper, is classical in comparison with intuitionistic negation. For classical negation $\sim$, the right side of (2.4) (or alternatively (2.7)) is an inferential characterization $\mathfrak{A}_\sim$, for which uniqueness holds. As classical negation is stronger than intuitionistic negation,

$$(3.2) \qquad \mathfrak{A}_\sim(A, A_1) \quad \Rightarrow \quad \mathfrak{A}_\neg(A, A_1)$$

is valid, which, according to the argument given above, yields

$$\sim A_1 \dashv\vdash \neg A_1,$$

if both classical and intuitionistic negations are available in the language considered.[14] If intuitionistic negation is introduced first, then the introduction of classical negation destroys conservativeness, as it enforces classical laws such as *excluded middle* to hold for intuitionistic negation.[15] The fact that, in the presence of classical negation, no distinct intuitionistic negation can be characterized, is not seen by Popper as a violation of any fundamental principle, but rather a significant discovery, showing that different negations cannot arbitrarily coexist. This makes good sense if Popper's basic aim is not

---

[14]See P5, pp. 113f. More precisely, (3.2) holds if there is a B available such that $\mathfrak{A}_\sim(B, A)$. If double negation is not available, intuitionistic negation does not necessarily collapse into classical negation.

[15]The proof in §2.3 above, that weak negation $\neg_w$ cannot be inferentially characterized, was already an application of this sort of reasoning. There weak negation collapsed into *two* stronger operations t and $\neg$, which were mutually contradictory.

semantic foundation, but *structural description*.[16] Koslow's theory (and also my own in Schroeder-Heister 1984a) differs from Popper's in that it can in principle be turned into a semantic theory. Due to the special form of Koslow's inferential characterizations, conservativeness is bound to hold. The fact that he can prove distinctness of operators is a consequence of that. Of course, conservativeness and distinctness do not make a semantic theory yet. But the idea that inferential characterizations start with elimination rules and characterize logical compounds as the weakest sentences for which the elimination rules are valid, suggests a semantics, according to which meaning is based on elimination rules and other valid rules are justified with respect to them by minimality conditions. This would be dual to verificationist semantics in the Dummett–Prawitz tradition, which extracts meaning from introduction rules and therefore from assertibility conditions, and justifies other valid inferences by principles which come close to maximality conditions.[17]

I am not claiming that Koslow is proposing a semantics in this sense. In fact, he makes it clear throughout that his structuralist theory does not give certain logics or certain logical operations preference over others. I just want to remark that Koslow's theory with its *specific form* of inferential characterizations *might be given* a semantic reading under *certain circumstances*,[18] in contradistinction to Popper, where their form remains unspecified. Popper's theory is a *radical* structuralist theory in that just the inferential role of logical compounds is uniquely described without any further constraints. This prevents a semantic reading as there are no special features like introduction or elimination rules, *in virtue of which* certain laws are valid, as might be required by a proof-theoretic semantics. On the other hand, by dealing with syntactically specified object-linguistic operations and using a bad terminology, Popper has failed to make his intentions sufficiently clear.

This is not intended as a defence of Popper's view. Conservativeness is a principle with strong grounding, as is the distinctness of operations characterized. There are good reasons to argue that, if operations are to be inferentially characterized at all, this should be done separately and independently for each of them, that is an inferential characterization of one operation (for example, classical negation) should not substantially alter that of another one given before (for example, intuitionistic negation). Therefore Koslow's structuralist approach might be preferable at the end. In any case, Popper's radical structuralist view is a coherent approach when properly reconstructed.

---

[16] Actually, in investigating various negations, some of which can be inferentially characterized whereas others cannot, and some of which can distinctly coexist, whereas others cannot (see P5, and P1, pp. 282f., note), Popper already considers the idea of combining logics, which only recently has gained significant attention (see, for example, Gabbay 1999).

[17] See Dummett (1991), Chapter 11, and Prawitz (1974), Schroeder-Heister (2006). In this tradition the dual approach based on elimination rules is occasionally mentioned as a possibility (see, for example, Prawitz 1971, Appendix A.2, and Dummett 1991, Chapter 13).

[18] Namely in cases where a syntactically specified object language is dealt with, and where the logical operations are represented in this language by syntactical operators.

4 Conclusion: A new view of logic?

Popper does not give new foundations for logic in the sense that he semantically justifies a logical system. Rather, the structuralist view is a descriptive approach, providing a framework in which various different logics (and even non-logics, as Koslow emphasized) can be defined as deducibility structures $\langle \mathcal{D}, \vdash \rangle$ with operations H_J that are inferentially characterized by conditions $\mathfrak{A}_J$. If providing such a framework is considered the basic task of logic, this is a new view of logic as a philosophical or mathematical discipline. Logic would then take a neutral stance towards competing logical systems, and just aim at comparing them with respect to their structural properties. This view not only is advocated by an outspoken structuralist such as Koslow, but has been present in certain areas of logic for two decades, especially in dealing with alternative logics. Examples are 'logical frameworks' in computer science describing various logics from a general (often type-theoretic) position,[19] and also the treatment of non-classical logics in terms of principles governing the consequence relation.[20] In this sense Popper's talking of 'new foundations' for logic would just be a misleading way of proposing a new orientation of logic as a descriptive rather than normative discipline.

This interpretation of Popper's logical papers is much in line with his other writings, in which he adopts a strong *anti-foundationalist* and *anti-justificationist* point of view (see Popper 1960). It would be extremely surprising if with respect to deductive logic Popper claimed just the opposite by *justifying* it and laying *new foundations* for it. Even though the logical writings were written much earlier than his papers against foundationalism, his main views have been there since *Logik der Forschung* (1935). Popper's later claim that classical logic is best suited for scientific reasoning, as it makes refutations easiest (Popper 1968, § 6 (3′), and 1970, § 4), thus fitting best with the idea of logic as the 'Organon of rational criticism' (Popper 1963, Chapter 1, appendix, paragraph (13)), also supports this view. Structural description of logical systems is one issue, the question of which logic to choose for a certain purpose is a different one, not belonging to philosophical logic any more. The latter question has to be answered by extra-logical reasons, yet on the basis of the structural evaluation of what the various possible systems can achieve.

Hence the structuralist reading, for which Koslow's theory is the best elaborated model, is not only perfectly *compatible* with Popper's general philosophical approach, but gives deductive logic a *clear-cut role* in his philosophical framework.

---

[19] See Huet & Plotkin (1991) and the references therein.

[20] See Gabbay (1994). An example is the treatment of consequence relations in non-monotonic logics, as in the classic paper of Kraus, Lehmann, & Magidor (1990).

Appendix 1: The axiomatization of absolutely valid rules

In P4, Popper tries to axiomatize the deducibility predicate '⊢' in such a way that the structural (= 'absolutely valid') rules for '⊢' become derivable. For deducibility $\Gamma \vdash A$, where Γ is now an ordered *list* (rather than a *set*) of sentences, he gives the following axioms, called *Basis I*:

(A.1) $B \vdash A \iff B, B \vdash A$

(A.2) $\Gamma \vdash A \ \& \ A, \Gamma \vdash C \implies \Delta, \check{\Gamma} \vdash C$

(A.3) $(\forall C)(\Gamma, A \vdash C \implies \check{\Gamma} \vdash C) \implies \Gamma \vdash A.$

Here $\check{\Gamma}$ results from Γ by putting its elements in reverse order, that is, if Γ is $\langle A_1, \ldots, A_n \rangle$, then $\check{\Gamma}$ is $\langle A_n, \ldots, A_1 \rangle$. The axioms are stated in my notation, using capital Greek letters for lists of sentences and understanding that the schematic letters A, B, C, Γ, Δ are universally quantified from outside. Popper's notation is less perspicuous. He combines (A.2) and (A.3) into a single axiom which is difficult to read. Under a formalist reading of deducibility statements, Axiom (A.3) can also be formulated as:

$$\Gamma \vdash A \text{ holds, if for every } C, \text{ the rule } \frac{\Gamma, A \vdash C}{\check{\Gamma} \vdash C} \text{ is admissible.}$$

Using (A.1), (A.2), and (A.3), Popper's reasoning in P4, Part I, can then be reconstructed as a derivation of all relevant structural rules.

It is difficult to see why elementary structural rules such as permutation, thinning, or cut should and could be reduced to something even more fundamental. It is very questionable whether the principles considered by Popper as a 'basis', are philosophically basic indeed. The standard structural rules appear more plausible and clearcut than principles (A.1)–(A.3). (A.1) is a special case of contraction and expansion (the dual of contraction), (A.2) combines cut with thinning and a special form of permutation, and (A.3) is a principle, which cannot even be formulated in the form of an inference rule, stating some sort of inverse to cut.

This is even more a problem for Popper's second axiomatization in P4, Part II, which combines purely structural aspects of '⊢' with properties of (object-linguistic) conjunction ∧, thus violating the idea that the structural base should be independent of the logical operations available.

Appendix 2: Deducibility with multiple succedents

At some places, Popper uses deducibility statements whose succedent is a finite set of formulas (P4, pp. 51-53). However, in contradistinction to Gentzen's approach, this is not considered a primitive notion. It is defined as follows:

$$\Gamma \vdash \Delta \ :\iff \ (\forall C)((\forall A \in \Delta)(A \vdash C) \implies \Gamma \vdash C).$$

Actually, the definition with context formulas

$$\Gamma \vdash \Delta \ :\Leftrightarrow\ (\forall \Gamma_1)(\forall C)((\forall A \in \Delta)(A, \Gamma_1 \vdash C) \Rightarrow \Gamma, \Gamma_1 \vdash C)$$

would be more general. The definition of deducibility with multiple succedents gives Popper the possibility to define the *refutability* of a list of formulas Γ as the limiting case where the succedent Δ is empty.

Using his definition of multiple succedent deducibility, in P5 Popper gives an inferential definition of classical negation as follows (p. 112):

$$A \dashv\vdash \sim A_1 \ \Leftrightarrow\ (A, A_1 \vdash\ \&\ \vdash A, A_1)$$

which would have to be spelled out as

$$A \dashv\vdash \sim A_1 \ \Leftrightarrow\ ((\forall C)(A, A_1 \vdash C)\ \&\ (\forall D)(A \vdash D\ \&\ A_1 \vdash D\ \Rightarrow\ \vdash D)).$$

This means that classical negation is characterized by the contradiction rule and by the *classical dilemma* (which corresponds to the law of *excluded middle*), or, as Popper puts it, 'the classical negation of b can be defined (as Aristotle might have defined it) as that statement which is at once contradictory and complementary to b' (ibidem).

Unfortunately, Popper only briefly mentions Gentzen's idea of multiple succedent sequents in a footnote (P4, p. 52).

Bibliography

Curry, H. B. (1948/1949). Reviews of P3, P1, P4, P5, P6. *Mathematical Reviews* **9**, 1948, p. 321, p. 486, pp. 486f., p. 487, and **10**, 1949, p. 422.

Dummett, M. A. E. (1991). *The Logical Basis of Metaphysics*. London: Duckworth.

Gabbay, D. (1999). *Fibring Logics*. Oxford: Clarendon Press.

————, editor (1994). *What Is a Logical System?* Oxford: Clarendon Press.

Gentzen, G. (1935). 'Untersuchungen über das logische Schließen'. *Mathematische Zeitschrift* **39**, pp. 176-210, 405-431. English translation in M. E. Szabo, editor (1969), 68-131. *The Collected Papers of Gerhard Gentzen*. Amsterdam: North Holland Publishing Company.

Hasenjaeger, G. (1949). Review of P6. *Zentralblatt für Mathematik und ihre Grenzgebiete* **31**, p. 193.

Hertz, P. (1923). 'Über Axiomensysteme für beliebige Satzsysteme. II. Teil. Sätze höheren Grades'. *Mathematische Annalen* **89**, pp. 76-102.

Huet, G. & Plotkin, G., editors (1991). *Logical Frameworks*. Cambridge: Cambridge University Press.

Kleene, S. C. (1947/1948). Review of P3. *Journal of Symbolic Logic* **13** (1947), pp. 173f. Review of P4, P5, and P6, ibidem **14** (1948), pp. 62f.

Koslow, A. (1992). *A Structuralist Theory of Logic*. Cambridge: Cambridge University Press.

Kraus, S., Lehmann, D., & Magidor, M. (1990). 'Nonmonotonic Reasoning, Preferential Models and Cumulative Logics'. *Artificial Intelligence* **44**, pp. 167-207.

Lejewski, C. (1974). 'Popper's Theory of Formal or Deductive Inference'. In Schilpp (1974), pp. 632-670.

McKinsey, J. C. C. (1948). Review of P1 and P2. *Journal of Symbolic Logic* **13**, pp. 114f.

Popper, K. R. (1935). *Logik der Forschung*. Vienna: Julius Springer Verlag.

———— (1947a). 'Logic without Assumptions'. *Proceedings of the Aristotelian Society* **47**, pp. 251-292. [**P1**]

———— (1947b). 'New Foundations for Logic'. *Mind* **56**, pp. 193-235. Corrections in *Mind* **57** (1948), pp. 69f. [**P2**]

———— (1947c). 'Functional Logic without Axioms or Primitive Rules of Inference'. *Indagationes Mathematicae* **9**, pp. 561-571. [**P3**]

———— (1948a). 'On the Theory of Deduction, I: Derivation and Its Generalizations'. *Indagationes Mathematicae* **10**, pp. 44-54. [**P4**]

———— (1948b). 'On the Theory of Deduction, II: The Definitions of Classical and Intuitionist Negation. *Indagationes Mathematicae* **10**, pp. 111-120. [**P5**]

—— (1949). 'The Trivialization of Mathematical Logic'. In E. W. Beth & others, editors (1949), pp. 722-727, p. 1259 (corrections). *Proceedings of the 10th International Congress of Philosophy.* Amsterdam: North Holland. [**P6**]

—— (1960). 'On the Sources of Knowledge and of Ignorance'. *Proceedings of the British Academy* **46**, pp. 39-71. Reprinted as the Introduction to Popper (1963).

—— (1963). *Conjectures and Refutations: The Growth of Scientific Knowledge.* London: Routledge & Kegan Paul. 5th edition 1989.

—— (1968). 'Epistemology Without a Knowing Subject'. In B. van Rootselaar & J. F. Staal, editors (1968), pp. 333-373. *Proceedings of the Third International Congress for Logic, Methodology and Philosophy of Science.* Amsterdam: North-Holland Publishing Company. Reprinted as Chapter 3 of Popper (1972).

—— (1970). 'A Realist View of Logic, Physics, and History'. In W. Yourgrau & A. D. Breck, editors (1970), pp. 1-30. *Physics, Logic and History.* New York: Plenum Press. Reprinted as Chapter 8 of Popper (1972).

—— (1972). *Objective Knowledge.* Oxford: Clarendon Press. 2nd edition 1979.

—— (1974). 'Lejewski's Axiomatization of My Theory of Deducibility'. In Schilpp (1974), pp. 1095f.

Prawitz, D. (1965). *Natural Deduction: A Proof-Theoretical Study.* Stockholm: Almqvist & Wiksell.

—— (1971). 'Ideas and Results in Proof Theory'. In J. E. Fenstad, editor (1971), pp. 235-308. *Proceedings of the 2nd Scandinavian Logic Symposium (Oslo 1970).* Amsterdam: North Holland Publishing Company.

—— (1974). 'On the Idea of a General Proof Theory'. *Synthese* **27**, pp. 63-77.

Schilpp, P. A., editor (1974). *The Philosophy of Karl Popper.* La Salle IL: Open Court Publishing Company.

Schroeder-Heister, P. (1984a). 'A Natural Extension of Natural Deduction'. *Journal of Symbolic Logic* **49**, pp. 1284-1300.

—— (1984b). 'Popper's Theory of Deductive Inference and the Concept of a Logical Constant'. *History and Philosophy of Logic* **5**, pp. 79-110.

—— (2002). 'Resolution and the Origins of Structural Reasoning: Early Proof-theoretic Ideas of Hertz and Gentzen'. *Bulletin of Symbolic Logic* **8**, pp. 246-265.

—— (2006). 'Validity Concepts in Proof-theoretic Semantics'. *Synthese* **148**, pp. 525-571.

Popper as a Philosopher of Mathematics

Eduard Glas

1 Introduction

Popper is not usually regarded as a philosopher of mathematics. As mathematical propositions fail to forbid any observable state of affairs, his demarcation criterion clearly separates mathematics from empirical science, and Popper was primarily concerned with empirical science. Speaking of a Popperian philosophy of mathematics, we mostly immediately think of Lakatos, who is usually considered to have applied and extended Popper's philosophy of *science* to mathematics. Like Lakatos, Popper saw considerable similarity between the methods of mathematics and of science — he held most of mathematics to be hypothetico-deductive (Popper 1992, Chapter 4, § III) — and he thought highly of his former pupil's quasi-empiricist approach to the logic of mathematical development (Popper 1972/1979, pp. 136f., 143, 165). His own views of the matter, however, are not to be identified with those of Lakatos, nor does their significance consist only in their having prepared the ground for the latter's methodological endeavours.

Popper never developed his views of mathematics systematically. However, scattered throughout his works, and often ancillary to other discussions, there are many passages that together amount to a truly Popperian philosophy of mathematics. This side of Popper's philosophy has remained rather underexposed, especially as compared with the excitement aroused by Lakatos's work, many of whose central ideas were developments of Popperian views, not only of science, but more specifically of mathematics as well. An earlier article of mine contains a detailed comparison between Popper's and Lakatos's views of mathematics, and an analysis of the Popperian roots of Lakatos's mathematical methodology (Glas 2001). In the present paper, I leave Lakatos aside and focus on Popper's own dialectic account of the growth of mathematical knowledge.

2 Fallibilism

Already in *Logik der Forschung* (1935), Popper had argued that we should never save a threatened theoretical system by ad hoc adjustments, 'conventionalist stratagems', that reduce its testability (Popper 1959, § 20) — a view

which was to be exploited by Lakatos to such dramatic effect in the dia-
logues of *Proofs and Refutations* (1963-1964/1976), under the heads of monster barring, exception barring, and monster adjustment. In *Conjectures and
Refutations* (1963), Popper showed how the critical method can be applied
to pure mathematics. Rather than questioning directly the status of mathematical truths, he tackled mathematical absolutism from a different angle.
Mathematical truths may possess the greatest possible (though never absolute) certainty, but mathematics is not just the accumulation of truths. Theories essentially are attempts at solving certain problems, and they are to be
critically assessed, evaluated, and tested, by their ability to solve adequately
the problems that they address, especially in comparison with possible rivals
(Popper 1963, Chapter 8, Chapter 10, § IX).

   This form of critical fallibilism obviously differed from Lakatos's quasi-
empiricism, among other things by avoiding the latter's considerable problems
with identifying the 'basic statements' that can act as potential falsifiers of
mathematical theories. Even so, Lakatos's referring to what he called Popper's
'mistake of reserving a privileged infallible status for mathematics' (Lakatos
1976, p. 139 footnote) seems unjust. Claiming immunity to one kind of refutation — empirical falsification — is not claiming immunity to all forms of
criticism, much less infallibility. As a matter of fact, Popper did not consider
anything, including logic itself, entirely certain and incorrigible (Popper, 1992,
Chapter 4, § III).

3 Objectivity

Central to Popper's philosophy of mathematics was a group of ideas clus-
tering around the doctrine of the relative autonomy of knowledge 'in the
objective sense' — in contradistinction to the subjective sense of the beliefs
of a knowing subject. Characteristic of science and mathematics is that they
are formulated in a descriptive and argumentative language, and that the
problems, theories and errors contained in them stand in particular relations,
independently of the beliefs that humans may have with respect to them.
Once objectivized from their human creators, mathematical theories have an
infinity of entailments, some entirely unintended and unexpected, that transcend the subjective consciousness of any human — and even of all humans,
as is shown by the existence of unsolvable problems (Popper 1972, Chapter 4,
§ 4). In this sense, no human subject can ever completely 'know' the objective
content of a mathematical theory, that is, including all its unforeseeable and
unfathomable implications.

   It is trivially true that knowledge in the said objective sense can subsist
without anybody being aware of it, for instance in the case of totally forgotten theories that are later recaptured from some written source. It also
has significant effects on human consciousness — even observation depends
on judgements made against a background of objective knowledge — and
through it on the physical world (for instance in the form of technologies).

Human consciousness thus typically acts as a mediator between the abstract and the concrete, or the world of culture and the world of nature. To acknowledge that linguistically expressed knowledge can subsist without humans, that it possesses independent properties and relationships, and that it can produce mental and also — indirectly — physical effects, is tantamount to saying that it in a way exists. Of course, it does not exist in the way in which we say that physical or mental objects or processes exist: its existence is of a 'third' kind. As is well known, Popper coined the expression 'third world' (or 'world 3', as he later preferred) to refer to this abstract realm of objectivized products of human thought and language.

Popper's insistence upon the crucial distinction between the objective (third-world) and the subjective (second-world) dimension of knowledge enabled him to overcome the traditional dichotomies between those philosophies of mathematics that hold mathematical objects to be human constructions, intuitions, or inventions, and those that postulate their objective existence. His 'epistemology without a knowing subject' accounts for how mathematics can at once be autonomous *and* man-made, that is, how mathematical objects, relations, and problems can be said in a way to exist independently of human consciousness *although* they are products of human (especially linguistic) practices. Mathematics is a human activity, and the product of this activity, mathematical knowledge, is a human creation. Once created, however, this product assumes a partially autonomous and timeless status: it possesses its own objective, partly unintended and unexpected properties, irrespective of when, if ever, humans become aware of them.

Popper regarded mathematical objects — the system of natural numbers in particular — as products of human language and human thought: acquiring a language means essentially being able to grasp objective thought *contents*. The development of mathematics shows that with new linguistic means new kinds of facts and in particular new kinds of problems can be described. Unlike what apriorists such as Kant and Descartes held, being human constructions does not make mathematical objects completely transparent, *clair et distinct*, to us. For instance, as soon as the natural numbers had been created or invented, the distinctions between odd and even, and between composite and prime numbers, and the associated problem of the Goldbach conjecture came to exist objectively: Is every even number greater than 2 the sum of two primes? Is this problem solvable or unsolvable? And if unsolvable, can its unsolvability be proved? And so on (Popper 1992, Chapter 1, § 2.XI). These problems in a sense have existed ever since humankind possessed a number system, although during many centuries nobody had been aware of them. Thus we can make genuine *discoveries* of independent problems and new hard facts about our own creations, and of objective (not merely intersubjective) truths about these matters.

Nothing mystical is involved here. On the contrary, Popper brought the platonist heaven of ideal mathematical entities down to earth, characterizing it as objectivized *human* knowledge. The theory of the third world at once

accounts for the working mathematician's strong feeling that he or she is
dealing with something real and explains how human consciousness can have
access to abstract objects. As we have seen, these objects are not causally
inert: for instance, by reading texts we become aware of some of their objective
contents and the problems, arguments, and other abstract entities that are
contained in them, so that the platonist riddle of how we can gain knowledge of
objects existing outside space and time does not arise. Of course, speaking of
causality here is using this notion in a somewhat peculiar, not in a mechanistic
sense. That reading texts causes in us a certain awareness of what is contained
in those texts is just a plain fact for whose acceptance no intricate causal
theory of language understanding is needed.

So, cultural artefacts like mathematics possess their own partially autonomous properties and relationships that are independent of our awareness
of them: they have the character of hard facts that are there to be *discovered*.
In this respect they are very much like physical objects and relations, which are
not unconditionally 'observable' either, but are apprehended only in a language that already incorporates many theories in the very structure of its usage.
Like mathematical facts, empirical facts are thoroughly theory-impregnated
and speculative, so that a strict separation between what traditionally has
been called the analytic and the synthetic elements of scientific theories is
illusory. The effectiveness of pure mathematics in natural science is miracu-
lous only to a logical positivist, who cannot imagine how formulas arrived at
entirely independently of empirical data can be adequate for the formulation
of theories supposedly inferred from empirical data. But once it is recognized
that the basic concepts and operations of arithmetic and geometry have been
designed originally for the practical purpose of counting and measuring, it is
almost trivial that all mathematics based on them remains applicable exactly
to the extent that natural phenomena resemble operations in geometry and
arithmetic sufficiently to be conceptualized in (man-made) terms of countable
and measurable things, and thus to be represented in mathematical language.
In mathematics and physics alike, theories are often put forward as mere speculations, mere possibilities, the difference being that scientific theories are to
be tested directly against empirical material, and mathematical theories only
indirectly, if and in so far as they are applied in physics or otherwise (Popper
1963, pp. 210, 331).

4 Logic, language, and criticism

It is especially the (dialectic) idea of *interaction* and partial *overlap* between
the three worlds that enables Popper's theory to transcend the foundationalist
programmes. Clearly, objective knowledge (world 3), that is, the objective contents of theories, can exist only if those theories have been materially realized
in texts (world 1), which cannot be written nor be read without involving human consciousness (world 2). Put somewhat bluntly, platonists acknowledge
only a third world as the realm to which all mathematical truths pertain,

strictly separated from the physical world; intuitionists locate mathematics in a second world of mental constructions and operations, whereas formalists reduce mathematics to rule-governed manipulation with 'signs signifying nothing', that is, mere material (first-world) 'marks'. In any case, reality is split up into at most two independent realms (physical and ideal or physical and mental), as if these were the only possible alternatives. Popper's tripartite world view surpasses physicalist or mentalist reductionism as well as physical/mental dualism, emphasizing that there are *three* partially autonomous realms, intimately coupled through feedback. The theory of the interaction between all three worlds shows how these seemingly incompatible mathematical ontologies can be reconciled and their mutual oppositions overcome (Popper 1992, § 3.XII; cp. Niiniluoto 1992).

I am not suggesting, of course, that Popper has given a final and exhaustive explanation of the nature of mathematical facts; his concern was primarily with the development of mathematical knowledge. Still, the three worlds distinction does much to clarify the said ontological problem, and provides a fruitful basis for further investigation.

The notion of a partially autonomous realm of objective knowledge has been criticized, most elaborately by O'Hear in his Popper monograph (1980). O'Hear does not deny that objectivized mathematical theories have partly unforeseeable and inevitable implications, but he does not consider this sufficient reason for posing what he calls 'an autonomous non-human realm of pure ideas'. Popper, of course, always spoke of a *partially* autonomous realm, not of 'pure ideas', but especially of fallible theories, problems, tentative solutions and critical arguments. O'Hear, however, argues that Popper's theory is misleading because it would imply that we are not in control of world 3 but are, on the contrary, completely controlled *by* it (pp. 183, 207). For relationships in world 3 are of a *logical* character, which is taken to mean that they are completely beyond our control. On O'Hear's construal, Popper allowed only a human-constructive input at the very beginning of the history of mathematics — the phase of primitive concepts connected with counting and measuring — after which logic took over and developments were no longer under human control. World 3 would be entirely autonomous rather than only partially autonomous, and mathematicians would be passive analysers rather than active synthesizers of mathematical knowledge — almost the opposite of Popper's earlier emphasis on the active role of the subject in observation and theory formation. I think that these conclusions rest on a misunderstanding of the logical character of relationships in world 3.

To stress the objective and partly autonomous dimension of knowledge is not to lose sight of the fact that it is created, discussed, evaluated, tested, and modified by human beings. Popper regarded world 3 above all as a product of intelligent human action, and especially of the human ability to express and criticize arguments in language. The objectivity of mathematics rests, as does that of all science, upon the criticizability of its arguments, so on language as the indispensable medium of critical discussion (Popper 1972,

Chapter 3, § 6 (1′)). Indeed, it is from language that we get the idea of 'logical consequence' in the first place, on which the third world so strongly depends. But mathematics is not *just* language, and neither is it *just* logic: there are such things as extra-logical mathematical objects. And although critical discussion depends on the use of discursive language, mathematics is not bound to one particular *system* of logic. O'Hear (1980, pp. 191-198) rightly argued that there is room for choices to fit our pre-systematic intuitions and even physical realities (he for instance discusses deviating logics to fit quantum mechanics). But the possibility of alternative logics does not invalidate the idea of logical consequence as such, it does not make one or the other of alternative logical systems illogical. The choice of a *specific* logical system for mathematics or science has itself to be decided by 'logical' argumentation (in the *general* sense of the term).

Although the third world arises together with argumentative language, it does not consist exclusively of linguistic forms but contains also non-linguistic objects. As is well known, the concept of number, for instance, can be axiomatically described in a variety of ways that, however, define it only up to isomorphism. That we have different logical explications of number does not mean that we are talking about different objects (nor that the numbers with which our ancestors worked were entirely different from ours). We must distinguish between numbers as third-world objects and the fallible and changing theories that we form about these objects. We have their various first-world representations on paper, their second-world representations in the minds of people, but over and above these also the objective third-world idea of number. That the third-world objects themselves are partly autonomous means that our theories about them are essentially incomplete, unable to capture fully their inexhaustible richness.

5 Popperian dialectic

The idea that the third world of objective mathematical knowledge is partly autonomous does not at all imply that the role of mathematicians is reduced to passive observation of a pre-given realm of mathematical objects and structures — no more than that the autonomy of the first world would reduce the role of physicists to passive observation of physical states of affairs. On the contrary, the growth of mathematical knowledge is almost entirely due to the constant feedback or 'dialectic' between human creative action upon the third world and the action of the third world upon human thought. Popper characterized world 3 as the (evolutionary) product of the rational efforts of humans who, by trying to eliminate contradictions in the extant body of knowledge, produce new theories, arguments and problems, essentially along the lines of what he called 'the critical interpretation of the (non-Hegelian) dialectic schema:

$$P_1 \Rightarrow TT \Rightarrow EE \Rightarrow P_2 \Rightarrow$$

(Popper 1972, p. 164). P_1 is the initial problem situation, that is, a problem picked out against a third-world background. *TT* is the first tentative theoretical solution, which is followed by error elimination (*EE*), its severe critical examination and evaluation in comparison with any rival solutions. P_2 is the new problem situation arising from the critical discussion, in which the 'experiences' (that is, the failures) of the foregoing attempts are used to pinpoint both their weak and their strong points, so that we may learn how to improve our guesses.

Every rational theory, whether mathematical or scientific or metaphysical, is rational on Popper's view exactly 'in so far as it tries to *solve certain problems*. A theory is comprehensible and reasonable only in its relation to a given problem-situation, and it can be rationally discussed only by discussing this relation' (Popper 1963, Chapter 8, § 2). In mathematics as in science, it is always problems and tentative problem solutions that are at stake. We are not interested just in truths (much less in truisms), but in truths that are relevant to an interesting problem (ibidem, Chapter 10, § IX): '[o]nly if it is an answer to a problem — a difficult, a fertile problem, a problem of some depth — does a truth, or a conjecture about the truth, become relevant to science. This is so in pure mathematics, and it is so in the natural sciences.' Popper clearly did not view mathematics as a formal language game, but as a rational problem solving activity based, like all rational pursuits, on speculation and criticism.

Although they have no falsifiers in the logical sense — they do not forbid any singular spatio-temporal statement — mathematical theories (as well as logical, philosophical, metaphysical and other non-empirical theories) can nevertheless be critically assessed for their ability to solve the problems in response to which they were designed, and accordingly improved along the lines of the *situational* logic or dialectic indicated above. In particular, mathematical and other 'irrefutable' theories often provide a basis or framework for the development of scientific theories that *do* have empirical falsifiers (Popper 1963, Chapter 8) — a view which later was to inspire Lakatos's notion of research programmes with an 'irrefutable' hard core (Lakatos 1978, p. 95).

Most characteristic of Popper's approach to mathematics was his focussing entirely on the dynamics of conceptual change through the dialectic process outlined, replacing the preoccupation of the traditional approach with definitions and explications of meanings. Interesting formalizations are not attempts at clarifying meanings but at solving concrete problems, such as the elimination of contradictions, and this has often been achieved by *abandoning* the attempt to clarify, or make exact, or explicate the intended or intuitive meaning of the concepts in question — as illustrated in particular by the development and rigorization of the calculus (Popper 1983, Addendum to Part I, Chapter IV). From his objectivist point of view, epistemology becomes the theory of problem solving, that is, of the construction, critical discussion, evaluation, and critical testing, of competing conjectural theories. In this enterprise, everything is welcome as a source of inspiration, including intuition, convention, tradition, and especially anything that suggests new problems. Most creative ideas are based on intuition, and those that are not are the result of criticism of intuitive ideas (Popper 1992, Chapter 4, §iii). There is no sharp distinction between intuitive and discursive thought. With the development of discursive language, our intuitive grasp has become utterly different from what it was before. This has become particularly apparent from the twentieth-century foundational crisis and the ensuing discoveries about incompleteness and undecidability: even our logical intuitions turned out to be liable to correction by discursive mathematical reasoning (ibidem §3).

There is a give-and-take between intuition, construction, convention, and criticism, but ultimately it is through language that we can lay out our thoughts objectively in symbolic form and then develop, discuss, test, and improve them. Humankind has used language to create a body of objective knowledge, stored in libraries and handed down from generation to generation, which enables us to profit from the trials and errors of our ancestors. The dialectic interplay between intuitive constructions in world 2, and their textual expression in world 1, necessarily involves us in the world 3 of objective problems and critical arguments.

Bibliography

Glas, E. (2001). 'The Popperian Programme and Mathematics'. *Studies in History and Philosophy of Science* **32**, pp. 119-137, 355-376.

Lakatos, I. (1963-1964). 'Proofs and Refutations'. *The British Journal for the Philosophy of Science* **14**, pp. 1-25, 120-139, 221-243, 296-342. Reprinted as I. Lakatos (1976). *Proofs and Refutations: The Logic of Mathematical Discovery*. Cambridge: Cambridge University Press.

———— (1978). *The Methodology of Scientific Research Programmes*. Cambridge: Cambridge University Press.

Niiniluoto, I. (1992). 'Reality, Truth, and Confirmation in Mathematics — Reflections on the Quasi-Empiricist Programme'. In J. Echeverria, A. Ibarra, & T. Mormann, editors (1992), pp. 60-77. *The Space of Mathematics*. Berlin & New York: De Gruyter.

O'Hear, A. (1980). *Karl Popper*. London: Routledge & Kegan Paul.

Popper, K. R. (1935). *Logik der Forschung*. Vienna: Julius Springer Verlag.

———— (1959). *The Logic of Scientific Discovery*. London: Hutchinson. English translation of Popper (1935).

———— (1963). *Conjectures and Refutations: The Growth of Scientific Knowledge*. London: Routledge & Kegan Paul. 5th edition 1989. London: Routledge.

———— (1972). *Objective Knowledge*. Oxford: Clarendon Press. 2nd edition 1979.

———— (1983). *Realism and the Aim of Science*. London: Hutchinson.

———— (1992). *In Search of a Better World*. London: Routledge.

PART 4
Science

B: Physics

Popper and
the Logic of Quantum Mechanics

Maria Luisa Dalla Chiara & Roberto Giuntini

Quantum mechanics (QM) has been a frequent object of investigation in the philosophical research of Karl Popper. At the same time, there are only few occasions where Popper devoted his attention to quantum logic (QL).

An important contribution is the article 'Birkhoff and von Neumann's Interpretation of Quantum Mechanics', which appeared in an issue of *Nature* in 1968. It is quite natural to ask: why such a late intervention, 32 years after the publication of Birkhoff & von Neumann's 'The Logic of Quantum Mechanics' (1936)? A partial answer is given by Popper himself: one is dealing with 'a paper which, after 32 years is still most influential'. In fact, the 1960s represented a 'renaissance period' for quantum logical investigations. We need think only of the fundamental contributions of Mackey, Jauch, Piron, Suppes, Mittelstaedt, and many others.

Popper's intention seems to be a radical criticism of the original roots of such approaches:

> My thesis is that Birkhoff and von Neumann's proposal is untenable. This is so partly ... because of some discoveries in lattice theory made by John von Neumann ... But it is so also ... because of certain very simple results of probability theory ....

In other words, the attempt is to reject Birkhoff & von Neumann's quantum logic by appealing to some of their algebraic results.

In order to follow Popper's argument, it will be expedient to recall some basic points of 'The Logic of Quantum Mechanics'. At the very beginning of their paper (1936, p. 823), Birkhoff & von Neumann observe:

> One of the aspects of quantum theory which has attracted the most general attention, is the novelty of the logical notions which it presupposes .... The object of the present paper is to discover what logical structures one may hope to find in physical theories which, like quantum mechanics, do not conform to classical logic.

Why does QM not conform to classical logic (CL)?

Both in classical and in quantum mechanics, *maximal* pieces of information about the physical systems under investigation are represented by *pure states*. There is, however, a basic difference between classical and quantum pure states. In classical mechanics (CM) any maximal information is *logically complete*: pure states *semantically decide all physical events* that may occur in our systems. The *semantic excluded middle principle* holds: any event E is either *true* or *false* for any pure state ψ.

In this framework, classical events can be mathematically represented by appropriate sets of pure states. As a consequence, the algebraic structure of all events turns out to be a *Boolean algebra*

$$\mathcal{C} = \langle \mathcal{E}_\nu, \wedge, \vee, ', \mathbf{1}, \mathbf{0} \rangle,$$

where

- $\wedge, \vee, '$ are the set-theoretic intersection, union, complement, respectively;

- $\mathbf{1}$ is the total set (representing the *certain event*), while $\mathbf{0}$ is the empty set (representing the *impossible event*).

According to a standard interpretation, $\wedge, \vee, '$ can be naturally regarded as a set-theoretic realization of the classical logical connectives *and, or, not*.

QM, instead, is essentially probabilistic. A pure state ψ generally assigns to a quantum event E a probability value $\psi(E)$ (a real number in the interval $[0,1]$). As a consequence, a quantum event may be semantically *indeterminate* for a given pure state, and the excluded middle principle is violated.

What about the algebraic structure of all quantum events? The most important novelty of Birkhoff & von Neumann's proposal is based on the following answer: the mathematical representative of any quantum event is a *closed subspace* of a special kind of abstract space called a *Hilbert space*. From an intuitive point of view, a Hilbert space $\mathcal{H}$ can be regarded as a kind of 'mathematical environment' for the physical system under investigation.[1]

The question arises: what do *negation, conjunction*, and *disjunction* mean in the realm of quantum events? As to the negation, Birkhoff & von Neumann's answer is the following: the mathematical representative E' of the *negative* of an event E is the *orthocomplement* of E. In other words, E' is the closed subspace that contains precisely all vectors that are *orthogonal* to all elements of E.

As to conjunction, Birkhoff & von Neumann notice that this can still be represented by the set-theoretic intersection (as in CM). For, the intersection of two closed subspaces is again a closed subspace. Disjunction, however, cannot be represented in the quantum case as set-theoretic union. For, generally, the union of two closed subspaces is not a closed subspace. In spite of this, we have at our disposal another good representative for the connective *or*: the *supremum* $E \vee F$ of two closed subspaces E, F, that is, the smallest closed subspace including both E and F.

---

[1] Closed subspaces of $\mathcal{H}$ are particular subsets of $\mathcal{H}$ that are closed under linear combinations and Cauchy sequences.

As a consequence, we obtain the following structure:

$$\mathcal{Q} = \langle \mathcal{E}\nu, \wedge, \vee, ', \mathbf{1}, \rangle,$$

where:

- $\wedge$ is the intersection, $\vee$ is the supremum, $'$ is the orthocomplement;

- $\mathbf{1}$ (the *certain event*) and $\mathbf{0}$ (the *impossible event*) correspond to the total space and to the null subspace, respectively.

The quantum structure $\mathcal{Q}$ turns out to simulate a 'quasi-Boolean behaviour'; however, it is not a Boolean. Something very essential is missing. Conjunction and disjunction are no longer distributive. Generally:

$$E \wedge (F \vee G) \neq (E \wedge F) \vee (E \wedge G).$$

The two events

- E and $(F$ or $G)$,

- $(E$ and $F)$ or $(E$ and $G)$

are not identical!

In fact, $\mathcal{Q}$ belongs to the variety of all *orthocomplemented orthomodular lattices*, which are not necessarily distributive.

1 An algebraic mistake of Birkhoff and von Neumann?

Popper's criticism of Birkhoff & von Neumann is primarily based on a mathematical argument: there must be something wrong in the quantum logical structure arising from the set of all closed subspaces of a Hilbert space. For, despite first appearances, such a structure turns out to collapse into a Boolean. The main steps of Popper's argument can be summarized as follows:

(1) The definition of the notion of *uniquely complemented lattice* is recalled: a lattice is uniquely complemented if & only if any element a has exactly one element x that is a 'good complement', satisfying the excluded middle and the non contradiction principle: $a \vee x = \mathbf{1}$; $a \wedge x = \mathbf{0}$.

(2) 'Birkhoff proved that every orthocomplemented lattice is a Boolean algebra, provided it is uniquely complemented.'

(3) In the case of the quantum lattice $\mathcal{Q}$: 'Birkhoff and von Neumann ... speak of ... "the" operation of complementation', implying that negation is unique. 'It is not always observed that ... a symbol like a' ... implies a unique operation, and that it leads to a contradiction if it is used where a has more than one complement.'

CONCLUSION: 'The lattice proposed by Birkhoff & von Neumann, and intended to be non-Boolean, is, in fact, Boolean.'

It is not difficult to discover where Popper's argument fails. In fact, the closed-subspace lattice in a Hilbert space is *at the same time orthocomplemented and not uniquely complemented*. Any non trivial element E (different from $\mathbf{0}$ and $\mathbf{1}$) has infinitely many good complements F such that $E \vee F = \mathbf{1}$ and $E \wedge F = \mathbf{0}$. The element F that is chosen as *the orthocomplement E'* of E is a particular element in this class of good complements. Unlike other possible complements, the operation $'$ further satisfies the following property (which is quite important for the physical interpretation):

$$\psi(E') = 0 \text{ if \& only if } \psi(E) = 1 \text{ and } \psi(E') = 1 \text{ if \& only if } \psi(E) = 0.$$

In other words, a pure state ψ assigns to the negation of an event E probability 0 (1) if & only if ψ assigns to the event E probability 1 (0).

Summing up: the mistake in Popper's argument is entirely contained in step (III), while (I) and (II) are clearly correct.

Apparently, Popper seems to have been deceived by a logical confusion between *explicit* and *implicit definitions* of operations. Suppose we want to introduce a new symbol (say $^\#$) for a unary operation, in a given theory. As is well known, we should first prove *an existence and a unicity condition*. In other words, for some formula $A(x,y)$ of the language we should prove:

for any x there exists exactly one y such that x and y satisfy the relation described by $A(x,y)$.

On this basis, we are allowed to state:

$$x^\# = y \quad =_{\mathrm{Df}} \quad A(x,y).$$

As a consequence, our new symbol $^\#$ turns out to be eliminable. However, operations can also be *implicitly defined* by means of *axiomatic systems*. In such cases, the corresponding symbols will not be, generally, eliminable. This is just what happens in the case of our orthocomplemented lattice $\mathcal{Q}$.

2   The probabilistic argument

Unlike the algebraic argument (which is trivially wrong), Popper's probabilistic critique deals with a crucial point of Birkhoff & von Neumann's approach. This concerns the introduction of a dimension function d that is defined on the set of all quantum events. The values of d are real numbers such that:

(∗)   if $E \subset F$ (E *implies* F), then $d(E) < d(F)$;

(∗∗) $d(E) + d(F) = d(E \wedge F) + d(E \vee F)$.

According to Birkhoff & von Neumann, conditions (∗) and (∗∗) 'partially describe the formal properties of probabilities'. What do they mean thereby? In fact, both conditions (∗) and (∗∗) are satisfied by any probability measure in a classical probability space, where events have a Boolean structure. Popper rightly notices that condition (∗∗) is quite strong: any orthocomplemented lattice of events with a convenient class of probability measures satisfying condition (∗∗) would automatically be Boolean. In his opinion, all this further confirms that Birkhoff & von Neumann were wrong, when claiming the non-Boolean character of the set of all quantum events. However, did Birkhoff and von Neumann really mean that condition (∗∗) is satisfied by quantum probability measures?

What are quantum probabilities? They correspond to *quantum states*: *statistical operators* that are *order-determining* with respect to the class of all quantum events. In other words, given two events E and F,

> $E \subseteq F$ if & only if all statistical operators assign to E a probability value
> that is less than or equal to the probability value assigned to F.

Birkhoff and von Neumann were pretty well aware that quantum probabilities cannot satisfy condition (∗∗). For, the following theorem holds:

> there is no quantum probability that satisfies condition (∗∗) for all pairs of quantum events E, F.

Why do they discuss the dimension function d (which cannot represent a quantum state)? The introduction of d seems to have a quite different aim: it is connected with von Neumann's attempt to elucidate a notion of *quantum probability space* that might be compatible with a *frequency interpretation* of probability. In particular, what von Neumann aimed at was establishing a quantum analogue of the concept of *classical probability space*. Such a space should consist of a pair $< \mathcal{E}, d >$, where $\mathcal{E}$ is an algebra of quantum events (not necessarily coinciding with the algebra $\mathcal{Q}$ of all closed subspaces) and d is a probability measure on $\mathcal{E}$ (called *a priori quantum probability*). The function d should satisfy conditions (∗) and (∗∗) and should be finite and non-negative. In other words, d should be a *finite dimension function*.

The modular property (which represents at the same time a weakening of distributivity and a strengthening of orthomodularity) is a direct consequence of the existence of a finite dimension function. In fact, it is not difficult to show that every lattice admitting a finite dimension function is modular. More importantly, von Neumann aimed at *deriving* the existence of a finite dimension function d from some *geometrical* properties of the structure of quantum events. This seems to be the main reason why the function d was called *a priori quantum probability* (von Neumann 1936, p. 93):

> We succeed in proving the existence of a unique numerical dimension-function, but all real numbers must be permitted as its values. ... It turns out that the *modular axiom* again plays a decisive rôle and that really very few new continuity assumptions are needed.

But what is the connection between our algebra of events (based on closed subspaces of a Hilbert space) and the existence of a finite dimension function? As is well known, the lattice of all closed subspaces of a Hilbert space satisfies the modular property if and only if the dimension of the Hilbert space is finite.

Thus, in the infinite dimensional case (which is essential for the mathematical formalism of QM) no finite dimensional function can be defined on the algebra of all quantum events. Von Neumann regarded this result as a 'pathological' property of the Hilbert space formalism. According to Rédei (2001), p. 158,

> it was largely because of this pathology that von Neumann expected the Hilbert space formalism to be superseded by a mathematical theory that he hoped would be more suitable for quantum mechanics.

In any case, what Birkhoff & von Neumann seem to require is just the existence of a finite dimension function and not of a *sufficiently rich* set of such functions (as Popper claims). It is worthwhile noticing that the assumption of the existence of a finite dimension function is consistent with the non-distributive nature of the structure of quantum events. The paper of Birkhoff & von Neumann leaves unanswered the question whether there exists a modular algebra of events (based on an infinite dimensional Hilbert space) admitting a finite dimensional function. The answer is contained in a joint article of Murray & von Neumann (1936), where they prove the existence of a non-distributive modular lattice of events (based on an infinite-dimensional Hilbert space) which admits an a priori probability. This paper originated what is now known as the 'dimension theory of von Neumann algebras'.

3   QL and Popper's interpretation of QM

Is there any general reason why Popper considered the quantum logical approach as an 'adversary' of his philosophy of QM? As is well known, Popper has on many occasion defended a strong statistical interpretation of the uncertainty principle: micro-objects may have values even for incompatible physical quantities, with a precision that goes beyond the limits asserted by Heisenberg's uncertainty relations. In a sense, Popper has anticipated the celebrated Einstein-Podolsky-Rosen argument (EPR). The *Gedankenexperiment* that he proposed might be regarded as a kind of 'ultra EPR', based on some physical mistakes. There is an interesting exchange of letters between Popper and Einstein on this subject: Einstein points out the wrong points in Popper's argument and Popper seems to accept his criticism. Further, Einstein repeats his well known position versus QM: '... zweitens glaube ich nicht, dass wir uns für die Dauer mit einer so *fadenscheinigen* Naturbeschreibung werden begnügen müssen'. Significantly enough, in the English edition of *The Logic of Scientific Discovery* (1959), Popper translated Einstein's German into English as follows: 'I do not believe that we shall have to be satisfied for ever with so loose and flimsy a description of nature', where the expression 'loose and flimsy' sounds even more negative than the original 'fadenscheinig'.

In the final part of his *Nature* paper Popper discusses the possible use of quantum logical tools in the investigation of the hidden variable question. Again, his position versus QL is radically negative: 'Note that it is a sheer weakening of the logical structure which they [Birkhoff & von Neumann] propose. ... [n]o conclusion — concerning ... the so called "hidden variables" —

can be derived within a system thus weakened, unless this conclusion can also be derived from the fuller classical system.'

This seems to be again a critical point. Of course, Popper is right, if he refers to the pure *logical systems*. QL is weaker than classical logic CL. As a consequence: no logical theorem can be proved within QL, without already being a theorem of CL. However, important arguments are not only *theoretical*, but even (and more often) *metatheoretical*. In fact, QL has proved to be a powerful metatheoretical tool just in the discussion of the hidden variable problem.

Does QT admit non-trivial deterministic completions, via hidden variables? This represents the crucial *physical completeness* question, which has been much investigated since the EPR paper. Roughly, physical completability via a non-contextual hidden variable theory means the following: any pure state ψ can be extended to a complete state $\langle \psi, \lambda \rangle$, where λ represents a *hidden part*. Further: (a) $\langle \psi, \lambda \rangle$ *decides* all quantum events (*determinism*); and (b) ψ and $\langle \psi, \lambda \rangle$ are logically and statistically consistent.

The physical completability question has turned out to be strongly connected with a metalogical property called *logical completability*. A logic **L** satisfies the logical completability property when any non-contradictory theory T, formalized in **L**, admits a *non-contradictory and logically complete* extension T^*. Logical completeness means that any sentence is *syntactically decided*: either proved or disproved. CL and many non-classical logics do satisfy the logical completability property, which is instead violated by QL. Physical and logical completability turn out to be deeply connected. In fact, one can prove the following result:

> QT admits a non-contextual hidden-variable completion if & only if the quantum logic associated with the system of all quantum events satisfies the logical completability property.

Since QL does not satisfy this property, one obtains, as a corollary, a pure logical proof of a 'no-go theorem' for non-contextual hidden variables (Giuntini 1991, p. 158).

Paradoxically enough, in spite of all his critical arguments against QL, Popper's propensity interpretation of probabilities seems to be deeply compatible with a 'quantum logical attitude'. In fact, the 'picture of the physical world' outlined in the proem to Chapter IV of *Quantum Theory and the Schism in Physics* (1982), might be shared by many quantum logicians:

> Indeterminism and the propensity interpretation of probability allow us to paint a new picture of the physical world. According to this picture, ... all properties of the physical world are dispositional, and the real state of a physical system, at any moment, may be conceived as the sum total of its dispositions — or its potentialities, or possibilities, or propensities. ...

> One of the main points of this approach is the suggestion that it may be possible, in this way, to give an indeterministic reinterpretation of Einstein's deterministic programme .... The aim is a picture of a world in which there is room for biological phenomena, for human freedom, and for human reason.

Bibliography

Birkhoff, G. & von Neumann, J. (1936). 'The Logics of Quantum Mechanics'. *Annals of Mathematics* **37**, pp. 823-843.

Giuntini, R. (1991). *Quantum Logic and Hidden Variables*. Mannheim: Bibliographisches Institut.

Murray, F. J. & von Neumann, J. (1936). 'On Rings of Operators'. *Annals of Mathematics* **37**, pp. 116-229.

von Neumann, J. (1936). 'Continuous Geometry'. *Proceedings of the National Academy of Sciences* **22**, pp. 92-100.

Popper, K. R. (1959). *The Logic of Scientific Discovery*. London: Hutchinson.

——— (1968). 'Birkhoff and von Neumann's Interpretation of Quantum Mechanics'. *Nature* **219**, 17.viii.1968, pp. 682-685.

——— (1982). *Quantum Theory and the Schism in Physics*. London: Hutchinson.

Rédei, M. (2001). 'Von Neumann's Concept of Quantum Logic and Quantum Probability'. In M. Rédei and M. Stöltzner, editors (2001), pp. 153-172. *Von Neumann and the Foundations of Quantum Mechanics*. Dordrecht: Kluwer Academic Publishers.

von Neumann, J. (1936). *See* Neumann.

Popper on
Irreversibility and the Arrow of Time[*]

Michael Esfeld

1 Irreversible processes

The laws of our basic physical theories describe all types of processes in such a way that they allow for these processes being reversed. Thus, if there is a process that leads from an event of the type A to an event of the type B, it is in accordance with the laws of our basic physical theories that there also is a process that leads from an event of the type B to an event of the type A. I take an event to be whatever is the content of a finite and continuous space-time region — in the last resort and more precisely, whatever there is at a space-time point — and a process to be a continuous sequence of events in this sense. On the other hand, many of the types of processes with which we are familiar seem to be irreversible: they happen only in one direction, but not in the reverse one. If, for instance, a wine glass falls on the floor, it is broken and does not go back into its former state. It never happens that scattered pieces of glass come together on their own to form a wine glass.

In the first part of this paper, I shall consider the following question: How can we bring the reversibility of all processes allowed for by the laws of our basic physical theories together with the irreversibility of many processes that we experience? The role of thermodynamics and radiation in this context will be examined. Based on an answer to this question, the second part of the paper will go into the relationship between irreversible processes and the so-called arrow of time in the sense of a flow of time. This relationship — and the issue of whether or not there is a flow of time — will be considered with respect to classical mechanics as well as special and general relativity. The paper will not take quantum theory into account.

The most widespread account of irreversibility refers to thermodynamics. According to the second law of thermodynamics, the entropy of a closed system increases in time (or remains constant), but never decreases. Entropy is a measure of disorder, whereby disorder is a way in which energy is dissipated

*For comments on the draft of this paper, I am grateful to Claus Beisbart, Christian Heinicke, Claus Kiefer, Vincent Lam, Christian Zemlin, and two anonymous referees for this book.

or scattered. When a wine glass falls on the floor and breaks into pieces, energy is scattered into many pieces whose motions are uncoordinated. Entropy has thus increased. The second law of thermodynamics describes the fact that such pieces do not come together on their own and form a wine glass. Thus, the second law of thermodynamics refers to irreversible processes.

The received view regards thermodynamics as being reducible to classical statistical mechanics.[1] Classical statistical mechanics, in turn, is reducible to classical mechanics. According to statistical mechanics, it is not impossible, but extremely unlikely, that the scattered pieces of a broken wine glass come together on their own to form a wine glass again. The reason is that it is very unlikely that the initial conditions for such a process, namely a coordinated motion of the pieces of the former wine glass, will ever be satisfied without external intervention. There are by far more states in which the motions of the pieces of the former wine glass are uncoordinated than states in which these motions are coordinated in such a way that the pieces come together to form a wine glass on their own. That is why the probability for the reversal of the process of the wine glass breaking into pieces — and thus the probability for a decrease in entropy — is negligible.

The common answer to the question how the reversibility that the fundamental laws allow is linked with the irreversibility that we hence experience is to say the following: Irreversibility is not a matter of fundamental laws; it is due to the fact that, in the cases of processes that we take to be irreversible, it is very unlikely that the initial conditions for a reversal of the processes in question will ever be met.

Popper challenges the received view. The focus of his challenge is the role of thermodynamics. In four short papers in *Nature* between 1956 and 1958, he argues that it is not true that all irreversible mechanical processes require an increase in entropy. There can be irreversibility without increase in entropy. Popper (1956) gives a simple example. He considers a pond into which a stone is dropped. The stone produces an outgoing wave of decreasing amplitude that spreads concentrically about the point of the stone's impact. Popper (1956) argues that this process is irreversible:

> Suppose a film is taken of a large surface of water initially at rest into which a stone is dropped. The reversed film will show contracting circular waves of increasing amplitude. Moreover, immediately behind the highest wave crest, a circular region of undisturbed water will close in towards the centre. This cannot be regarded as a possible classical process. (It would demand a vast number of distant coherent generators of waves the co-ordination of which, to be explicable, would have to be shown, in the film, as originating from one centre. This, however, raises precisely the same difficulty again, if we try to reverse the amended film.)

---

[1] For recent refinements and elaborations of this view, see, however, Sklar (1993), Chapter 9, Callender (1999), and Albert (2000), Chapters 2-4.

Although Popper claims that the water wave is an example of an irreversible process independent of thermodynamics, he grants that any experimental realization of such a process involves an increase in entropy.[2] His point is that the increase in entropy is not the reason for the process being irreversible: The reason is that the conditions for the reversal of this process cannot be established — independently of whether or not the reversal of this process would also involve a decrease in entropy.[3]

Furthermore, when Popper claims that the described process of contracting circular waves is not a possible physical process, he does not intend to deny that such a process is permitted by the laws of classical mechanics. In a later paper, he says:[4]

> The problem before us ... is the clarification of the notion of a 'causally irreversible physical process'; or more precisely, of a process that is (*a*) 'theoretically reversible', in the sense that physical theory allows us to specify conditions which would reverse the process, and at the same time (*b*) 'causally irreversible', in the sense that it is causally impossible to realize the required conditions.

Hence, the reversal of the process in question is physically possible in the sense that it is not ruled out by physical law. According to the use of terminology that is now widely accepted, anything that is permitted by the laws of physics is physically (or nomologically) possible. However, the initial conditions for the reversal of the process in question cannot be brought about. Therefore, there are processes that are de facto irreversible, independently of whether or not an increase in entropy is involved. Popper (1956) takes this result to be general: although irreversibility is not implied by the fundamental equations, he maintains that it characterizes most solutions. Consequently, according to Popper, irreversible processes have a cosmic significance.

A generalization of Popper's argument is proposed by Hill & Grünbaum (1957). They show that there are some de facto irreversible processes of radiation in any open, infinite system. This result applies to the universe as a whole as well, if we take the universe to be an open, infinite system. They say:[5]

> In open systems there always exists a class of allowed elementary processes the inverses of which are unacceptable on physical grounds by requiring a *deus ex machina* for their production. For example, in an open universe, matter or radiation can travel away indefinitely from the 'finite' region of space, and so be permanently lost. The inverse process would require matter or radiant energy coming from 'infinity', and so would involve a process which is not realizable by physical sources.

---

[2]See Popper (1958), p. 403.
[3]See also Grünbaum (1974), p. 778.
[4]Popper (1957a), p. 1297.
[5]Hill & Grünbaum (1957), p. 1296.

It is debatable whether the universe is an open, infinite system; it may be more plausible to regard it as a closed system. However that may be, Hill & Grünbaum are right in so far as they point out that the example of an irreversible process that Popper discusses illustrates a general phenomenon: what applies to the water waves in Popper's example is true of all kinds of wave-producing phenomena — including electromagnetic waves in particular — and holds on a cosmic scale. In the literature, all these phenomena are discussed as the irreversibility of radiation.

Thus far, Popper has argued that (a) there are processes that are irreversible and whose irreversibility is not due to an increase in entropy and that (b) such processes have a cosmic significance, that is, are relevant on a cosmic scale. These claims made in Popper's contributions to *Nature* between 1956 and 1958 are compatible with the view that (a*) there are processes that are irreversible and whose irreversibility is due to an increase in entropy and that (b*) such processes have a cosmic significance, too. Radiation may simply include further cases of irreversible processes in addition to processes that are irreversible owing to an increase in entropy. In a later paper in *Nature*, however, Popper goes further and attacks the significance of irreversible thermodynamic processes. He claims that:[6]

> With very few and short-lived exceptions, the entropy in almost all known regions (of sufficient size) of our universe either remains constant or decreases, although energy is dissipated (by escaping from the system in question).

Popper does not give any reasons or evidence in support of this claim. Consequently, he denies that the second law of thermodynamics has any importance on a cosmic scale.[7] According to Popper, irreversible processes of radiation are the *only* sort of irreversible processes that have a cosmic significance.

We can thus distinguish three theses that Popper puts forward:

(1) There are irreversible processes of radiation (wave-producing phenomena), and these processes are relevant on a cosmic scale.

(2) The irreversible processes of radiation are independent of the irreversible processes of thermodynamics.

(3) The irreversible processes of thermodynamics are not relevant on a cosmic scale.

The first of these theses is widely accepted. It is not in dispute that there are irreversible processes of radiation and that these processes have a cosmic significance. The third thesis is the least plausible one. Popper's argument of 1965 has been countered by Grünbaum among others.[8] A large majority of physicists and philosophers today assume that entropy increases on a cosmic scale. The second thesis is hotly debated until now: Popper's view that the

---

[6]Popper (1965), p. 233.
[7]See also Popper (1957b).
[8]See, in particular, Grünbaum (1974), § 5.

irreversible processes of radiation are independent of the irreversible processes of thermodynamics is a minority view. But it has some prominent supporters. Adolf Grünbaum, for one, agrees with Popper. Although he rejects Popper's third thesis, he maintains on the basis of the argument in Hill & Grünbaum (1957) that the irreversible processes of radiation are more important than the thermodynamic ones.[9] Huw Price, to mention another example, argues in his book on time that the irreversibility of radiation is independent of thermodynamics.[10] The majority view, however, is that the irreversibility of radiation can be traced back to thermodynamic irreversibility.[11]

I shall not take a stance on Popper's three theses here. Instead, I should like to examine the significance of Popper's challenge to what was and still is the majority view. According to the majority view, irreversibility is of thermodynamic origin, consisting in an increase in entropy, and thermodynamics is in some sense grounded in statistical mechanics. Irreversibility and thus increase in entropy are global phenomena: there is an increase in entropy on a cosmic scale. Therefore, the majority view is committed to admitting an initial state of the universe that is a state of comparatively low entropy. The commitment to such an initial state arises whatever the basic laws may in the last resort be: if one bases thermodynamics upon a particular interpretation of quantum mechanics instead of classical mechanics, one can argue that the fundamental laws provide for irreversible processes.[12] Nonetheless, the assumption of a low entropy initial state of the universe is needed in any case in order to account for the global increase in entropy.[13]

The problem for the majority view is to justify that assumption about the initial state of the universe. One can object that, on the majority view, the problem of giving an account of why some processes are irreversible is simply shifted back: as it stands, an initial state of the universe with low entropy is as improbable as anything that is rejected as being extremely improbable. That the scattered pieces of a broken wine glass do not on their own come together to form a wine glass again is explained on the basis that the initial conditions for such a process are extremely unlikely to obtain. That explanation takes us in the last resort to an initial state of the universe with low entropy. But that such a state is the initial condition of the universe seems to be at least as improbable as the fulfilment of the initial conditions for the scattered pieces of a broken wine glass to come together to form a wine glass again without external intervention. That is to say, states with a low entropy constitute only

---

[9]Grünbaum (1973), p. 277. For a discussion of Popper's and Grünbaum's claims see Zenzen (1977).

[10]See Price (1996), Chapter 3, in particular p. 72.

[11]See, in particular, Zeh (2001), Chapter 2, especially p. 36. But see also Frisch (2000), pp. 399-404.

[12]See Albert (2000), Chapter 7.

[13]See the overview in Price (2002).

a very small minority among the physically or nomologically possible initial states of the universe.[14]

However, Popper's alternative account runs into the same problem. If the irreversibility of radiation (wave phenomena) holds on a cosmic scale, it is in the last resort to be explained by referring to initial conditions of the universe. There have to be specific initial conditions at the beginning of the universe that lead to sources of outgoing radiation, stones that can be thrown into ponds to produce outgoing waves, and so on. But then we have the same problem again: the required conditions at the initial state of the universe that lead to coordinated outgoing waves among other things seem to be as improbable to obtain as the initial conditions that would be required for the outgoing waves in Popper's example to contract. As Price puts it,[15]

> Why are conditions so exceptional in (what we call) the past? In particular, why does the universe contain the kinds of events and processes which provide the *sources* for the outgoing radiation we observe around us? Why does it contain stars, radio transmitters, otters slipping into ponds, and so on?

The same point applies if we take the universe to be an open, infinite system (as Hill & Grünbaum 1957 do in their extension of Popper's argument): coherent radiation coming in from infinity in contrast to coherent radiation being emitted into infinity can be ruled out only on the basis of certain special initial conditions holding in the universe.[16]

Hence, the point at issue is in the last resort not whether the irreversibility of radiation can be traced back to thermodynamic irreversibility or whether both sorts of irreversibility are independent of each other or whether, as Popper claims, radiation is the only source of irreversibility on a cosmic scale. The point at issue is to justify the assumption about the initial conditions of the universe to which one is committed if one takes any of these views. Thus, in the last resort, neither thermodynamics nor radiation provides any explanation of irreversibility. The appropriate place to look for such an explanation, if there is any, is cosmology and quantum gravity in particular. There are a number of ideas how to justify the assumption of an initial state of the universe that is at the origin of the irreversible processes that we experience.[17] None of these ideas, however, is as yet wholly convincing.

Alternatively, one can argue that the call for a justification of this assumption about the initial state of the universe is inappropriate. One may reject this call on empirical grounds, claiming that our empirical evidence may guide us to a particular assumption about the initial state of the universe, but that the total empirical evidence that we can acquire cannot provide any basis for

[14]See Penrose (1989), Chapter 7, for a calculation of the probability of such a state. Compare also Price (1996), Chapter 2, in particular pp. 27, 36-40.

[15]Price (1996), p. 57. See also Arntzenius (1994), § 4; Zeh (2001), p. 16; Callender (2001), § 2.2.

[16]See, for instance, Sklar (1993), pp. 305f.

[17]For a philosophical assessment of these ideas, see, for instance, Sklar (1993), Chapter 8, and Price (1996), Chapter 4.

an explanation of the particular features of the initial state of the universe. Another possibility is to call into question the distinction between laws and initial conditions against the background of which the assumption of a particular initial state of the universe is seen not as a matter of law, but as a matter of initial conditions. On the best-system view of laws,[18] that assumption may well acquire the position of an axiom. One can then argue that if this assumption is an axiom of the best system and thus lawlike, any further explanation is neither required nor possible.[19]

2 The arrow of time

Let us now inquire into the relationship between irreversible processes and the so-called arrow of time. Let us take for granted that there are irreversible processes that are relevant on a cosmic scale, whatever their ground may in the last resort be. Popper's motivation for suggesting that (a) there are irreversible processes that do not have thermodynamic origins and that (b) these are the foremost example of irreversible processes, is that he considers a statistical theory of the arrow of time to be unacceptable.[20] He thereby assumes that thermodynamics is reducible to statistical mechanics. He sees the arrow of time as having a cosmic significance[21] and regards it as a fundamental feature of the universe.[22] He takes the existence of de facto irreversible processes to be sufficient for speaking of the arrow of time and the flow of time.[23] As he makes clear in his reply to Grünbaum, he means by the arrow or flow of time a temporal view of the universe: the universe is in time in the sense that there is a present state of the universe and that the universe develops from past states via the present state to future states (so that time flows from past states of the universe via the present state to future states):[24]

> I conjecture that it is part of the structure of our spatiotemporal universe that time is not only anisotropic but has in addition a direction; that there is not only the relation of betweenness in its topology, but also the relation of before and after. And that the *words* 'before' and 'after' are of course as conventional as the numerals by that we may characterize time, but that the relation denoted by these words is part of the structure of reality, so that time has an arrow. ... I shall say something in defence of the usefulness of the notions of the past, present, and future for the description of reality. ... 'The present age of the universe' is a perfectly good term in cosmology. ... In other words, the past, present, and future are perfectly good terms in cosmology and astronomy ....

---

[18]See, for instance, Lewis (1986), pp. XI-XVI, 121-131.

[19]Compare Callender (2001), § 2.8, Callender (2004), § 6, and see also Albert (2000), pp. 160f.

[20]See Popper (1958), p. 403; Popper (1965), p. 233.

[21]See, in particular, Popper ibidem.

[22]See, in particular, Popper (1967).

[23]See, for instance, Popper (1956) and Popper (1965), p. 233.

[24]Popper (1974), pp. 1141-1143. See also Popper (1998), Essay 7, § 17.

Note, however, that this view as such does not imply that only the present
state of the universe exists. Note furthermore that Popper's use of the expression 'the arrow of time' says more than what most physicists and philosophers
today mean by their rather loose use of this term:[25] whereas Popper means
by the expression 'the arrow of time' a temporal view of the universe, most
physicists and philosophers mean by the expression 'the arrow of time' no
more than that there are irreversible processes in time.

Popper makes clear in the quotation above that the temporal view of the
universe goes beyond the admission of irreversible processes. In addition to
irreversibility, there is a direction of time in the sense of a flow of time from
past via present to future. Let us therefore examine whether the existence of
irreversible processes on a cosmic scale is necessary and/or sufficient for the
arrow of time, as conceived by the temporal view of the universe. If there are
irreversible processes, there are processes that are asymmetric or anisotropic
in time. The asymmetry or anisotropy of processes in time is conceptually
not the same thing as the asymmetry or anisotropy of time. Properties of
something in time cannot be regarded as properties of time itself without
further argument.[26] Moreover, the property in question here — irreversibility
— seems to be a matter of fact rather than a matter of a fundamental physical
law. Hence, even before it comes to the conclusion from the anisotropy of time
to the flow of time, the first step is to go from anisotropic processes in time
to the anisotropy of time itself. Nonetheless, one may justify this step on the
basis of the view that time is not an entity over and above what there is in
time. If one takes this view of time, one may consider irreversible processes
on a cosmic scale to be sufficient for speaking of the anisotropy of time.

Popper does not employ the notion of the anisotropy of time in his papers
in *Nature*. Grünbaum makes use of this notion in his discussion of Popper's
claims, and Popper then takes up this notion in his reply to Grünbaum quoted
above. Grünbaum regards irreversible processes of radiation and/or thermodynamics as sufficient for taking time itself to be anisotropic. He maintains,
however, that the anisotropy of time is all that can be built on irreversible
processes.[27] Following Grünbaum, my thesis in this part of the paper is that
drawing attention to irreversible processes — such as the ones of radiation
and/or thermodynamics — does not provide an argument for assuming an
arrow of time in the sense of a temporal view of the universe.

Imagine a Newtonian world. In this world, there is a universal time in the
sense of an unequivocal temporal ordering of all events: For any two events
e_1 and e_2, e_1 is either simultaneous with e_2 or earlier than e_2 or later than
e_2. Moreover, assume that Newton's philosophy of time holds in this world:
there is absolute time. Absolute time has an arrow in the sense that it flows
from past via present to future. There is a present state of the universe as
well as past and future states. Note, however, that this philosophy of time is

[25]Compare, for instance, the title of Savitt (1995).

[26]Compare Horwich (1987), in particular pp. 45-47.

[27]See Grünbaum (1973), pp. 209f., 314f., and Grünbaum (1974), § 2.

not required for Newtonian physics. Let us, furthermore, assume that there are no irreversible processes in this world. This assumption is consistent with Newtonian mechanics as well as with Newton's philosophy of time. Nonetheless, absolute time is anisotropic in this world — its flow cannot be reversed, although, in this imagined Newtonian world, all processes are reversible in time. Hence, irreversible processes are not necessary for the metaphysics of an arrow of time in the sense of a temporal view of the universe. (Nevertheless, such processes may be necessary for our experience of what is called the flow of time.)

When it comes to today's physics of time, we have to consider relativity theory. Special relativity, as introduced by Einstein (1905), is based on two principles: (a) All inertial systems are physically equivalent. That is to say, the physical laws are independent of which inertial systems are employed to define a reference frame in which physical events and processes are described. (b) In any inertial system, light expands in the same way, independently of the state of motion of the source from which the light is emitted. This is the principle of the constancy of the velocity of light. Starting from this principle, Einstein is able to conceive dynamics without employing the notion of an absolute time. Simultaneity has to be defined on the basis of this principle without invoking the notion of an absolute time. The result is that there is no universal simultaneity. For any two events e_1 and e_2 that are simultaneous relative to one reference frame, there is another reference frame relative to which e_1 is earlier than e_2 and yet another reference frame relative to which e_1 is later than e_2. Temporal duration, as well as spatial length, is relative to a reference frame. There is no universally preferred reference frame. Nonetheless, for any two events, a spatio-temporal distance can be defined that is independent of any reference frame: it remains the same whichever reference frame is considered.

Einstein's considerations result in the famous light cone structure of special relativity: For any event e_n at a space-time point, there are a future light cone and a past light cone that contain all and only those events at space-time points that can be reached from e_n with a velocity that is lower than the velocity of light. Thus, for any event e_n at a point in space-time, there are a relative future and a relative past. The events in both the future and the past light cone are all separated from e_n by a timelike distance. The events in the future light cone are later than e_n and the events in the past light cone are earlier than e_n in all reference frames. Furthermore, there are events that could be connected with e_n only by a velocity that is higher than the velocity of light. These events lie outside the light cone of e_n. They are separated from e_n by a spacelike distance. There is no objective temporal order of these latter events. Which of these events are simultaneous with, earlier than, or later than e_n depends on the choice of a frame of reference.

If simultaneity is relative to a reference frame and if there is no universally preferred reference frame, then there is no universal present. Any point in space-time can count as here-now. Special relativity therefore speaks against a temporal view of the universe. Since there is no unique temporal order that encompasses all events, there is no flow of time. The resulting view is known as the conception of a *block universe*, that is, an atemporal view of the universe: everything exists at a space-time point or region, and all there is in space-time simply exists.[28]

This conception leaves open what the content of the so-called block universe is: The block universe admits not only events at space-time points and processes, which have temporal parts, but also things that exist as a whole for a certain time and that do not have temporal parts.[29] For instance, only a thing can be in motion, and only a thing can be accelerated. It is sometimes claimed that the block universe does not admit time and change. This is not quite correct: the block universe is not in time in the sense that it does not develop in time; but it includes time. Furthermore, it may contain things whose properties can change. What the block universe lacks is one unequivocal temporal order for all events.

The conception of a block universe is not committed to determinism. The definition of determinism that is now widely accepted is this one: take all those possible worlds in which the same natural laws as in our world obtain, that is, all nomologically possible worlds. Consider any two such worlds and imagine a distinction between space and time for both worlds such that we define a unique temporal order that is the same for both worlds. These worlds are deterministic if and only if the following holds: if these two worlds agree at any time, then they agree for all times.[30] Determinism thus is a metaphysical thesis that is independent of whether and to what extent predictions are possible. Possible worlds that are a block universe need not satisfy this definition.[31]

For any point in space-time, there are a past and a future light cone. There are no causal relations between events that lie outside each other's light cones. Let us assume, for the sake of argument, that causation is asymmetric in the sense that only events in its past light cone can be causally relevant to an event. The conception of a block universe leaves open whether and to what extent the event at a given space-time point is determined by events in its past light cone. In the same way, this conception leaves open whether and to what extent events in the future light cone are determined by the event at the space-time point under consideration. The claim that the events in the future light cone are as determinate as the events in the past light cone does not imply that these events are also determined.[32] Given some unique temporal order relative to a reference frame that is the same for two worlds that are a block universe, these worlds may agree up to a certain point of time and then

[28]See, for instance, Price (1996), pp. 12-15.

[29]See, for instance, Mellor (1981), pp. 128-132.

[30]See Earman (1986), p. 13.

[31]See Dorato (1995). Popper (1982), § 26, by contrast, takes the view of a block universe to imply metaphysical determinism.

[32]But compare Popper (1998), Essay 7, § 19.

diverge. Hence, the issue of determinism versus indeterminism is independent of the issue of an atemporal versus a temporal view of the universe. As the above mentioned example shows, there can be a flow of time in a deterministic Newtonian world. As the considerations in this and the preceding paragraph show, a block universe may admit indeterminism.

General relativity combines special relativity as a theory of space-time with a theory of matter insofar as matter is a source of gravitation. Matter-energy influences the geometrical structure of space-time: as a result of the presence of matter-energy, space-time is curved. Gravitation (the gravitational field) and the curvature of space-time are the same thing. General relativity is relevant to cosmology in particular. The mainstream interpretation of the data in cosmology is that all galaxies move away from each other, whichever point in space-time one considers and if one uses a local reference frame that is in free fall in the gravitational field. This is the basis for the majority view in cosmology according to which the universe is expanding and its expansion can be traced back to a singularity, the so-called big bang. It is an open question whether expansion continues indefinitely or whether there may be a state of maximal expansion, which is followed by contraction. The cosmological theory of an expanding universe adds geometrical structure to the concept of a block universe in that space-time is regarded as being curved. However, this theory does not presuppose that there is a universally preferred reference frame. Although there are considerable changes in general relativity as regards the treatment of time, what special relativity says about the relativity of simultaneity and the relativity of temporal durations and spatial lengths remains valid in general relativity. Consequently, general relativity is no basis for claiming that there is an arrow of time in the sense of a flow of time. Furthermore, if the expansion of the universe is seen as one big process, that process may even be reversible, as long as contraction of the universe cannot be excluded. If the expansion of the universe turns out to be reversible, however, this does not imply that entropy will decrease; an increase in entropy is possible even in a contracting universe.

The irreversible processes of entropy increase and radiation can be incorporated into the concept of a block universe that special relativity can be taken to suggest, as well as into all the cosmological models to which general relativity gives rise. Consider an event e_2 at a space-time point. Imagine that there is a process from an event e_1 in the past light cone of e_2 to e_2. If this process is irreversible, then, without any external intervention, there is no process from e_2 to an event e_3 in its future light cone that is of the same type as e_1. Such restrictions may be ubiquitous in a block universe. They may even be lawlike. Irreversible processes do not imply one unique temporal order for all events any more than the expansion of the universe that is at the core of today's mainstream cosmological theory implies this. Hence, there can be irreversible processes such as the ones described by thermodynamics as well as the theory of radiation on a cosmic scale — and there may even be an irreversible process of the expansion of the universe — without there being a physical basis for an arrow of time in the sense of a flow of time as an objective feature of the universe.

Consequently, in contrast to what Popper claims, irreversibility and the arrow of time in the sense of a temporal view of the universe are logically independent of each other: there can be an arrow of time in this sense (flow of time) without irreversible processes occurring in time as in the imagined Newtonian world. And there can be irreversibility without an arrow of time in this sense as in the described block universe. To make a case for a physical basis of an arrow of time as an objective feature of the universe, other arguments are needed than Popper's argument drawing on irreversible processes. It may be possible to integrate into general relativity a cosmological model that contains a universally preferred reference frame, and considerations in connection with the notorious quantum measurement problem and quantum non-locality may speak in favour of such a model. A cosmological model that contains one unequivocal temporal ordering of all events due to a universally preferred reference frame would certainly be a physical basis for a philosophy of time that assumes an arrow of time in the sense of a flow of time without, however, implying such a philosophy of time. But arguments for such a model are another topic.

To conclude this paper, we can sum up the main results in the following two theses:

(1) Whatever may be the source of the irreversible processes with which we are familiar, whether thermodynamics or radiation or both, if these processes are relevant on a cosmic scale, the problem is to give an account of why there are the specific and very improbable initial conditions of the universe that give rise to these processes (or to make plausible why the call for such an account is misplaced).

(2) Irreversible processes are not a physical basis for the philosophical position that there is an arrow of time in the sense of a flow of time. Such processes are neither necessary nor sufficient for an arrow of time in this sense.

Popper's merit is to have drawn attention to processes whose irreversibility may not be due to an increase in entropy. However, he did not consider the problem of the initial conditions of the universe that are necessary for these processes to obtain, and he is wrong in conceiving a link between such processes and a flow of time as an objective feature of the universe.

Bibliography

Albert, D. Z. (2000). *Time and Chance*. Cambridge MA: Harvard University Press.

Arntzenius, F. (1994). 'The Classical Failure to Account for Electromagnetic Arrows of Time'. In T. Horowitz & A. I. Janis, editors (1994), pp. 29-48. *Scientific Failure*. Lanham: Rowman & Littlefield.

Callender, C. (1999). 'Reducing Thermodynamics to Statistical Mechanics: The Case of Entropy'. *Journal of Philosophy* **96**, pp. 348-373.

——— (2001). 'Thermodynamic Time Asymmetry'. *Stanford Encyclopedia of Philosophy*. http://www.science.uva.nl/~seop/entries/time-thermo/

——— (2004). 'Measures, Explanations and the Past: Should "Special" Initial Conditions be Explained?' *The British Journal for the Philosophy of Science* **55**, pp. 195-217.

Dorato, M. (1995). *Time and Reality. Spacetime Physics and the Objectivity of Temporal Becoming*. Bologna: Cooperativa Libraria Universitaria Editrice Bologna.

Earman, J. (1986). *A Primer on Determinism*. Dordrecht: D. Reidel Publishing Company.

Einstein, A. (1905). 'Zur Elektrodynamik bewegter Körper'. *Annalen der Physik* **17**, pp. 891-921.

Frisch, M. (2000). '(Dis-)Solving the Puzzle of the Arrow of Radiation'. *The British Journal for the Philosophy of Science* **51**, pp. 381-410.

Grünbaum, A. (1973). *Philosophical Problems of Space and Time*. 2nd edition. Dordrecht: D. Reidel Publishing Company. Originally published 1963.

——— (1974). 'Karl Popper's Views on the Arrow of Time'. In Schilpp (1974), pp. 775-797.

Hill, E. L. & Grünbaum, A. (1957). 'Irreversible Processes in Physical Theory'. *Nature* **179**, pp. 1296f.

Horwich, P. (1987). *Asymmetries in Time. Problems in the Philosophy of Science*. Cambridge MA: MIT Press.

Lewis, D. K. (1986). *Philosophical Papers*, Volume 2. New York & Oxford: Oxford University Press.

Mellor, D. H. (1981). *Real Time*. Cambridge: Cambridge University Press.

Penrose, R. (1989). *The Emperor's New Mind. Concerning Computers, Minds, and the Laws of Physics*. Oxford: Oxford University Press.

Popper, K. R. (1956). 'The Arrow of Time'. *Nature* **177**, 17.iii.1956, p. 538.

——— (1957a). Reply to E. L. Hill and A. Grünbaum. *Nature* **179**, 22.vi.1957, p. 1297.

——— (1957b). 'Irreversibility; or, Entropy since 1905'. *The British Journal for the Philosophy of Science* **30**, pp. 151-155.

——— (1958). Reply to R. C. L. Bosworth. *Nature* **181**, 8.ii.1958, pp. 402f.

—— (1965). 'Time's Arrow and Entropy'. *Nature* **207**, 17.vii.1965, pp. 233f.

—— (1967). 'Structural Information and the Arrow of Time'. *Nature* **214**, 15.iv.1967, p. 322.

—— (1974). 'Grünbaum on Time and Entropy'. In Schilpp (1974), pp. 1140-1143.

—— (1982). *The Open Universe: An Argument for Indeterminism*. London: Hutchinson.

—— (1998). *The World of Parmenides*. London: Routledge.

Price, H. (1996). *Time's Arrow and Archimedes' Point. New Directions for the Physics of Time*. New York & Oxford: Oxford University Press.

—— (2002). 'Boltzmann's Time Bomb'. *The British Journal for the Philosophy of Science* **53**, pp. 83-119.

Savitt, S. F., editor (1995). *Time's Arrows Today. Recent Physical and Philosophical Work on the Direction of Time*. Cambridge: Cambridge University Press.

Schilpp, P. A., editor (1974). *The Philosophy of Karl Popper*. La Salle IL: Open Court Publishing Company.

Sklar, L. (1993). *Physics and Chance. Philosophical Issues in the Foundations of Statistical Mechanics*. Cambridge: Cambridge University Press.

Zeh, H. D. (2001). *The Physical Basis of the Direction of Time*. 4th edition. Berlin: Springer. Originally published 1989.

Zenzen, M. J. (1977). 'Popper, Grünbaum and de facto Irreversibility'. *The British Journal for the Philosophy of Science* **28**, pp. 313-324.

46

The Arrow of Time:
Experienced rather than Explained*

Daniela M. Bailer-Jones †

I agree with Michael Esfeld's conclusion that a 'flow of time', with a sense of *before* and *after* (Popper 1974), needs to be distinguished from the existence of irreversible processes in physics. In the following, I shall first emphasize the importance of human experience for the conception of a 'flow of time'. Then I shall criticize the examples that Esfeld employs when he argues for an independence of irreversible processes and an 'arrow' or 'flow' of time. Finally, I question whether the second law of thermodynamics can *explain* irreversibility and whether the direction of time can be rooted in physics as it currently stands.

1 The human experience of irreversibility

Irreversible processes provide asymmetry in physics and thus what physicists might call an arrow of time. But this is not what Popper calls an arrow of time. His notion is one of a flow of time that is, as I see it, almost invariably tied to the human experience of past, present, and future. In his first *Nature* communication, Popper (1956) presents his understanding of the arrow of time in terms of the idea of watching a film of a physical process and being able to tell whether the film is watched backwards or forwards. For this distinction, the issue is not only whether certain physical processes are reversible in theory. It is also important whether *it is our experience* to observe these processes in a certain way and direction (they may be what Popper calls 'irreversible in practice'). Watching concentric water waves contracting towards a common centre and culminating in a stone being ejected upwards, leaving behind a perfectly still water surface, is simply not our experience and would therefore strike anyone as unusual and against the 'flow of time', no matter how physically conceivable it may be according to certain symmetric laws of physics (cp. Penrose 1989, p. 304).

Emphasizing the perceptions that constitute our experience is not to deny that there is something in physics that can contribute to or account for these

---

*This paper was given at KARL POPPER 2002 as an invited commentary on Michael Esfeld's lecture 'Popper on Irreversibility and the Arrow of Time' (this volume, pp. 57-70).

perceptions. Time-asymmetry may be a kind of minimum requirement of what physics must supply in order to contribute to the human conscious perception of the flow of time. Introducing Boltzmann's view, Popper says: 'the time coordinate itself has no arrow, no direction; but whenever there is a major fluctuation in some part of the world, then any live organism, any observer, will *experience* a direction of time: he will experience that the future lies in the direction of entropy increase' (Popper 1998, Essay 7, § 17). So, potentially there is a strong link between asymmetry in physics and the experience of the flow of time. I want to endorse this link. I need to add, though, that I doubt that physics can supply anything more to an understanding of time than the statement of the asymmetry of certain physical processes.

Irreversibility is the basis for observing asymmetry. It is because certain events follow other events and not the reverse that makes it possible to distinguish directions in time. Our experience of a passage of time is, for instance, moulded by the experience of loss: that the glass is irretrievably lost if it falls off a table, just as a person is irretrievably lost after she dies. Or, in Popper's words, '[o]ur own lives and deaths should teach us that some, if not all, natural processes are in fact irreversible' (Popper 1998, Essay 7, § 21). For processes to be irreversible means that there is no going back to certain earlier states and the experience thereof.

When we experience the asymmetry of entropy increase, then this is unrelated to whether entropy is to decrease at some future point in time (for example, during a big crunch, as Huw Price (1996) hypothesizes) and even if we cannot explain *why* entropy increases. Similarly, when we consider the concentric waves produced by a stone having been dropped into water, then it is enough that this process is irreversible *in practice*. Irreversibility then features as at least an apparent property of the flow of time. This is so even if the possibility of the reverse process is not excluded by the laws of physics (cp. Frisch 2000). The human temporal experience of certain processes in nature is that they 'happen' to be anisotropic in certain ways, and correspondingly we do not experience in reality everything that we may encounter in a film watched backwards. Irreversible physical processes provide an opportunity to observe asymmetry and distinguish a direction of time, but are not themselves the 'flow of time'.

2 Esfeld's argument concerning irreversibility and a flow of time

Now, while I agree with Esfeld that irreversible processes are not to be identified with a 'flow of time', I am not convinced that his examples support this distinction. Esfeld builds his argument for an independence of irreversible processes and an 'arrow of time', that is, a flow of time with a sense of *before* and *after*, on two examples. The first is one of a Newtonian world in which there exists an unequivocal temporal ordering of all events and also no irreversible processes, consistent with Newtonian mechanics. Esfeld assumes in addition that Newton's philosophy of time holds in that there is an absolute time that flows from past via present to future. He then infers from this example the possibility of an arrow of time without there being irreversible processes. My problem with this example is that Newton's assumption of an arrow of time is simply superimposed and not part of the physics that manifests the conditions in this imagined world. The arrow of time has simply been put in and assumed to exist — and therefore been found to exist. Newton was presumably guided by his human experience of time when he conceived his philosophy of time, but from the point of view of a disembodied Newtonian physics, there *is* no arrow of time in this world. Therefore we cannot conclude from this example that there can be an arrow of time without irreversibility. The example is set arbitrarily rather than based on physical theory only. Even if there were people who observed the unequivocally ordered events in Esfeld's Newtonian world, it is still not clear whether these inhabitants would be capable of making out a flow of time without observing irreversibility. For example, there would be no preference for people to grow old and die rather than get younger and become unborn. How can we assume that people in this world will experience time, other than just by asserting this? So, Esfeld's proposed Newtonian world may in truth be one without irreversibility *and* without an arrow of time.

Esfeld's second example concerns a block universe in which there is irreversibility, but no unique temporal ordering of events. The latter is due to special relativity according to which simultaneity is relative to a reference frame 'and if there is no universally preferred reference frame, then there is no universal present' (Esfeld, this volume, p. 65). The lack of a unique temporal ordering is here taken to mean that there is no arrow of time. However, even if there is not one unequivocal temporal order for all events in all reference frames, there certainly is a temporal order for events in each reference frame, and from the point of view of our human experience, only our individual reference frame is of interest. So, from the point of view of an individual's reference frame, unambiguous earlier-later relationships can be experienced, probably based on irreversible processes that occur among the temporally ordered events in the reference frame. So, in my sense of the flow of time depending on human experience, there can be an arrow of time even in a block universe. Consequently, Esfeld's block universe world need not be one without a flow of time. On the contrary, once one allows for human perceivers of an order of events, this order is present, even in a block universe, so the block universe is not by definition devoid of an arrow of time.

In short, my critical remarks on Esfeld's examples indicate why his examples of (a) a Newtonian world without irreversible processes, but *with* an arrow of time and of (b) a block universe with irreversible processes, but *without* an arrow of time do not, in my opinion, serve as arguments for the independence of irreversibility and an arrow of time.

3 Explaining irreversibility

In various places, Esfeld talks about the second law of thermodynamics *explaining* why, for example, the shattered pieces of a wine glass will not come back together to form a wine glass. Elsewhere he says that neither thermodynamics nor radiation provides an *explanation* for irreversibility. I wonder how much a law such as the second law can explain. The second law of thermodynamics states that in a closed system the entropy does not decrease, or rather that this is extremely unlikely. This is a law in the sense that it is based on what is observed in nature.[1] Such laws express, at an abstract level, some regularity in nature, a regularity that is stated on the basis of 'fact' rather than on the basis of an explanatory account. To say that something happens regularly in a certain way is not to say why it happens in that particular way. Correspondingly, laws do not automatically provide far-reaching explanations. We can, for instance, use Newton's laws to account for planetary motion, and planetary motion is an illustration of Newton's laws, but anybody would be hard-pressed to go further and say *why* it is that Newton's law of gravity holds. There is no argument for Newton's laws derived from some more general principles, and if there were, we would then be equally hard-pressed to prove or explain these more general principles.[2]

Laws may be used to motivate why certain aspects of a process are connected in a certain way, so laws can be employed in constructing an account, sometimes called a mechanism (Glennan 1996), that explains a process. However, reference to a law does not automatically provide the illumination expected of explanation. For this, some understanding of why a law holds is at least desirable. Explaining irreversibility by reference to the second law does not help much and borders on the tautological. There is a level at which reference to a law may help to explain a phenomenon or a particular process in nature, such as planetary motion. This is because reference to the law helps to put the phenomenon or process into the wider context of physical theories thought to hold in nature. Irreversibility is, however, not an individual (local) phenomenon or an individual (local) process, but rather a general principle. To say that the second law of thermodynamics explains irreversibility would be to replace one principle (irreversibility) with another (entropy increase). This would help only if the latter principle were able to do explanatory work.

---

[1] It, just like other physical laws, is not based directly on the data that result from experiment or observation, but on data that are analysed and interpreted to the effect that they support the law (Bogen & Woodward 1988).

[2] Nonetheless, some explanations or laws are more satisfying than others, for example if they encompass a wider range of phenomena or apply under a wider range of conditions, or if they are stated in a particularly simple or readily applicable form. In this sense it may not be in vain to want to *explain* the second law of thermodynamics. But assuming that the second law cannot be reduced to any other existing law, this 'explanation' could be successful only in the sense that we may come up with some other law that encompasses the second law. In this case we simply shift the burden of explanation on to the new law (or even an initial condition, such as very low initial entropy in a universe of finite age).

But this is not so. As I said before, the second law is based on 'fact'. It is taken to hold because this is what continues to be observed in nature.[3]

Quoting the initial conditions of the universe provides a constraint that makes it possible to encounter the law, but does not explain it. Indeed, Popper was concerned with initial conditions and summarizes his efforts in his 1950s *Nature* communications as follows: 'The asymmetry I tried to point out was one that affects the realizability of *initial conditions*, in contradistinction to an asymmetry of the theories or laws' (Popper 1998, Essay 7, § 25). However, with regard to entropy increase, the issue is not whether or not a low entropy state at the beginning of the universe is realizable as an initial condition. It clearly is, because it looks as if low entropy is the state encountered *in practice* if entropy is to increase afterwards. Popper refers to this as 'Boltzmann's "assumption A"' (ibidem, § 17), and characterizes it as a cosmological assumption outside statistical mechanics. It is clearly important for us to establish that our big-bang models are consistent with the assumption of low entropy in the universe, and it certainly looks as if the initial conditions of these models must have been in agreement with this. In the case of radiation, Popper argues that we cannot create the initial conditions for the reverse process of contracting waves. For such initial conditions to occur would be unbelievably unlikely *and* not something encountered *in practice*. In the case of the early universe, in turn, we are confronted with the opposite situation: The universe clearly did produce the, albeit unlikely, low entropy conditions *in practice*.

Exploring the low entropy conditions of the early universe is all very well; it provides us with conditions and constraints for our big-bang models.[4] Yet, this is nowhere near providing an *explanation* of irreversibility. Maybe the explanatory onus of where irreversibility comes from has been shifted, but a detailed account of the big bang does not answer the question of why irreversibility is observed. It merely gives some conditions under which irreversibility can be observed. Physics *states* that there is entropy increase and consequently irreversibility in the world as we find it. Moreover, irreversibility is probably a major factor in the human experience of a flow of time, just as Popper seems to imply, yet this does not mean that the direction of time is explained by physics.

---

[3]This is not to suggest that a law cannot be explained, just that a law on its own does not do any explanatory work. For instance, one may seek to explain irreversibility by classical statistical mechanics.

[4]Penrose does indeed explore the conditions and constraints on the creation of the universe, but his account is no stronger than the following: '*For some reason*, the universe was created in a very special (low entropy) state, with something like the WEYL=0 constraint of FRW-models imposed upon it' (Penrose 1989, p. 339, my emphasis). He also speaks of an impasse that has been reached where we do not understand 'why space-time singularities have the structure that they appear to have' (p. 345).

Bibliography

Bogen, J. & Woodward, J. (1988). 'Saving the Phenomena'. *The Philosophical Review* **97**, pp. 303-352.

Frisch, M. (2000). '(Dis-)Solving the Puzzle of the Arrow of Radiation'. *The British Journal for the Philosophy of Science* **51**, pp. 381-410.

Glennan, S. (1996). 'Mechanisms and the Nature of Causation'. *Erkenntnis* **44**, pp. 49-71.

Penrose, R. (1989). *The Emperor's New Mind. Concerning Computers, Minds, and the Laws of Physics.* Oxford: Oxford University Press.

Popper, K. R. (1956). 'The Arrow of Time'. *Nature* **177**, 17.iii.1956, p. 538.

———— (1974). 'Grünbaum on Time and Entropy'. In P. A. Schilpp, editor (1974). *The Philosophy of Karl Popper*, pp. 1140-1143. La Salle IL: Open Court Publishing Company.

———— (1998). *The World of Parmenides.* London: Routledge.

Price, H. (1996). *Time's Arrow and Archimedes' Point. New Directions for the Physics of Time.* New York & Oxford: Oxford University Press.

47

A New Look at Popper's Pond

Mathias Frisch

In a famous letter to the journal *Nature* Karl Popper argued that wave phenomena exhibit a temporal asymmetry distinct from the thermodynamic asymmetry that entropy never decreases (Popper 1956a). Popper illustrates this asymmetry through the following example. After a stone is thrown into a large body of water whose surface was initially still, circular waves diverge from the point of impact. The time-reversed phenomenon of circularly converging waves — imagine a film showing the diverging wave run backwards — does not occur. This asymmetry raises two questions. First, the fundamental equation governing wave phenomena is time-symmetric. Where, then, does the asymmetry come from? And second, even if the wave asymmetry is indeed distinct from the thermodynamic asymmetry, are the two asymmetries in any way related?

Often Popper is taken to have argued that the answer to the second question is 'yes'. For example, Huw Price argues in his book *Time's Arrow and Archimedes' Point* (Price 1996) that Popper believed that both the wave asymmetry and the thermodynamic asymmetry share a common origin. That is, on the view Price attributes to Popper, neither of the two temporal arrows is reducible to the other, yet both can be explained in terms of a third, cosmological asymmetry. In this paper I will sketch what I take to be Popper's view on the asymmetry, which he presented in his letter to *Nature* and in replies to a series of responses to the letter in the same journal (Popper 1956b, 1957, 1958), and argue that this standard interpretation is mistaken. My motivation in this paper is more than merely to contribute to the project of Popper-exegesis. The view Popper advocates — which might also have been the view of Albert Einstein, whom Popper cites — has virtually no adherents among experts writing on the subject today. This, I believe, is unfortunate since it is in fact the most satisfactory account of the wave asymmetry.[1]

I shall first briefly summarize important features of the physics of the thermodynamic and wave asymmetries and shall then present what I take to be Popper's account of the latter asymmetry.

The thermodynamic arrow is today commonly explained by an appeal to a *de facto* asymmetry between initial and final conditions. Standard microphysical arguments seem to show that any relatively low entropy state evolves with overwhelming probability into a state of higher entropy. But since the

---

[1]For a detailed defence of this view, see Frisch (2005), Chapter 7.

underlying microphysical laws are time-symmetric, the same argument also appears to show that a low entropy state evolved from a higher entropy past, contrary to what is the case. This symmetry is broken by postulating as initial conditions at the beginning of the universe an extremely low entropy state (and hence, intuitively, an extremely improbable state). According to Price, Popper's account of the wave asymmetry proceeds similarly: In the light of time-symmetric laws the asymmetry of wave phenomena is explained by an appeal to time-asymmetric de facto initial conditions. Some such account of the wave asymmetry has in fact become the received view: most physicists and philosophers writing on the subject argue that the asymmetry needs to appeal to either statistical or even thermodynamical considerations of some sort.

What then does physics tell us about the wave asymmetry? The wave equation used to represent wave phenomena is a differential equation that can be solved either in terms of an initial or a final value problem. More specifically, the equation allows us to determine a wave in a certain region, given the wave at an initial time together with the trajectories of all wave sources in that region, or equivalently given the wave at a final time together with the trajectories of sources. If the wave is represented in terms of an initial value problem, then the waves mathematically associated with each wave source are diverging waves (or so-called *retarded waves*). The total wave is given by these diverging waves together with the incoming wave. If, however, the wave is represented in terms of a final value problem the waves mathematically associated with each source are converging (or *advanced*) waves. The total wave, again, is obtained by adding the wave associated with sources to any source-free outgoing wave. It is important to stress that it is one and the very same wave that can be represented either as a combination of diverging and source-free incoming waves or a combination of converging and source-free outgoing waves. Of course this means that the diverging waves in one representation have to be written as a combination of converging and free waves in the other and vice versa.

So far the mathematical representations of waves in the presence of wave sources, or wave generators, are completely symmetric. Whether the wave associated with an individual generator is diverging or converging merely depends on whether we choose to represent the wave in terms of an initial or a final value problem. In what sense, then, are wave phenomena asymmetric? They are asymmetric in that the total wave often can be represented entirely as a sum of diverging waves with zero incoming waves (such as the wave produced by a stone on a pond whose surface is initially still), but there are (almost) no circumstances where the total wave is fully converging with zero outgoing waves. That is, the wave asymmetry is an asymmetry between prevailing initial and final conditions: Initial conditions can usually be chosen to involve zero incoming waves, but final conditions cannot be so chosen. The problem of the wave asymmetry, then, is to account for this asymmetry in initial conditions.

Now, we can see immediately that the proposal Price attributes to Popper is problematic. According to that proposal the *explanation* of the asymmetry invokes asymmetric initial conditions. But, as we have just seen, the *explanandum* in the case of the wave asymmetry (unlike the thermodynamic case) involves just such an asymmetry. So merely stating that initial conditions are asymmetric is in danger of begging the question. Nevertheless, there might appear to be some evidence in favour of Price's reading of Popper. Thus, Popper emphasizes that the asymmetry is not 'implied by the fundamental equations' of the theory (Popper 1956a). And there is Popper's reference in (Popper 1956b) to Albert Einstein, who, as Price quotes, in one place said that the irreversibility of wave phenomena is not lawful but is 'exclusively based on reasons of probability' (Ritz & Einstein 1909, p. 324).

Nevertheless, it seems to me that Price is misinterpreting Popper's view. For Popper draws a clear contrast between wave phenomena and thermodynamics. While he takes the former to show that 'irreversible classical [that is, non-statistical] processes exist', he says that 'on the other hand, in statistical mechanics all processes are in principle reversible, even if the reversion is highly improbable' (Popper 1956a). Thus, for Popper there is a crucial difference between the two asymmetries: the wave asymmetry is a *strict* asymmetry, while the thermodynamic asymmetry is not. And this difference must be reflected in differences in the explanations of the asymmetries. But how, one might ask, can this be squared with Popper's claim that the asymmetry is not implied by the fundamental equations? How can it be that the wave-asymmetry is strict and at the same time not implied by the fundamental equations governing wave phenomena?

In a later reply to a reply (Popper 1957) Popper distinguishes what he calls 'theoretical reversibility' from 'causal reversibility' and characterizes a radiation process as

> a process that is (*a*) 'theoretically reversible', in the sense that physical theory allows us to specify conditions which would reverse the process, and at the same time (*b*) 'causally irreversible', in the sense that it is causally impossible to realize the required conditions.

That is, while the wave equation is time symmetric and allows for both diverging and converging waves associated with a wave source, converging waves, according to Popper, violate a causal constraint; they are 'causally, and therefore physically, impossible' (Popper 1958, p. 403).

Popper here seems to be appealing to the notion of the wave physically associated with a source: even though the mathematical representation of the wave may change, depending on whether we are dealing with an initial or a final value problem, physically the wave associated with an individual wave generator is a fully divergent wave. The wave physically associated with a wave source is that component of the total wave that would be absent if the source were absent. If this component is fully diverging, then changes to the state of a source have an effect on the wave in the future but not the past.

This, then, provides us with an explanation of the wave asymmetry. We find fully diverging waves, but not fully converging waves, since past waves are usually damped or absorbed eventually, so that there are many circumstances in which incoming waves can for practical purposes be set equal to zero. Introducing a wave source then leads to a fully divergent wave.

The notion of the physical contribution of a wave source arguably is a causal notion: sources causally influence the state of the wave medium, and this influence cannot be spelled out entirely in terms of how the wave equation determines the state of the wave, given specific initial or final conditions. The wave equations alone does not tell us how changes to the state of a source would affect the wave. What we need to know in addition is how the initial or final conditions are affected by that change. The causal condition that wave generators physically contribute fully diverging waves partially determine what the correct boundary conditions are: given that sources contribute diverging waves, we know that interventions into the state of the source affect the wave in the future, and hence the final conditions, but not wave in the past and initial conditions.

Thus, we see how wave phenomena can be both theoretically reversible and causally irreversible: On the one hand, as far as the laws of the theory are concerned, which take the form of differential equations and determine how the state of a wave evolves from given initial or final conditions, the theory is completely symmetric. Yet, on the other hand, the physical contribution of each source to the total wave is diverging or fully retarded. Thus, Popper argues that circularly converging waves 'cannot be regarded as a possible classical process', for this (Popper 1956a, p. 538)

> would demand a vast number of distant coherent generators of waves the co-ordination of which, to be explicable, would have to be shown, in [a film depicting the process] ..., as originating from the centre. This however, raises precisely the same difficulty again, if we try to reverse the amended film.

And in his second letter (Popper 1956b, p. 382) he adds:

> we are led to an infinite regress, if we do not wish to accept the coherence of the generators as an ultimate and inexplicable conspiracy of causally unrelated conspirators.

Now, Price maintains that Popper took this generator argument as an argument for the asymmetry of the elementary wave processes, instead of assuming the asymmetry as a premise in order to account for the asymmetry of the total waves, as I have suggested. In fact, it is not unequivocally clear from the text whether Popper meant to use the regress argument to *establish* the causal asymmetry or whether he makes use of the claim that there is a causal asymmetry as a *premise* in his argument. But a principle of charity would suggest that we interpret Popper as taking the asymmetry of the individual generators as given. For Price's criticism of any attempt to argue for the causal asymmetry is right on the mark. As he points out, to claim that the existence of coherently oscillating wave generators, producing a converging wave, would constitute an inexplicable conspiracy is to presuppose that the waves associated with generators are fully divergent. For to assume that only divergent waves but not convergent waves (if they were to exist) could be the source of coherent motion is to be guilty of a temporal 'double standard fallacy' (Price 1996, p. 55). If we did not, as I am suggesting, assume from the outset that the generators produce diverging waves, we would have to treat diverging and converging waves on a par and both could account for correlations.

Popper says that converging waves are physically impossible. But should it not be in principle possible to set up coherent generators that produce a concentrically converging wave? Popper argues that such a setup would have to be orchestrated centrally, but this of course does not show that it is strictly impossible. I think we can make sense of Popper's views here, if we pay careful attention to the distinction between the total wave and the elementary processes that give rise to that wave. Popper's view appears to be that the *individual* generators of the wave are asymmetric, and this asymmetry indeed is a strict causal asymmetry. The asymmetry of the individual generators can then help to explain the asymmetry of the total wave. The latter asymmetry, however, is not strict as far as local regions are concerned: if we were to set up things carefully enough and rigged up enough generators in the right way, we could produce converging waves. But if we included the generators of the converging wave in the picture, the original asymmetry is again restored: the converging wave is shown to be the result of multiple diverging waves.

Thus Popper's argument for why converging waves do not occur involves an appeal to initial conditions: initial conditions necessary for the existence of converging waves do virtually never obtain. But one should note that the role of initial conditions in this argument is rather different from that in standard arguments for the thermodynamic asymmetry. In the latter case, the asymmetry of entropy flow is accounted for by postulating what are under some standard measure extremely improbable initial conditions. Some have argued that this presents a problem for the standard account, since it has to leave the improbable initial conditions themselves unexplained. But there is no similar problem for Popper's account, since most 'initial' configurations of generators will not lead to coherent converging waves. Thus, while the thermodynamic case relies on an appeal to improbable initial conditions, Popper only needs to assume that very probable initial conditions obtain — initial conditions where the individual generators are not delicately coordinated. Moreover, since the asymmetry in the case of wave phenomena is ultimately explained by an appeal to an asymmetry characterizing the individual wave generators, there need not be any asymmetry between initial and final arrangements of generators.

As a last bit of support for my reading of Popper I want to point out that it fits rather well with Popper's reference to Einstein. Einstein's writings on the issue present an interpretive problem, since he characterized the radiation asymmetry in seemingly contradictory ways on different occasions. But in the passage to which Popper refers, Einstein unequivocally says that elementary radiation processes are asymmetric and that 'the reverse process [that is, that of a spherically converging wave] does not exist as elementary process' (Einstein 1909, p. 819). In fact, Price's support for his own interpretation of Popper seems to rest partly on getting Popper's reference to Einstein wrong, since Price mistakenly thinks Popper is referring to the joint paper (1909) with Ritz in which Einstein claims that 'the irreversibility is exclusively based on reasons of probability'.

I have presented what I take to be the best possible coherent interpretation of Popper's view on radiation. But I want to end with presenting a certain problem for my interpretation of Popper (or perhaps a problem for the internal coherence of Popper's views). For Popper's own views on the methodology of science do not appear to leave any room for his distinction between what is *theoretically* and what is *causally* possible. For in Popper (1935), § 12, he maintains that

> [t]o give a *causal explanation* of an event means to deduce a statement which describes it, using as premises of the deduction one or more *universal laws*, together with certain singular statements, the *initial conditions*.

And further down he says (ibidem):

> The 'principle of causality' is the assertion that any event whatsoever *can* be causally explained — that it *can* be deductively predicted.

Thus, Popper's own view does not allow for a distinction between what follows nomically from certain initial conditions and what is causally possible. In the case of wave phenomena the wave equation allow us to predict what, in the light of specific initial or final conditions is physically possible. And Popper tells us that making this kind of prediction simply is what we mean by explaining an event causally. But then it becomes a mystery how wave processes can be theoretically reversible in that they are describable both in terms of an initial and a final value problem with the help of time symmetric laws, *and at the same time* can be causally irreversible. There simply is no asymmetry of deductive prediction for wave phenomena.

In this debate between Popper the methodologist and Popper the philosopher of physics I suggest we should side with the latter. In fact, I want to suggest that Popper's views on the wave asymmetry show much more finely honed scientific intuitions than his general methodological writings sometimes seem to indicate.

Bibliography

Einstein, A. (1909). 'Über die Entwicklung unserer Anschauung über das Wesen und die Konstitution der Strahlung'. *Physikalische Zeitschrift* **10**, pp. 817-825.

Frisch, M. F. J. (2005). *Inconsistency, Asymmetry, and Non-locality: A Philosophical Investigation of Classical Electrodynamics*. New York & Oxford: Oxford University Press.

Popper, K. R. (1935). *Logik der Forschung*. Vienna: Julius Springer Verlag. 2nd edition 1966. Tübingen: J. C. B. Mohr (Paul Siebeck). 10th edition 1994. English translation, Popper (1959).

———— (1956a). 'The Arrow of Time'. *Nature* **177**, 17.iii.1956, p. 538.

———— (1956b). Reply to Richard Schlegel. *Nature* **178**, 18.viii.1956, p. 382.

———— (1957). Reply to E. L. Hill and A. Grünbaum. *Nature* **179**, 22.vi.1957, p. 1297.

———— (1958). Reply to R. C. L. Bosworth. *Nature* **181**, 8.ii.1958, pp. 402f.

———— (1959). *The Logic of Scientific Discovery*. London: Hutchinson.

Price, H. (1996). *Time's Arrow and Archimedes' Point. New Directions for the Physics of Time*. New York & Oxford: Oxford University Press.

Ritz, W. & Einstein, A. (1909). 'Zum Gegenwärtigen Stand des Strahlungproblems'. *Physikalische Zeitschrift* **10**, pp. 323f.

48

Theoretical Models and Theories in Physics
A Rejoinder to Karl Popper's Picture of Science[*]

Andrés Rivadulla

1 Some doubts on Popper's position in the debate between instrumentalism and realism

The realism–instrumentalism debate has been the most important issue in the history of western epistemology since Plato. Karl Popper's approach to this question in his paper 'Models, Instruments, and Truth' is: '[A]re scientific theories *nothing but* instruments, or should they, as I suggest, be regarded as attempts to find the truth about our world, or at least as attempts to get nearer to the truth?' (1994, Chapter 8, § 8). Popper (1982a, § 15) himself answers: 'I see our ... theories as human inventions — nets designed by us to catch the world. ... Theories are not *only* instruments. What we aim at is truth: we test our theories in the hope of eliminating those which are not true. In this way we may succeed in improving our theories — even as instruments: in making nets which are better and better adapted to catch our fish, the real world.'

Realism and instrumentalism interlace in Popper's understanding of science. Indeed, he claims to be a realist, but as to the capability of theories to represent the world, Popper (ibidem) recognizes that 'they will never be perfect instruments for this purpose. They are rational nets of our own making, and should not be mistaken for a complete representation of the real world in all its aspects; not even if they appear to yield excellent approximations to reality.' Moreover, as to the question of approximation to truth or to reality, Popper failed to provide a rational procedure for the comparison of theories by their verisimilitude, as many philosophers of science, and I myself (1987, § 2), showed some years ago.

[*]This paper is part of research project BFF2002-01244 on *Theoretical Models in Physics*, which has been supported by the Spanish Ministry of Science and Technology. I thank two anonymous referees for encouraging and critical comments on a previous version of this paper.

But it is in the third volume of the *Postscript* where Popper sheds serious doubts on whether realism is truly his main message in philosophy of science (1982b, Introductory Comments, § IX. I have italicized the final sentence):

> The decisive thing about Einstein's theory, from my point of view, is that it has shown that Newton's theory ... *can* be replaced by an alternative theory which is of wider scope, and which is so related to Newton's theory, that every success of Newtonian theory is also a success for that theory, and which in fact makes slight adjustments to some results of Newtonian theory. *So for me this logical situation is more important than the question which of the two theories is in fact the better approximation to the truth.*

In my view the existence of *limiting cases* in physics — a fact that Popper himself has been supporting since *Logik der Forschung* (1935, § 79) — provides indeed the way for the comparison among competing theories. If furthermore the *predictive balance* is overwhelmingly favourable to one of the theories, then there can be no doubt about whether, without resorting to truth or verisimilitude, the better one has been rationally chosen. Thus it seems reasonable to doubt that Popper's realism is firmly founded.

2 Popper on theoretical models in physics

The main idea underlying the use of *theoretical models* in science is the assumption that we do not have direct access to Nature, but that in spite of this fact we can propose some conjectures intended to represent natural processes and empirical phenomena. We construct a theoretical model when we conceive mathematically of the physical relationships among the alleged elements of Nature appearing in our alleged images of reality.

In modern epistemology discussion of the role played by theoretical models goes back at least to Pierre Duhem, who in *Aim and Structure of Physical Theory* (1906, Part I, Chapter IV, et passim) discussed the fruitfulness of models for discoveries, and other related matters. Mary Hesse (1966) took part in the dispute between Duhem and N. R. Campbell on the role of theoretical models, and Max Black (1962) classified the different types of models. Nancy Cartwright, Bas van Fraassen, Ronald Giere, Lawrence Sklar, and Giovanni Boniolo, among others, have made important contributions as well to the questions raised by the use of theoretical models in science.

Given the instrumentalist component in Popper's epistemology — theories as instruments —, it is not strange that he has emphasized the role played by theoretical models in physics. Without developing a detailed account of *theoretical models* of physics, there are places in his work where he presents different features of models: (a) models consist of certain elements related to each other by some universal laws of interaction; (b) models may be called theories, but not all theories are models; (c) models cannot be completely true, since they are necessarily rough, schematic, and vast oversimplifications and approximations; (d) models omit much, they overemphasize much, and they do not represent the facts truly, and so on. However, claiming to be a realist, Popper affirms that we can decide, by testing, which of two competing models is the better one. Better in the sense of *better approximation to truth*.

The use of theoretical models has found widespread application throughout the natural and the social sciences. This is accepted by Popper himself (1994, Chapter 8, § 2): 'It will suffice to remind you that Ptolemy, Copernicus, and Kepler were all makers of models, and that Newton's theory arose partly as an attempt to solve the problem of explaining how Kepler's model was "animated".'

Popper (1972, Chapter 4, § 9, and Appendix, § XI) conceives of Copernicus's and Ptolemy's theories essentially as cosmological geometrical models. And in volume I of the *Postscript* he discusses the question of the truth of models (1983, Part I, § 4, pp. 58f.): 'Most of us today strongly believe — and have reason to believe — in the Copernican model of the solar system (as revised by Kepler and Newton): ... But what are our reasons for believing in the truthlikeness of this theory? (To be sure, we do not believe in its complete truth, since it is only a model and therefore bound to be an over-simplification and approximation ...'

Can any model be true? Popper answers this question roundly (1994, Chapter 8, pp. 172f.): 'I do not think so. Any model, whether in physics or in the social sciences, must be an over-simplification. It must omit much, and it must overemphasize much. ... it seems to be quite unavoidable in the construction of models, both in the natural and in the social sciences, that they over-simplify the facts, and thus do not represent the facts truly.'

In spite of this, Popper claims, models can be compared with each other in regard to their verisimilitude. But this comparison is affected by the same difficulty that affects the comparison of theories by their verisimilitude: ignorance about the truth. In fact, Popper affirms (1983, Part I, § 4, p. 61):

> Though we may reasonably believe that the Copernican model as revised by Newton is nearer to the truth than Ptolemy's, there is no means of saying *how* near it is: even if we could *define* a metric for verisimilitude (which we can do only in cases which seem to be of little interest) we should be unable to *apply* it unless we knew the truth — which we don't. We may think that our present ideas about the solar system are near to the truth, and so they may be; but we cannot know it.

Moreover, a further difficulty arises in relation to the truthlikeness of models, which is novel in relation to the issue of the verisimilitude of theories. According to Popper (1994, Chapter 8, § 4), it is not easy to test a model. This is due to the fact that 'models are always and necessarily somewhat rough and schematic over-simplifications. Their roughness entails a comparatively low degree of testability. For it will be difficult to decide whether a discrepancy is due to the unavoidable roughness, or to a mistake in the model.'

Despite these shortcomings, Popper (ibidem) concludes that 'we can sometimes decide, by testing, which of two competing models is the better'. And, in order to instantiate his claim, he asserts (ibidem, §10) that 'Copernicus' model appears to be a better approximation to the truth than Ptolemy's, Kepler's a better approximation than Copernicus', Newton's theory a better approximation still, and Einstein's better again.'

My aim below will be to discuss whether models are the kind of constructs of which it can be affirmed justifiably that they are more or less truthlike.

3 The place of theoretical models in the debate between instrumentalism and realism

3.1 Pros and contras of the celestial model of Newtonian mechanics

Although the Newtonian model of the solar system is, like all models, according to Popper, a vast oversimplification, it predicts accurately phenomena such as planetary motion, tides, free fall, and so on, and has been very successful as well in predicting comets' orbits. For instance Edmond Halley (1656-1742) determined for the first time in 1705 the orbit of the comet that bears his name. Isaac Newton himself suggested to him that the comets observed in 1456, 1531, 1607 and 1682 might be regular appearances of the same body. This model allowed also the discovery of new planets, such as Neptune by Johann Gottfried Galle on 24 September 1846, following precise instructions by Le Verrier.

The success of Newtonian celestial mechanics captivated minds such as Laplace, who in the Introduction to his *Essai philosophique sur les probabilités* (1819) expressed in the following way the confidence that Newtonian mechanics inspired in him:[1]

> Une intelligence qui pour un instant donné connaîtrait toutes les forces dont la nature est animée et la situation respective des êtres qui la composent, si d'ailleurs elle était assez vaste por soumettre ses données à l'analyse, embrasserait dans la même formule les mouvements des plus grands corps de l'univers et ceux du plus léger atome: rien ne serait incertain pour elle, et l'avenir comme le passé serait present a ses yeux.

In spite of its big success, the Newtonian model cannot be considered empirically acceptable. The Newtonian model of the universe accounts only approximately for the light deflection by the Sun. Newton (1704, Book III, Part I, Query I; 1952, p. 516) himself asked in his *Opticks* whether the trajectory of a light ray passing through the Sun's gravitational field might be deflected by it: 'Do not bodies act upon light at distance, and by their action bend its rays; and is not this action (*coeteris paribus*) strongest at the least distance?' The same question was also posed by Kant in *Opus postumum*, Volume XXI,

---

[1]'An intelligence that at any given moment knew all the forces that animate nature and the mutual positions of all the entities that compose it, if moreover this intelligence were vast enough to submit its data to analysis, it could embrace in the same formula the movements of the largest bodies of the universe and those of the lightest atom; nothing would be uncertain for it, and the future and the past would be present before its eyes.'

p. 404 of his *Gesammelte Schriften*, and Georg von Söldner (1776-1833) obtained for the light bending the value of $0''.87$. Clifford Will (1989, pp. 110f.) reports the first calculations of light deflection in the 19th century. In fact, let m_p be the mass of a photon coming near the Sun, and r_0 the distance of the photon from the Sun's centre. If we denote by ν_x and F_x respectively the x-components of the photon's velocity and of the force of the Sun upon the photon in the position (r_0, y), then (cp. Kittel, Knight, & Ruderman 1965, Chapter 149)

$$F_x = -G_N m_S m_p \cdot \frac{r_0}{(r_0^2 + y^2)^{3/2}}.$$

Since from $m_p \nu_x \approx \dfrac{1}{c} \displaystyle\int_{-\infty}^{\infty} F_x dy$ we obtain $\nu_x \approx \dfrac{-2G_N m_S}{c r_0}$, then when r_0 is the Sun's radius r_S, the bending angle α is so small, that

$$\Delta\alpha \approx \frac{|\nu_x|}{c} = \frac{2G_N m_S}{r_S c^2} \text{ radians} = 0''.87.$$

Unfortunately, this is only half of the observed value. Einstein's general relativity claims (cp. Landau & Lifshitz 1951, § 11.8) that the bending of the light ray is given by

$$\Delta\alpha = \frac{4G_N m_S}{r_s c^2},$$

from which an angular deviation of $1''.75$ follows. Clifford Will (1993, § 7.1, and Update § 14.3) presents results of light deflection measurements taken between 1920 and 1990, which show agreement with general relativity to 0.1%.

In accounting for planetary perihelion precession the Newtonian model was not very successful either. The advance of the perihelion of any planet consists in the fact that the main axis of the planet's ellipse rotates around the focus occupied by the Sun. According to observations, reported by Misner, Thorne & Wheeler (1973, Box 40.3, pp. 112f.), Mercury's perihelion shows an advance of circa $5600''$ per century. Newtonian mechanics can account for about $532''$ as an effect of the perturbation of the planets, and for nearly $5025''$ more caused by the rotation of the Earth, where the observatory is placed. There remain approximately $43''$, which the Newtonian model cannot account for. Einstein's relativity theory accounts for them as a typical relativistic effect, due to the proximity of Mercury to the Sun, by virtue of which this planet suffers the effects of the solar gravitational field most severely.

Albert Einstein (1917, § 29) claims explicitly that both observational results (the light deflection by the Sun, and Mercury's perihelion precession) represent a failure of classical mechanics.

In conclusion, even if some models have been very successful in earlier applications, Popperian verisimilitude — and even non-Popperian probability of truth — does not give any explanation of the role played by theoretical

models in the methodology of physics. Does it make any sense to claim that
Newtonian mechanics, which has failed in many applications, is less truthlike
than relativity theory, whose predictions have not yet been 'falsified'? No, it
does not, because, even if the *predictive balance* is overwhelmingly favourable
to relativity, this does not imply that it is true, or even more truthlike than
Newtonian mechanics. Empirical success is not an indicator of truth or of
verisimilitude.

3.2 Accounting for magic numbers in atomic and nuclear physics

There are in microphysics two sets of numbers, which, for the reasons to be
given below, are called *magic numbers*. These are 2, 10, 18, 36, 54, 86, [118] in
atomic physics, and 2, 8, 20, 28, 50, 82, 126 in nuclear physics. The models to
be presented below do account satisfactorily for them, without pretending to
be a complete or even a truthlike representation of Nature at the microphysical
level.

3.2.1 The atomic central field shell model

The well-known Bohr model for hydrogen atoms was unsuited for the investigation of many-electron atoms. In order to study two-electron atoms, helium
atoms, the simplest intended approach was the so-called *independent-particle
atom model*, in which electrons were assumed to move independently from
each other. In this model the Hamiltonian of the total system was merely
the sum of two hydrogenic Hamiltonians, with the repulsion term of the interaction between the electrons being neglected. Now, the energy of helium
atoms in the fundamental state predicted by this model was much bigger
than the experimentally observed value. Thus this model had to be rejected
as empirically inadequate.

Following a suggestion by Douglas Rayner Hartree (1897-1958) in 1928, the
model was refined assuming a *central field approximation*, where each electron
moves independently from the other one in a net central potential $V(r)$, which,
according to Bransden & Joachain (1983, pp. 265f.), 'represents the attraction
of the nucleus plus some average central repulsive potential due to the other
electron'. In case of many-electron atoms, each electron moves independently
in an effective spherically symmetric potential $V(r)$ created by the nucleus
and all the other $N-1$ electrons. Developed by Hartree, together with John
Clarke Slater (1900-1976), the central field model was able to account for the
magic numbers and for the periodic table of elements as well.

Two basic assumptions are needed to develop this model. The first one is
Wolfgang Pauli's exclusion principle, according to which no two electrons in
an atom are allowed to have the same set of quantum numbers: n (principal),
l (orbital), m_l (magnetic), m_s (spin). The other is that the total energy of
the atom depends only on the number of electrons occupying each of the
individual energy levels E_{nl}. Electrons having the same value of n and l —
where $n = 1, 2, 3, 4, \ldots$ and $s : l = 0$; $p : l = 1$; $d : l = 2$; $f : l = 3$; $g : l = 4$,

and so on — are said to belong to the same *subshell*. The maximum number of electrons allowed by Pauli's exclusion principle to occupy a subshell is $2(2l+1)$. Electrons having the same value of n are said to belong to the same *shell*. The maximum number of electrons in a shell is $2n^2$. Electrons occupy the available lower energy levels, filling them according to Pauli's principle. When a subshell is complete, electrons begin to occupy the next energy level. Thus in the central field approximation, electrons are disposed in successive shells of energy nl around the atomic nucleus.

Magic numbers are nothing but the *atomic numbers* of *noble gases*. Each magic number results from the sum of the total electron number in each shell and the previous magic number. Since 2 is the atomic number of Helium, it is the first magic number. Noble gases are inert, that is, they are electrically neutral and do not interact with other atoms to form chemical compounds. According to the *central field shell model* this is due to their outer shell being filled with electrons. This atom model thus *saves* the existence of *magic numbers*.

3.2.2 Theoretical models in nuclear physics

There is not yet a complete theory of the atomic nucleus, since the analytic form of the relationships between nuclear forces and the parameters that cause them is still unknown. Therefore nuclear physicists are compelled to resort to nuclear models, in order to account for limited domains of intended applications. There are two main kinds of models: collective models and models of independent particles.

3.2.2.1 The *liquid drop* model of the nucleus. The first nuclear model was proposed independently by Niels Bohr and Jakov Ilich Frenkel (1894-1952) in 1936. Assuming a spherical symmetry for the atom nucleus, all computation methods lead to the conclusion that the radius R of the nucleus is given by $R = r_0 A^{1/3}$, where A is the nuclear mass and $r_0 = 1.2 \sim 1.5 \times 10^{-13}$ cm. Moreover, the density of nucleons (protons and neutrons) in the atom nucleus is given by

$$n = \frac{A}{4\pi R^3/3} = \frac{3}{4\pi r_0^3} \approx 10^{38} \text{ nucleons/cm}^3$$

Furthermore if we denote by m the mass of a nucleon, then the mass density in one atom nucleus is $\rho = n \times m \approx 1.45 \times 10^{14}$ g/cm^3. Finally (cp. Sivoukine 1989, p. 125)

$$d = \sqrt[3]{\frac{4\pi R^3}{3A}} = \sqrt[3]{\frac{4\pi}{3}} r_0 \approx 2.3 \times 10^{-13} \text{ cm}$$

gives the value of the average distance among nucleons. Now, as can be seen directly n, ρ, and d are constants. Moreover the nuclear binding energy is proportional to the mass, due to the fact that $\Delta E/A \approx$ constant. These facts support the idea of a *liquid drop model* of the atomic nucleus, because of the analogy of nuclei with macroscopic drops of incompressible liquids.

The big success of the nuclear liquid drop model was to save the so-called semi-empirical mass formula for the nuclear binding energy, which was proposed by Carl Friedrich von Weiszäcker in 1935, and thus it was very appropriate for the calculation of the masses of more than 200 nuclei, except those with small A. Unfortunately neither Weiszäcker's formula, nor the liquid drop nuclear model, could account for the unusually high stability of so-called magic nuclei.

3.2.2.2 The *shell* model of the nucleus. The binding energy is an index of the stability of nuclei: the higher it is, the more stable are nuclei. In this sense the liquid drop model was empirically adequate. However there are some nuclei that are unusually stable. These nuclei, whose values of Z and/or N are: 2, 8, 20, 28, 50, 82, 126, are called *magic nuclei*. One important feature of *magic nuclei* is that they are the most abundant nuclei in nature.

Robert Eisberg & Robert Resnick (1974, p. 576) state that:

> The analogy between nuclear and atomic magic numbers prompted many people to look for an explanation of the nuclear phenomenon that was similar to the explanation of the atomic phenomenon. ... However, when the nuclear magic numbers were first being discussed seriously, around 1948, it seemed very difficult to understand how nucleons could move independently in a nucleus. The reason was that the liquid drop model had been dominant for a number of years, and it seemed basic to this model that a nucleon in a nucleus (of density $\sim 10^{18} \mathrm{Kg/m^3}$!) would constantly interact with its neighbours through the strong nuclear force. If so, the nucleon would be repeatedly scattered in travelling through the nucleus, and it would follow an erratic path, resembling Brownian motion much more than the motion of an electron moving independently through its orbit in an atom.

A further reason for scepticism regarding the applicability of the atomic independent particle shell model to the nuclear phenomenon was the non-existence of a central force capable of creating a central symmetry. But in spite of these difficulties Maria Goeppert-Mayer (1906-1972) and Hans D. Jensen proposed independently of each other a *shell model of the nucleus*, and published it together in *Elementary Theory of Nuclear Shell Structure*, 1955. Both were awarded in 1963 the Nobel Prize for Physics.

The main difference introduced by the shell model of the atom is that for the nuclear phenomenon it was necessary to consider the interaction spin-orbit. In the shell model of the nucleus each level is denoted by nl_j, where n and l are as before, and $j = l + 1/2$ or $l - 1/2$ is the quantum number of the total angular momentum $\mathbf{J} = \mathbf{L} + \mathbf{S}$ of a nucleon. The order of filling levels: $1s\ 1p\ 1d\ 2s\ 1f\ 2p\ 1g\ 2d\ 3s\ 1h\ 2f\ 3p\ 1i\ 2g$, accounts for nuclear magic numbers, since these are the numbers of nucleons accumulated in the last subshell of each shell. Further properties of nuclei like nuclear spin, nuclear parities, and so on, are also predicted by this shell model of the nucleus. In spite of the empirical success of nuclear models, both collective and independent, the impossibility for models to be more or less truthlike than other ones is made clear by Eisberg & Resnick (1974, p. 591, my italics), who claim:

> The shell model is based upon the idea that the constituent parts of a nucleus move independently. The liquid drop model implies just the opposite, since in a drop of incompressible liquid the motion of any constituent part is correlated with the motion of all the neighbouring parts. The conflict between these ideas emphasizes that a *model* provides a description of only a *limited set* of phenomena, *without regard to* the existence of contrary models used for the description of other sets.

In similar terms Boniolo, Petrovich & Pisent (2002), p. 447 affirm that:

> The microscopic models (like the shell models) deal with independent particles with long mean free path, while collective models justify the treatment of nuclear matter as a continuum, by assuming nucleons as strongly correlated particles with very short mean free path. The crash between these two approaches is evident, but it becomes less dramatic if we consider them just as mental attitudes useful to draw mathematical models apt to save the phenomena.

Nuclear physics supplies excellent examples of theoretical models intended as devices for saving phenomena. Truth and truthlikeness are out of place here.

3.3 Mathematical models and deterministic chaos

In *deterministic chaos theory* it is usual to call *chaotic* the solutions of equations that evolve in completely different ways, although they derive from nearly identical initial conditions. Actually they are solutions of deterministic equations, but they are called chaotic, according to Herbert Goldstein (Goldstein, Poole, & Safko 2002, p. 483), '[b]ecause, although deterministic, they are not predictable because they are highly sensitive to initial conditions ... Specific solutions change exponentially in response to small changes in the initial conditions.

A characteristic example of deterministic chaos is the so-called *logistic equation*. It is the non-linear equation $x_{n+1} = ax_n(1-x_n)$, which is intended to offer a model of the evolution of a population. In this equation x_{n+1} denotes the number of individuals in the next generation, a symbolises the growth factor, x_n is the number of individuals of the present generation, and $1-x_n$ is a correction factor that contributes to slowing down the population increase.

The logistic equation works as a quadratic iterator. x_n takes firstly any value in the interval $[0,1]$, and we solve the equation for any value of a, that is, we obtain the corresponding value of x_{n+1}. Next we take for x_n precisely the value just obtained for x_{n+1}, and we solve the equation again. And so forth. The representation in a diagram of the logistic equation offers amazing results. In case $x_0 = 0.3$ and $a = 3$, the equation's graph oscillates among values near 0.69 and 0.63, which shows that the population grows and decreases regularly. In case $x_0 = 0.3$ and $a > 3.5$ the graph begins to behave chaotically. Accordingly the population loses stability, and prediction becomes impossible. Still more surprising is the case when, maintaining the same value of a, the value of x_0 is slightly modified, that is, when the initial number of individuals scarcely changes; under these conditions the graph is chaotic, as it was before, but completely different from the former one (cp. Bublath 2001, p. 132). This shows that the mathematical model of the logistic equation is extraordinarily sensitive to small changes in the initial conditions. The problem lies in the non-linear character of the logistic equation. Non-linear mathematical models of nature are not reliable for the predictive task of science. They are prone to chaos.

Galileo Galilei wrote in *Il Saggiatore*, in 1623, that natural philosophy, that is, physics, is written in the extraordinary book open in front of our eyes, the Universe. But this book cannot be read, if we do not know the language in which it is written. It is written in mathematical language, and its characters are triangles, circles, and other geometric figures, without which it is impossible to understand anything. Four centuries after Galileo we have to moderate our enthusiasm in the empirical applicability of mathematics. Nature, more chaotic than regular, refuses to obey the dictates of models, which are, as Popper recognized, merely schematic and vast oversimplifications of reality.

Bibliography

Black, M. (1962). *Models and Metaphors*. Ithaca NY: Cornell University Press.

Boniolo, G., Petrovich, C., & Pisent, G. (2002). 'Notes on the Philosophical Status of Nuclear Physics'. *Foundations of Science* 7, pp. 425-452.

Bransden, B. H. & Joachain, C. J. (1983). *Physics of Atoms and Molecules*. Harlow, Essex: Addison Wesley Longman Ltd.

Bublath, J. (2001). *Chaos im Universum*. Munich: Droemer.

Duhem, P. M. M. (1906). *La théorie physique. Son objet et sa structure*. Paris: Chevalier & Rivière, Editeurs. 2nd edition 1914. Paris: Marcel Rivière. English translation 1954. *The Aim and Structure of Physical Theory*. Princeton NJ: Princeton University Press.

Einstein, A. (1917). *Über die spezielle und allgemeine Relativitätstheorie*. Reprinted in A. J. Fox, M. J. Klein & R. Schulmann, editors (1966). *The Collected Papers of Albert Einstein*, volume 6: *The Berlin Years, 1914-1917*. Princeton NJ: Princeton University Press.

Eisberg, R. & Resnick, R. (1974). *Quantum Physics of Atoms, Molecules, Solids, Nuclei, and Particles*. New York: John Wiley and Sons.

Goldstein, H., Poole, C. P., & Safko, J. L. (2002). *Classical Mechanics*. 3rd edition. San Francisco CA: Addison Wesley.

Hesse, M. B. (1966). *Models and Analogies in Science*. Notre Dame IN: University of Notre Dame Press.

Kittel, C., Knight, W. D., & Ruderman, M. A. (1965). *Mechanics*. New York: McGraw-Hill Book Company.

Landau, L. & Lifshitz, E. (1951). *The Classical Theory of Fields*. Cambridge MA: Addison-Wesley Press.

Misner, C., Thorne, K. S., & Wheeler, J. A. (1973). *Gravitation*. New York: W. H. Freeman and Co.

Newton, I. (1704). *Optics*. Reprinted in I. Newton & C. Huygens (1952), pp. 545-619. *Mathematical Principles of Natural Philosophy; Optics (Newton); Treatise on Light (Huygens)*. Edited by R. M. Hutchins. Chicago: Encyclopaedia Britannica. 4th printing 1993.

Popper, K. R. (1935). *Logik der Forschung*. Vienna: Julius Springer Verlag.

——— (1972). *Objective Knowledge*. Oxford: Clarendon Press.

——— (1982a). *The Open Universe. An Argument for Indeterminism*. London: Hutchinson.

——— (1982b). *Quantum Theory and the Schism in Physics*. London: Hutchinson.

——— (1983). *Realism and the Aim of Science*. London: Hutchinson.

——— (1994). *The Myth of the Framework. In Defence of Science and Rationality*. London: Routledge.

Rivadulla, A. (1987). 'Kritischer Realismus und Induktionsproblem'. *Erkenntnis* **26**, pp. 181-193.

Sivoukine, D. (1989). *Physique atomique et nucléaire*. Deuxième partie. Moscow: Mir.

Will, C. (1989). 'Experimental Gravitation from Newton's *Principia* to Einstein's General Relativity'. In S. W. Hawking & W. Israel, editors, pp. 80-127. *300 Years of Gravitation*. Cambridge: Cambridge University Press.

——— (1993). *Theory and Experiment in Gravitational Physics*. Revised edition. Cambridge: Cambridge University Press.

49

An Instrumentalist Criticism of Popper's Propensities

Manuel Bächtold

1 The Propensity Interpretation

Karl Popper has argued for his own interpretation of quantum mechanics, the *propensity interpretation*. In his view, interpreting this theory in an appropriate manner consists, first of all, in providing a relevant interpretation of *quantum probabilities* — that is, probabilities deduced, thanks to Born's rule, from the state vector associated to a physical system. He claims that '*the interpretation of the formalism of quantum mechanics is closely related to the interpretation of the calculus of probability*' (1982b, Introduction, § 3).

Popper argues against a *subjectivist* interpretation of quantum probabilities. He considers what he calls 'the intrusion of subjectivism into physics' as one of the main reasons for the present 'crisis of understanding' in physics (ibidem, Preface 1982). The use of probabilities in quantum mechanics, he asserts, does not at all express an *epistemological* limitation, as Heisenberg had suggested at first, when he established the so-called 'uncertainty relations' (Popper ibidem, Preface 1982, § II; Heisenberg 1927).

Why is quantum mechanics probabilistic? According to Popper, 'the kind of *problems* which the theory is supposed to solve ... are essentially *statistical problems*', yet '*statistical questions demand, essentially, statistical answers.* Thus quantum mechanics must be, essentially, a statistical theory.' (Ibidem, Introduction, § 3.) That is to say, probabilities do not originate from the human *impossibility* of a strictly deterministic description, but from the *demand* for a statistical description imposed by the problems we are facing in physics.

This justification of the probabilistic character of quantum mechanics agrees with a *frequentist* interpretation of probabilities. Quantum probabilities should then be identified with the relative frequency of a given outcome in an infinite sequence of repeated measurements. Such an interpretation was supported by Popper in Chapter VIII of *Logik der Forschung* (1935). In his later publications, however, Popper considered it as unsatisfactory: quantum probabilities do not merely concern measurement outcomes. He argued that the unavoidable use of probabilities in physics expresses a feature of the physical world in itself. In other words, quantum probabilities have to be assigned an *ontological* status. They represent what Popper calls 'propensities': not *categorical* properties — that are actual and well-defined at each instant —, but *dispositional* properties — that *might* become actual in the future. (In this paper, 'actual' and 'actuality' will be taken to refer to *something that exists as a matter of fact*, see Aristotle, *Metaphysics*, book IX, 1048a. The typical example will be a measurement outcome.) Popper here asserts his clear metaphysical commitment: he conceives the world as 'a world of propensities' (Popper 1990). This world view walks hand in hand with his conception of the world as being intrinsically *indeterministic* (see Popper 1982a). For, if the state of the world at a given instant is characterized by propensities, this means that its state in the future is only partially determined. What of the relative frequencies of outcomes observed in repeated experiments? They are observable consequences of propensities inherent to the physical reality involved in those experiments: propensities, are interpreted by Popper, as 'tendencies to produce relative frequencies on repetition of similar conditions or circumstances' (Popper 1982b, Introduction, § 3, eighth thesis).

2 To what are propensities attributed?

What are propensities the properties of? Concerning this question, Popper seems to support a rather ambiguous view. On the one hand, he maintains that propensities are properties of a *whole physical situation*, including a physical system (say, an electron) *and at the same time* the environment surrounding this system (for instance, an experimental device that enables us to carry out a measurement on the electron). Propensities are inherent not exclusively in *observable* physical situations (that is, experimental situations), but indeed in any physical situation of the objective world — 'objective' here meaning *independent of any human being*. He writes (1982b, Introduction, § 3, note 63):

> My theory of propensities was always intended as a completely objective physical theory. The propensities refer to any physical situation. Propensities are then not properties of the particle but of the objective physical situation; for example of an experimental situation. Of course the objective situation will *normally* be one that has arisen in the physical world without human interference, although it *may* be due to man, and perhaps even to a physicist who has built an apparatus. In the latter case we speak of 'experimental arrangement'.

On the other hand, if propensities are conceived of as properties of the world in itself, nothing prevents one from attributing propensities to a physical entity with arbitrarily defined boundaries. As a consequence Popper sometimes waves aside the idea that propensities are properties of a whole physical situation. He then attributes propensities to isolated physical systems. For instance he speaks of the 'propensities of *particles* to take up a certain state under certain conditions' (1982b, Chapter II, § 11), or maintains that 'the real state of *a physical system*, at any moment, may be conceived as the sum total of its dispositions [or] propensities' (ibidem, Chapter IV, my emphasis).

Two conceptions of the attribution of propensities seem to be in competition here. Yet, there might be one way to avoid contradiction. It could be argued that (a) propensities are *assigned* to an isolated physical system (say, an electron), although (b) they are *determined* by the whole physical situation to which this system belongs.

Let us assume that propensities can be conceived of as properties of physical systems. The following question then arises: What *kind* of physical systems can be identified as the recipient of propensities? Particles such as electrons or photons, as Popper suggests? As concerns *quantum field theory*, such an answer is problematic. For, in the case of a quantum vacuum — where there is no particle — this theory predicts that the measurement of some physical magnitudes can yield non-zero values. This is expected to happen, for instance, when measuring the square of the quantum field operator (see Teller 1995, pp. 108f.). If the non-zero values obtained in such experiments are interpreted as the actualization of some propensities, then these propensities cannot be attributed to a physical system anymore — just because there is no physical system in the case of a quantum vacuum.

Are these unexpected experiments an indicator of the existence of a 'new ether', namely the quantum vacuum (the expression is due to Parrochia 1997)? Should we then identify the latter itself as the recipient of propensities? Before drawing such a conclusion, we should pay attention to another odd feature of the quantum vacuum. Let us consider the quantum vacuum in Minkowski space-time, that is, an inertial frame of reference. According to the predictions of quantum field theory, any particle-detector that is motionless relative to this inertial frame of reference will detect zero particles, and this with a probability equal to 1. Whereas any particle-detector that is uniformly accelerated, being in a 'Rindler space-time', will detect with certainty one or several particles (see Unruh and Wald 1984). These particles are called 'Rindler particles', by contrast with the 'Minkowski particles'. The formal relation between the two situations is as follows: the vacuum eigenvector of the Minkowski-observable 'number of particles' can be reformulated as a superposition of the eigenvectors of the Rindler-observable 'number of particles' — each of these latter eigenvectors being associated to a number of particles different from zero.

Starting from Bohr's theory of complementarity, Rob Clifton and Hans Halvorson (2001, pp. 456f.) have offered a convincing interpretation of this phenomenon:

> [W]e may think of the choice of an observer to follow an inertial or Rindler trajectory through spacetime as analogous to the choice between measuring the position or momentum of a particle. Each choice requires a distinct kind of coupling to the system, and both measurements cannot be executed on the field simultaneously and with arbitrarily high precision. Moreover, execution of one type of measurement precludes meaningful discourse about the values of the observable that the observer did not choose to measure.

According to this interpretation, there is no *absolute* quantum vacuum. The vacuum state vector is always relative to a given frame of reference. Which is to say that 'quantum vacuum' is a meaningful expression only with regard to a given experimental context.

Because of the great empirical success of quantum field theory, it is often alleged that the ultimate substrate of the world is composed of*quantum fields* (this is the opinion, for example, of Clifton and Halvorson ibidem). Following Popper's way of interpreting quantum mechanics, one should then identify the quantum fields as the recipient of propensities. This is what Clifton and Halvorson have suggested: they view 'a quantum field as a collection of correlated "objective propensities" to display values of the field operators in more or less localized regions of space-time, relative to various measurement contexts' (p. 460).

Advocating such a view involves the belief that quantum field theory deals with *physical fields*. However, Paul Teller has shown that the use of the notion of field *in quantum field theory* must be considered merely as an accident in the history of the theory. Teller indicates two distinct ways to derive quantum field theory. The historical way consists in starting with classical fields, and in representing them by means of Fourier expansions. The quantization rule is then applied to the Fourier components — they become operators satisfying commutation relations (Teller 1995, pp. 70-73). The second way to derive the formalism of quantum field theory consists in starting with the Fock space theory, which deals with 'quanta' and not with 'fields', and then to switch from the momentum basis to the position basis (ibidem, pp. 54-59). In this second formulation of quantum field theory, we can leave the notion of field aside.

To put it radically, the concept of *physical field* hardly suits quantum field theory. A 'field' in classical physics corresponds to a physical magnitude defined at each space-time point. As Teller argues, this does not hold in the case of a 'quantum field operator'. Indeed, the latter belongs to a non-commutative mathematical structure, and does not possess, in the general case, a well-defined value at each space-time point (ibidem, p. 97). Consequently, it seems quite inappropriate to interpret the 'quantum field operator' as the formal representative of a 'physical field'. Under these circumstances the problem remains of determining to what the propensities are attributed.

Teller offered another propensity interpretation of quantum field theory that seems less problematic than Popper's. In his opinion the Fock space formalism 'does not attribute states to objects in the world. Instead states [of quantum mechanics] simply characterize propensities for what will be manifested with what probability under various activating conditions' (ibidem, p. 105). Propensities are related to the set of possible outcomes that *can* occur in the context of a given experimental arrangement. They are not properties of an independent reality. According to this interpretation, it is irrelevant to try to identify the substrate of the world to which the propensities could be assigned. In other words, the ontological problem of determining the recipient of propensities is here 'dissolved'.

3 Propensities and actualities

To conceive propensities as related to a given experimental device is the first step towards an *instrumentalist* interpretation of quantum mechanics. The second step amounts to acknowledging that behind the concept of 'propensities', there is nothing more than a reference to what is 'actual' for us in the context of an experiment — that is, the outcomes we can observe. This leads us to claim that *the content of our knowledge concerning propensities is reducible to the content of our knowledge concerning what is actual for us*. Indeed, we do not have direct access to propensities. We cannot observe them. The manifestation of a propensity remains parasitic on the setting up of a measurement device. Propensities are intrinsically and implicitly defined by what appears to us as actual. Insofar as they are associated to the state vectors of quantum mechanics, one has to admit that the propensities are inferred from what has been actual for us at the time of past experiments, and yield information about what will be actual for us at the time of future experiments.

Let us consider a given measurement. Before the occurrence of the outcome, we have no direct access to the physical reality under investigation. And notwithstanding the fact quantum mechanics enables us to make predictions concerning the outcome of this measurement, these predictions are only probabilistic. Now, Popper infers from the probabilistic predictions statements concerning the world as it is in itself, namely the existence of propensities. However, no experimental verification of this claim is possible. To use Popper's own criterion, this claim is not 'falsifiable' (see Popper 1935/1959, Chapters IV and VI). The only empirical content attached to propensities is relative to the measurement outcomes. Indeed, a supporter of the propensity interpretation will infer the existence of a given propensity only if he or she knows that a corresponding outcome can actually occur in the physical situation being considered. For this reason, describing the world in terms of propensities is, at best, a way of *reformulating* the description of what can be actual for us in the context of an experiment.

Propensities correspond to a reification of the possible — that is, the possible outcomes of a measurement. But what is possible itself depends on what is actual, and can be reduced to it. In *Fact, Fiction, and Forecast*, Nelson Goodman agrees with this idea (1954, Chapter II, § 4, pp. 56f.):

> ... discourse, even about possibles, need not transgress the boundaries of the actual world. What we often mistake for the actual world is one particular description of it. And what we mistake for possible worlds are just equally true descriptions in other terms. We have come to think of the actual as one among many possible worlds. We need to repaint that picture. All possible worlds lie within the actual one.

In fact, Goodman reveals here a mistaken and common inversion, which Popper seems to make. One should consider the actual world as a starting point, and admit that any discourse about what is possible takes its origin in this actual world. Instead, Popper ascribes to the possibilities (for instance, possible events) an ontological primacy, and views the actual world merely as one instantiation of these possibilities.

This inversion is exposed also by Henri Bergson (1930, pp. 109f.; my translation). He criticizes the idea

> that the possible is less than the actual, and that, for this reason, the possibility of things precedes their existence. Thus they could be represented in advance; they could be thought before being realized. But it is the reverse that is the truth ...: the possible is only the actual with, as an addition, an action of the mind that rejects the image of it in the past once it has occurred.

Popper has developed a strategy of defence to counter this kind of instrumentalist criticism. This strategy consists in weakening the status of what is said to be 'actual' in the context of a measurement. To do so, he uses one of the main arguments against logical positivism. Indeed, he asserts that the distinction between *observational terms* and *theoretical terms* is not clear-cut. The observational terms are always 'theory-laden'. He contends that because of its theoretical weight, each so-called 'observational term' cannot be *directly* observable. The more significant the theoretical weight of the term is, the more the indirectness of its observability increases. This leads Popper to write 'that most observations are more or less indirect, and that it is doubtful whether the distinction between directly observable incidents and whatever is only indirectly observable leads us anywhere' (1963, Chapter 3, §6). This conclusion is relevant to the problem of propensities. According to Popper, nothing can justify the view of 'propensities' as secondary as compared to what is said to be 'actual'. 'Actualities', as well as 'propensities', are in some degree theoretical and at the same time, similarly observational. That is why rather than giving credence only to actualities, Popper proposes to assume, at least as a conjecture, 'the reality of the dispositions [*i.e.* the propensities]' (ibidem).

As was remarked above, however, the conjecture of the existence of propensities is not falsifiable. This conjecture can possibly have a meaning only within a metaphysical framework. Nevertheless it is of no use in the real practice of physicists, who, when making predictions by means of quantum mechanics or quantum field theory, do not have to refer to propensities.

Moreover, Popper's argument concerns not so much the measurement outcomes — what is here identified as the 'actual' — as the *theoretical interpretation* of these outcomes. Indeed, one can make a distinction between the *outcome* that we encounter at the end of a measurement and the underlying *physical event* that is supposed to have occurred during the measurement. For instance, the outcome can be the position of a pointer on the measurement apparatus, and the physical event can be the value of a photon's momentum detected during the measurement. The physical event amounts to an interpretation of what our eyes observe. In this respect, what should we say about propensities? When Popper refers to them, it is only at the time of the interpretation of the outcomes. In the case of the former example, he could infer from the position of the pointer that the photon's *propensity* to have this momentum has been actualized. The point is that a measurement outcome can, in principle, be acknowledged by all physicists. (Every physicist will agree on the position of the pointer.) Whereas propensities do not satisfy this criterion of intersubjective acknowledgment. Few physicists will agree on the existence of dispositional properties belonging to the studied photon. Consequently, it does not seem justified to consider that propensities have the same status as actualities. To support the existence of propensities involves, at least, the knowledge of what can be actual when making experiments.

4 Conclusion

Popper's aim was to answer this question: How could the world be the way quantum mechanics says it is? This is still the aim of many specialists of quantum mechanics (see Healey 1989, p. 6, and van Fraassen 1991, p. 4). However, is this the right way to understand quantum mechanics? Problems arise when we try to offer an image of the world that takes quantum mechanics into account. The purpose of this paper was precisely to point out two problems that are inherent to Popper's propensity interpretation. (a) What are the recipients of propensities? With regard to quantum field theory, there is no satisfying answer to this question. (b) Do propensities correspond to an independent reality? This is a quite problematic point given that the content of our knowledge concerning propensities is reducible to the content of our knowledge concerning what is actual for us in the context of an experiment.

How then can we interpret quantum mechanics? Instead of making any metaphysical statement, we could try to understand quantum mechanics *as a theory that belongs to a specific research activity*. In this respect, we should grasp, in a precise manner, the *function* of each part of the theory, for example, the function of the state vector, the function of Schrödinger's equation, and so on. Such an instrumentalist approach has become more and more popular in recent years (see Peres 1993). It is impossible here to develop this approach, yet we might emphasize the fact that probabilities in quantum mechanics can be viewed merely as a prediction tool about what can become actual at the end of a given measurement. Why do we deal with probabilistic predictions rather than with deterministic ones? This might be a result of the existence of incompatible observables. There is nothing to make us think that these probabilities represent some dispositional properties belonging to an independent world.

Bibliography

Aristotle. *Metaphysics*. In J. Barnes, editor (1984). *The Complete Works of Aristotle*, Volume II. Princeton NJ: Princeton University Press.

Bergson, H. (1930). 'Le possible et le réel'. Reprinted in *La pensée et le mouvant: Essais et conférences*. 12th edition 1941. Paris: PUF.

Clifton, R. & Halvorson, H. (2001). 'Are Rindler Quanta Real? Inequivalent Particle Concepts in Quantum Field Theory'. *The British Journal for Philosophy of Science* **52**, pp. 417-470.

van Fraassen, B. (1991). *Quantum Mechanics: An Empiricist View*. Oxford: Clarendon Press.

Goodman, N. (1954). *Fact, Fiction, and Forecast*. London: Athlone Press.

Healey, R. A. (1989). *The Philosophy of Quantum Mechanics: An Interactive Interpretation*. Cambridge & elsewhere: Cambridge University Press.

Heisenberg, W. (1927). 'Über den anschaulichen Inhalt der quantentheoretischen Kinematik und Mechanik'. *Zeitschrift für Physik* **43**, pp. 172-198.

Parrochia, D. (1997). 'Le vide quantique est-il un nouvel éther?' In E. Gunzig & S. Diner, editors (1997), pp. 94-104. *Le vide, univers du tout et du rien*. Bruxelles: Complexe.

Peres, A. (1993). *Quantum Theory: Concepts and Methods*. Dordrecht: Kluwer Academic Publishers.

Popper, K. R. (1935). *Logik der Forschung*. Vienna: Julius Springer Verlag. English translation, Popper (1959).

——— (1959). *The Logic of Scientific Discovery*. London: Hutchinson.

——— (1963). *Conjectures and Refutations: The Growth of Scientific Knowledge*. London: Routledge & Kegan Paul. 5th edition 1989. London: Routledge.

——— (1982a). *The Open Universe: An Argument for Indeterminism*. London: Hutchinson.

——— (1982b). *Quantum Theory and the Schism in Physics*. London: Hutchinson.

——— (1990). *A World of Propensities*. Bristol: Thoemmes.

Teller, P. (1995). *An Interpretive Introduction to Quantum Field Theory*. Princeton NJ: Princeton University Press.

Unruh, W. & Wald, R. (1984). 'What Happens When an Accelerating Observer Detects a Rindler Particle'. *Physical Review D* **29**, pp. 1047-1056.

van Fraassen, B. (1991). *See* Fraassen.

50

Karl Popper's Propensity
Interpretation of Probability[*]

Jacob Rosenthal

The propensity interpretation of probability was developed by Karl Popper in the 1950s as a successor to the frequency interpretation he had formerly adhered to.[1] According to the propensity interpretation, probabilities are properties of certain experimental arrangements, namely, tendencies of those arrangements to produce certain outcomes. More exactly: imagine a random experiment with possible outcomes $A_1, A_2, \ldots, A_n$. That outcome A_i occurs with probability p_i means, according to the propensity interpretation, that the experimental set-up is endowed with a tendency or propensity of relative strength p_i to produce the outcome A_i. This is, of course, in need of expli-cation, if 'propensity' or 'tendency' is supposed to be more than merely a new word for 'probability'. To give content to his conception, Popper offers us three main ideas: propensities are, first, dispositions of a certain kind, second, they are generalized physical forces or causes, and third, they are weighted possibilities. I will discuss these ideas in turn. The upshot will be that they all fail for the same reason: They presuppose, in one way or another, the concept of probability that should be interpreted by introducing the concept of propensity. They all lead to a conceptual circle.

First, propensities as dispositions. If a thing shows under certain typical circumstances a certain characteristic behaviour, we ascribe a corresponding disposition to the thing, as a persistent property of it. 'Something x is dis-posed at time t to give response r to stimulus s if and only if, if x were to undergo stimulus s at time t, x would give response r' (Lewis 1997, p. 143). A standard example for a disposition is solubility in water. Every lump of sugar would dissolve if put into water under normal circumstances, so every sugar lump has the permanent property of water solubility. The dissolution is the manifestation or display of this disposition. Dispositions are character-ized through the corresponding displays. So, if propensities are dispositions of experimental arrangements, the question is: Dispositions to what? What are their characteristic manifestations?

---

[*]Thanks to two anonymous referees for valuable comments and criticisms.

[1]See the three articles Popper (1957), (1959), and (1967), the *Postscript* to his *Logic of Scientific Discovery*, on which he worked in the 1950s and 1960s, but which was not published before 1982-1983, and finally the small book Popper (1990).

There are two answers to this question contained in Popper's works. According to the first, the manifestation of a propensity is a characteristic relative frequency in the long run (Popper 1957, p. 67; 1959, p. 35; 1967, pp. 32f.). That a certain experimental arrangement has a propensity, or tendency, of relative strength p to produce the outcome A, means that, if the experiment were repeated very often (or even infinitely many times), the outcome A would occur in approximately (or even exactly) $100p\%$ of the cases. So propensities are dispositions of experimental arrangements to produce the possible outcomes with certain characteristic relative frequencies in the long run.

The problem with this answer is that it presupposes a non-probabilistic connection between probabilities and relative frequencies, which definitely does not exist. Imagine a fair die, which, if thrown under normal circumstances, has equal probability for each number. If you throw the die repeatedly, each sequence of outcomes is possible, and in particular it is possible that each throw results in the same number. Since the different throws are independent, the second throw can of course have the same result as the first, the third the same result as the second, and so forth. This possibility is already implicitly contained in the characterization 'independent repetitions of the same (random) experiment'. So it is simply not true that a fair die would, upon repetition, lead to a series of outcomes in which each number occurs (exactly or approximately) with the relative frequency $1/6$. That such a 'regular' series of outcomes occurs, is only highly probable, and it is the more probable the more often the experiment is repeated, but other series are nevertheless possible and remain so even in the (hypothetical) limiting case of an infinite number of repetitions.

To be a little bit more precise: if a fair die is thrown n times and the throws are independent, then every possible sequence of outcomes occurs with the same probability $(1/6)^n$. In particular, the series that consists only of sixes occurs with this probability. Its chance is no less than that of any other particular series of outcomes. With increasing n the proportion of such 'irregular' series (that is, of series in which the six numbers are not approximately evenly distributed) among all series diminishes more and more, and so the probability of getting a regular series increases ('weak law of large numbers'). In the limiting case of an infinite number of throws the proportion of irregular outcome series to all series is zero, and so you get with probability 1 a series in which each number occurs with relative frequency $1/6$ ('strong law of large numbers'). But this does not mean that you would get such a series for sure, because the irregular series are still there, and each of them has the same chance to occur as each of the regular series. Only the measure-theoretic proportion of the irregular series among all possible series is zero.

So, if a propensity is characterized as a disposition to produce certain frequencies in the long run, it is a disposition that is only probabilistically connected to its manifestations. The statement 'in the long run there would result such-and-such relative frequencies' is either false or to be understood as shorthand for 'in the long run there would *with high probability* result such-and-such frequencies'. But now a conceptual circle has emerged: Popper characterizes probabilities as propensities, and propensities as dispositions of experimental arrangements to produce certain relative frequencies in the long run. But since these occur only with high probability, the concept of probability that should be explicated via the idea of propensity is in fact presupposed by it. You cannot say what kind of disposition a propensity is if you do not refer to probabilities. Of course there could be dispositions that are only probabilistically connected to their respective manifestations, and of course you are free to call such dispositions 'propensities' (see, for example, Mumford 1998), but then you cannot interpret probability statements via reference to propensities.

The same problem emerges at once, and more obviously, if the manifestations of the propensities are not understood as certain relative frequencies in the long run, but rather as the outcomes of single experiments. This is the second answer contained in Popper's works as to what the manifestations of propensities are (1957, pp. 67f.; 1959, pp. 28, 37). The propensity of an experimental arrangement to produce the outcome A is displayed if and only if this outcome actually occurs upon carrying out the experiment. But since A occurs only with a certain probability p, the disposition of the experimental arrangement to produce A is, under the relevant circumstances, displayed only with a certain probability. Therefore the concept of probability is again presupposed.

So the result is that you cannot on the one hand give a propensity interpretation of the concept of probability, and on the other hand introduce propensities as certain dispositions. As dispositions are characterized through their manifestations, and probabilities are only probabilistically connected to observable events, each alleged candidate for a manifestation of a disposition called 'propensity' occurs, under the relevant circumstances, only with a certain probability. But it is this very concept of probability (in the context of physical theories) that should be interpreted by the idea of propensity, so it cannot be presupposed in an explanation of what propensities are.

Second, Popper compares propensities to physical forces (1957, pp. 68-70; 1959, pp. 27f., 30f., 37f.; 1967, pp. 41f.; 1982a, pp. 93-95, 105; 1990, pp. 12-14, 18-20). Doing this, he has more in mind than just that propensities are theoretical entities. He speaks of 'the idea of propensity as a kind of generalization of — or perhaps even an alternative to — the idea of force' (Popper 1982a, p. 95; 1990, pp. 12, 14), and he compares his introduction of propensities to the introduction of classical forces into physics by Newton (Popper 1957, p. 70; 1990, pp. 13f.). The propensity interpretation of probability is in his opinion a new physical theory or hypothesis. But his further remarks on this point are too vague to be really helpful. Some suggest that he sees propensities as forces that vary probabilistically in strength or direction. That would indeed be a generalization of the idea of force, but there is no physical

theory that uses this concept of randomly varying forces, and anyway, even
if there were such a theory, the question of what probabilities in physics are
would be as open as ever. The idea of probabilistically varying forces would
be just another application of the concept of probability, and not an interpretation of it. So Popper's second idea, that propensities are something like
generalized forces, is not very convincing either. One cannot say that Popper
has proposed a new physical theory, or a modification of an existing one. What
he does propose is a certain interpretation of the probabilities in physics or at
least in quantum mechanics, an interpretation that makes these probabilities
objective and applicable to the single case and that makes probability statements testable by means of relative frequencies. But it is one thing to aim
at such an interpretation, and another thing really to develop it, and neither
the concept of force nor the concept of disposition has proved helpful for this
task.

Analogous remarks apply to the view of the propensity theory as a generalized theory of causality, that is, to the characterization of propensities as a
generalization of deterministic causes (Popper 1990). According to this view,
propensities are causes or causal links of a certain strength. But what does it
mean that an experimental arrangement is endowed with, say, a strong causal
tendency to produce outcome A and with a weak tendency to produce outcome B? Does it mean that, upon carrying out the experiment, outcome A
must occur? Does the stronger cause always beat the weaker one? This is, of
course, not intended, for it is the situation of a typical random experiment we
want to understand and model by the concept of propensity. So we have to
say that the stronger cause is the one that succeeds with higher probability or
the one that succeeds more often, and in either case we hit on the concept of
probability. (Remember that, in a random experiment, everything that can
be said about relative frequencies is qualified by probabilities.) Propensities,
then, are causes or causal links that bring about the respective effects not
necessarily, but only with a certain probability. Such a probabilistic theory
of causality is evidently just another application of the concept of probability
and not an interpretation of it.

Third, Popper says that propensities are weighted, or weights of, physical
possibilities (Popper 1967, p. 32; 1990, pp. 9f.). From this point of view the
propensity theory appears to be an improvement of the classical conception
of probability, according to which the probability of an event is the ratio of
'favourable' to 'equally possible' cases. One shortcoming of this idea is that in
many examples there simply are no equally possible cases, for instance, when
a loaded die is thrown. So you may generalize the classical conception by saying that the possible cases need not be equally possible, that some cases can
be 'more possible' or 'easier to realize' than others, that, in general, 'weights'
are attached to the possible cases and that the probability of an event is the
sum of the weights of the favourable cases. And, if you like, you can call these

weights, or possibilities thus weighted, 'propensities'. But this can hardly be called an interpretation of probability. 'Probability' is simply replaced by new words with the same meaning. Remember here a second well-known shortcoming of the classical conception, namely that 'equally possible' means exactly the same as 'equally probable', so that the definition of probability as the ratio of favourable to equally possible cases involves a conceptual circle. This criticism applies equally to Popper's propensity theory, if it is presented in this way. That a certain possible outcome has 'greater weight' than another is just to say that it occurs with greater probability. If you try to avoid this conceptual circle by referring to frequencies instead, that is, by saying that 'greater weight' means 'occurs more often', you are again confronted with the problem that relative frequencies are only probabilistically connected to probabilities, or propensities, or weighted physical possibilities, or whatever you want to put in this place, so that you are, after all, still caught in the conceptual circle.

I conclude that Popper has not succeeded in providing a suitable interpretation of probability in the context of physics. 'Propensity' or 'tendency' are no more than pictorial names for objective single-case probabilities or objective chances. If one thinks about probabilities in nature, one may have the idea that there are 'tendencies' in the world that pull in different directions with different strengths. No wonder that the idea of force also comes to mind in this context. But if you want to leave the level of mere associations and develop an interpretation of probability based on these ideas, you immediately become involved in a conceptual circle. For what can it mean that a certain possible outcome of a random experiment has a greater tendency or propensity to become actual than another possible outcome? It means either that the first outcome occurs with higher probability, in which case the circle is most obvious. Or it means that the outcome would, upon repetition, occur more frequently, which is either false or to be taken as shorthand for 'would with high probability occur more frequently', in which case the conceptual circle emerges again. Popper's various attempts to explicate his talk of 'propensities' or 'tendencies' of experimental arrangements all lead back to this dilemma.

Does this mean that the propensity interpretation of probability has to be dismissed? Not necessarily. First, one could say that according to the propensity interpretation, 'probability' is just a fundamental, irreducible concept that cannot be explicated any further by reference to other concepts. One would then drop the talk about dispositions, forces, weighted physical possibilities and so on and simply say that propensities are real, physical entities, objective and applicable to the single case, and ascribable to experimental arrangements by means of relative frequencies — period. The problem with this answer is that it leaves the crucial properties of propensities unexplained: Why do propensities obey the probability calculus? Why are they connected to observable relative frequencies, and how do they explain the occurrence of those frequencies? There is no suitable bridge principle that connects propensities and relative frequencies, as there is in other cases where a theoretical entity is connected to an observable one, because any such connection would have to be qualified by higher-order probabilities that must be interpreted in turn.

Second, following Popper, other writers have developed varieties of the propensity interpretation that are perhaps more promising. Among these, I want to mention Mellor (1971) and Lewis (1980). Both of them introduce propensities, or objective chances, not via their connection with relative frequencies, but via their connection with subjective probabilities, or rational degrees of belief. Popper would certainly not have approved of that, because from their point of view the subjective concept of probability, that is, the concept of probability as rational credence, is fundamental. But it seems clear, first, that there are such things as subjective degrees of belief, measurable through betting quotients, and that coherent betting quotients obey the calculus of probability. Second, it seems plausible that this or a similar concept of probability must be fundamental, because 'probable', 'probability', and related notions are first of all epistemic notions that have their origin in our limited knowledge in general, and that the idea that there are probabilities in nature comes only later. Third, it is clear that if there are such things as objective chances, that is, probabilities in nature, they certainly constrain rational credence, or more precisely: the objective chance of an event provides the appropriate degree for the belief in its occurrence. Otherwise the term 'objective probability' would simply be out of place. Whatever it is in nature that is given the name 'objective probability', it certainly would not deserve this name if it did not constrain rational credence. So it seems to be a promising idea to found a concept of objective chance on a theory of subjective probability plus a bridge principle of the indicated kind that connects chance and credence.

This programme was carried out concisely by David Lewis (1980, 1986, 1994). Its problem is that according to it we know nothing about objective chances or propensities except that they are entities that constrain rational credence. Everything else follows from that. To model a chance phenomenon according to the propensity interpretation means to assume that the world contains entities that provide appropriate degrees of belief. How they manage to do that remains obscure. Chances or propensities have a certain normative power that is not further explained, and we know nothing about them except that they have this power. Or, to put it the other way round: chance is nothing but objectified credence, subjective probability inscribed into nature. This is no doubt very strange, but attempts to do better by connecting propensities to certain observable entities have failed so far. Of course there might be other observable entities than relative frequencies to which propensities are connected. What immediately comes to mind here are physical symmetries, symmetries in nature. But first, there is no indication that suitable symmetries, from which the objective chances can be inferred, always exist, and second, there may well be several different symmetries that lead to different probabilities (Bertrand's paradoxes). So physical symmetries are not promising candidate either to provide us with a general and non-probabilistic connection between objective chances (propensities) and observable entities. But without such a connection objective chances (propensities) remain obscure entities.

Bibliography

Lewis, D.K. (1980). 'A Subjectivist's Guide to Objective Chance'. In R.C. Jeffrey, editor (1980), pp. 263-293. *Studies in Inductive Logic and Probability, Volume II*. Berkeley: University of California Press. Reprinted with a postscript in Lewis (1986), pp. 83-132.

—— (1986). *Philosophical Papers, Volume II*. New York: Oxford University Press.

—— (1994). 'Humean Supervenience Debugged'. *Mind* **103**, pp. 473-490.

—— (1997). 'Finkish Dispositions'. *Philosophical Quarterly* **47**, pp. 143-158.

Mellor, D.H. (1971). *The Matter of Chance*. Cambridge: Cambridge University Press.

Mumford, S. (1998), *Dispositions*. Oxford: Oxford University Press.

Popper, K.R. (1957). 'The Propensity Interpretation of the Calculus of Probability, and the Quantum Theory'. In S. Körner, editor (1957), pp. 65-70 and 88f. *Observation and Interpretation, Proceedings of the Ninth Symposium of the Colston Research Society, University of Bristol*. London: Butterworths. Reprinted as selection 15 in K.R. Popper (1985). *Popper Selections*. Princeton NJ: Princeton University Press.

—— (1959). 'The Propensity Interpretation of Probability'. *The British Journal for the Philosophy of Science* **10**, pp. 25-42.

—— (1967). 'Quantum Mechanics without "The Observer" '. In M. Bunge, editor (1967), pp. 7-44. *Quantum Theory and Reality*. Berlin, Heidelberg, & New York: Springer Verlag. Reprinted as the Introduction to Popper (1982b).

—— (1982a). *The Open Universe. An Argument for Indeterminism*. London: Hutchinson.

—— (1982b). *Quantum Theory and the Schism in Physics*. London: Hutchinson.

—— (1990). *A World of Propensities*. Bristol: Thoemmes.

51

Single Event Probabilities in Popper's Propensity Account

Melis Erdur

Probabilistic statements are common in science. However, what these statements exactly mean is a matter in dispute. A myriad of interpretations have been proposed. The propensity account is one of them. It was put forward by Karl Popper, a former proponent of the frequency interpretation, who believed that the propensity interpretation handled single event probabilities much better than the frequency account. Despite the arguments Popper provided in favour of the propensity account, many philosophers remained suspicious of its success. The major objection to his view is that it suffers from the *reference class problem*, which was originally a problem for the frequency account, and thus, like its rival, fails to make sense of single event probabilities.

Having observed the problem, some philosophers have suggested possible solutions to save the propensity interpretation. However, it has also been noted that such solutions imply either that the propensities are not fully objective or that statements concerning propensities are not testable. Both of these implications are highly problematic for Popper because the objectivity of propensities and the testability of propensity statements are crucial for his philosophy of science in general.

In this paper, I shall first examine the reference class problem applied to the propensity account. Then I shall briefly discuss the suggested solutions, which I believe are hardly acceptable for Popper. Finally, I shall argue that the propensity account is not committed to any of these unacceptable solutions because, properly understood or interpreted, it does *not* face the reference class problem at all. Let me then start by explicating the reference class problem as it is raised against the frequency view.

The frequency interpretation equates probability with relative frequenies, and to the extent that they are meaningful, it assigns single events probabilities according to the sequence of events to which they belong. For instance, the event of getting a '6' in the next throw with a regular die is assigned 1/6 because the relative frequency of the throws whose outcomes are '6' in a sequence of throws with a regular die is 1/6.

The reference class problem arises in assigning single events to sequences. Consider, for instance, the probability of getting a '6' in a particular throw of a certain die at a certain time. We can classify that throw as *a throw with this die* or as *a throw with this die thrown in this way* or as *a throw with any die from this height*, and so on. Recall that the frequency view assigns probability to a single event on the basis of the relative frequency of its occurrence in a certain sequence of events. Now note that the *relative* frequency of an event depends on the sequence taken as reference. Moreover, the sequence taken as reference is determined according to the way an event is classified or described. Hence the probability of a single event depends on the way it is classified or described. If, for instance, the relative frequency of '6' in the sequence consisting of *throws with the die d from height h* is 1/6, then when the single event is classified as *a throw with the die d thrown from height h*, the probability of the next throw is assigned 1/6. However, if the relative frequency of '6' in the sequence consisting of *throws with the die d thrown in the manner m* is 1/3, then when the single event is classified as such, it is assigned the probability 1/3. In this way, the single event probability depends on the way the event is classified, and thus it cannot be assigned a unique value. This is the reference class problem. Let me then turn to the propensity interpretation.

Popper's propensity account takes 'as fundamental *the probability of the result of a single experiment*, with respect to its *conditions* rather than the frequency of results in a sequence of experiments' (1957, p. 68). The basic motivation for the shift from the frequency view to the propensity view is that proper assignments of single events to sequences are primarily based on the conditions under which they occur. For instance, suppose that there are two dice, one regular and the other biased such that the probability of getting a '1' is 1/4. Now consider the sequence consisting of throws with the biased die except for a few throws with the regular die. Since a few throws do not affect the relative frequenies, the relative frequency of getting a '1' in that sequence will be 1/4. However, as Popper argues, it will be wrong to assign the probability 1/4 to getting '1' in the throws with the regular die although they actually belong to a sequence in which the relative frequency of that event is 1/4. The probability of getting a '1' in the throws with the *regular* die should be assigned 1/6. This shows, according to Popper, that it is the experimental conditions that probabilities of single events depend on, and not belonging to this or that sequence (1957).

Although originally raised against the frequency view, it is not hard to apply the reference class problem to the propensity view. In Popper's propensity view, the probabilities of single events are assigned *with respect to the conditions* under which they occur. But what are *the conditions* of a single event? As Wesley Salmon asks: 'Are we talking about the toss of any old die, biased or unbiased? Or about any method of tossing? Or tossing by means of a dice cup? Or by a left handed person?' (1979, p. 197). Since it is the experimental conditions that produce propensities for the realization of single events, these singular probabilities will depend on the conditions chosen. In that case, the propensity view will suffer from the reference class problem as the frequency view does, that is, it will fail to assign a unique value to single events.

Observing the problem that Popper's propensity view seems to face, Donald Gillies (2000, pp. 814f.) suggests that the single event probabilities should be subjective. He states:

> We can certainly introduce objective probabilities for events A which are outcomes of some sets of repeatable conditions **S**. When, however, we want to introduce probabilities for single events, these probabilities, though sometimes objectively based, will nearly always fail to be fully objective because there will in most cases be a doubt about the way we should classify the event, and this will introduce a subjective element into the singular probability.

In fact, as Henry Kyburg points out, there are many passages in Popper's works that suggest that he already lets such subjective elements into his view. As Kyburg observes, Popper states that propensities 'are relational properties of the experimental arrangement — the conditions *we intend* to keep constant' (1959, p. 37, my italics). However, as Kyburg notes, such subjectivity makes propensities 'anomalous' for Popper's philosophy of science. He says (1974, p. 361):

> Popper makes much of the objectivity of propensity statements, and decries at great length the 'subjectivism' of both subjective and logical probability. But here we find that propensities are properties of conditions we *intend* to keep constant. ... Thus that of which probabilities are predicated depends on our intentions ... and since the values of probabilities and the strengths of propensities depend on what it is they are predicated of, these values and strengths in turn depend on our intentions ...

Making single event probabilities subjective is a possible solution to the reference class problem. For in that case *the proper conditions* with respect to which the probabilities are assigned will simply be those that we intend to keep constant. However, such an idea hardly counts as a solution for Popper because, as Kyburg notes, the objectivity of probability is the very idea he has defended in all his works, as his general philosophy of science demands.

Another idea to save the propensity view could be qualifying *the conditions* that produce propensities. Some followers of Popper appeal to this idea. For instance, it is suggested by David Miller (1994, pp. 185f., my italics) that

> every propensity ... must be referred to *the complete situation of the universe* ... at the time. ... Only in this way do we attain the specificity required to resolve the problem of the single case.

James Fetzer (1982, p. 195, my italics) offers a similar suggestion:

> It should not be thought that propensities for outcomes ... depend, in general, upon the complete state of the world at a time rather than upon *a complete set of ... relevant conditions* ... which happens to be instantiated in that world at that time.

In fact, Popper seems to endorse an idea quite similar to the above ones in his later work. As Gillies notes, Popper states that 'propensities in physics are properties of *the whole physical situation* and sometimes the particular way in which a situation changes' (Popper 1990, p. 17).

However, as Gillies points out, if propensities are ascribed to the complete situation of the universe or to the complete set of relevant conditions at a time, then we lose the testability of hypotheses concerning propensities. The complete situation of the universe is never repeated, and both formulating and testing a conjecture about a complete set of relevant conditions are almost impossible (Gillies 2000, p. 824). Given that testability is so central in Popper's philosophy of science, the above suggestions do not qualify as *solutions* to the reference class problem for him.

Is it the case, then, that Popper cannot provide an account of objective single event probabilities that satisfies the basic requirements of his philosophy of science? I believe that a certain understanding of propensities, which can be extracted from his works on the subject, allows genuine objective single event probabilities and testable hypotheses about them. To see how, consider what Popper says about singular probability statements (1983, Part II, § 26, my italics):

> [the propensity view] interprets singular probability statements as statements that attribute probabilities to single events, or *more precisely, to a single event and a set of circumstances* under which the event in question is supposed to happen.

Hence, according to him, a propensity statement is not merely about a single event, it is about a single event *and* a set of conditions. According to him, propensities are 'objective *relational* properties of the physical world' (1957, p. 70, my italics) or '*relational* properties of the experimental arrangement' (1959, p. 37, my italics). That is why, he states, propensities are similar to forces (1983, Part II, § 20, p. 3593):

> propensities ... resemble forces, or fields of forces: a Newtonian force is ... a relational property of at least two things; and the actual resulting forces in a physical system are always a property of the whole physical system. Force, like propensity, is a relational concept.

In the light of what he says about propensities and their resemblance to forces, we can conclude that it is not appropriate to talk about *the* propensity of a single event. *Every* set of conditions under which a single event takes place produces *a* certain propensity for the single event. We can talk about *the propensity of throwing with this die to realize the event of getting a '6' in the next throw*, or *the propensity of throwing with this method to realize that event*, and so on. Every part of the situation has an effect on the realization of the single event, and propensities are the measures of that effect. That is how they are relational properties of the whole physical situation.

Consider the force metaphor again. Given a group of objects, say, a, b, c, d, the force exerted on a by b exists, as well as the force exerted on a by c *and d*, and so on. There exists a force between *any* two objects as well as a force exerted on an object by the combination of *any* set of objects. In a physical situation, *all* these forces exist. Similarly, there exists *a* propensity of *any* set of conditions to produce a certain single event.

Now, let us turn back to the reference class problem. Recall that it arises because the set of conditions relative to which the probability of a single event is referred cannot be defined, and that is why the single event cannot be assigned a unique propensity value. In the light of the above clarifications, it is obvious that this problem simply does not apply to Popper's propensity view, because the latter makes no claim to provide *absolute* single event probabilities. As we have seen, Popper talks about a *relation* of the event under a set of conditions and a single event, and *not* about a single event by itself. Since his account does *not* even *allow* absolute or unique propensity values for single events, it will not make sense to criticize it for not achieving that.

Moreover, once it is understood that propensities are relational properties, it becomes clear that their objectivity is not jeopardized. A propensity exists between a single event and any set of conditions under which the event occurs; but *given* a set of conditions and a single event, the propensity between them is an objective aspect of the world. 'Taller than' is a relation, and we can talk only about a person's being taller than another. However, given any two people, who is taller than the other is an objective fact of the world. In a similar way, depending on our intentions and the scientific problem at hand, we may consider one particular event and one particular set of conditions rather than another. However, the propensity between the event and the set of conditions in question is an objective aspect of the world, and does not depend on our intentions.

Furthermore, the relational nature of propensities renders the hypotheses concerning them testable. Given a hypothesis about the propensity of a set of conditions to realize a single event, we can test it by keeping the selected set of conditions constant, and observing the relative frequency of the outcome. That relative frequency will indicate the effect of the specified set of conditions on realizing the event in question. If, for instance, the propensity of throwing with the die d from a height h to realize the event of getting a '3' in the next throw is $1/4$, then it is expected that the relative frequency of '3' in a sequence of throws with that die from that height is sufficiently close to $1/4$. Note that once the hypotheses concerning propensities involve both single events and *specified* sets of conditions, testing such hypotheses by repeating the experiment while keeping the specified set constant becomes legitimate.

It may be argued that although the objectivity of the propensities and the testability of the hypotheses concerning them are maintained, Popper's propensity account is not better off than the frequency account as far as the reference class problem. One may argue that the reference class problem arises precisely because of the need for *absolute* single event probabilities, and

Popper's account, in so far as it does not provide them, does suffer from the reference class problem whether or not it has such an aim.[1]

Is this a legitimate objection to Popper's account? Does the inability to provide absolute single event probabilities by itself count as a defect of a probability account? I do not think that it does. Probabilities are aspects of physical reality, and there seems to be no particular reason for them to be absolute rather than relational. There are many relational properties of physical reality. For instance, as Popper observes, Newtonian forces are relational properties among objects. Therefore, it would make no sense to criticize Newtonian theory for not providing an account of absolute forces. In a similar way, relations such as 'taller than' are defined between two things. It would make no sense to criticize a view for not providing an absolutist account of the 'taller than' relation. In short, providing a relational account of something is not by itself a defect.

I believe that the reference class *problem* within the frequency account of probability is rather the fact that single event probabilities depend on the way the events are *classified* or *described*. This by itself can perfectly well be considered as a defect for an account. For the dependence of probability values on the way events are described indicate that probabilities are not *real* aspects of the physical world. And this would be a problem for an account that claims to explain certain *objective* aspects of the world. If, for instance, the force exerted on an object by another depended on the way the objects were described, then this would indicate that forces were not *real* or *objective* aspects of the physical world. In this sense, a physical theory that aims to account for forces as objective aspects of the physical world can be criticized for such a dependence on the way objects are described.

That is why the reference class problem is a problem for the frequency account but *not* for the propensity account. The former is unable to assign probability values to single events independently of the way they are classified or described. Given that the frequency account aims to explain probabilities as objective aspects of the world, this counts as a serious problem. On the other hand, the propensity account is *able* to provide objective single event probabilities, that is, to assign probability values to single events independently of the way they are described. This allows propensities to be objective aspects of the physical world, as it is aimed by the propensity account. In this sense, the propensity account *is* better off than the frequency account regarding single event probabilities. The fact that propensities are relational is, by itself, not a defect of Popper's account. On the contrary, if in fact propensities *are* relational, it is an important merit.

---

[1] Here I am indebted to the comments of the referees.

Bibliography

Fetzer, J. H. (1982). 'Probabilistic Explanations'. In P. D. Asquith & T. Nickles, editors (1982), pp. 194-207. *PSA 1982*, Volume 2. East Lansing MI: Philosophy of Science Association.

Gillies, D. A. (2000). 'Varieties of Propensity'. *The British Journal for the Philosophy of Science* **51**, pp. 807-835.

Kyburg, H. E., Jr (1974). 'Propensities and Probabilities'. *The British Journal for the Philosophy of Science* **25**, pp. 358-375.

Miller, D. W. (1994). *Critical Rationalism: A Restatement and Defence*. Chicago & La Salle IL: Open Court Publishing Company.

Popper, K. R. (1957). 'The Propensity Interpretation of the Calculus of Probability, and the Quantum Theory'. In S. Körner, editor (1957), pp. 65-70 and 88f. *Observation and Interpretation, Proceedings of the Ninth Symposium of the Colston Research Society, University of Bristol*. London: Butterworths. Reprinted as selection 15 in K. R. Popper (1985). *Popper Selections*. Princeton NJ: Princeton University Press.

——— (1959). 'The Propensity Interpretation of Probability'. *The British Journal for the Philosophy of Science* **10**, pp. 25-42.

——— (1983). *Realism and the Aim of Science*. London: Hutchinson.

——— (1990). *A World of Propensities*. Bristol: Thoemmes.

Salmon, W. C. (1979). 'Propensities: A Discussion Review'. *Erkenntnis* **14**, pp. 183-216.

PART 4
Science

C: Biology

52

The Emergent Character of Life

Josep Corcó

I should like to begin by mentioning that Popper, in his intellectual autobiography, suggested that he first became interested in writing about biology when he read a book by Erwin Schrödinger. That book was entitled *What is Life?* (Schrödinger 1944). It is well known that Popper disliked questions beginning with 'What is ...?' — yet he liked Schrödinger's book. At one point Popper even called the book 'a marvel'.

However, Popper disagreed with certain important points. For instance, he objected to Schrödinger's statement that negative entropy is the answer to the question, 'what is the characteristic feature of life?'(Popper 1974/1976, § 30). Popper thought that Schrödinger's answer was a mistake and he tried to give a better one, as we shall see. Another disagreement Popper harboured but did not mention in *Unended Quest*. Schrödinger accepted that physics and chemistry could not explain the structure of living matter at that moment, but he hoped that new and unknown physical theories would do so eventually. Behind this hope, there was the Vienna Circle's idea of the unity of sciences and of physicalism. All sciences must be reduced to physics, some members of this circle insisted. Popper questioned physicalism in general terms, and he thought that biology in particular would not necessarily be reducible to physics. In *Objective Knowledge* he expressed it this way (1972, Chapter 8, § I):

> as a rationalist I wish and hope to understand the world and ... I wish and hope for a reduction. At the same time, I think it quite likely that there may be no reduction possible; it is conceivable that life is an *emergent* property of physical bodies.

Popper then proceeded to propose an emergentist cosmology, such that in the evolution of the universe, new things appear. We all know Popper's distinction between World 1 (the physical world), World 2 (the world of subjective knowledge) and World 3 (the world of human thought contents). We also know that World 2 emerges *from* — *out of* — World 1, and World 3 emerges *from* World 2. Popper says that living beings belong to World 1. But within World 1, he distinguishes between inert things and living beings. So life has emerged from a lifeless world, a physico-chemical, inert world. Popper is not a vitalist, however (Popper 1974/1976, § 37). I think that Popper uses the term emergence in a very concrete way: it means novelty, unpredictability, and irreducibility. Thus life is a novelty in a physico-chemical world. We cannot predict life from the standpoint of a physico-chemical world. And life is irreducible to it.

Popper pointed out that this view is opposite to a reductionist one that tries to find the explanation for a new level by looking at the structure and interaction of elements on the lower level. Popper knew that the reductionist programme is very important for science and he conceded its achievements. Nevertheless, he gave up hope of its final success, especially in the investigation of life. The new level cannot be completely explained by the rules and laws of the level from which it emerges, he insisted. One of his main arguments was that the higher level is able to act on the lower level: there is 'downward causation', an expression that Popper took from Donald T. Campbell (Campbell 1974).

In *The Self and Its Brain* (Popper & Eccles 1977) Popper discussed the examples he felt make the existence of downward causation evident. They involved the survival of complex organisms and ecological systems. They pose problems for the reductionist position, he said (ibidem, Chapter P1, § 7):

> An animal may survive the death of many of its cells, and the removal of an organ, such as a leg (with the consequent death of the cells constituting the organ); but the death of the animal leads, in time, to the death of its constituent parts, cells included.

For Popper, downward causation could exist only if the lower level is not completely determined, but indeterminism is insufficient to make downward causation possible. The lower level must also be open to the action of the higher level. Popper saw organisms as hierarchical systems of plastic controls — with a certain degree of control from the higher to the lower systems, with biological systems controlling physico-chemical ones. Such control would be plastic because there would be feedback from the controlled system to the controller system. Thus, upward causation also exists, such that it is possible for there to be physico-chemical systems that affect biological ones. I should say there are interactions between levels. Still, for Popper, because downward causation exists, we cannot expect to find a comprehensive theory of life in physico-chemical terms. That is to say, we cannot expect to reduce life to a physico-chemical theory. Biology, then, may be regarded as an enrichment of physico-chemistry, and this will explain why biology is partly but not wholly reducible.

Opposed to this vision we find the determinist's point of view, Popper pointed out. Determinism accepts only a subjectivist interpretation of the probability of single events: thus, what we can understand by indeterminacy shows only that we have insufficient knowledge of reality. In the deterministic position, there are no truly indeterminate events. Against this, Popper proposed an objective interpretation of probability, namely a propensity theory. The propensities are real, but they do not determine the future: they are just

tendencies of a situation to change. Popper thought that there is real indeterminacy in all three worlds. Indeterminacy makes it very difficult to predict
many processes — such as life, for instance. He accepted Monod's argument
on the origin of life (Popper 1982, addendum 2, § X):

> Monod's suggestion is that life emerged from inanimate matter by an extremely
> improbable combination of chance circumstances, and that this may not merely
> have been an event of low probability but of zero probability — in fact, a *unique*
> event.
>   ... [a]s Monod points out, the machinery by which the cell (at least the
> non-primitive cell which is the only one we know) translates the [genetic] code
> 'consists of at least fifty macromolecular components *which are themselves coded
> in DNA*'. Thus the code cannot be translated except by using certain products of
> its translation. This constitutes a really baffling circle: a vicious circle, it seems,
> for any attempt to form a model, or a theory, of the genesis of the genetic code.

Popper thought that if the origin of life is a unique event with a probability near zero, it is therefore not predictable. The relationship between
probability and predictability is not clear, however. Popper pointed out that
even if Monod's suggestion were refuted, and we could produce life under
replicable conditions, we might be doing so without a complete understanding of physico-chemical processes. In that case, said Popper, the properties of
life would remain, still, unpredictable. Furthermore, Popper thought that the
evolutionary process of life is unpredictable. In the evolution of life there are
many possibilities and only some of them take place. When some take place,
new possibilities appear. The development of life, therefore, is just as unpredictable as life itself. Thus, Popper saw life as a unique, creative process full of
unpredictable events. When Popper in *In Search of a Better World* described
the results of the process, his words suggest wonder. He is astonished (1992,
Chapter 1, § IV):

> The first cell is still living after billions of years, and now even in many trillions
> of copies. Wherever we look, it is there. It has made a garden of our earth
> and transformed our atmosphere with green plants. And it created our eyes and
> opened them to the blue sky and the stars. It is doing well.

Popper accepted that life is, basically, a net of metabolic processes, that
there are no constituents other than chemical ones. Nevertheless, life has properties that are different from those of the chemical world. Popper reminded us
that problems, knowledge, and values appear in the universe along with the
origin of life. Therefore, he proposed as a distinction between inert things and
life the fact that only organisms have problems and try to solve them. In his
intellectual autobiography, he said that the organism's problems are typically
not physical problems and that organisms themselves are not physical things
(Popper 1974/1976, § 37). Rather, living beings are physico-chemical structures that solve problems, and because of that, they are not merely physical.

Life is a novelty in a physico-chemical world, and problems are essentially involved (1982, Addendum 2, section XI):

> Problems and problem solving seem to emerge together with life. Even though there is something like natural selection at work prior to the origin of life — for example, a selection of the more stable elements due to the radioactive disintegration of the less stable ones — we cannot say that, for atomic nuclei, survival is a 'problem' in any sense of this term. ... Indeed, we can describe life, if we like, as problem solving, and living organisms as the only problem solving complexes in the universe.

The most basic problem life has is to adapt to the environment, to survive, and Popper thought that any attempt to adapt presupposed an attempt to know the environment. Thus, adaptation by means of trial and error is a kind of knowledge of the general or specific conditions of the environment. Popper said that the organism, with its structure and its behaviour, would be like a theory that could be accepted or refuted by the environment (1972, Chapter 6, § XVIII). When an organism survives and leaves offspring, the organism has solved a problem with a new theory. Moreover, this knowledge must be an anticipation of environmental conditions for life (Popper 1999, Chapter 4, the section entitled 'Adaptation and Darwinism', p. 49):

> Life must be adapted to the future conditions of the environment; *and in this sense general knowledge comes earlier than momentary knowledge*, than special knowledge. Right from the start, life must be in this way equipped with general knowledge, with the knowledge we usually call knowledge of the laws of nature. Of course, this is not knowledge in the sense of conscious knowledge.

Thus, when Popper asserted that organisms have problems, he did not want to say that they are necessarily conscious of them. Popper looked at the apparently tentative behaviour of living beings and posited the idea of dispositions. In living beings we find behavioural dispositions to action that are linked to unconscious expectations. Popper placed expectations and dispositions to action in World 2, as a kind of subjective knowledge, and he believed that they involve a certain degree of freedom. Living beings can make decisions about their behaviour. Even when behaviour is partially determined by genetics, all organisms have some capacity to choose. Popper said that, in making choices, living beings not only change in and of themselves — they also try to transform the environment in favour of life. Popper says that all living beings are looking for a better world when they actively look for the best conditions for life. In this search, they have transformed many aspects of the Earth. He said it this way (1977, Chapter P1, § 6):

> The theory of organic evolution starts from the fact that all organisms, but especially the higher organisms, have a more or less varied repertoire of behaviour at their disposal. By adopting a new form of behaviour the individual organism may change its environment. ... By this individual action, the organism may 'choose', as it were, its environment; and it may thereby expose itself

and its descendants to a new set of selection pressures, characteristic of the new environment.

So, life changes the environment for its purposes, even as life itself changes through mutations in its genetic material, some of which would be adaptive to the regularities in the environment. In this process, we must remember, Popper said that a species includes in its constitution some knowledge of its environment. The selection of mutations, however, will come from the ecological niche elected or constructed by the behaviour of organisms. This is the reason why Popper says that the structures of an organism could be considered objective products of tentative behaviour. Thus, with the words 'objective products', we now seem to be in World 3. Just as World 3 is the product of human activity, the structures of organisms are products of activity by organisms. And like some of the products of World 3, organisms' structures are objective knowledge embodied. Therefore, I suggest that we should expand our interpretation of World 3, to include the organisms' structures, as the products of life itself. They are objective knowledge, but not always correct, Popper said (1990a, pp. 46f.; 1999, Chapter 5, p. 70):

> I think that, say, 99 per cent of the knowledge of all organisms is inborn and incorporated in our biochemical constitution. ...
>
> Thus, all our knowledge is hypothetical. It is an adaptation to a partly unknown environment. It is often successful and often unsuccessful, the result of anticipatory trials and of unavoidable errors, *and of error elimination.* Some of the errors that have entered the inheritable constitution of an organism are eliminated by eliminating their bearer; that is, the individual organism. But some errors escape, and this is one reason why we are all fallible: our adaptation to the environment is never optimal, and it is always imperfect.

Popper admitted that the attribution of knowledge to all living beings is an anthropomorphic idea. But he answered that anthropomorphism is indispensable for understanding the theory of evolution. We must relate some aspects of man to some aspects of other living beings, thinking in terms of homologies. He established a homology between the expectations incorporated within an organism's constitution and scientific theories, for example. The difference is that man can eliminate the false scientific theories with critical thinking, whereas false expectations embodied in other living beings are eliminated by death. I think that this homology between the constitution of living beings and scientific theories makes it possible to think of the constitution of living beings in terms of World 3, as objective knowledge.

In my view, the three worlds of Popper's cosmology help us to distinguish three aspects of life. First, living beings, as inhabitants of World 1, have physico-chemical properties. Then, in World 2, the active attitude of living beings includes dispositions, expectations, and decisions that comprise subjective knowledge. And finally, knowledge is incorporated into the biological constitutions of living beings, and that knowledge might be compared to the objective knowledge that belongs to World 3. By looking at the differences between life in World 1, life in World 2, and life in World 3, the emergent character of life is clarified. There is no knowledge in the physico-chemical world, yet knowledge is characteristic of life. This is possible because knowledge is an emergent property. Popper expressed this principle in a lecture in 1989 (1990a, p. 39; 1999, Chapter 5, pp. 64f.):

> the origin and the evolution of knowledge may be said to coincide with the origin and the evolution of life, and to be closely linked with the origin and evolution of our planet earth. Evolutionary theory links knowledge, and with it ourselves, with the cosmos; and so the problem of knowledge becomes a problem of cosmology.

In that article, Popper recalled that Heraclitus compared life with fire in order to say that life is a process, like fire. But, I would like to suggest a symbolic meaning for this comparison. To understand the symbol, we must consider the analogous meaning of fire. Fire has two main aspects: it gives light and it heats. The second aspect, fire's power to heat, symbolizes the idea of solidarity, the idea of love, as I suggested in a paper discussing similarities between Popper and Peirce (Corcó 2001). The first aspect, however, the power to light, is more relevant to Popper's view of the emergent character of life. Fire's light-giving power symbolizes knowledge. Popper said that Heraclitus was right: living beings are not things, they are flames. I should add that living beings are flames because they are knowledge.

Popper's view, then was emergentist. Nevertheless it was not *anti*-reductionist, for he conceded that life is a physico-chemical process. He thought that before trying or insisting upon reduction, however, we need to know very well what we are trying to reduce. This means that we need to work first on the level to be reduced. He considered that we cannot solve the problems linguistically, by eliminating some entities through refusing to talk about them. We must be, initially, pluralistic, trying to work through the arguments for emergence, as Popper did. Furthermore, we may continue to desire reduction and explore it.

I should like to close by referring again to Popper's own words from the first quotation I mentioned, because they underline his openness to dialogue. He expressed himself in terms of his own real, natural desire: '...as a rationalist I wish and hope to understand the world and ...I wish and hope for a reduction.' Popper then faced up to the discomfort that irreducibility poses to a rationalist by embracing emergence (1972, Chapter 8, §1): 'At the same time, I think it quite likely that there may be no reduction possible; it is conceivable that life is an *emergent* property of physical bodies.'

Bibliography

Campbell, D. T. (1974). ' "Downward Causation" in Hierarchical Organized Biological Systems'. In F. Ayala, & T. Dobzhansky, editors (1974), pp. 179-86. *Studies in the Philosophy of Biology. Reduction and Related Problems*. London: Macmillan.

Corcó, J. (2001). 'La selección natural en Popper y Peirce'. *Anuario Filosófico* **34**, pp. 139-155.

Popper, K. R. (1972). *Objective Knowledge*. Oxford: Clarendon Press. 2nd edition 1979.

———— (1974). 'Intellectual Autobiography'. In P. A. Schilpp, editor (1974), pp. 1-181. *The Philosophy of Karl Popper*. La Salle IL: Open Court. Reprinted as *Unended Quest* (1976). London & Glasgow: Fontana/Collins.

———— (1982). *The Open Universe*. London: Hutchinson.

———— (1990a). 'Towards an Evolutionary Theory of Knowledge'. In K. R. Popper (1990b), pp. 29-51. Reprinted as Chapter 5 of Popper (1999).

———— (1990b). *A World of Propensities*. Bristol: Thoemmes.

———— (1992). *In Search of a Better World*. London: Routledge.

———— (1999). *All Life is Problem Solving*. London: Routledge.

Popper, K. R. & Eccles, J. C. (1977). *The Self and Its Brain*, Berlin: Springer International.

Schrödinger, E. (1944). *What is Life? The Physical Aspect of the Living Cell*. Cambridge & elsewhere: Cambridge University Press. Reprinted in E. Schrödinger, *What Is Life? & Mind and Matter*, 1967. Cambridge & elsewhere: Cambridge University Press.

53

Popper's Darwinism

Peter Munz †

The term 'Darwinism' is used nowadays (when social Darwinism has disappeared below the horizon) for at least two totally different paradigms of thought. There is Popper's Darwinism on one side; and the Darwinism of evolutionary psychology and evolutionary epistemology, on the other. These two paradigms not only have nothing to do with each other but are also diametrically opposed to each other. The second paradigm is an ill-informed attempt to rehabilitate some kind of induction as a justification of knowledge by maintaining that knowledge is the end product of observations and/or experiences. This Darwinism was started by Konrad Lorenz (1941) and, in a different form, is enjoying a heyday in the voluminous, widely acclaimed writings of Tooby and Cosmides (for example, Barkow, Cosmides, & Tooby 1992). Darwin had dismissed Locke's *tabula rasa* mind and radical empiricism out of hand. But given the concept of adaptation, Lorenz and his many followers began to argue that our sense organs, having been selected must be adapted, that is, are trustworthy sources of knowledge. This argument has been taken to salvage Locke or, as one might say, Darwinize Locke. True, our mind is not a *tabula rasa*, but it has evolved, thanks to natural selection, complete with the ability to pick up correct information. As Lorenz put it, our knowledge is phylogenetically a posteriori; but ontogenetically a priori. In other words: our sense organs (Lorenz) or our mental modules (Tooby and Cosmides), being the products of natural selection, are adapted to get things right. While this argument has proved valid for the kind of information that paramecia and mallard ducklings come into the world with, it is hopelessly ill-informed when applied to humans. Neuroscience has shown that the human brain is not a single organ capable, with a few exceptions, of responding unequivocally to stimuli. It registers colour, position, size, time, location, shape, and other inputs separately and thus creates a binding problem that has to be solved before a single representation can emerge. As Popper, anticipating this neuroscientific evidence, put it, we cannot learn by simply staring at the world (1959, § 30). We first need a theory that has to be exposed to falsification even as biological organisms are proposals made to the environment and then exposed to natural selection. Popper's Darwinism is therefore diametrically opposed to the Darwinism of both evolutionary epistemology and evolutionary psychology. Instead of Darwinizing Locke, Popper took from Darwin the general idea that in biological evolution there are chance mutation and selective retention, and applied it to the evolution of knowledge. His epoch-making alternative to conventional positivism consisted in the fact that he saw a complete continuity from the amoeba to Einstein. It can be documented (Munz 2004, pp. 39f.) that Popper's *Darwinism*, unlike the other type, was initially developed without reference to or reliance on Darwin.

I want to explain the precise nature of Popper's Darwinism and make sure it is distinguished from other widely acclaimed forms of Darwinism. Darwinism, in general, is both a research programme and a paradigm — a Lakatosian research programme and a somewhat un-Kuhnian paradigm. As a research programme it has proved phenomenally progressive; and as a paradigm, it is remarkably un-Kuhnian because it is falsifiable. If we were to find a fossil of *homo sapiens* which is two thousand million years old, Darwinian evolution would have been refuted. Being rich, Darwinism comes in many shapes and has inspired different ways of thought, not all always distinguished. The American philosopher Daniel Dennett, for example, mentions with approval the Popperian Darwinian explanation of the growth of knowledge and in the very same book praises evolutionary psychology, a very different Darwinian research programme that is conceived in order to be incompatible with the Popperian variety of Darwinism. Since a third version known as 'Social Darwinism' has disappeared below the horizon, let me focus on two of the best known Darwinisms of the present time, that is, on the characteristics of Popperian Darwinism and on the kind of Darwinism that is used to underwrite both the evolutionary epistemology of Konrad Lorenz and the evolutionary psychology of John Tooby and Leda Cosmides, and is highly commended by such acclaimed thinkers as Steven Pinker, Daniel Dennett, Mike Corballis, and Henry Plotkin.

Darwin himself made two pregnant pronouncements on philosophy. He dismissed Locke's radical empiricism and the idea of the mind as a *tabula rasa*, out of hand. He endorsed Plato's conception that we have a priori knowledge, as long as we understand that it is derived by inheritance from our simian ancestors, not from our pre-existence in Plato's transcendental world of ideas. On the face of it, Darwin's judgements on Locke and Plato are mutually exclusive. Either you are partially right in siding with Plato; or you are completely wrong in siding with Locke. But closer scrutiny reveals that if there is evolution by natural selection of the most adaptive organs, one might argue that since our sense organs have to be taken to be adaptive, Locke's radical empiricism could be justified: it relies on our sense organs which are selected to take in the real world that has shaped them. With such an amendment, the mind comes to be seen not as a Lockean *tabula rasa*, but as reliably equipped at birth to watch and observe correctly. I would call this line of thinking a Darwinization of Locke. Locke had simply *assumed* that our senses are reliable and that our knowledge is consequently reliable, provided we do not go beyond our senses. Now, with the Darwinization of this argument, we *know* why they are reliable.

Without going into historical details, I take it that this kind of reasoning was first put forward by Konrad Lorenz in the forties of last century. The term 'evolutionary epistemology' was first introduced by Donald Campbell in 1966, in his contribution (1974) to the Schilpp volume about Popper, to describe Popper's way of thinking of the growth of knowledge as a form of critical selection from an abundance of invented falsifiable hypotheses. It was appropriated with acknowledgement by Lorenz in his *Die Rückseite des Spiegels* (1973) but narrowed to apply to nothing but his own Darwinization of Locke. As he put it: the knowledge about the world we pick up is phylogenetically a posteriori and ontogenetically a priori. This means that as a species evolved, gradually, those of the sense organs of its members that pick up correct information are selected and end up as hereditary adaptations. Hence, where species are concerned, their knowledge of the world comes *after* their experience of the world. But where individual organisms are concerned, they come into the world with the ability ready installed and, hence, their knowledge is a priori: it precedes experience. As this argument stands, it looks like a piece of impeccable Darwinism. But it comes in two parts. First, Lorenz observed, it shows that the radical Kantian distinction between phenomena and noumena is wrong. If sense organs have evolved in response to the real world, whatever it is they pick up cannot just be features of the *phenomenal* world. Kant's transcendental idealism is, from a Darwinian point of view, seriously flawed. Organisms that have been naturally selected must reflect the real world; that is, the world as it is in itself, because it is *that* world that has done the selecting. That world must be the real and only world. However, I should mention that this anti-Kantian argument has been qualified by Gerhard Vollmer in a sophisticated manner. Vollmer distinguishes between the microcosm, the macrocosm, and the mesocosm, and argues that since we have evolved in the mesocosm, the only world we can understand is the world of the mesocosm. Microcosm and macrocosm are known only inferentially by calculation (Vollmer 1985).

Second, Lorenz proved in a series of breathtaking experiments, that all manner of organisms, from paramecia to mallard ducklings, do indeed come into the world ready programmed to pick up correct information. He even demonstrated that as a result of such programming, one could fool mallard ducklings. They are born with the ability to recognize their mother and to follow her. When Lorenz placed himself in front of the newly hatched baby ducklings, and waddled in order to pretend to be their mother, they would mistake him for their mother and, what is more, become imprinted to follow Lorenz rather than their mother for the rest of their lives. This shows that the ducklings are not endowed with the ability to recognize their mother; but only with the ability to detect things that waddle in front of them. This experiment is the most perfect example of a Darwinized Lockean empiricism. It salvaged Locke's empiricism and explained why this kind of empiricism was the right way to explain knowledge. Nevertheless Lorenz's expression that knowledge is phylogenetically a posteriori is infelicitous, because it suggests that natural selection is a sort of inductive process in which experiences are accumulated and in which that accumulation is installed in the genes. But over and above this misleading expression, there was a catch that Lorenz himself never really addressed. His experiments about ontogenetically a priori knowledge were all done with pre-human organisms. He never really addressed the question of humans. It is all very well for a paramecium to respond to a stimulus in an unequivocal manner, for it has been naturally selected to do so.

But the human brain is different. It is not a single organ that has evolved in response to features of the environment to which it is adapted. It is not only very large but also sub-divided into billions of neurons that, in turn, are linked in billions of ways. With a few notable exceptions, humans do not just respond to a stimulus. Because of their large brains, they first have to make a representation that is achieved by combining many separate neuronal registrations and binding them together. If one sees a chair, the location, the size, the time, the colour, the shape, and so on are all registered in different parts of the brain. Since different parts of the cortex deal with the analysis of different parts of a visual stimulus, one has to ask how it is all put together again. For a representation to take place, there has to be simultaneous processing of different aspects of the visual stimuli in different cortical regions. There is a real division of labour. How are the colour information in one place, the shape information in another place, and the motion information in yet another place, assembled *accurately*, that is, how is the decision that the several registrations belong together, made? This division of labour creates what neuroscientists are calling the binding problem and it is this problem that proves that the simple Darwinization of Locke will not work, at least not for humans. Whatever it is one is taking in, is so fragmented in different parts of the brain that those fragments first have to be bound together before a response can take place — and this demonstrates that empiricism, even a Darwinized empiricism, cannot explain how it is that one comes to have knowledge of the chair. Lorenz's project of an evolutionary epistemology can be plausible only in organisms in which a stimulus triggers a simple response. But where humans are concerned, it is quite wrong. If it had succeeded, it would, among other things, have rehabilitated the method of arriving at generalizations by induction. For if our sense observations are veridical because our sense organs have been naturally selected to pick up correct information, all that is needed to take the first step towards induction, is the repetitive occurrence of these correct pieces of information. For it would be reasonably legitimate to infer that the repetitions will continue.

In spite of the flaw in Lorenz's project, the project has been taken up with a vengeance. It has changed its name. In the shape it is given by John Tooby and Leda Cosmides, it is no longer called evolutionary epistemology, but evolutionary psychology. For the accent now is not on the sense organs as trustworthy sources of information. The knowledge that is now alleged to be phylogenetically a posteriori and ontogenetically a priori consists not of the adaptiveness of our senses, but of the adaptiveness of mental modules, genetically programmed to pick up friendship, hostility, horses, evenings, people who cheat, and what have you. The argument is based on the idea that these psychological dispositions are inherited from our foraging ancestors in whom they have been installed by natural selection. For example, a Palaeolithic person unable to detect a social cheat, could not have survived and did not survive for long — at least not long enough to leave many offspring. Lorenz's phylogenetic a posteriori knowledge was collected many thousands of years ago and has produced us modern people, complete with the modules we require for orientation and survival.

To begin with, this argument suffers from the same flaw as Lorenz's argument. The ability to detect a social cheat is not the result of observing a social cheat. When one is watching a social cheat, one's brain, even the brain of one of our foraging ancestors, registers location, size, colour, tone of voice, body language and so on, in different locations. Before there can be the ability to detect a cheat, these several registrations have to be bound together, so that simple observation by itself cannot possibly have led to the cheat detection module. Given the ways in which the brain's labour is divided, it would have been necessary, first, for there to have been a socio-cultural habit or convention of bringing several diverse registrations together to make their presence felt as 'cheat detection'. In addition there is also something quite nebulous about the concept of a mental module. Does it consist of a part of the brain that is separate from all other parts ? Or is it a spiritual event that our brains cannot but pick up? I find the idea that there are mental modules no more credible than the idea that there are angels or demons. In view of the neurological binding problem, it is highly implausible that an entire, complex mental disposition to observe social cheats or horses or friendship, should be installed in the brain by natural selection. One way or another, both evolutionary epistemology and evolutionary psychology are attempts to justify the old belief that true knowledge is derived from the accumulation of observations and that knowledge is true if and only if it is so derived. Both arguments use Darwin in order to explain why observations are a reliable source of knowledge.

Popper started at the opposite end. He did not use Darwinism to warm up an old, conventional explanation of how we come to have knowledge. *His* Darwinism, as I shall explain presently, was more like an after-thought, an end-product. He did not use the idea of natural selection and of adaptation to justify our reliance on observation. On the contrary, he began by *questioning* the possibility of observation as a source of knowledge. For this reason he did not even consider whether a Darwinian derivation of observation might make observation an acceptable source of knowledge. When Popper, following Hume, discovered that induction is not a viable way of arriving at general laws, he also realized that simple observations, which always must lie at the roots of inductive inferences, are not an acceptable starting point for induction. His criticism did not just concern induction, but also the bricks induction claims to be using. The crucial passage is in the second paragraph of (1959), § 30. He wrote that we cannot learn anything by unprejudiced, unguided, uninformed staring at the world. The passage is well known and I need not enlarge on this argument. It follows, he continued, that before we can observe and watch we have to have a *theory* in our mind that tells us where to look. The formation of a hypothesis must precede, not follow, observation. The next step in the argument was to insist that such a hypothesis must be falsifiable. If it is not, it remains an empty and idle speculation that refers to nothing at all and is not worth being put forward.

The evolutionary psychology of Tooby and Cosmides claims that humans, whatever they do and think, are doing and thinking so without having been nurtured. They maintain that any attempt to explain behaviour and knowledge as resulting from or being influenced by the culture people are living in, is superfluous. They claim that it is a mistake to pursue social science, that is, to study the ways in which people are being nurtured, because nurture does not take place; or, in so far as there is nurture, it makes no difference. The inherited modules that have been selected naturally, provide all the knowledge we need to guide our behaviour, determine our beliefs, and to recognize horses, friends, pigs, houses, and so on, and so on. Therefore, the widely held belief that we must study cultures because they provide the forms of nurture that influence our cognition, our beliefs, and our behaviour, is misguided. By contrast, in Popper's Darwinism, for the selection of falsifiable but unfalsified hypotheses to take place, it is essential that we live in, and are nurtured by, a free and open politico-cultural environment so that the hypotheses we keep inventing are exposed to incessant and unrestricted criticism. A closed culture must protect at least some hypotheses dogmatically and make them immune to criticism. In such closed cultures knowledge cannot develop. The non-genetically determined politico-cultural environments make all the difference between a Darwinian progression towards knowledge and the absence of a progression towards knowledge. The shape of a culture is vitally important and has to be studied by sociology and anthropology.

At this point I want to make two observations. First, though Popper himself never realized this, the later Wittgenstein in his *Philosophical Investigations* (1953), right at the beginning, put forward a very similar argument. He pointed out that when we are speaking, we cannot define what we mean when we are saying something, ostensively. That is, we cannot define our meanings by pointing at certain events or objects. When we do, there is endless opportunity for misunderstanding. As Quine explained soon after, when we say 'rabbit' and point at one running past, we could be taken to mean 'rabbithood', or 'mammal', or 'four-legged animal', or 'speed', or many other things. In short, we cannot define what we are saying by making a silent observation and cannot confirm what we mean by pointing. Wittgenstein's argument began at the other end from Popper's. Instead of explaining, as Popper had done, that we cannot derive our knowledge from observations, he explained that whatever knowledge we happen to have, cannot be justified by pointing at an observation. I believe it is one of the tragedies of modern philosophy that Popper and Wittgenstein never realized that they were barking up the same tree.

My second observation concerns Popper's remarkable prescience. Just as Darwin never knew that the discovery of the molecular structure of DNA would corroborate and enlarge his theory, Popper did not anticipate that modern neuroscience would bear out his rejection of observation as a basis for knowledge. For, as I indicated above, neuroscience has found that our brains are such that they cannot register what we see. Each stimulus, whether it comes from a chair or from a car crash, is broken up into many component parts and registered in a different part of the brain. For this reason simple input cannot possibly be the foundation of our knowledge of the chair or the car crash. In this way, neuroscience has, in a very important manner, underwritten Popper's argument that we cannot start with observation. And, for that matter, it has at the same time, underwritten Wittgenstein's parallel demonstration that we cannot end with observations. The neuroscientific evidence in favour of Wittgenstein's and Popper's arguments that we cannot count on observations strikes me as so important that I will quote a passage from Semir Zeki's *A Vision of the Brain* (1993, p. 321):

> The problem is that of determining that it is the same (or a different) stimulus which is activating different cells in a given visual area or in different visual areas. Suppose that three cells in area V3, all responsive to the horizontal orientation ... are activated by the same horizontal stimulus, for example the upper edge of a fence gate. Suppose further that these three cells receive inputs from twelve cells in area VI with corresponding orientation that, in turn, are responding to the same stimulus. The task is here to ascertain that the three cells in V3 and the twelve cells in VI are all responding to the same, and not to different stimuli.

What Zeki is saying is that something more than reliance on or recourse to observation is needed. Simply staring at the world will not yield much information about the world. There has to be an ability to decide which registrations belong together and which registrations belong somewhere else. Both Popper and Wittgenstein would be pleased to know that their philosophical argument against using observation as a basis for knowledge has been confirmed by neuroscientific evidence.

Without neuroscientific evidence, Popper argued that we gain knowledge by making a wild and imaginative proposal, and by making it in such a way that we can always tell what observation would falsify it. The proposal or the hypothesis or the theory *precedes* the observation and dictates what observations we ought to make. The proposal itself is not determined by prior observation and could almost, at least in principle, be seen as a random event. If a proposal fails to be falsified, it can be regarded provisionally as a true theory that will yield true predictions. The term 'provisional' is important, because there is no knowing whether in future there may not turn up an observation that falsifies the proposal. Nowadays, when we are all accustomed to think in Darwinian terms, it does not take much imagination to spot the analogy between Darwinian evolution and this theory of knowledge. (a) The proposal is not dictated by prior events. (b) The proposal is imaginative and its truth (or, in biology, its adaptiveness) can emerge only by its failure to be falsified, *after* it has been made. (c) The requirement that a viable proposal must be falsifiable, implies that it must be exposed to the world, which might reject it. (d) Only those proposals that, though falsifiable, remain unfalsified, are selected for retention. (e) A falsifiable but unfalsified theory is provisionally true and should therefore be called verisimilar rather than true. The concept of verisimilitude (truthlikeness) corresponds to the concept of adaptation. Adaptations are rarely perfect. To be selected, a feature only needs to be more adapted than the features possessed by its competitors. In biology one could form the concept of adaptation-likeness to parallel Popper's concept of truthlikeness. Every one of these five features of Popper's philosophy of knowledge is an echo of the Darwinian theory of evolution. (a) The proposal corresponds to a mutation the occurrence of which is not determined by prior events. (b) Truth corresponds to adaptation. (c) In biology, every mutation is automatically falsifiable although, in the absence of suitable competition, not always falsified; in knowledge, one has to take care to make nothing but falsifiable proposals. (d) Unfalsified hypotheses are retained because they yield the most explanations, that is, the best predictions. (e) Very few adaptations are perfect. If there are no or only few competitors, even a poor adaptation can allow its bearer to survive and reproduce. Adaptation-likeness, like truthlikeness, is usually sufficient. The difference, however, is that when we have adaptation-likeness, there is no need to go further; but when we have mere truthlikeness, there is an inevitable drive to search for improvement, that is, for greater likeness.

While there was no trace of Darwin in the *early* formulation of Popper's theory, Popper himself gradually woke up to the fact that his account of the growth of knowledge implied that it was a continuation of Darwin's account of evolution. For every one of the five features listed above can be found in Darwinian evolution. It is remarkable that Popper took some time to realize this and to understand that in his account the growth of knowledge was to be seen as a continuation of biological evolution. When he finally acknowledged this fact he himself gave it two very poignant formulations. He wrote that all evolution, from the amoeba to Einstein proceeded by the trials and errors of hypotheses (1972, pp. 24f., 70, 246-248, 261, 265, 347); and that there is only one important difference when evolution proceeds from biological organisms to linguistically formulated theories. When a species presents itself as a falsifiable but falsified proposal, one has to wait for several generations for that species to die out because of diminishing offspring, diminishing at least by comparison to its competitors in the same environment. With *linguistically* formulated proposals we are more fortunate. When they are falsified, we can eliminate them at the drop of a hat and do not have to wait for their holders to die out gradually. We can make the theories, he said, die in our stead (ibidem, pp. 70, 122, 244, 261).

The fact that Popper's progress towards explicit Darwinism was slow can be documented. In the first German edition of 1935 of *Logik der Forschung*, he wrote in § 30 in terms that are clearly not Darwinian. He wrote that those theories are to be preferred that, in competition, stand up best because they can be tested most severely. Standing up, they are seen as having been selected. The careless reader may think that the use of the term 'selection' (=*Auslese*) is Darwinian. But a perusal of the many German translations of Darwin's *Origin of Species* makes it quite clear that it is not, at least not to German readers and speakers. I have taken the trouble of consulting seven German translations of Darwin's work and found that in all cases the titles do not mention natural selection at all. They all translate Darwin's title as 'The Origin of Species by Natural Breeding' or '. . . by choice resulting from natural breeding'. There is no mention of the German term (*Auslese*) for 'selection'. It would follow, therefore, that when Popper in 1935 wrote of the 'selection' of theories, it would be extremely unlikely that he and his readers would have been thinking of Darwin, let alone have their attention drawn to Darwin.

But when we look at the first English translation of *Logik der Forschung* of 1959. the Darwinian terminology of the same passage is totally obvious: 'We choose the theory which best holds its own in competition with other theories; the one which, by natural selection, proves itself the fittest to survive.' Here we get not only 'selection' but 'natural selection'; and the term 'survival of the fittest' — which was not Darwin's original text but has since Spencer assumed an unmistakable Darwinian connotation. There is no point in arguing that the Darwinian terms crept in inadvertently through the minds of the two translators, Julius and Lan Freed. As anybody who knew Popper knows, Popper would never allow a single word in translation that he had not scrupulously vetted himself. To top the story, there is something even more remarkable than the gradual approach to Darwinism by 1959. When further German, revised, editions appeared in 1966 and 1969, the original un-Darwinian text was preserved. It was not until 1972 when Popper's *Objective Knowledge* (1972) appeared, that the Darwinian feature of Popper's philosophy was made fully explicit.

To return to the main topic. Popper's Darwinism was not planned. It simply emerged that his independently developed theory of the growth of knowledge saw that growth as a continuation of Darwinian biological evolution. The other two Darwinisms that I discussed above used Darwin as proof that their views of how we get knowledge must be correct. Popper did not use Darwinism to prove that he was right. On the contrary, he developed his explanation of the growth of knowledge independently and only began to understand *after* it had been developed, that in his explanation, the growth of knowledge had emerged as a continuation of Darwinian evolution. I myself like to think of this continuity in terms I take to be truly Popperian: theories are like organisms. Since all organisms evolve as a result of their knowledge of their environment, I see them as embodied theories. By the same token, in order to underline the continuity of evolution from the amoeba to Einstein, we should call our theories disembodied organisms (Munz 1993, pp. 162f., 165, 167f., 202, 207).

Bibliography

Barkow, J. H., Cosmides, L., & Tooby, J., editors (1992). *The Adapted Mind*. New York: Oxford University Press.

Campbell, D. T. (1974). 'Evolutionary Epistemology'. In P. A. Schilpp, editor (1974), pp. 413-463. *The Philosophy of Karl Popper*. La Salle IL: Open Court Publishing Company.

Lorenz K. (1941). 'Kants Lehre vom Apriorischen im Lichte gegenwärtiger Biologie'. *Blätter für deutsche Philosophie* **15**, pp. 94-125.

—— (1973). *Die Rückseite des Spiegels*. Munich: Piper. English translation 1977. *Behind the Mirror. A Search for a Natural History of Human Knowledge*. London: Methuen.

Munz, P. (1993). *Philosophical Darwinism*. London: Routledge.

—— (2004). *Beyond Wittgenstein's Poker*. Aldershot: Ashgate.

Popper, K. R. (1935). *Logik der Forschung*. Vienna: Julius Springer Verlag. English translation, Popper (1959).

—— (1959). *The Logic of Scientific Discovery*. London: Hutchinson.

—— (1972). *Objective Knowledge*. Oxford: Clarendon Press. 2nd edition 1979.

Vollmer, G. (1985). *Was können wir wissen?* Stuttgart: S. Hirzel Verlag.

Wittgenstein, L. J. J. (1953). *Philosophical Investigations*. Oxford: Blackwell.

Zeki, S. (1993). *A Vision of the Brain*. Oxford: Blackwell Scientific Publications.

54

Making Sense of Knowledge in the Light of Evolution
Popper and the Collapse of the Modern Epistemological Project

Renan Springer de Freitas

The collapse of the modern foundational epistemological project has led some authors to claim that epistemology is dead. There has been either a retreat to a pragmatic approach to knowledge, according to which there is nothing to be said about knowledge except what can result from an investigation about how people's beliefs are actually formed, or a Kantian–Heideggerian inspired attempt to 'overcome epistemology' by making explicit the untenable anthropological premises that underlie the Cartesian failed quest for apodictic knowledge.[1] It has rarely been noted, however, that Popper pioneered all this discussion on the feasibility of the modern foundational enterprise without thereby concluding that any conceivable epistemological project is necessarily doomed to failure. He envisaged a solution in Darwin's evolutionary thought. The remarkable Russian geneticist Theodosius Dobzhansky titled one of his articles: 'Nothing in Biology Makes Sense except in the Light of Evolution'.[2] Popper would perhaps add that the same obtains in epistemology. In this paper, I argue that making sense of knowledge in the light of evolution — something, by the way, that even the very distinguished Darwinian biologist Ernst Mayr failed to do, *malgré lui*, in his monumental *The Growth of Biological Thought* — allows us to avoid both the modern (Cartesian) anxiety for ultimate foundations to validate knowledge claims, and the untenable requirement, that in fact underlies both the pragmatist retreat and the Kantian-Heideggerian inspired attempt to overcome epistemology, that every piece of knowledge be encapsulated in its own time or, in other words, that the past become irrelevant to the present.

I am afraid that the route that has led to the now widely adopted pragmatist retreat was opened two centuries ago by David Hume. Hume, as is well

---

[1] 'Overcoming Epistemology' is, by the way, the title of a paper by Charles Taylor originally published in Bayes, Boham, & MacCarthy (1987).

[2] Dobzhansky (1973).

known, fought the Cartesian aspiration to doubt-free knowledge by postulating that there is no knowledge other than that which may result from the unreflective habit of establishing connections between (past) experiences and (future) expectations. If all knowledge results from the acquisition of certain habits (such as that of expecting water to quench our thirst, food to placate our hunger, the sun to rise tomorrow, and ourselves to remain ourselves at dawn), then all there is to be investigated about it is how our minds must operate to make such acquisition possible. From this perspective, talking about knowledge amounts to talking about the nature of the human mind, that is, it amounts to investigating what our minds must be like so that we can continue having expectations that no evidence or reasoning authorizes us to have.

In postulating that no evidence or reasoning can establish any connection between past and future, Hume dealt a blow to more than just the Cartesian aspiration for certainty. He also disputed the feasibility of any conceivable epistemological project. I believe that this questioning, just hinted at in the eighteenth century, reappeared with full strength in the twentieth century, under a behaviourist guise. This is visible in the sociological approach to knowledge adopted by Thomas Kuhn,[3] in the holistic naturalism proposed by W. V. Quine, and in the Wittgensteinian pragmatism of Richard Rorty, to mention only those whom I see as the most stimulating variations of the pragmatic manner of rejecting epistemology. In all these cases, there appears the guiding principle — actually absent from Hume's sceptical empiricism, but capable of being traced traced back to him — that there is nothing to be said about knowledge beyond what an account of behaviour can offer.

In parallel to all this, we have recently witnessed another manner of rejecting epistemology, whose basis is found, somewhat surprisingly, in Kant's transcendental philosophy. What I refer to is Charles Taylor's proposal to 'overcome epistemology' by means of an argument whose content is basically the following: the Cartesian epistemological project rests on a set of untenable anthropological notions — especially that of 'detachment'. Let us render these notions explicit, as they constitute the very conditions of possibility for any epistemology, and we will then be showing the unfeasibility of such a putative area of investigation. I suspect that there is an enormous affinity between this proposal and Foucault's project, expressed in *The Order of Things*, of 'bringing to light' the conditions of possibility for our claims to knowledge. However, Taylor wants to go beyond Foucault. He wants to take a step that, though necessary, Foucault could not allow himself to take, namely, to make it possible to compare knowledge claims made under the dominion of different traditions of thought, world views or, to make use of his own term, *epistēmes*. Taylor, unlike Foucault, while intending to 'overcome epistemology', admits the possibility of there being a real gain in knowledge when

---

[3]I cannot fail to mention that Kuhn, in his later writings, for example (1991) expressed, in an implicitly self-critical manner, his deep dissatisfaction with approaches to science that draw sweeping philosophical conclusions solely on the basis of historical or sociological studies. I thank an anonymous referee for calling my attention to this.

there is a transition from one world view to another, and of this gain being accessible to rational evaluation. Hence, he strives to show how it is possible to evaluate, at the margin of any discussion of an epistemological nature, what can be gained, in cognitive terms, through such transitions. He delved into the transition from Aristotelian physics to modern physics to argue that we can better understand the fragility of the former if we ignore the criteria usually established by epistemologists to adjudicate between theories.[4]

My main objection to this line of argument is that it prevents, at the outset, Aristotelian physics from having any cognitive relevance beyond the period in which it dominated the epistemological scene — something that in principle it could have, despite its obvious fragility.[5] In more general terms, Taylor's approach to transitions retains what I consider to be the main deficiency of the pragmatic way of rejecting epistemology: it makes whatever happens in the past irrelevant to whatever comes to happen at a later time, whether such later time is a less remote point in the past, or the present or even the future. Thus, although Taylor, unlike Foucault, would not refrain from discussing what has been gained through a transition such as, say, that that occurred from Lamarck's 'instructionism' to Darwin's 'selectionism', his perspective would nonetheless prevent, at the outset, the Lamarckian 'instructionism' from having any cognitive relevance beyond the eighteenth century.

This is where Darwin — via Popper — must enter the scene. Their evolutionary thought can help us answer questions that one will be entirely prevented from even entertaining if one rejects epistemology in either Hume's or Taylor's Kantian way. I refer here to questions such as these: Why is it an error to encapsulate the scientific thought of, say, Aristotle in the Middle Ages or, say, of the naturalist Cuvier in the eighteenth century? Why should we see such thoughts (or any past thought) as much more than mere historical relics?

The general lines of my answer run as follows. The scientific thought of an Aristotle or of a Cuvier — or any thought said to be scientific, for that matter — consists in a set of theoretical propositions that may prove themselves true or false, on top of a non-explicit set of meta-theoretical (or even metaphysical) concepts that are placed safely away from the action of the *modus tollens*, and constitute the 'background' of those propositions. These two sets are joined in a single block.[6] When a given block comes crumbling down — as when the Aristotelian 'block' collapsed in the seventeenth century, or as when the 'block' represented by Cuvier's creationist thought followed suit in the nineteenth century —, it is possible that one or another of its parts, that is, some of the aforementioned meta-theoretical concepts, and one or another

---

[4]Taylor discusses the 'non-epistemological' way of showing the fragility of Aristotelian thought in a chapter entitled 'Explanation and Practical Reason' in his (1995).

[5]See, for example, Elliot Sober's 'Evolution, Population Thinking, and Essentialism', published as Chapter 11 of his (1994).

[6]Before any reader acquainted with Lakatos's or Quine's writings decides to charge me with plagiarism, I promptly wish to confess that, up to this point, I have said nothing that those two have not said themselves. My own contribution, I hope, begins in the next phrase.

theoretical proposition that may have survived the *modus tollens*, acquire autonomy and, at a later moment, comes to settle elsewhere. As a possible result of this process, evolutionary changes — herein understood, Popper style, as the emergence of new problems — can then be triggered. From this perspective, these migratory fragments (that is, these pieces coming off crumbled 'blocks') would be sources of potentially evolutionary variations in traditions or systems of thought that come to accommodate them, in the same way as a genetic mutation is a source of potentially evolutionary variations in living organisms carrying a mutant gene. In this way, while the pragmatic approach to knowledge simply forbids us beforehand from trying to say anything about the scientific interest (or, if one prefers, lack of interest) presented by, say, Aristotelian thought, and while Taylor wants to teach us to acknowledge the fragility of such thought — inviting us to see how incapable it actually is in comparison with modern rationalist thought, of clearly perceiving the assumptions supporting it — Darwin (whose perspective does not allow us to see any incompatibility between acknowledging how the seventeenth century's foundational enterprise is in vain and hoping to keep epistemology alive, that is, hoping that there are still important things to be said about knowledge beyond what can be offered by either an effort to 'bring to light' the premises that are at the root of our claims to knowledge, or by a description of behaviour) would invite us to identify fragments that have been detached from said Aristotelian thought and become articulated, at a later moment, to other fragments originating from any other source, so as to trigger the emergence of new problems and, therefore, evolutionary changes in existing corpora of knowledge.

It is precisely this kind of exercise, namely, showing the scientific importance of a past system of thought — bizarre as it may seem to our eyes — by retracing the route of fragments that may have been detached from such a system so as to make it possible for a new problem to emerge, that the evolutionary approach to knowledge proposed by Popper invites us and allows us to undertake.

As an example, let us consider the problem around which biological thought itself started to revolve, in these two last decades or so: understanding how *ontogeny and phylogeny articulate themselves in the evolutionary process*.[7] How could this problem emerge? This is what we will be, at the outset, prevented from investigating if we reject epistemology either via Hume, or via Taylor's Kant, because, in both cases, we would be led to overlook the important role played by past thoughts — in the case under consideration, those of Cuvier (1769-1832) and Aristotle — as a result of encapsulating them in their own time.

I am afraid that the roots of the problem in question can be found in something that would, in our days, be the target of the most merciless mockery: Cuvier's so-called 'catastrophism'. Well into the eighteenth century,

---

[7]See Thompson (1988); Maynard Smith (1998); Raff (1996); Gilbert, Opitz, & Raff (1996); Webster & Goodwin (1996).

when naturalists such as Buffon (1707-1788) and Lamarck (1744-1829) already pointed toward evolutionary thought,[8] Cuvier insisted in stating that species were fixed and could be created or extinguished only at a single stroke (via natural catastrophes).[9] This led historians of science (said to be 'traditional') to oppose Cuvier (whose perspective was creationist) to Lamarck and Darwin. Foucault objects to that. To him, this is a very superficial way of seeing things. It is true that Cuvier had a 'fixist' view of species. It is true also that Lamarck and Darwin shared an evolutionary view of species. But from this — argues Foucault — it does not follow that Darwin's thought would be closer to Lamarck's than to Cuvier's, and even less, that Lamarck and Darwin stood on the side of truth whereas Cuvier was in error. It suffices, Foucault goes on to argue, that we examine the epistemological 'grid' that is at the root of these naturalists' different claims for us to conclude that Cuvier's thought, despite its 'fixist' concept, is much closer to Darwin's evolutionary thought than to Lamarck's.[10]

Even if we admit that Foucault is right (if he is not, this was certainly a brilliant mistake), he fails anyway, as he keeps, if involuntarily, Cuvier's 'catastrophism' encapsulated in the eighteenth century. The most Foucault allows himself to concede to Cuvier's thought is the role of 'Darwin's relay'. Therefore, notwithstanding his commendable and successful effort to save Cuvier from the blemish of being an obscurantist, he eventually holds the latter's thought irrelevant for any period after the eighteenth century. The cost of such encapsulation, as I wish to suggest, is precisely that of rendering unfeasible any understanding of the process that culminated in the emergence of the problem that now moves biological thought forward.

To demonstrate that Cuvier's 'catastrophism' — this formidable metaphysical construct that collapsed altogether in the nineteenth century — plays a relevant role in the referred to process, it would be necessary to identify some fragment that may have been detached from this construct and, at a later moment, joined to other fragments from other demolished 'constructs', or, alternatively, settled on to some other 'construct' already established, in such a way as to trigger changes that could culminate in the emergence of the problem under consideration. I suspect that Cassirer's monumental work may lead us to such a fragment.[11] It has to do with the notion of *Bauplan* — the idea according to which the diversity of animal forms is an outcome of the existence of four fixed created plans of organization of bodies. My hypothesis is that this notion is at the root of the current inquiry into the evolutionary role played by ontogenetic development — and, therefore, of the problem of how phylogeny (genetic descent) and ontogeny (embryonic development) relate to each other in the evolutionary process.

---

[8]See, in this regard, Mayr (1982) and Hull (1967).

[9]See, in that regard, Haeckel (1911), p. 45. Incidentally, Haeckel praises Lamarck for not letting himself be influenced by Cuvier's catastrophism.

[10]Foucault (1985), Chapters V and VIII.

[11]Cassirer (1948).

There is, however, a hurdle in the way. Such an inquiry, one could legitimately object, is not new. Actually, it dates back to the second half of the nineteenth century. Shortly after Darwin published *The Origin of Species*, in 1859, the German morphologist Ernst Haeckel (1834-1919) was already mobilizing himself to understanding the evolutionary role played by ontogenetic development. Haeckel knew Cuvier's thought deeply, as few others would, and it would never occur to him to make any use of the 'catastrophist' concept. If — the objection could go on — the notion of *Bauplan* could have no ties even in the nineteenth century to the emergent inquiry into the evolutionary role of ontogenetic development, why would it now, when it sounds all the more bizarre?

My answer is this: if, on the occasion when Haeckel presented his criticism of Cuvier, the referred to Cuvierian notion was no more than a bizarre antique, this was mostly due to the fact that it then found itself 'floating' freely, without being joined to anything. In other words, this was only because it had been detached from the catastrophist construct without having, as a counterpart, been connected to any other notion(s). If, however, at some later moment, such a connection should come to happen, then it would be perfectly possible that it would cease being a mere historical relic and would trigger evolutionary changes in some established bodies of knowledge. I conjecture that this is precisely what happened. At this point, I once again resort to Cassirer. He traced the route of the referred to notion up until at least a century later, when it was joined to the 'vitalism without vital force' proposed by Uexküll, whose connection with the inquiry into the evolutionary role of ontogenetic development seems to be quite clear. So, the Darwin–Popper evolutionary perspective, instead of confining the notion of *Bauplan* to the eighteenth century (as would both Taylor's Kantian Heidegger, and those who recommend a pragmatist retreat), invites us to retrace the route of this notion from the point where Cassirer left it.

The proposal not to confine Cuvier's thought to the eighteenth century can actually be seen as a special case of a more general proposition: one should not confine the pre-Darwinian typological concept of species to the nineteenth century. It is usually stated that the advent of the theory of evolution by means of natural selection and, more specifically, of the evolutionary synthesis of the 1930s, once and for all removed a major hurdle hampering the progress of biological knowledge: the typological concept of species, according to which there is something inherent in the individuals of the same given species that makes each one what each one is. According to such reasoning, in the same way as it is impossible to understand, say, what the scientific revolution of the seventeenth century was, without understanding what the Aristotelian metaphysical system brought down by Galileo was, it is likewise impossible to understand what was the referred to evolutionary synthesis — which incidentally, so to speak, saved Darwinian tradition from extinction — without understanding what exactly was the metaphysical system it brought down, namely, the typological thought underlying the idealist biology of the nineteenth century.

Although I have no objection against such reasoning, one should not lose sight of the fact (as one would be led to, if one rejected epistemology in any of the ways previously mentioned) that in the same way that the Einsteinian revolution rehabilitated certain concepts originating from Aristotle's cosmology, that Galileo had left behind,[12] there is a search going on now, in biology, for a 'new synthesis' that could recover some of the concepts originating from the typological thought that the evolutionary synthesis left behind, notably the notions of *homology* — sponsored by R. Owen, Darwin's fierce adversary —, itself a legacy of the Aristotelian notion of 'unity of plan', and that of *morphogenetic field*, inherited from the vitalist embryology of the 1920s. One now seeks to recover these two notions and thereby make it possible for biology to fulfil a promise that, supposedly, the evolutionary synthesis could not make it able to fulfil, namely, to provide an explanation for macro-evolution, that is, the formation of species of higher categories from species of lower categories — for example, an amphibian from a fish, or a bird from a reptile.[13]

There is a considerable literature trying to demonstrate how the Darwinian tradition can (and should) accommodate the referred to notions so as not to come to a dead end.[14] But this involves the serious problem of how to make the Darwinian tradition compatible with pieces of knowledge inherited from the typological view — and specially with the essentialist concept of species presupposed by this view. In a strictly Darwinian view, species are not, as they are in typological thought, natural kinds. They are just the result of the precarious stabilization of given gene pools. This statistical concept of species entailed pioneer works in population genetics, produced by Fisher, Haldane, Wright (and later by Dobzhansky), and classic works on the formation of new species, produced by Mayr and the paleontologist George Simpson in the 1940s. But this was not enough to meet the need to explain macro-evolutionary processes from micro-evolutionary processes — for which typological thought after all provides an answer (the 'saltationalist' one), whether satisfactory or not. How can the Darwinian tradition advance as far as this problem is concerned, if not by relying on help from the previously rejected metaphysical concepts derived from typological thought? To the extent that I understand it, this is the deadlock in which the Darwinian tradition finds itself today. Were we to follow the anti-epistemological recommendations rooted in either Hume's or Kant's thought we would be led to miss a crucial point like this.

Perhaps we owe to the monumental 1982 work written by the aforementioned German biologist Ernst Mayr, *The Growth of Biological Thought*, the

---

[12]See, in this regard, the splendid lecture by Alexandre Koyré, 'On the Influence of Philosophical Conceptions on the Evolution of Scientific Theories', delivered in Boston, at the American Association for the Advancement of Science 1954 Meeting. This paper appears in his (1971).

[13]See, in this regard, Gilbert, Opitz, & Raff (1996).

[14]I shall limit myself to mentioning just two collections whose contributions move in that direction: Ho & Sanders (1985) and Depew & Weber (1985).

knowledge that it would be inconceivable to reach any synthesis of Mendelian genetics and the theory of evolution through natural selection, had not the typological concept of species (which prevailed in the nineteenth century and early twentieth century) been abandoned in favour of a population concept of species. Until such substitution occurred, Mendel's laws constituted a major obstacle to, rather than a primary condition for, the advancement of the Darwinian theory of evolution. In other words, in order for Mendel's laws and the theory of evolution by natural selection to merge into an 'evolutionary synthesis', it was necessary that species were no longer seen as the actualization or realization of pre-determined morphological types (as in the typological view) but, rather, and in radical contrast, as mere populations or aggregates of highly diversified, genetically unique individuals. Without this concept of species as an unstable aggregate of genetically unique individuals sharing a common gene pool, the idea of natural selection makes no sense whatsoever — and the concept was not available until the early twentieth century. The fact is, therefore, that until then biological thought was markedly anti-selectionist.

Hardly anyone would dispute all this nowadays. But does all this mean that typological thought should, at the outset, be confined to the nineteenth and early twentieth century? Mayr's answer is an unequivocal yes.[15] He seems to have thought, in curious, involuntary tune with all contemporary efforts to 'overcome epistemology', that, since the typological concept of species underlying nineteenth century's idealist morphology is utterly unsustainable, then such morphology cannot bear any cognitive relevance beyond its own time. As a consequence, he concentrated on the first Mendelian anti-selectionists (de Vries, Bateson, and Goldschmidt) and on the idealist morphologists of the nineteenth century, notably Owen, Saint-Hilaire and Cuvier, and failed to envisage the possibility of there being a continuous line between the metaphysical concepts of these morphologists and, for example, the important discovery by Hans Spemann, made in the 1920s, that a part of the embryo exerts influence on the development of a neighboring part.[16] In fact, an embryologist of the stature of Spemann is not even included in the cross index of Mayr's 974-page book. Mayr cited him but only with a passing criticism of the typological flavour of his thought, while veritable giants of twentieth century embryology, such as Paul Weiss, de Beer, and Waddington, were not even mentioned, nor did they deserve even the briefest criticism addressed to Spemann.

I really doubt that there is a single historian of science who would escape the accusation of neglecting some important name. But, as far as one, at the outset, encapsulates some thought in its own time, one is not just led to neglect

---

[15]On the other hand, Sober's answer is an unequivocal no. He goes as far as to suggest that the Aristotelian Natural State Model, which lies at the heart of the typological view, 'is not wholly without a home in contemporary biology; in fact, the way in which it finds an application there highlights some salient facts about what population thinking amounts to' (1994, p. 204).

[16]Pioneer studies by Hans Spemann on embryonic development gained a vast literature. I restrict myself to citing Waddington (1996).

one or another name, but can be led to overlook entire research programmes. This is what happened in the case of Mayr. He was led to overlook the entire tradition of 'rational morphology', that had its apogee in the 1920s, saw a timid revival in the 1960s, and, in the 1980s, came to its culmination as one of the bases of what is known today as Developmental Biology — that is, the study of the relations existing between embryonic development and evolution.

I suspect that the book *Embryos, Genes and Evolution*, by Rudolf Raff & Thomas Kaufman, published in 1983, is one of the cornerstones in this recent effort to explain evolutionary change not only in genetic terms but also in terms of patterns of embryonic development. Having published his book in 1982, Mayr could not have cited Raff & Kaufman's book. Nonetheless, had he been in tune with Popper's evolutionary thought, he would have been led to ask how the thought of a de Beer, or of a Spemann, both relevant for the 1920s, managed to find fertile grounds to flourish later on, in the 1980s. He would then have been led to question how the ground was prepared so that the rational morphology of the 1920s, which has its roots in nineteenth-century typological thought and, more remotely, in the Aristotelian notions of 'unity of plan' and 'homology', could be revived and, more important, could be (or fail to be) incorporated by the Darwinian tradition in the late twentieth century.[17]

We therefore face an entire agenda of very important issues that we would necessarily be, at the outset, prevented from addressing if, instead of trying to replace the modern, seventeenth-century foundational epistemological project by another, of evolutionary character, we contented ourselves with just decreeing the unfeasibility of any conceivable epistemological project. More than that, for all I have said throughout this paper, such a choice would imply an irremediable and potentially catastrophic divorce between philosophy and the history of science.

---

[17]There is a curious irony here. Mayr is a fierce adversary of theories of evolution by leaps in biology — that is, of the idea that dates back to the first Mendelians and according to which new species appear by chance, abruptly. Goldschmidt's famous thesis of the 'hopeful monster' is the perfect expression of this view. Mayr became notable for his arguments against Goldschmidt, as he demonstrated the continuous and incremental character of the formation of new species. However, his silence on the aforementioned embryologists of the 1920s somehow betrays a 'saltationist' epistemology or, in other words, the premise according to which it was through a leap, an act of chance, that fragments of the typological thought of the nineteenth century came back to the scientific scene almost a century later. In that case, nothing would have prepared the terrain on which such a return could occur and bear fruit. One cannot, from the start, discard the possibility of there simply having been such a leap, but one cannot, simply subscribe either, without further ado, to the saltationist epistemology underlying Mayr's thought.

Bibliography

Cassirer, E. (1948). *El Problema del Conocimiento IV*. Mexico City: Fondo de Cultura Económica. Originally published as *Das Erkenntnisproblem in der Philosophie und Wissenchaft der neueren Zeit, IV*. English edition 1950. *The Problem of Knowledge*, Volume 4. *Philosophy, Science, and History since Hegel*. New Haven CT: Yale University Press.

Depew, D. & Weber, B., editors (1985). *Evolution at a Cross-Road*. Cambridge MA: The MIT Press.

Dobzhansky, T. (1973). 'Nothing in Biology Makes Sense except in the Light of Evolution'. *American Biology Teacher*, March 1973, pp. 125-129.

Foucault, M. (1985). *The Order of Things*. London: Tavistock Publications.

Gilbert, S., Opitz, J., & Raff, R. (1996). 'Resynthesizing Evolutionary and Developmental Biology'. *Developmental Biology* **173**, pp. 357-372.

Haeckel, E. (1911). *Historia da Creação Natural*. Porto: Livraria Chardro Editora. 1st English edition 1876. *The History of Creation*. London: Henry S. King. First German publication 1868.

Ho, M. & Sanders, P., editors (1985). *Beyond Neo-Darwinism*. London: Harcourt.

Hull, D. (1967). 'The Metaphysics of Evolution'. *The British Journal for the History of Science* **3**, pp. 309-337.

Koyré, A. (1971). *Études d'Histoire de la Pensée Philosophique*. Paris: Éditions Gallimard.

Kuhn, T. S. (1991). 'The Road Since Structure'. In A. Fine, M. Forbes, & L. Wessels, editors (1991), pp. 3-13. *PSA 1990: Proceedings of the 1990 Biennial Meeting of the Philosophy of Science Association*, Volume 2. East Lansing MI: Philosophy of Science Association.

Mayr, E. (1982). *The Growth of Biological Thought*. Cambridge MA: Harvard University Press.

Raff, R. (1996). *The Shape of Life: Genes, Development and the Evolution of Animal Form*. Chicago: University of Chicago Press.

Raff, R. & Kaufman, T. (1983). *Embryos, Genes and Evolution*. New York: Macmillan & Co.

Smith, J. Maynard (1998). *Shaping Life. Genes, Embryos and Evolution*. New Haven CT: Yale University Press.

Sober, E. (1994). *From a Biological Point of View. Essays in Evolutionary Philosophy*. Cambridge: Cambridge University Press.

Taylor, C. (1987). 'Overcoming Epistemology'. In K. Bayes, J. Boham, & T. MacCarthy, editors (1987). *After Philosophy*. Cambridge MA: MIT Press.

———— (1995). *Philosophical Arguments*. Cambridge MA: Harvard University Press.

Thompson, K. S. (1988). *Morphogenesis and Evolution*. New York: Oxford University Press.

Waddington, C. H. (1996). 'Fields and Gradients'. In M. Locke, editor (1996). *Major Problems in Developmental Biology*. New York: Academic Press.

Webster, G. & Goodwin, B. (1996). *Form and Transformation: Generative and Relational Principles in Biology*. Cambridge: Cambridge University Press.

55

Darwinism is the Application of Situational Logic to the State of Ignorance*

David Miller

1 Introduction

My topic today lies, I suppose, within the field known as evolutionary epistemology, a field to which I have not before attempted to contribute more than the occasional incidental remark. This is not because I have imagined that evolutionary considerations are of no importance in a comprehensive theory of human knowledge. On the contrary, it is clear that they provide a descriptive underpinning to the valuable idea that the knowledge possessed by humans is both continuous with, and radically different from, the knowledge possessed by animals and by plants. By installing human knowledge, especially objective human knowledge, in its proper niche within biological evolution, we can come to appreciate without difficulty and without discomfort that there is no place in the world for the kind of knowledge of which philosophers traditionally speak. We can appreciate, that is to say, that the sceptical tradition, which always had better arguments than its opponents had, had also a better conclusion within its grasp. (It had only to avoid nihilism.) But to reach this conclusion there is of course no need to take any detour through biology, fascinating as it is. It is a logical conclusion (Miller, 1994, Chapter 1), rendered more agreeable perhaps, but not more correct, by evolutionary illustration.

Hence my past reluctance to proceed further into evolutionary epistemology. I have never been dismayed or scandalized by the conclusion that our knowledge is, as Xenophanes described it, 'but a woven web of guesses'. I am not kept awake at night by the fear that my bed is unsupported, although

*This paper originated, under an inappropriate title, as a presentation to the international workshop *Evolutionary Epistemology and Karl Popper's Conception of the Open Society: Karl Popper's First Visit to St Petersburg* held in St Petersburg, Russia, from 5 July to 8 July 1999. The full version of the paper, entitled 'The Only Way to Learn', was delivered (in Spanish) as an invited lecture to the X Congreso Nacional de Filosofía in Argentina, held in Huerta Grande (Córdoba) from 24 November to 27 November 1999. It was completed in peace and seclusion at the lakeside house of Profesora Patricia Morey in Los Molinos, to whom I offer my profound thanks.

I know that the support that it appears to have is ultimately illusory; and I am not kept awake either by the fear that our knowledge of the world is unsupported.

But as we shall see, evolutionary epistemology is perhaps not the best place to locate the ideas that I wish to put before you. For more interesting than the now widely accepted thesis that the growth of knowledge is a proper part of biological evolution is the converse thesis that biological evolution is a part, but only a proper part, of the growth of knowledge. All adaptation, according to this thesis, amounts to a revision of the state of knowledge of the species, or organism, or organ, that undergoes the adaptation. On the other hand, the growth of objective knowledge is not biologically adaptive, even if we prescind from the idea that adaptation is invariably advantageous. Objective knowledge — the knowledge that we hold in libraries and databases, and only in fragments in our heads — is plainly not biologically embodied. This thesis that the growth of knowledge is a more general phenomenon than is biological adaptation is one that I wish to defend. But I should not be understood to imply that the growth of knowledge outruns evolutionary explanation. That is to say, it should not be concluded that the explanatory power of the theory of evolution is restricted to biological phenomena. Of course, it all depends on what you mean by the theory of evolution. The principal thesis of this lecture is that we do well to see as crucial to evolution, as opposed to life, not the biological categories of survival and reproduction but the logical categories of conjecture and refutation. This allows us to give an explanation of natural selection, rather than an explanation couched in terms of natural selection.

No claim to originality is made here. As the terms *conjecture* and *refutation* make obvious, my remarks are little more than an elaboration of some of Karl Popper's fundamental ideas. This is true in at least four respects.

(1) Popper was the first to offer a systematic theory of learning by trial and error.

(2) Popper was the first to endorse a thoroughgoing rational scepticism.

(3) Popper was the first to point to the significance of disembodied objective knowledge.

(4) Popper was one of the originators of evolutionary epistemology.

My lecture will attempt to weave together these four strands of Popper's philosophy, in a manner that, I hope, will reveal its ability to illuminate both human knowledge and animal knowledge; to show that they are similar, and to show where they are different. Along the way I shall somewhat unsystematically counter various criticisms that have been given at various times. Of course I take full responsibility for my interpretation of Popper's philosophy, knowing well that many of his other followers have often disagreed with me.

As I have already hinted, my primary aim is to give some substance to the doctrine that our investigations of the world are not very different from any of our other activities in the world. We learn only by trial and error — but this is unsurprising because everything that we undertake is an instance of trial and error. My thesis is that trial and error epitomizes the situational logic of a state of ignorance. What distinguishes human beings, and even scientists, from other beings is not a superiority in avoiding errors, but a superiority in replacing them.

2 Situational logic in a state of ignorance

In this section I try to explain the idea that the method of trial and error is an obvious way to proceed if we do not know how else to proceed.

Let me begin with the following remarks from § 37 of Popper's autobiography *Unended Quest* (Popper 1974/1976):

> Let there be a world, a framework of limited constancy, in which there are entities of limited variability. ...
>
> Add to this the assumption of the existence of a special framework — a set of perhaps rare and highly individual conditions — in which there can be life or, more especially, self-reproducing but nevertheless variable bodies. Then a situation is given in which the idea of trial and error-elimination, or of Darwinism, becomes not merely applicable, but almost logically necessary....
>
> I do not think that Darwinism can explain the origin of life. ... But this does not affect the view of Darwinism as situational logic, once life and its framework are assumed to constitute our 'situation'.
>
> ... Indeed its [Darwinism's] close resemblance to situational logic may account for its great success, in spite of the almost tautological character inherent in the Darwinian formulation ....

Similarly in § 16 of Chapter 2 of *Objective Knowledge* (Popper 1972) we read:

> ... a considerable part of Darwinism is not of the nature of an empirical theory, but is a *logical truism*.
>
> Let us make clear what is empirical in Darwinism and what is not. ...
>
> ... given living organisms, sensitive to environmental changes and changing conditions, we can say something like the following. Only if the organisms produce mutations, some of which are adjustments to impending changes, and thus involve mutability, can they survive: and in this way we shall find, as long as we find living organisms in a changing world, that those which happen to be alive are pretty well adjusted to their environment. If the process of adjustment has gone on long enough, then the speed, finesse, and complexity of the adjustment may strike us as miraculous. And yet, the method of trial and of the elimination of errors, which leads to all this, can be said not to be an empirical method but to belong to the *logic of the situation*. This, I think, explains (perhaps a little too briefly) the logical or *a priori* components in Darwinism.

Doubtless these explanations are indeed a little too brief. John Watkins was one who was not convinced. Having announced in a lecture given in 1995 his dissent from those 'people who saw evolutionary epistemology as a major

new turn in Popper's philosophy' (1995, p. 191), he says of the idea that
Darwinism is an application of situational logic (ibidem, p. 194):

> I find this baffling. What he [Popper] had called 'situational logic' involved an
> agent in a well-defined situation, for instance a buyer in a market, where the
> agent's situational appraisal and preferences jointly prescribe a definite course
> of action. What has that to do with the theory of evolution? There is no in-
> consistency in supposing both that all creatures always behave in accordance
> with the logic of their situation, *and* that all species are descended unchanged
> from their original prototypes. Situational logic has nothing to say about the two
> assumptions that differentiate Darwin's theory from contemporary alternatives
> to it, namely that heritable variations occur and that a successful variation may
> get preserved.
>
> Nor does situational logic say anything about an assumption that differen-
> tiates Popper's theory of the growth of scientific knowledge from Humean and
> other empiricist views, namely that science essentially involves *intellectual inno-
> vation.* ...
>
> I don't think that Popper ever came up with a satisfactory answer to the
> question, 'Why is Darwinism important?'

Let us try.

The expression 'situational logic' is perhaps an unfortunate one, since it
suggests something much more rigid than the idea that agents act appropriately to the situations in which they find themselves; whereas the term
'situational analysis', also commonly used, plainly belongs to the methodology of explanation rather than to any explanatory empirical theory. The term
'rationality principle', on the other hand, is frequently understood as a sub-
stantive principle of individual psychology, and is better avoided. Situational
logic, like common sense, is not supposed to be mysterious or grand. Let us
see if we can make satisfactory progress without any good name for what we
are doing.

First I should like to ask you to accept a less severe and less deterministic
understanding of situational logic than is suggested by Watkins's words 'in
a well-defined situation ... the agent's situational appraisal and preferences
jointly prescribe a definite course of action'. Despite the looming presence
of the deductive model of explanation, according to which an event is not
explained unless its description is deduced from some congeries of universal
laws and initial conditions, I have never understood situational analysis to prescribe 'a definite course of action' if 'definite' means anything like 'unique'.
A generic action may indeed be prescribed, but its actual method of imple-
mentation be left generously open. Tolstoy can be perfectly right 'when he
describes how it was not decision but "necessity" which made the Russian
army yield Moscow without a fight and withdraw to places where it could
find food' (Popper 1945/1957, § 31), yet — as the final phrase indicates —
not include within the scope of 'necessity' the exact disposition of the troops
after the withdrawal. Situational logic, seen positively, is more of a satisficing

activity than a maximizing one. But it may be better to see it, as Popper's philosophy sees logic itself, as something negative, the organon of criticism, not of proof (Popper 1963, Chapter 1, appendix, paragraph (13); 1983, Part I, § 27). Situational logic proscribes courses of action as inappropriate or irrational; it prescribes them only when there is a sadly limited repertoire of possibilities at the agent's disposal.

In brief, it should be no part of situational logic that an agent should act completely appropriately to his situation, even to the situation as he sees it. For in most situations in which rational deliberation is possible one most important thing that the agent sees is that he does not see everything. Not only does he act in a state of imperfect knowledge, he knows that he so acts. He is bewildered, not just deluded. There is accordingly always some looseness in what his own situational analysis enjoins. The greater the agent's ignorance of the situation, the greater the looseness. It should now be reasonably clear that in many situations the agent knows so little that very little is enjoined. Blind trial-and-error activity — eventually 'intellectual innovation' — becomes more appropriate to the situation of ignorance than any other activity. But although we always know something, we are almost always to some extent ignorant.

It is in this sense, I suggest, that the method of conjectures and refutations is a kind of situational logic. Since Darwinism is the application of conjectures and refutations at the genetic level, and perhaps at higher levels, it too partakes of the triviality of situational logic. If you really have very little idea of what is happening, a good policy, though it may kill you, is to try to find out what is happening; and finding out implies guessing. Watkins makes a sorry mistake in restricting situational logic entirely to the behavioural level, and in supposing that intellectual or behavioural innovation is not itself often appropriate behaviour. And since a change in genetic make-up is little short of a message from Heaven, the only way that you can do something to improve your adaptation to the environment, or even that of your descendants, is to move to or create a new environment. If you are lucky enough to be able to survive your mistakes, your progeny may flourish too. If active Darwinism is right, therefore, situational logic does indeed say something about the Darwinian assumption that 'a successful variation may get preserved'. It perhaps says less about the assumption that 'heritable variations occur', but it does not say nothing. A copying system that is not 100% perfect is a successful variation that did indeed get preserved.

I know of course that the assumption of perfect information is a standard assumption within economics. It may serve a useful purpose there, but only a pragmatist could believe that it is generally true. Bayesians have at least recognized that most decisions are made in the absence of complete knowledge, and have produced in response a theory of decision making under uncertainty; that is, of decision making in a state in which the agent's probability distribution is not wholly concentrated at a single atom. Yet it is not possible to represent within the Bayesian formalism a state of complete ignorance (or even a state of complete ignorance with regard to any proposition). This does make sense within the theory of belief functions of Dempster and Shafer (Shafer 1976), to be sure, but this theory too has nothing to say about decision making in such a state of ignorance.

3   The universality of evolutionary explanation

Much of the criticism that evolutionary epistemology has attracted has been directed at the somewhat naive, though admittedly appealing, view of the growth of scientific knowledge as a struggle for survival among competing hypotheses. Critics have rightly objected to this as anything more than a metaphor. Hypotheses do not breed or form populations, for instance; indeed, they partake of rather few specifically biological characteristics. Even Peter Munz, whose (1993) is one of the most interesting and valuable books in the field, describes hypotheses as 'disembodied organisms' (p. 162; see also this volume, p. 140).

But hypotheses are not organisms. Knowledge, especially human knowledge, is instead quite literally a generalized organ; not an endosomatic organ, to be sure, in the case of most human knowledge, but an exosomatic or disembodied organ, one developed outside the skin. To call it only an analogue of an organ would be like calling aviation an analogue of flight. This way of looking at knowledge makes it pretty clear that it is the prime material on which evolution works; the evolution of species may be the gross phenomenon, the biological veneer, but what is really the subject of evolution is knowledge. As I suggested in § 1, *knowledge = adaptation*, an equation often used by Popper, by Wächtershäuser, and others to drive the point home. It provides an entirely different picture of the relevance of evolutionary theory to the theory of knowledge than that conjured up by the fantasy of hypotheses battling to survive in a hostile environment of refutational forces.

I am therefore not moved by the attempt by Anthony O'Hear (1997) to challenge the wisdom of evolutionary explanation of the higher mental, aesthetic, and moral faculties, on the grounds that they do little to aid, and perhaps much to frustrate, the purely biological needs of survival and reproduction. This anti-evolutionary pessimism is obviously a reaction to the excesses of sociobiology; but a natural child also of an equally unacceptable pro-evolutionary optimism that goes back at least to Lorenz, namely the naive doctrine that biological pressures have so moulded our everyday cognitive faculties that they must give us overall a pretty accurate picture of the world; so that we may conclude, for instance, that (with a handful of well known exceptions) sense perception is veridical. (Even Popper once said something like this.) It is recognized of course that it would be circular to use this argument to provide any empirical support for Darwinian theory itself. But it is cited every so often as an explanation, or a sketch of an explanation, of the success of science, and even as a way of rebutting scepticism.

The mirror image of this complacent view — with which, I should emphasize, I do not agree — is the disappointing reflection that in mathematics and in philosophy, in morality, and in art, we have no reason at all to suppose that we are well adapted to discovering the truth. The theory of evolution, it is urged, is concerned fundamentally with survival and reproduction, and if we humans have somehow transcended these biological needs then we cannot expect the theory of evolution to be able to discriminate the shafts of light from the surrounding darkness. That is to say, there can be no proper evolutionary explanation of much characteristically human activity. From an evolutionary perspective we cannot explain why we study mathematics or cosmology, or play string quartets; nor does our evolutionary past give us any reason to think that we do any of these things well — and that means, in the case of science, that there is no evolutionary reason to think that we have any ability to discover the truth. But it is time that we became accustomed to scepticism — though not to nihilism — at every level, from rational theology to matters of survival and reproduction. Moreover, as I have unoriginally suggested, we misread the theory of evolution, even at the level of what used to be called the lower organisms, if we restrict its compass to matters of survival and reproduction. There is more to Darwin's theory of evolution than the doctrine of natural selection. We may read on p. 57 of Popper (1994):

> This is a generalization of the Darwinian idea that organisms have constantly to solve survival problems. According to my theory there are lots of problems which are not survival problems. When a tree puts out its roots, or arranges its foliage, it solves specific local problems posed by the stones and rocks in the earth and by the conditions of access to light. An organism may develop a preference for a certain kind of food, but may be able to survive on other kinds. To get the preferred food poses a problem. But it is not necessarily a survival problem. It may, for example, develop a certain food because, let us say, the food is easy of access or something like that.

Of course survival and reproduction patrol the boundaries, for all of us. Still, most species have obtained a tenuous hold on the second of these essential activities; and though the first is sometimes threatened by man, often there is no genetic or biological development that can arrive in time to overcome the threat. Active problem solving is at the heart of evolutionary development, both amongst the lowest organisms and amongst the highest. There is accordingly nothing to prevent us from giving evolutionary explanations — that is to say, explanations that make use of indeterministic situational logic — of all our intellectual activities, even (as rightly emphasized by Watkins 1970, § 6.3) those that do not succeed.

Bibliography

Miller, D. W. (1994). *Critical Rationalism. A Restatement and Defence*. Chicago & La Salle IL: Open Court Publishing Company.

Munz, P. (1993). *Philosophical Darwinism. On the Origin of Knowledge by Means of Natural Selection*. London: Routledge.

O'Hear, A. (1997). *Beyond Evolution*. Oxford: Clarendon Press.

Popper, K. R. (1945). 'The Poverty of Historicism III'. *Economica* NS **XII**, pp. 69-89. References are to the book edition 1957. *The Poverty of Historicism*. London: Routledge & Kegan Paul.

—————— (1963). *Conjectures and Refutations. The Growth of Scientific Knowledge*. London: Routledge & Kegan Paul. 5th edition 1989. London: Routledge.

—————— (1972). *Objective Knowledge*. Oxford: Clarendon Press. 2nd edition 1979.

—————— (1974). 'Intellectual Autobiography'. In P. A. Schilpp, editor (1974), pp. 1-181. *The Philosophy of Karl Popper*. La Salle IL: Open Court. Reprinted as *Unended Quest* (1976). London & Glasgow: Fontana/Collins.

—————— (1983). *Realism and the Aim of Science*. London: Hutchinson.

—————— (1994). *Knowledge and the Body–Mind Problem*. London: Routledge.

Shafer, G. (1976). *A Mathematical Theory of Evidence*. Princeton NJ: Princeton University Press.

Watkins, J. W. N. (1970). 'Imperfect Rationality'. In R. Borger & F. Cioffi, editors (1970), pp. 167-217. *Explanation in the Behavioural Sciences*. Cambridge & elsewhere: Cambridge University Press.

—————— (1995). 'Popper and Darwinism'. In A. O'Hear, editor (1995), pp. 191-206. *Karl Popper: Philosophy and Problems*. Cambridge & elsewhere: Cambridge University Press.

PART 4
Science

D: Social Sciences

56

Methodenstreit oder Ideologiedebatte?
Ein Rückblick auf den „Positivismusstreit"

Evelyn Gröbl-Steinbach

1 Worum ging es im Positivismusstreit?

Der Positivismusstreit der 60er Jahre präsentiert sich in der Literatur als eine in erster Linie methodologische Auseinandersetzung. Kritische Theoretiker und kritische Rationalisten stritten sich um eine adäquate Konzeption der Sozialwissenschaften, vor allem der Soziologie. Auf den ersten Blick ging es dabei primär um Fragen wie: was sind die richtigen Methoden der Soziologie, beobachtet oder interpretiert sie, welche Rolle spielen dabei die wissenschaftlichen Werte der Wertfreiheit und der Objektivität, wie sieht die Prüfung sozialwissenschaftlicher Theorien aus und so weiter.

Tatsächlich aber prallten zwei unterschiedliche philosophische Ansätze gegeneinander: eine historisch-dialektische Philosophie der Gesellschaft, die sich selbst als eine Form der Praxis auffasst und den Anspruch hat, der Gesellschaft die richtigen Zielsetzungen auf wissenschaftliche Weise angeben zu können und eine realistische Philosophie kritischer Rationalität, die Wissenschaft und politisches Engagement unterscheidet und die Ziele und Interessen der Gesellschaft von jenen der Wissenschaft getrennt halten will. Von beiden Seiten wurde zwar Kritik an der gegnerischen Wissenschaftsauffassung geübt, die aber tatsächlich Kritik am anderen philosophischen System als einer Ideologie ist. Die gegnerische Auffassung über die Methodologie der Sozialwissenschaften wurde von jeder Streitpartei zum Instrument erklärt, die von der anderen Position zu ideologischen Zwecken eingesetzt wird. Das, was die gegnerische Position als Sozialwissenschaft vertritt, so der wechselseitige Vorwurf, mache adäquates Wissen von gesellschaftlichen Zusammenhängen unmöglich, weil die Auffassung von Rationalität, die ihr zugrunde liegt, dazu führt, dass die Sozialwissenschaften politischen Interessen dienen bzw. dass Sozialwissenschaften benutzt werden können, Herrschaftsstrukturen zu verschleiern. Es war ein Streit, den die kritische Theorie verloren hat. Für ihr Scheitern ist die Kritik des kritischen Rationalismus durchaus maßgeblich gewesen.

2 Die konträren Positionen

Der Positivismusstreit begann mit den Referaten von Popper und Adorno auf
der Tübinger Arbeitstagung der Deutschen Gesellschaft für Philosophie im
Oktober 1961 (Dahms 1994, pp. 323-350). Allerdings gab es dort keine Konfrontation der Ideen des kritischen Rationalismus mit jenen der kritischen
Theorie. Popper stellte vielmehr 27 Thesen auf, in denen er seine Wissenschaftsauffassung darlegte und sich gegen den (Neo-)Positivismus wandte
(Popper 1969). Seine eigene Auffassung charakterisierte er als eine fallibilisti-
sche Erkenntnistheorie, die auf sichere Grundlagen verzichtet, kennzeichnete
die Methode der Wissenschaften generell als die von Versuch und Kritik und
verteidigte die wissenschaftliche Objektivität im Sinne intersubjektiver Ko-
operation. Kritisch wandte er sich gegen Naturalismus und Szientismus in den
Sozialwissenschaften, aber auch das Selbstverständnis eines Teiles der dama-
ligen Soziologie als einer sozialen Anthropologie der westlichen Lebensweise,
die auf Theorien mit allgemeinem Erklärungsanspruch verzichtet so wie gegen
den Kontextualismus und Relativismus der Wissenssoziologie Mannheims.

Auf die eigene Sicht der Sozialwissenschaften bzw. Soziologie ging Popper
nur in wenigen Punkten ein und zwar auf die Autonomie der Soziologie gegen-
über der Psychologie und die objektiv-verstehende Methode der Situations-
logik (Popper 1969, pp. 119-122) als Methode der Soziologie. Die Wertfreiheit der Wissenschaft zu behaupten, bezeichnete Popper als paradox, betonte
dabei aber die Notwendigkeit, wissenschaftliche von außerwissenschaftlichen
Werten zu unterscheiden. Mit den Grundannahmen der kritischen Theorie
setzte sich Popper in keinem einzigen Punkt auseinander. Die Namen Adorno
und Horkheimer, aber auch Hegel und Marx, wurden nicht erwähnt. Wenn
man nach den Gründen fragt, so scheint Popper der Meinung gewesen zu sein,
mit der Kritik an der Wissenssoziologie auch Hegel zu treffen und damit den
marxistischen Hegelanhänger Adorno (Dahms 1994, p. 344). Dies war aber
ein Irrtum, denn Adorno hatte Mannheim ebenfalls bereits in einem Aufsatz von 1937 scharf kritisiert (Adorno 1953), allerdings nicht den Historisten
Mannheim, sondern Mannheim als Positivisten. Adorno verfuhr ähnlich. Er
kritisierte in seinem Koreferat seinen Vorredner keineswegs, sondern stellte
vielmehr die Gemeinsamkeiten ihrer beider Auffassungen heraus, die sowohl
in der Zurückweisung des Positivismus und der Wertfreiheitsthese als auch in
der Ablehnung des Relativismus bestanden. Darüber hinaus ging Adorno in
seinem Koreferat „Zur Logik der Sozialwissenschaften" (Adorno 1969c) zwar
auf Poppers Thesen ein, formulierte aber keine Gegenposition, sondern bes-
tenfalls gewisse Unterschiede in ihrer beider Auffassungen, wobei er den Eindruck entstehen ließ, dass die Übereinstimmungen zwischen ihnen überwogen.
Zweifellos wäre die Tübinger Tagung vergessen worden und der Positivismusstreit würde in der deutschen Wissenschaftsgeschichte nicht als die bedeu-
tendste Auseinandersetzung über die Sozialwissenschaften der 60er Jahre gel-
ten, hätten sich nicht zwei Personen eingemischt: Jürgen Habermas und Hans
Albert. Sie sind es, die jene Debatte geführt haben, die heute als „Positivismusstreit" bekannt ist. Erst Habermas formulierte den Streitpunkt: die Frage nach

den Aufgaben und den Zielsetzungen der Sozialwissenschaft aus der Sicht der „analytischen Wissenschaftstheorie" und stellte die Position der Frankfurter systematischer dar als Adorno es auf seine aphoristische Weise getan hatte. Und erst die engagierte und detaillierte Beschäftigung Alberts mit dem hier zu Tage tretenden Theorieverständnis der Frankfurter Schule, in dem traditionelle marxistische Auffassungen tradiert und verändert wurden, ließ eine Auseinandersetzung entstehen. Allerdings war diese Konfrontation keineswegs frei von Missverständnissen, weil beide Parteien weder dem Selbstverständnis der anderen Seite folgten noch die Darstellung der eigenen Position durch die gegnerische Auffassung akzeptieren konnten.

3 Historisch-dialektische Geschichtsphilosophie versus Wissenschaftslehre

Habermas hat die Eigenarten der kritischen Theorie sowie die zentralen Punkte, in denen er den Unterschied zum kritischen Rationalismus sah, zum ersten Mal ein Jahr später in einem Aufsatz herausgearbeitet, der zunächst als Beitrag in einer Festschrift zum sechzigsten Geburtstag Adornos erschien und 1969 in dem Sammelband *Der Positivismusstreit in der deutschen Soziologie* (Adorno u.a. 1969) zusammen mit den Beiträgen von Popper, Adorno, Albert und anderen wieder abgedruckt wurde (Habermas 1969a). Dabei hielt er sich in seiner Darstellung der kritischen Theorie relativ eng an die Vorgaben von Horkheimer, der bereits 1937 in seinem Aufsatz „Traditionelle und kritische Theorie" das Programm einer kritischen Sozialwissenschaft entworfen hatte (Horkheimer 1937). Mit der Abgrenzung einer „kritischen" von einer „traditionellen" Theorie hatte Horkheimer die spätere Unterscheidung zwischen kritischer und positivistischer Sozialwissenschaft in gewisser Weise vorweggenommen. *Traditionell* nennt Horkheimer die neuzeitliche Wissenschaftsauffassung, die seit Descartes als Paradigma von Erkenntnis gilt. Es trennt die Wissenschaft und ihre Methode von der gesellschaftlichen Lebenspraxis mit ihren Interessen und Wertungen. Wissenschaft ist hier ein rein auf das Ziel der Erkenntnisgewinnung ausgerichtetes Unternehmen, das nicht beachtet, dass die Verwertung ihrer Ergebnisse von gesellschaftlichen, primär ökonomischen, Interessen gelenkt wird. *Kritisch* dagegen nennt er eine Wissenschaftsauffassung, für die Wissenschaft nur einen Teil des gesellschaftlichen Gesamtzusammenhanges ausmacht und ein Produkt des menschlichen Arbeitsprozesses ist. Eine kritische Wissenschaft hat deshalb nicht nur das Ziel, die sozialen Phänomene zu beschreiben und zu erklären, sondern ist Ausdruck eines „kritischen Verhaltens" und hat die Funktion, die Gesellschaft im Sinne „vernünftiger Zielsetzungen" praktisch-politisch zu verändern, womit Horkheimer eine sozialistische Gesellschaftsordnung meinte. An die damalige Konzeption von kritischer Theorie knüpfte Habermas an. Er zählte die Besonderheiten der kritischen Theorie der Gesellschaft auf: Ihre Methode, die — in der Tradition der Marxschen Ansatzes — historisch und dialektisch ist, ihr Untersuchungsgebiet: Gesellschaft als Totalität, d.h. ein Zusammenhang, der von den Wissenschaftlern und den untersuchten Personen nicht strikt unterschieden werden kann, sondern dessen Grundsätze und Strukturmechanismen sich in den Erfahrungen und Handlungen aller Gesellschaftsmitglieder ausdrücken. Die kritische Theorie ist kein deduktiver Zusammenhang von Aussagen, denn die Gesetzmäßigkeiten der Gesellschaft sind nach Habermas nicht so beschaffen, dass sie in unbeschränkten Allsätzen formuliert werden könnten. Anders als der Kausalzusammenhang in der Natur verändere sich die Struktur der Gesellschaft im Verlauf der geschichtlichen Entwicklung. Diese systematische Veränderung könnte nur — und hier wiederholte er eine marxistische Grundannahme — durch historische Bewegungsgesetze erfasst werden, die den objektiven Sinn des historischen Prozesses enthalten (Habermas 1969a, p. 163), den Habermas allerdings nicht spezifizierte. Insofern sei das Schema von Hypothesenformulierung und Konfrontation mit der Erfahrung nach den präzise definierten Regeln einer empirischen Methode der Soziologie für die Erklärung der Gesellschaft unpassend.

Ausführlich beschrieb er die charakteristischen Merkmale einer dialektisch verfahrenden Theorie. Zunächst habe sie einen doppelten Anspruch: sowohl die historische Gesetzmäßigkeit des objektiven gesellschaftlichen Zusammenhanges zu erfassen wie auch sich auf empirische gesellschaftliche Ereignisse als historisch einmaliger individueller Ereignisse in einem unumkehrbaren Entwicklungsprozess zu beziehen. Insofern werden einzelne empirische Vorkommnisse in der Gesellschaft als Konkretisierungen eines universalen historischen Bewegungsgesetzes aufgefasst. Dies erfordere eine andere Sichtweise des Verhältnisses zwischen Theorie und Praxis und zwischen Erkenntnissen und Werten als der kritische Rationalismus sie habe. Nachdem dieser die lebenspraktischen Fragen des Wertens und Entscheidens aus dem Aussagenzusammenhang wissenschaftlicher Theorien heraus halten will und unter Praxis nur die experimentelle Bewährung von Hypothesen verstehe, rechnet ihn Habermas zum Positivismus. Für diesen sei ein Irrationalismus und Subjektivismus der Werte charakteristisch. Praxis sei für das Wissenschaftsprogramm des kritischen Rationalismus nichts als Technik, denn Prognosen könnten nur als sozialtechnische Empfehlungen umgesetzt werden (Habermas 1969a, p. 171). Hingegen enthält eine dialektisch gewonnene Erkenntnis der Gesellschaft notwendig wertende Entscheidungen über gesellschaftliche und politische Zielsetzungen, da es ihr Ziel ist, die Lebenspraxis der Menschen zu verändern. Sie hält die Zukunft der Gesellschaft für praktisch veränderbar und formuliert deshalb keine Prognosen, sondern gesellschaftspolitische Programme. Ihre Bewährung bestehe nicht darin, dass empirische Prüfsätze gefunden werden, die ihr nicht widersprechen, sondern in einer gelingenden Lebenspraxis der Gesellschaftsmitglieder.

Alberts Antwort ließ nicht lange auf sich warten. Sie erschien 1964 in der *Kölner Zeitschrift für Soziologie und Sozialpsychologie*. Er präzisierte in seiner Antwort (Albert 1969a) die Punkte, die der kritische Rationalismus ablehnt.

Es sind dies:

(1) Das dialektische Verfahren, das die Grenzen formaler Logik überschreitet. Albert bemängelt, dass die kritischen Theoretiker nicht angeben können, was sie eigentlich tun, wenn sie dialektisch verfahren.

(2) Der Begriff der „gesellschaftlichen Totalität", die weder als organisches Ganzes aufzufassen sei noch als Klasse, die sich umfangslogisch bestimmen lässt und somit beliebig interpretierbar ist sowie die Problematik eines historischen Gesetzes. Albert lehnt die Möglichkeit solcher Gesetze rundheraus ab, da eine Aussage, die sich auf die konkrete gesellschaftlich — geschichtliche Totalität bezieht, nichts weiter sein kann als eine singuläre Aussage.

(3) Die Bezugnahme auf eine Alltagserfahrung, die aus der Perspektive der kritischen Theorie schon vor der Prüfung der Theorie für ihre Gültigkeit spricht. Albert besteht darauf, dass die Abstammung einer Theorie — wenn sie z. B. aufgrund einer moralischen Erfahrung sozialer Ungerechtigkeit entwickelt wird — nicht über ihre Wahrheit entscheidet.

(4) Ein Theorie-Praxis-Verhältnis, das es ermöglicht, aus dem objektiven historischen Geschehen ein praktisches Ziel der Gesellschaft abzuleiten, also einen objektiven Sinn der Geschichte zu ermitteln. Die kritische Theorie ist nicht fähig, die Struktur einer Theorie als wissenschaftlich zu erweisen, die zu so etwas fähig zu sein beansprucht. Die Möglichkeit, auf wissenschaftliche Weise einen objektiven Sinn der Geschichte zu ermitteln, weist er mit Hinweis auf Poppers *The Poverty of Historicism* (Popper 1957) zurück.

(5) Eine sozialwissenschaftliche Erkenntnis, die im Aussagenzusammenhang Werturteile enthält, also etwa Aussagen von der Art enthält, dass Gesellschaft ein „Verblendungszusammenhang" (Adorno 1969b, p. 83) sei. Zwar stehen Forscher in normativen Bezügen, und im Forschungsbetrieb existieren gesellschaftliche und ökonomische Interessen. Aber diese haben nach Auffassung des kritischen Rationalismus keinen Einfluss auf die Aussagenstruktur der Ergebnisse.

(6) Die instrumentalistische Deutung der Erfahrungswissenschaft, die das Verhältnis von Theorie und Praxis als Sache der sozialen Legitimation aufzufassen gezwungen ist und die Frage der Wahrheit wissenschaftlicher Erkenntnis unter den Tisch fallen lässt (Albert 1969a, pp. 216-220).

Den Positivismusvorwurf weist er zurück. Er erinnert Habermas daran, dass der kritische Rationalismus keine theorieunabhängige Basis kennt und dass die Theorieimprägniertheit der Basissätze sicherlich kein positivistisches Element darstellt. Und er erklärt Habermas' Einschätzung der kritisch-rationalistischen Trennung von Tatsachen und Wertungen als positivistisch mit einer Verwechslung von analytischen Ebenen. Die von Habermas angeführten Interessen der Forscher fallen demnach in den Bereich der Wissenschaftssoziologie, die nicht mit den Regeln der Methodologie verwechselt werden dürften: Nur letztere ermöglichen einen reinen, nämlich an der Idee der Wahrheit orientierten Erkenntnisbegriff.

4 Habermas' neuer Ansatz: transzendentaler Pragmatismus

Habermas' Positivismusvorwurf gegen den kritischen Rationalismus ließ auf jeden Fall erkennen, dass der jüngste Vertreter der kritischen Theorie einen neuen Ansatz vertrat, den seine Lehrer nicht teilten. Weder Horkheimer noch Adorno hatten Popper für einen Positivisten gehalten. (Erst in der Jahre später hinzugefügten „Einleitung" folgt Adorno der Einschätzung von Habermas; vgl. Adorno 1969a, p. 7, Anmerkung 1.) Habermas verwendet den Begriff „Positivismus" als Kampfbegriff. Zwar war er sich darüber im Klaren, dass Popper nicht die Position des älteren Positivismus oder des logischen Empirismus vertritt. Als Positivismus deutet er den kritischen Rationalismus, weil dieser für eine einheitliche Methode für die Natur- und die Sozialwissenschaften, sowie auch für die Geisteswissenschaften eintritt. Dies wird mit dem logisch-positivistischen Programm einer Einheitswissenschaft identifiziert. Alle empirischen Wissenschaften werden unterschiedslos als interessefreie theoretische Tatsachenwissenschaften ausgewiesen, für die eine einheitliche Wissenschaftslogik, die eine einheitliche Methode postuliert, zuständig ist. Diese Auffassung von einer einzigen Methode der empirischen Wissenschaften wird von den kritischen Theoretikern auch „Szientismus" genannt (Adorno 1969a, p. 9). Bei Habermas steht die Bezeichnung zusätzlich für eine Position, die die Soziologie zu den empirischen Wissenschaften rechnet und Erfahrung als systematische Beobachtung versteht. Er bewegt sich in dieser Zeit bereits in die Richtung einer transzendental-pragmatistischen Erkenntnistheorie, die eine neue Auffassung über unterschiedliche Erfahrungsbereiche von Natur- und Sozialwissenschaften enthält.

Adorno hatte seine Sicht der Erfahrung noch anders, nämlich als Zweifel an der sozialwissenschaftlichen Brauchbarkeit von Fakten formuliert, die unabhängig von der gesellschaftlichen Totalität sind. Er lehnte objektive Fakten aber mit marxistischen Argumenten ab, wegen des Verdachts der „Verdinglichung" (Adorno 1969a, p. 23), also weil sie der dialektischen Annahme nicht entsprachen, dass jede einzelne Erfahrung von der gesellschaftlichen (kapitalistischen) Totalität vorgeprägt ist. Zwar folgte daraus, dass singuläre Sätze über einzelne Fakten keine prüfenden Instanzen für die kritische Theorie darstellen konnten, weil diese nur das als Erfahrungsbasis zuließ, was die „antagonistische Beschaffenheit der Gesellschaft" (Adorno 1969a, p. 23) enthielt. Aber Adorno machte noch nicht eine a priori notwenige Differenz der Erkenntnisweisen dafür verantwortlich wie Habermas, der nun einen prinzipiellen Unterschied im Erkennen von physikalischen Dingen und Ereignissen und dem Erkennen von menschlichen Subjekten und ihren symbolischen Ausdrucksweisen sah. Für Adorno war einfach das historisch-existenzielle Engagement der Subjekte in der Erfahrungsbasis der Theorie notwendig. Horkheimer lehnte den Pragmatismus ab. In einem Aufsatz, der allerdings erst nach der Debatte zwischen Habermas und Albert erschien, setzte er den Pragmatismus mit dem Positivismus gleich (Horkheimer 1967, p. 51).

Habermas bezog in dem Aufsatz, „Gegen einen positivistisch halbierten Rationalismus" (Habermas 1969b), mit dem er auf Albert antwortete, zum ersten Mal eine Position, die eine eigene, nämlich transzendental-pragmatistische Umdeutung der kritischen Theorie andeutete, die er später in dem Buch *Erkenntnis und Interesse ausführte* (Habermas 1968).

Dass der kritische Rationalismus ein halber Positivismus sei, versuchte Habermas nochmals anhand folgender Streitpunkte zu zeigen: der unterschiedlichen Deutung von Erfahrung, dem Basisproblem, dem Verhältnis der methodologischen zu den empirischen Aussagen und am Dualismus von Tatsachen und Werten (Habermas 1969b, p. 237). Warum er den kritischen Rationalismus in die positivistische Ecke stellte, machte er bereits auf den ersten Seiten deutlich. Nun ging es nicht mehr um den Vorwurf, der kritische Rationalismus verweigere sich einer dialektischen Methode und ihm fehle der Blick aufs Ganze der Gesellschaft — das war noch die Terminologie der marxistisch inspirierten Version Adornos der kritischen Theorie gewesen. Jetzt hieß der Vorwurf, dass der kritische Rationalismus die philosophische Reflexion auf seine eigenen methodologischen Regeln bzw. sein eigenes Wissenschaftsverständnis unmöglich mache, weil er — wie der logische Empirismus — Philosophie in der objektivierenden Einstellung der Wissenschaften betreibe, sie also bloß als Metatheorie wissenschaftlicher Theorien verstünde und nicht — wie Habermas' Vorstellung es nahe legte —, als philosophische Erkenntnistheorie, die die Standards, die sie den Wissenschaften vorschreibt, als notwendige begründen zu können beansprucht. Dieser Mangel an Selbstreflexion der kritisch-rationalistischen Methodologie sei positivistisch. Sie sei nicht in der Lage, die Rationalität ihrer methodologischen Regeln ihrerseits zu rechtfertigen (Habermas 1969b, p. 252). Positivistisch sei auch das Missverständnis der Methodologie für das, was Erfahrung sei. Vom kritischen Rationalismus werde Erfahrung auf die wiederholbare Beobachtung empirischer Vorgänge reduziert. Er habe keinen Blick dafür, dass er mit der Auszeichnung einer einzig möglichen Form des empirischen Zugangs zur Welt auch den Geltungssinn empirischer Aussagen festlege (Habermas 1969b, p. 238). Habermas spricht damit sein eigenes pragmatistisches Verständnis empirisch überprüfbarer Aussagen aus; die pragmatistische Interpretation von Erkenntnis setzt die Wahrheit von Aussagen mit ihrer experimentellen Bewährung gleich. Die empirische Basis, die der kritische Rationalismus zulasse, sei positivistisch, denn es sei gar nicht möglich, eine Theorie an theorieunabhängigen Tatsachen zu prüfen. Dass er die falsifizierenden Basissätze, die ja nur die Erfahrungen der Forscher mit der Welt wiedergeben, mit an sich existierenden Tatsachen gleich setze, an denen eine Theorie geprüft werde, zeige klar, dass Popper ebenso wie der Positivismus die beobachtbare Welt für die einzig wissenschaftlich erforschbare Wirklichkeit halte und die transzendentale Reflexion auf die Konstitutionsproblematik der Erfahrung außer Acht lasse. Hingegen stelle eine pragmatistische Theorie wissenschaftlicher Erkenntnis die Frage nach den Bedingungen, unter denen eine empirische Aussage über die Welt überhaupt möglich sei. Ihr Thema sei die Weise wie der Mensch die beobachtbare und technisch behandelbare Welt zum

Gegenstand wissenschaftlicher Forschung macht; es sei das erkenntnisleitende
„...Interesse an der möglichen informativen Sicherung und Erweiterung er-
folgskontrollierten Handelns ..." (Habermas 1969b, p. 244). Alberts Feststel-
lung, dass Instrumente nur erfolglos angewendet, aber nicht als falsch widerlegt werden können, lässt Habermas zwar unwidersprochen, betont aber dennoch, dass mit der Art der Prüfungsbedingungen für eine Theorie auch schon
festgelegt sei, in welcher Region der Wirklichkeit sie allein widerlegt werden
könne. Und experimentell wiederholbare Beobachtungen seien nun einmal nur
bei Sätzen möglich, die etwas über den Bereich der technisch bearbeitbaren
Wirklichkeit aussagen.

Habermas hat damit einen Ansatz formuliert, der anders als die kritische Theorie Horkheimers und Adornos den Unterschied der praktischen
Verwendbarkeit naturwissenschaftlicher und kritisch sozialwissenschaftlicher
Aussagen erkenntnistheoretisch rechtfertigt. Während in der experimentellen
Bewährung naturwissenschaftlicher Theorien ein technisches Erkenntnisinteresse zum Ausdruck kommt, ist in den Sozialwissenschaften auf Grund ihres unterschiedlichen Erfahrungsbezugs ein Interesse an der praktischen Lebenssitu-
ation der untersuchten Objekte enthalten. Damit hat Habermas dem gesellschaftlichen Engagement der kritischen Theorie eine neue, erkenntnistheo-
retische Basis gegeben (Habermas 1969b, p. 261), die nicht mehr die des
Marxismus ist.

5   Umfassende Vernunft versus kritische Rationalität

Es ist wichtig, sich klar zu machen, dass dennoch erst Habermas' neue pragmatistische Erkenntnistheorie es ermöglichte, der kritischen Theorie den ak-
tivistischen, auf die Veränderung der Gesellschaft abzielenden, Impuls der
30er Jahre zurückzugeben, als Horkheimer und Adorno noch der marxistischen Überzeugung von einer proletarischen Revolution anhingen. Diese Er-
wartung hatten sie inzwischen aufgegeben. Unter dem Eindruck der Schre-
ckensherrschaft des Nationalsozialismus hatten sie 1947 das Buch *Dialektik der
Aufklärung* (Horkheimer & Adorno 1947) publiziert. Pessimistisch stellten sie
hier die gesamte menschliche Geschichte als Selbstzerstörung der menschlichen
Vernunft dar. Das einzige, was noch an Marx erinnert, ist die Geschichtsphilosophie, die aber Marx geradezu umkehrt. Am Ende der Geschichte steht
nicht die Befreiung, sondern der unvermeidliche Untergang der Menschheit.
Horkheimer und Adorno bezeichnen den Fortschritt an wissenschaftlicher Er-
kenntnis und technischen Beherrschung der Natur in ihren Anfängen zwar als
Befreiung. Zunächst habe das wissenschaftliche Denken aufklärend gewirkt,
weil es die Mythen zerstörte und die Menschen zu einer autonomen Lebens-
führung befähigte. Aber die wissenschaftliche Rationalität habe nicht nur
Religionen zu Mythen erklärt, sondern auch die objektiven Grundlagen der
Moral zerstört. Indem die Aufklärung Werte und Normen auf menschliche
Verträge und Beschlüsse zurückführte, reduzierte sie die Vernunft auf eine in-
strumentelle bzw. Zweck- Mittel-Rationalität. Dadurch wurde die Aufklärung

durch Wissenschaft von einer befreienden zu einer unterdrückenden Weltsicht. Als Emanzipation gelte heute nur mehr der Zuwachs an empirischem Wissen und die Entwicklung von Technologien, die nicht nur die Natur, sondern auch den Mensch beherrschen. Insofern ist der geschichtliche Prozess der „Selbstbefreiung durch das Wissen" für Horkheimer und Adorno ein Vorgang, der in Unterdrückung und Ohnmacht endet.

Adorno und Horkheimer haben hier zwar zum ersten Mal ein Konzept von technischer bzw. instrumenteller Rationalität entworfen, das auch Habermas später verwendet, aber sie hatten Rationalität grundsätzlich als Instrument der Versklavung des Menschen denunziert. Eine *kritische,* nämlich die Gesellschaft verändernde, Theorie war auf der Basis der „Dialektik der Aufklärung" grundsätzlich nicht mehr möglich.

Habermas war damals zwar noch weit von seiner „Theorie der kommunikativen Rationalität" entfernt, dachte aber bereits in die Richtung eines neuen Rationalitätskonzepts indem er von einer Art von Vernunft sprach, die über die wissenschaftliche Rationalität hinausgehe (Habermas 1971ba pp. 307-335). Diese neue Rationalitätskonzeption sollte rationales Handeln nicht auf technologisches Handeln reduzieren und eine Kritik wissenschaftlicher Theorien nicht mehr nur im Zusammenhang mit experimenteller Bewährung ermöglichen.

In den Sozialwissenschaften handle es sich nicht um Gegenstände und kausal ablaufende Prozesse, sondern um Personen und Gruppen, die sich selbst interpretieren und in einem irreversiblen Geschichtsprozess stehen. Wenn man die Beziehungen zwischen Menschen in derselben Einstellung untersuche wie die gesetzmäßigen Beziehungen zwischen Dingen und Ereignissen, dann würden Menschen als Objekte behandelt, über welche die Wissenschaft verfügen will. Das wissenschaftstheoretische Programm des kritischen Rationalismus habe eine Auffassung von Sozialwissenschaft zur Folge, deren Ziel in der Sicherung und Erweiterung der Herrschaft über die Menschen bestünde.

Eine solch unreflektiert sich als Erfahrungswissenschaft deutende Soziologie nehme keine Rücksicht auf die Bedürfnisse und das Selbstverständnis von Menschen. In einer so verstandenen Soziologie komme nur ein technisches Erkenntnisinteresse zum Ausdruck. Hingegen orientiere sich die kritische Theorie an einer umfassenden Rationalität, die nicht nur die Methoden der Erfahrungswissenschaft als rational auszeichnen kann, sondern auch die Handlungsziele und normative Einstellungen von Menschen in ihrem Lebensalltag. (Habermas 1969b, p. 263). Während der kritische Rationalismus, diese Art von Rationalität ausblenden muss, würde sie in einer kritischen Sozialwissenschaft zum Ausdruck kommen. Allerdings meinte Habermas damals noch immer, dass es die dialektische Methode sei, durch die diese intersubjektiven Rationalität der Kommunikation zugänglich werde (Habermas 1969b, p. 264), ohne jedoch, worauf Albert in seiner Replik auf Habermas hinwies, ihr Verfahren verdeutlicht und ihre Funktion für den neuen, pragmatistischen Ansatz erläutert zu haben (Albert 1969b, p. 298).

6 Ideologieverdacht

Beide Positionen unterzogen einander einer massiven Ideologiekritik. Diese Ideologiekritik wurde jedoch von beiden Seiten nicht als Kritik an politischen Ideen und Überzeugungen geführt, sondern als Kritik an der Art, wie die jeweils andere Seite Philosophie betrieb und an der Absicht, die sie verfolgten. Diese sahen beide Seiten beim Gegner als identisch. Es war die Art, wie beabsichtigt wurde Wissenschaft für — oder gegen — die Interessen der Menschen einzusetzen. Dies ist auf den ersten Blick deshalb erstaunlich weil beide philosophische Richtungen derselben Tradition entstammen. Beide knüpfen an die europäische Aufklärung des 18. Jahrhunderts an. Diese hat zum ersten Mal die Idee entwickelt, dass die Vernunft die Fähigkeit des Menschen ist, autonom, ohne Zuhilfenahme übernatürlicher Mächte, die Welt zu erkennen und sein Leben nach eigenen Vorstellungen zu gestalten, dass die Vernunft die Erfahrung braucht, um die Welt zu erkennen, und dass die Menschen frei sind und über unveräußerliche Rechte verfügen (Kant).

Sowohl der kritische Rationalismus wie die (ursprüngliche) kritische Theorie vertreten das Konzept eines gesellschaftlichen Fortschritts durch Vernunft. Und sie sehen beide — wie die Denker der europäischen Moderne von Bacon und Descartes bis Kant, dass die modernen Wissenschaften durchaus eine Emanzipation von undurchschauten Schicksalsmächten und Aberglauben bewirken können. Der kritische Rationalismus glaubt wie Kant an eine „Selbstbefreiung (der Menschheit) durch das Wissen" (Popper 1961). Popper schließt an die Forderung Kants an, niemals blind irgendwelchen Autoritäten zu glauben, sondern die eigene Vernunft als kritische Instanz zu verwenden. Wissen ist auch im kritischen Rationalismus eine unverzichtbare Bedingung von sozialer und politischer Emanzipation. Wissenschaftliches Wissen ist zur Korrektur von Vorurteilen imstande, ermöglicht rationale Handlungsorientierungen und setzt dadurch die Menschen in Stand, gesellschaftlich herrschende Meinungen durch sachliche Kritik in Frage zu stellen und zu überwinden. Für die Anwendung der kritischen Rationalität gibt es keine Beschränkungen. Kritik hat insofern eine subversive Kraft: sie unterhöhlt alles, was Absolutheitsansprüche hat, alles Unhinterfragte, Tradierte, ob es nun aufgrund von Macht oder von Tradition Geltung hat. Die kritische Theorie vertritt nichts anderes, meint aber, die emanzipatorische Funktion der Naturwissenschaften hängt aber davon ab, welchen Gebrauch die Menschen davon machen. Insofern sei es notwendig, dass komplementär zu den Naturwissenschaften in die Geistes- und Sozialwissenschaften die intersubjektive Verständigung über Werte und Ziele Eingang finden sollte.

Insofern war die Methodendiskussion zwischen kritischem Rationalismus und kritischer Theorie ein Streit um die richtige Art einer „Selbstbefreiung durch Wissen": um die Freiheit der Wissenschaft von gesellschaftlich-politischer Korrumpierung auf der Seite Alberts, ein Beharren auf dem notwendigen gesellschaftspolitischen Mandat der Sozialwissenschaften auf der Seite der kritischen Theoretiker.

Albert führte den Antifundamentalismus des kritischen Rationalismus ins Feld, die Zurückweisung des Unfehlbarkeitsanspruchs von philosophischen

Sätzen und plädierte für die Durchsetzung eines grundsätzlich fallibilistischen Selbstverständnisses auch der Philosophie und für eine Zurückweisung privilegierter und spezifischer Erkenntnismethoden, wie eben der Dialektik.

Es ist kein Zufall, dass Popper die Theorien von Freud, Hegel und Marx als Paradigmata der Unwissenschaftlichkeit und als ideologische Selbstimmunisierungen von Pseudoerkenntnis hervorgehoben hat (Popper 1979, pp. 38-48). Gemeinsam ist ihnen, dass sie nicht widerlegt werden können. Indem die Theorie jede Einzelerfahrung von vornherein so in den theoretischen Rahmen integriert, dass sie auf jeden Fall mit ihm vereinbar ist, kann jeder empirische Befund zu einer Bestätigung erklärt werden. Wenn in der Psychoanalyse der Analysand noch so überzeugt ist, dass der Analytiker falsch liegt, für die Theorie ist es bloß der Widerstand, den sie selbst vorhergesagt hat. Ebenso erlaubt es die Geschichtsphilosophie marxistischer Herkunft, jede mögliche historische Entwicklung als Indiz für das Zutreffen ihrer Entwicklungsprognosen zu interpretieren. Die totalisierende Tendenz dieser Theorien, einfach alles in ihr theoretisches Gebäude zu integrieren, macht sie zu einer Ideologie der Gegenaufklärung. Theorien dieser Art lassen die Möglichkeit einer theorieunabhängigen Erfahrung nicht zu. Alternative Hypothesen sind für sie nur innerhalb ihres theoretischen Rahmens zulässig, der Rahmen selbst jedoch kann nicht in Frage gestellt werden. Falls man es dennoch versucht, hat man sich zum Gegner der betreffenden Theorie erklärt, der nicht bereit ist, ihren besonderen Wissensanspruch zu akzeptieren und dessen Argumente von den Vertretern dieser Theorie folglich nicht mehr ernst genommen werden.

Albert sieht die kritische Theorie in diesem Sinne als gigantisches Projekt, um eine kritische Vernunft auszuschalten (Albert 1969b, pp. 267-305). Er kritisiert an Adorno und Habermas die metaphernreiche, fast dichterische Sprache und unklare, vieldeutige Aussagen. Er sieht in der dialektischen Methode die Logik außer Kraft gesetzt zugunsten rhetorischer Kunstgriffe. Er fordert die Einhaltung der Maßstäbe einer rationalen Diskussion und Argumentation, was die Formulierung verständlicher und nicht-widersprüchlicher Sätze meint. Dem kritischen Rationalismus erscheint die dialektische Methode ideologieverdächtig, weil er vermutet, dass damit der Gegenstandsbereich der sozialen Tatbestände, Beziehungen und Prozesse dem Erklärungsanspruch der Erfahrungswissenschaften entzogen werden soll. Er unterstellt den Frankfurtern einen Vernunftbegriff, der mit der Beschwörung der gesellschaftlichen Totalität dem (politischen) Totalitarismus Vorschub leistet, weil er sachliche Kritik unmöglich macht. Für den kritischen Rationalismus sind hier alle Bedingungen eines ideologischen Denkens erfüllt: Die Kritische Theorie ist nicht nur nicht widerlegbar, sie verhindert kritisches und klares Denken, sie ist Obskurantismus. Was ihrer Idee gesellschaftlicher Emanzipation widerspricht, wird von ihr als Verbündung mit den Herrschaftsinteressen des Kapitals politisch denunziert. Die kritische Theorie war aus der Sicht des kritischen Rationalismus, ob nun pragmatistisch oder nicht, noch immer Geschichtsphilosophie in praktischer Absicht, nämlich an der Abschaffung von Demokratie und liberaler Marktwirtschaft interessiert.

Hingegen war und blieb der kritische Rationalismus in der Sicht von Habermas eine Philosophie, die naiv, nämlich unreflektiert das Programm einer reinen, nämlich interessefreien Wissenschaft vertrat. Sein Verständnis von Wissenschaft definiere sie ausschließlich als „Science". Und diesem Verständnis der Wissenschaft warf er vor, es leiste einer bürokratischen und technokratischen Gesamtverfassung der Gesellschaft Vorschub und verhindere eine rationale Reflexion des Gesamtzusammenhangs von Wissenschaft, Wirtschaft und Gesellschaft als unwissenschaftlich. Seine Argumentation lautete folgendermaßen: Sozialwissenschaftliche Erkenntnisse sind ideologisch, wenn sie die gesellschaftliche Wirklichkeit nur erklären oder einzelne soziale Ereignisse vorhersagen, denn die bestehende Gesellschaft ist eine unfreie und ungerechte Gesellschaft. Empirisch prüfbare nomologische Hypothesen lassen alles in der Gesellschaft wie es ist. Die Erfahrung, die hier Prüfinstanz ist, lässt die gesellschaftliche Unterdrückung nicht einmal sichtbar werden. Deshalb beteilige sich eine erfahrungswissenschaftliche Soziologie an einem Gesamtsystem der Unterdrückung und die Philosophie, die für eine wertfrei empirische Soziologie argumentiert, legitimiere damit soziale Ungerechtigkeit und Unfreiheit.

Diese Rekonstruktion der Argumentation der beiden Streitparteien zeigt, dass es im Streit zwar um das gemeinsame Thema: Sozialwissenschaft und ihre gesellschaftliche Rolle ging. Aber de facto konnten die Frankfurter zur Zeit des Positivismusstreits den Argumenten Alberts keine konsistente Position entgegenstellen. Adorno und Horkheimer vertraten in dieser Zeit keine kritische Gesellschaftstheorie auf historisch-dialektischer Grundlage mehr, Habermas vertrat zwar einen neuen Ansatz, verwendete aber zum Teil noch die alte Terminologie und wiederholte die alten Zielsetzungen, die nicht unbedingt mehr zu seinem Pragmatismus passten. Insofern war die von Albert beklagte Unklarheit der anderen Position kein Zufall.

7 Kritische Rationalität

Vernunft oder Rationalität ist für den kritischen Rationalismus die Fähigkeit zur Prüfung von Aussagen oder Behauptungen anhand von Logik und Erfahrung in Diskussionen, die an der Idee der Wahrheit orientiert sind. Der Form nach dürfte Popper dabei die Situation eines Diskurses vor Augen gehabt haben, in dem alle, die sich daran beteiligen, gleich berechtigt sind und frei, ihre Meinungen zu äußern. Er beschreibt eine Einstellung, die zugibt, „... dass ich mich irren kann, dass du recht haben kannst und dass wir gemeinsam vielleicht der Wahrheit auf die Spur kommen werden" (Popper 1973, p. 276). Wesentlich für die kritisch-rationalistische Position ist, dass die Vernunft vor nichts halt macht. Sie muss sich zutrauen, alles zu prüfen, auch die ersten oder fundamentalen Annahmen der Philosophie selbst. Die kritische Theorie dagegen unterstellt ein Vernunftkonzept, das es ermöglichen soll, Werte, Ziele und den objektiven Sinn der Geschichte zu erkennen, nicht nur, diese Ziele in Diskussionen unter Erwägung des Für und Wider zu beschließen.

(Der kritische Rationalismus würde versuchen, Werte auf diese Weise zu behandeln.)

Aufgrund ihres Konzepts von Vernunft meinte die kritische Theorie erkennen zu können, dass die bestehenden gesellschaftlichen Verhältnisse die Menschen in Unfreiheit und Unterdrückung halten. Von ihren eigenen normativen Maßstäben hingegen, die in die Gesellschaftskritik Eingang fanden, aber nirgends offen gelegt wurden, unterstellte sie, dass sie Ausdruck einer objektiv historischen bzw. umfassenden Vernunft seien und insofern absolut und unwiderlegbar. Kritik war für die kritische Theorie die Einsicht der Vernunft selbst in die objektiv falschen Verhältnisse und insofern Kritik an einer Wissenschaft, die eine solche Einsicht nicht erlaubt.

Ebenso unvereinbar sind die Auffassungen über Aufklärung und Emanzipation. Der kritische Rationalismus hält an der Idee der Aufklärung fest, dass autonomes, kritisches Denken und gut geprüftes wissenschaftliches Wissen die Menschen fähig macht, ihre Lage zu erkennen und zu verändern. Die kritische Theorie wollte aber genau diese aufklärerische Überzeugung über sich selbst aufklären. Ihr Argument war aber nicht, dass wissenschaftliche Erkenntnis ein geeignetes Mittel zur Unterdrückung von Menschen sein kann — das hätte wohl auch der kritische Rationalismus unterschrieben —, sondern dass sie unvermeidlich ein Mittel der Unterdrückung sein muss, wenn sie sich nicht in den Dienst einer Kritik der falschen Gesellschaftsordnung stellt, die den Maßstäben der kritischen Theorie zu entsprechen hatte.

Der kritische Rationalismus unterscheidet hingegen die Frage nach wissenschaftlicher Erkenntnis von der Frage, wie Menschen miteinander leben wollen, also von Zielsetzungen und Werten. Er ist nicht bereit, für die Beantwortung von Wahrheitsfragen moralische oder politische Maßstäbe heranzuziehen. Der entscheidende Punkt aber ist, dass er keine unfehlbaren Maßstäbe einer gerechten oder richtigen sozialen Ordnung anerkennt. Er akzeptiert keine unfehlbare Vernunft, die der Rationalität der einzelnen Menschen überlegen ist. Nach kritisch rationalistischer Auffassung sind es die Betroffenen selbst, die nach kritischer Prüfung der Sachlage von Fall zu Fall selbst entscheiden, in welcher Sozialordnung sie leben wollen.

Es war der Irrtum der kritischen Theorie, die Vernünftigkeit letzter Zwecksetzungen mittels einer geschichtsphilosophisch bzw. auch kommunikationstheoretisch angeleiteten Soziologie wissenschaftlich ermitteln zu wollen. Sie ist damit gescheitert.

Literatur

Adorno, T. W. (1953). „Das Bewusstsein der Wissenssoziologie', In R. Tiede-
mann u. a., Hrsg. (1953), pp. 31-46. *Adorno, Gesammelte Schriften*, Bd.
10.1. Frankfurt/Main: Suhrkamp.

——— (1969a). „Einleitung". In Adorno u.a. (1969), pp. 1-81.

——— (1969b). „Soziologie und empirische Forschung". In Adorno u.a. (1969),
pp. 81-101.

——— (1969c). „Zur Logik der Sozialwissenschaften". In Adorno u.a. (1969),
pp. 125-143.

Adorno, T. W., Albert, H., Dahrendorf, R., Habermas, J. & Popper, K. R.
(1969). *Der Positivismusstreit in der deutschen Soziologie.* Neuwied &
Berlin: Hermann Luchterhand Verlag GmbH. 2. Auflage 1970.

Albert, H. (1969a). „Der Mythos der totalen Vernunft". In Adorno u.a. (1969),
pp. 193-234.

Albert, H. (1969b). „Im Rücken des Positivismus?" In Adorno u.a. (1969),
pp. 267-305.

Dahms, H.-J. (1994). *Positivismusstreit. Die Auseinandersetzung der Frankfurter Schule mit dem logischen Positivismus, dem amerikanischen Pragmatismus und dem kritischen Rationalismus.* Frankfurt/Main: Suhrkamp.

Habermas, J. (1968). *Erkenntnis und Interesse.* Frankfurt/Main: Suhrkamp.

——— (1969a). „Analytische Wissenschaftstheorie und Dialektik". In Adorno
u.a. (1969), pp. 155-191.

——— (1969b). „Gegen einen positivistisch halbierten Rationalismus". In
Adorno u.a. (1969), pp. 235-266.

——— (1971a). „Dogmatismus, Vernunft und Entscheidung — zu Theorie
und Praxis der verwissenschaftlichten Zivilisation". In Habermas (1971b),
pp. 307-335.

——— (1971b). *Theorie und Praxis.* 4. Auflage, Frankfurt/Main: Suhrkamp:
1. Auflage 1963.

Horkheimer, M. (1937). „Traditionelle und kritische Theorie". *Zeitschrift für
Sozialforschung* **6**, pp. 245-294.

——— (1967). *Zur Kritik der instrumentellen Vernunft,* Frankfurt/Main:
Fischer.

Horkheimer, M. & Adorno T. W. (1947). *Dialektik der Aufklärung.* Amsterdam: Querido.

Popper, K. R. (1957). *The Poverty of Historicism.* London: Routledge &
Kegan Paul.

——— (1961). „Selbstbefreiung durch das Wissen". In L. Reinisch, Hrsg.
(1961), pp. 100-116. *Der Sinn der Geschichte.* München: C. H. Beck.

——— (1969). „Logik der Sozialwissenschaften". In: Adorno u.a. (1969),
pp. 103-123.

———— (1973). *Die offene Gesellschaft und ihre Feinde*, Bd. 2, 3. Auflage, Bern: Francke.

———— (1979). *Ausgangspunkte. Meine intellektuelle Entwicklung*. Hamburg: Hoffmann & Campe.

57

Karl Popper and the Reconstitution of the Rationalist Left

Steve Fuller

1 Introduction: Picking up the pieces of Popper's vision

Karl Popper will be remembered as the twentieth-century figure who most successfully used a theory of science to launch a full-blown general normative philosophy. The republic of science was designed to provide the blueprint for institutionalizing civic republican democracy in society at large (Jarvie 2001). My own social epistemology increasingly draws inspiration from Popper's project (Fuller 2000a, Chapter 1; Fuller 2002, Chapter 4). Nevertheless, Popper's own aspirations have generated no end of misunderstanding, from both intended targets and potential allies. To be sure, Popper was always swimming against the current in two senses. First, he was a resolutely dialectical thinker. Most of his supposedly positive views were really negative ones in disguise: his deductivism was anti-inductivism, his liberalism anti-authoritarianism, his individualism anti-holism. Consequently, Popper often presented his views as critical sketches that presuppose acquaintance with the details and history of what is being criticized. Second, the twentieth century has accelerated the 'outsourcing' of philosophical problems, if not to the special sciences themselves, at least to philosophical sub-disciplines (or sub-philosophical disciplines?) that shadow those sciences. Thus, the readers of Popper who are interested in, say, his falsificationist methodology, his political liberalism, his philosophy of social science, and his evolutionary epistemology tend to fall into four distinct camps — none with an interest in trying to put all the pieces together.

Popper was, of course, not alone in having his legacy suffer from such fragmentation. His great nemesis of the 1960s, Frankfurt School doyen Theodor Adorno, was a similarly dialectical thinker whose high modernist aesthetics, Hegelian epistemology, Marxist sociology, and post-Holocaust ethics have also tended to attract four discrete audiences. Indeed, contrary to the tenor of the so-called *Positivismusstreit* that beset German social theory from 1961 to 1969, Popper and Adorno resembled each other much more than either resembled, respectively, the analytic philosophers of science and the cultural studies practitioners with whom they are superficially associated today. This point suggests just how much the unregulated division of labour in the sciences has undermined the quest for a holistic philosophical vision. Moreover,

in the case of Popper and Adorno, the changing political fortunes of Marxism
have added to the confusion. The result has been to divide the forces of what
I call the 'Rationalist Left' into 'critical theory' (Adorno and his Marxist followers) and 'critical rationalism' (Popper and his more liberal followers). That
such a potentially unified Rationalist Left had originally existed — at least
in Popper's mind — comes through in a series of books that have shifted the
ideological locus of Popper's thought from his professorial career in London
(allegedly under the gaze of Friedrich von Hayek) to the 'Red Vienna' of his
youth (Shearmur 1996, Notturno 1999, Hacohen 2000).

My assessment of Popper's contribution should be understood as part of
an attempt to reconstitute this Rationalist Left, wherein (I believe) lies the
fate of the premier autonomous knowledge-producing institution, the university, the governance of which provided the concrete context for the *Positivismusstreit* (Adorno et al. 1976). The failure of Adorno and Popper to resolve
— or even effectively articulate — their differences opened the door to the
rightward anti-rationalist drift that has characterized the so-called 'postmodern condition' that currently threatens the university's future. The rest of
the paper proceeds as follows. In § 2, I argue that the postmodern condition
repeats much of the cultural diversity and intellectual eclecticism present in
the Weimar Republic, which in turn bred several oppositional movements designed to provide a needed focus and direction to inquiry. Popper and Adorno
were junior members of two such oppositional movements. Both recognized
the dangers inherent in knowledge enterprises simply being allowed to follow
their inertial tendencies without concern for the larger humanizing goals of inquiry. In § 3, I show how the critical sensibility shared by Popper and Adorno
emerged from theology as the first 'scientific' form of inquiry to challenge institutionalized dogma in the eighteenth century. The logical positivists who
originally boosted Popper's philosophical reputation intended to complete this
critical process by wrenching the ideals of science from disciplinary dogmas
dressed up as metaphysics. In § 4, I provide a didactic account of the *Positivismusstreit*, highlighting where Adorno and Popper both agreed and disagreed
with each other. I conclude by showing how their generally unremarked agree-
ments provide a basis from which to launch a counter-attack on contemporary
postmodern ideology.

2 Back to Weimar? The recurrent philosophical crisis of institu-
tionalized knowledge

The idea that all philosophy is philosophy of a special science had been born
of neo-Kantian professionalization in the late nineteenth century. Once Kant
declared that ultimate reality was unknowable, the door was open to specify
the scope of inquiry in terms of human interests (Habermas 1971). Hegel
(in)famously advanced the ultimate unity of human interests. Similarly, and
to their credit, the positivists did not accept academic specialization as a
reliable indicator of distinct human interests. Not surprisingly, every self-

declared positivist — from Comte to Carnap — was an academic *persona non grata*, at least in the university systems of Europe that depended on the illusion that academic bureaucracy recapitulates scientific epistemology. And why was there this dependency? For the most part, specialization had provided academics with what biologists call 'protective coloration' from an otherwise repressive political environment: one spoke freely only about what one was qualified to speak. The cost of this strategy, however, was that it gave philosophers little incentive to rise above specialist commentary to address comprehensively — if controversially — the ends of knowledge.

The politically correct assumption at the time was that the ends of knowledge were either transcendentally presupposed by the sort of inquiry in which one was engaged or explicitly provided by the state. Both were politically safe options because neither invited critical reflection on the social conditions of one's own knowledge production. At the dawn of the twentieth century, the distinction was epitomized in Germany, respectively, by the philosopher Heinrich Rickert and the economist Gustav Schmoller (Ringer 1969). At the dawn of the twenty-first century, European science policy gurus have virtually reproduced the distinction between the transcendental and instrumental orientations in terms of 'Mode 1' and 'Mode 2' knowledge production (Gibbons et al., 1994). What is missing in both versions of the distinction is the idea of an autonomous institution that is oriented toward knowledge but is not beholden to either its resident specialists or external clients. That institution is normally called a *university*. The twentieth century's most eloquent defender of academic inquiry, Max Weber, reaffirmed 'science as a vocation' in response to the excesses represented by Rickert and Schmoller. Weber, in turn was a formative influence on Popper's sense of science's social and epistemic responsibilities.

Even if 2002 repeats the normative shortsightedness that had been on display in 1902 (the year of Popper's birth), what transpired between this repetition enabled Popper to be part of the opposition to the neo-Kantian academic establishment. The signature event was Germany's defeat in World War I, despite the wholehearted support of its scientific community, which was generally regarded as the world leader. Thus, the 1920s witnessed the revival of more searching inquiries into the ends of knowledge, often with an eye to avoiding excessively technological conceptions. This concern united the three principal movements that revolted against the neo-Kantian orthodoxy: logical positivism, the Frankfurt School, and existential phenomenology. The positivists differed from the other two in terms of their relative optimism that normatively desirable ends could be secured for knowledge without a radical rejection of the recent history of science. Whereas in the name of philosophical hygiene, Adorno and Horkheimer (1972), writing in 1943, would have us return to a time — somewhere between 1630 (Bacon) and 1830 (Comte) — just before the Enlightenment function of science shaded into an instrumental positivism; and Heidegger would take us all the way back to the pre-Socratics; those associated with logical positivism and its aftermath — Carnap, Popper,

Feyerabend, Lakatos, and Kuhn — seemed to believe that science started to
lose its way only when applications were allowed to overtake theory development, which coincided with science's entanglement in the German military-
industrial complex in the years leading up to World War I.

This difference in the depth of diagnosis — what Edmund Husserl was
calling in the 1930s 'the crisis of the European sciences' — led to a variety
of solutions to respecifying the ends of knowledge. Most radically, Heidegger
would have us 'unthink' the last two-and-a-half millennia of Western thought
by pursuing the etymological roots of fundamental philosophical concepts. The
Frankfurt School more mercifully advocated an 'ideology critique' that would
identify the sustaining forces of political economy behind the deformation of
the sciences. These were conceptualized as 'structural contradictions', which
once revealed could be resolved through some yet-to-be-disclosed political
process that, following Marx's own apocalyptic rhetoric, was sometimes called
'revolution' (though not to be confused with any of the revolutions actually
declared in the name of Marx). The logical positivists dwelled still closer to the
linguistic surface, seeing not so much a contradiction as an *underdetermination*
of knowledge claims by the evidence claimed on their behalf. Thus, on the one
hand, latter-day followers of the Frankfurt School — say, Herbert Marcuse —
might charge contemporary physics with uncritically continuing a discourse
from an earlier era when it was free inquiry into the nature of things, even
though it was now captive to the military-industrial complex. On the other
hand, latter-day followers of logical positivism — say, W. V. O. Quine — would
limit their criticism to the fact that any scientific finding might be explained in
terms of various alternative frameworks, not simply the one that has come to
be historically associated with it for whatever reason, including the ideological
ones that the Frankfurt School suspected.

The subsequent histories of mainstream analytic philosophy of science and
the Popperian heresy may be understood in terms of the radically different
conclusions they drew from what Quine (1960) called the 'underdetermination
of theory choice by data'. The mainstream — ranging from Quine to Kuhn
— has stressed the role of historical presumption, or what Nelson Goodman
(1954) called 'entrenchment', in determining how organized inquiry should
proceed. Thus, both Quine and Kuhn believed that science was an inherently
conservative process that favours local adjustments to research programmes
with proven track records — that is, until the adjustments themselves become too ad hoc or contrary to trained intuition. In short, science sticks to its
conceptual framework until it self-destructs. From this standpoint, the philosophical urge to question fundamental assumptions is most unscientific. But
whereas the analytic orthodoxy increasingly leaned on the 'empiricist' side
of logical empiricism (as logical positivism came to be known in the United
States) to offer guidance to scientific theory choice, the Popperian heterodoxy
relied on the sharpening of insight offered by the 'logical' side, which in turn
stressed the continuity of philosophy and science as forms of inquiry. Most
strikingly, Popper identified the scientific enterprise with the construction

of 'crucial experiments' designed to reveal contradictory theoretical assumptions, from which the scientist is then forced to choose. In this context, the past performance of competing research programmess is accorded much less weight, mainly because — as both Imre Lakatos and Paul Feyerabend were later to stress — track records are rational reconstructions that selectively draw from history for self-serving purposes. These histories require at least as much criticism as the scientific theories legitimated by them.

Popper's proactive strategy for challenging dominant scientific theories — including his critical attitude toward the histories that legitimate those theories — was mobilized in aid of rendering science as *game-like* as possible. The full import of this point has been rarely appreciated, mainly because it has not been taken literally, perhaps even by Popper himself. (Popper's most maverick student, Feyerabend, actually took the master's words most literally.) It means that rational decisions about science as a form of inquiry cannot be taken, unless two general conditions are met. First, tests are designed not to be biased toward the dominant theory. This is akin to ensuring that two opposing teams operate on a level playing field during a match, regardless of the differences in their prior track records. Second, the tests must not be burdened with concerns about the costs and benefits of their outcomes, especially as these pertain to the political and economic prospects of the scientists or their supporters. Allowing such considerations to influence the course of play would invite the equivalent of match-fixing. Once these two conditions of the game-like character of science are met, it becomes clear that the sense of 'progress' relevant to science is modelled on improved gamesmanship, as reflected in periodic changes in the game's rules, typically in response to tendencies that have emerged over several test matches. In short, a game advances if its players' performance expectations rise.

It is easy to see how the gaming metaphor would make science continuous with philosophy, which has also become more sophisticated over time without achieving a final goal or even accumulating results. Nevertheless, the metaphor also reveals just how remote this normative ideal of science is from actual scientific practice. In the first place, the track records of competing theories are normally brought to bear in evaluating a scientific experiment, thereby placing a much greater burden on the upstart to produce an outcome that exceeds the expectations of the orthodoxy. Secondly, an anticipated low benefit-to-cost ratio of overturning an established theory may be invoked as grounds for not even allowing an upstart's formal challenge, especially when the relevant experiment would require large public expenditures. Finally, while the norms governing scientific practice have palpably changed over time, these changes have been rarely the result of formal legislation; rather, they have reflected a statistical drift toward imitating the practice of acknowledged winners. The overall effect of these three non-game-like features of science has been to impede any global evaluation of the state of organized inquiry in relation to its putative goals. One is simply encouraged to follow the inertial tendencies of tradition. In this very important respect, science has become 'de-philosophized'.

From a strict Popperian standpoint, contemporary 'Big Science' is a regressive form of organized inquiry. This is *not* to deny that science may succeed as an economic productivity multiplier or, for that matter, a Keynesian job-creation scheme for the surplus of overeducated people. To be sure, science serves several social functions at once, but rarely all equally well. Indeed, science's success as a source of societal governance and economic growth has been at the expense of its progress as an epistemic institution. At this point, a comparison of the history of science and the history of politics may help to clarify the Popperian normative horizon. If the history of politics has made any cognitive progress at all, it has been by the introduction of periodic elections for fixed terms of office. This institution, associated with the civic republican roots of democracy, forced societies on a regular basis to think about what they have done and what they want to do next, with an explicit invitation to have someone else take them in a different direction. Of course, the citizenry may decide to retain the incumbent, but elections force this decision to be explicitly justified and not simply be allowed to proceed uncritically, as in the case of a royal dynasty. In contrast, as science has acquired more secular power, it has come to resemble just such a dynasty, in which the dominant research programmes are pursued by default, which Robert Merton (1973) has dignified as the 'principle of cumulative advantage'. The great symbol of such regressive science politics is the fixed discipline-based, peer-review structure of the US National Science Foundation, the cognitive function of which can be disturbed only 'externally', say, when Congress registers a budget deficit.

It is worth underscoring that, like most historic monarchies, the scientific establishment continues to enjoy widespread public support on most matters. Consequently, it could be claimed that it already represents 'the will of the people', and hence requires no further philosophical schemes for democratization. At this point, Popper's anti-majoritarian approach to democracy — his civic republican sensibility — comes to the fore. Many authoritarian regimes, especially the twentieth-century fascist and communist ones, could also persuasively claim widespread popular support, at least at the outset and in relation to the available alternatives. For Popper, however, the normative problem posed by these regimes is that their performance is never put to a fair test. In this respect, a disturbing feature of twentieth-century intellectual history is that the dominant figures of the two main European philosophical traditions — Ludwig Wittgenstein and Martin Heidegger — have promoted a conformist vision of social practice that accords exaggerated metaphysical significance to sheer inertia. Moreover, this point is not only anti-Popper but also anti-Adorno, though Popper and Adorno managed to stereotype each other as philosophical agents of conformity. Nevertheless, to the critical turn that both Popper and Adorno urged, Wittgenstein and Heidegger would have said, 'If it ain't broke, don't fix it'.

3 A genealogy of the critical spirit: From theology to science

An intriguing feature of Popper's epistemology that appears early in his career is the claim that we possess *a priori false beliefs*, the revision and replacement of which provides the need for the systematic pursuit of inquiry, or science. What is striking here is the idea that humanity's special interest in knowledge arises not from the spirit of curiosity but from our having been born out of sorts with reality. (For an excellent account that traces this sensibility to Popper's training in educational psychology see Hacohen 2000, Chapters 3f.) Most epistemologies presuppose more auspicious origins. For example, Descartes and Leibniz believed that our fundamental ideas — and most of our derivative ones — must be true because God created us to be in harmony with the rest of nature, indeed with the capacity to reflect its structure in our minds. As the deity receded from view in the eighteenth century, humanity lost its preordained harmony with nature but not its capacity for thriving in it. Kant granted that we have no special access to the order of nature, but in practice that implied that nature had no order other than that which our minds imposed. Of course, even if indeterminate, nature may provide considerable resistance to our impositions, which then cause us to redouble our efforts. Soon we arrive at Freud's psychic defence mechanisms. But with the development of Darwinism in the twentieth century, a happier vision of humans has returned — one common to both Jean Piaget and E. O. Wilson. It resurrects the old biological doctrine of epigenesis, so that each organism is a repository of multiple (though not indefinitely many) genetic potentials that the environment actualizes to varying degrees. Leibniz would be pleased — but not Popper, whose views were much closer to that great nemesis of Leibniz, Voltaire. In this context, we may say that Popper follows Voltaire in regarding the quest for knowledge as bearing the mark of Original Sin, albeit in a secularized form. Specifically, the price of knowing anything at all is that it will be fallible.

Here Popper continues the Enlightenment tendency to admit a broadly *tabula rasa* conception of the mind, only then to invoke it to dismiss the gullibility of first-hand reports. The controversial Biblical criticism of the period inspired by Pierre Bayle can be understood in this fashion, as well as Hume's equanimity at being an empiricist who nevertheless was sceptical toward inductive proof. Nowadays cognitive psychologists would say that the Enlightenment wits had a very vivid sense of 'confirmation bias': *The price of acquiring any knowledge at all is that it will be somehow distorted by the conditions of its acquisition; hence, criticism is the only universally reliable method.* Moreover, criticism was seen as a thoroughly *moral* stance to adopt toward a witness to some past event. For example, whereas Biblical scholars had previously regarded the Apostles' testimony of Christ's Resurrection as simply a statement of fact in which the Apostles' personal histories were epistemically irrelevant, the Enlightenment critics took seriously the Apostles' role in constructing the event as significant — and the long-term epistemic cost that heightened awareness may have incurred, even for those who take the general truth of Christianity as uncontroversial. The history of Biblical criticism, then, was one long exercise in unpacking the universal dimension of Christ's message from its historical baggage. But, as the critiques of Lessing, Kant, Hegel, and Feuerbach made increasingly clear, the very identity of Christ himself may be part of this historical baggage, which continued the historic alienation of human beings from the full realization of their species potential. The logical conclusion of this line of thought was an open endorsement of humanism, which pitted the academic pursuit of theology against the dogma of the established Christian churches. This conflict reached a head with the requirement of religious loyalty oaths for university appointments — a condition that momentously excluded the young Karl Marx from an academic life.

However, this turn of events set a precedent that went beyond Biblical criticism. When Wilhelm von Humboldt founded the University of Berlin in 1810 as an institution devoted to the unity of teaching and research, theology was included as an autonomous field of inquiry protected not *by* but *from* church doctrine. Indicative of theology's protected status was its application of the critical method to ideas that, outside the academic context, would be promulgated as part of the pastoral mission of the churches to stabilize the social order. What had not been anticipated was that the churches might be just as much in need of protection from academic criticism as vice versa; hence, the academic exclusion of the likes of Marx. By the end of the nineteenth century, a version of the same problem had begun to haunt science itself, as it started to assume religion's traditional legitimatory role in political and educational arenas. In this context, Ernst Mach extended the critical-historical method from theology and the human sciences into the natural sciences (Fuller 2000b, Chapter 2). His version of 'positivism' was largely an application of science's critical outlook to science itself. It demystified the legitimatory pretensions of science promoted by Auguste Comte's original positivism by showing that the spirit of science, no less than that of religion, is susceptible to captivity by its dominant institutions, or as we would now say, 'paradigms'. Specifically, contingencies are rewritten as necessities in the official histories of science, as uncertain tradeoffs are presented as clear decisions that presciently anticipated their consequences. Mach's critical-historical remedy was to unearth these forgotten alternatives and their unanswered objections to the dominant trajectories.

Mach's critical-historical impulse has come down to contemporary philosophers of science in a desiccated form as 'instrumentalism', the doctrine that theories are important only as summaries of established phenomena that can be used to predict and control other phenomena. The radical implication of this doctrine left unexplored is that the dominant scientific theories are not the only ones that could be used for these purposes, and indeed the theories may not have been themselves instrumental in establishing the phenomena that underwrite their current dominance. In that respect, instrumentalism was meant to be a liberating doctrine. But, as the positive face of the underdetermination thesis noted above, it has suffered a similarly conservative fate. Thus, instrumentalism's reluctance to draw specific theoretical conclusions beyond the phenomena has been read *not* as a studied agnosticism toward all theories — Mach's own view — but rather a bias toward the theories currently most closely associated with the phenomena. (Thus, in reaction, 'realism' became the self-appointed guardian of science's progressive tendencies.) It was precisely this conservative reading of instrumentalism that Popper demonized as 'inductivism'. Moreover, there is evidence that Popper himself was alive to the theological roots of Mach's critical-historical perspective, which Feyerabend (1979) made explicit in his Luther-like call for the institutional disestablishment of science. In the note to the Introduction to *The Open Society and Its Enemies* (1945) Popper acknowledges his debt to Henri Bergson for the phrase 'open society', through which Bergson (in his 1932 book, *The Two Sources of Morality and Religion*) captured the periodic phase of spiritual renewal and institutional reformation that he believed marks the history of all religions.

Mach may have failed to stem science's increasing dogmatization in the twentieth century, what both Bergson and Popper would have recognized as the 'closed society' of experts and adepts who engage in what Kuhn would later sanitize as 'normal science'. Nevertheless, Mach succeeded in instilling the critical spirit in the generation of German-speaking philosophical scientists and scientific philosophers born in the last quarter of the nineteenth century. Here I mean to include Einstein, Heisenberg, Wittgenstein, Carnap, as well as Popper — each of whom, in his own way, saw the need to break out of institutionalized modes of thought. But perhaps the most indelible legacy of Mach's influence on the philosophy of science has been the distinction between the contexts of *discovery* and *justification*. It is here that Popper and the logical positivists revealed their Enlightenment credentials most clearly. Like the Bible, an historical account of a scientist's discovery is an alloy of blindness and insight whose decontamination must precede its evaluation. The logical positivists believed that this decontamination would involve the rewriting of the original account in symbolic notation that revealed its logical structure. Popper and his followers remained sceptical of this appeal to notation, preferring instead to specify the conditions under which the account would be shown false, regardless of the authority conveyed in its original expression. In either case, these secularizations of the critical-historical method should be seen in sharp contrast with a corresponding secularization that occurred to the *hermeneutical method*, which had been traditionally used to maximize the coherence of a body of legitimatory knowledge, typically a set of canonical texts and exemplary decisions.

While the critical-historical method flourished in a university environment where knowledge *of* religion was kept separate from knowledge *for* religion, hermeneutics routinely blurred the distinction, given its aim of producing knowledge to justify the decisions taken by civil and ecclesiastical courts (Gadamer 1975). It would be difficult to overestimate the difference in outlook that resulted from this difference in the context of knowledge production. On the one hand, the critical-historical method continually strove to *disembed* truth from its specific textual and institutional containers so as to make it universally available. In this respect, the Enlightenment took over the prose-lytizing mission of Christianity. On the other hand, the hermeneutical method sought to *embed* truth in traditions of lived experience so as to consolidate the community of believers. The former understood the power of knowledge to lie in the freedom one was afforded from the domination of others, the latter in the relative advantage over others afforded to the possessor of know-ledge. In both cases, the content of knowledge may be the same, but the spirit in which one acquires and disposes of such knowledge could not be more different. Hermeneutics is ultimately backward-looking, seeking reasons for believing what is already believed, whereas critique is forward-looking, seeking reasons not to reach premature closure on belief. As we shall now see, one of the great disappointments of the contemporary period is the failure of Popper and Adorno to see themselves on the same side, as opposed to the epistemological foundationalists in both analytic and continental philosophy.

4   The Rationalist Left divided against itself: How Popper and Adorno misrecognized their common cause — and a hint on how to go forward

The *Positivismusstreit* was supposed to be about the methodology appropriate for social science research (Fuller 2003, Chapters 13f.). But as to be expected from such 'world-historic' debates, much more was said about general epi-stemological attitudes than protocols for sociological research. My account is a reflection on what is reported in Adorno et al. (1976).

After the original exchange at the 1961 meeting of the German Socio-logical Association, the rapporteur, Ralf Dahrendorf, observed that there was remarkably broad agreement between Popper and Adorno, especially in terms of targeted foes, such as the style of empirical research spawned by structural-functionalist sociology. Moreover, there was even agreement over the tendency of experimental psychology and theoretical economics to obscure, if not out-right deny, the background social conditions that ultimately determine the validity of their generalizations. In short, Dahrendorf found *both* Popper and Adorno to be staunch anti-positivists. What probably made this initial out-come seem so surprising — especially to younger listeners (Dahrendorf himself was only 32 in 1961) — was the vivid opposition between Marxism and liberal-ism that characterized the Cold War political landscape. Yet, here it is worth recalling the free intercourse between Marxism and liberalism that transpired under the rubric of 'social democracy' in the 1920s, the formative period for both Popper and Adorno (Shearmur 1996, especially Chapter 1).

What turned out to be the point of rupture between Popper and Adorno was adumbrated in their manner of expression. But even then, both Popper and Adorno shared the critic's tendency to presuppose that the audience already knows the target of criticism in some detail, so that one's own discourse becomes a series of reflections on the hidden opponent. This common feature of their discourse made it frustrating for listeners who sought constructive advice on the conduct of social research. Nevertheless, Popper and Adorno expressed their critiques in radically different forms. Popper provided a list of theses, with which he wanted Adorno to agree or disagree. In response, Adorno, seeing very little with which to disagree in what Popper had said, decided instead to dwell on the care with which one needs to formulate epistemological claims in the human sciences so that they are not captured by an unreflective and potentially oppressive positivism. In other words, Adorno could be read as criticizing Popper for not being sufficiently 'reflexive' in considering how his words might be used to legitimize projects to which he (and Adorno) would be opposed. In the second round of the debate, in which Popper and Adorno were themselves replaced by members of the younger generation — Hans Albert and Jürgen Habermas — Adorno's friendly criticism of Popper was magnified into a major ideological dispute. Habermas especially drove home the idea that Popper's 'straight-talking' approach was politically and intellectually naïve, especially during a period of increasing social unrest. It was after this explicit assertion of the *superiority* of the Frankfurt School's 'dialectical' critique that Popper's defenders began to demonize Adorno's followers as irrationalists and totalitarians. Soon thereafter came the dissolution of the Rationalist Left, in whose aftermath we labour today.

In Tables 1 and 2, I have summarized the points of disagreement and agreement between Adorno and Popper. I regard the disagreements as an 'inhouse dispute' between heirs to the critical-historical tradition in philosophy who happen to draw on different conceptual and empirical resources to stake their claims. On the other hand, the spirit that animates their common foes is radically opposed to that tradition. I shall now comment on some of the distinctions drawn in these two tables. Perhaps the most significant difference between Adorno and Popper is the source of their theories of inquiry, or sense of 'logic'. Adorno relies on Hegel, whereas Popper is clearly influenced by Frege (via Carnap and Tarski). Adorno presumes that we start with a false sense of connectedness to reality (via empiricism), which gives us a limited sense of how the world can be. In other words, we know some things only at the expense of others. Thus, the aim of inquiry becomes first to show that our empirical understanding of reality is spurious (via criticism) and then to establish a normatively acceptable understanding. However, how exactly one reaches that final stage is left radically unclear. For his part, Popper also presumes that we start with a false sense of connectedness, but it is expressed more through untested knowledge claims than unexamined experiences. Thus, in the context of testing knowledge claims, one comes to realize the extent to which our words (or concepts) distort our understanding of reality. Yet, the continual recognition of this difference, through iterations of the critical turn toward our claims, is the closest ever Popper comes to realizing an aim for inquiry. Nevertheless, while neither Adorno nor Popper provides an especially

Table 57.1   TWO MODES OF CRITIQUE:
POPPER AND ADORNO AS ENEMIES

	ADORNO	POPPER
AIM OF INQUIRY	Reunite Mind and World	Distinguish Mind and World
TEST OF A PROPOSITION	What is omitted by p that could have been said?	Under what conditions can p be falsified?
NATURE OF TRUTH	Gradually emerges in the whole	Emerges first in a part which informs the whole
STATE OF KNOWLEDGE	All disciplines are mutually alienated	Some disciplines are more self-conscious than others
NORMATIVE FUNCTION OF CONTRADICTION	Means to a higher-order synthesis	Means to a decision between alternatives
VALUE OF DIALECTICS	Self-consciousness of presuppositions	Self-consciousness of consequences
NATURE OF SOCIAL SCIENCE	Persuasive definitions that motivate social action	Hypotheses that are testable outside the context of action
PHILOSOPHICAL FLAW	Obscurantist tautology: spurious depth	Naïve falsificationism: spurious transparency
POLITICAL THREAT	Totalitarianism of the concept	Imperialism of the concept

satisfactory overall vision of inquiry for the social researcher, Popper is more sanguine than Adorno about the precedent set by the success of the physical sciences. However, Popper operates with a rather sophisticated and somewhat idealized understanding of scientific method that, for example, refuses to see empirical regularities as necessarily indicative of scientific laws, if they have not been first subjected to rigorous experimental tests.

To be sure, Adorno understood this feature of Popper's view, but (rightly, I believe) equally saw that it could be easily misunderstood as endorsing a mindlessly positivist conversion of regularities to laws. Here one could imagine Adorno asking Popper: 'If your view of physics as the vanguard of inquiry applies only under ideal experimental conditions — which hardly ever obtain in the social sciences — then what good is it as a normative standard?' But Popper could respond with his own probing query about the wisdom of Adorno's stress on the 'reflexive' dimension of social science, especially that one should assert only that which one believes will do less harm than good. From Popper's (again, equally valid) standpoint, Adorno seemed to be guilty

Table 57.2   MY ENEMY'S ENEMY IS MY FRIEND:
POPPER AND ADORNO AS ALLIES

THEIR COMMON ENEMY	THEIR COMMON AGREEMENT
Language therapy: Philosophy interrogated by common sense	*Enlightenment critique*: Philosophy interrogates common sense
The neo-Kantian disunity of science thesis, and the 'underlabouring' approach to philosophy promoted by it	Disciplinary boundaries are not epistemically significant; rather they inhibit an independent critical judgement on the state of knowledge
The logical positivist asymmetry of facts (cognitive) and values (non-cognitive)	Neither facts nor values can ever be epistemically justified though both may be vindicated in their consequences
The Mannheimian restriction of the socio-historical conditioning of knowledge to the social sciences, since the natural sciences are universal	Categories of the natural sciences are no 'closer' to reality than those of the social sciences; both involve choices that should be evaluated against their consequences
Sharp division of labour between philosophy and sociology (that is, rational versus irrational)	The relationship between philosophy and sociology is more like mind versus body (that is, form versus matter)
Philosophy degree zero: The positionless 'jargon of authenticity' (Heidegger) or 'neutral observation language' (Carnap)	Philosophy emerges dialectically against the dominant discourses of the day
Psycho-social essentialism: Society is the sum of its atomic individuals *or* individual is the sum of social roles	*Anti-essentialism*: The potential of individuals is realized in a social world that is defined by countervailing tendencies

of letting his reluctance to defend autonomous institutions of free inquiry influence his views about what is appropriate to be said. In other words, in the guise of reflexivity, Adorno allowed a dialectical point to mask his political pessimism, which only served to lay the groundwork for an esoteric elitism.

Not surprisingly, Adorno and Popper captured each other's weak points beautifully but failed to address their own. For the many social and natural scientists who found in Popper a source of legitimation, he was regarded as an accessible positivist who could be used to justify what Kuhn called 'normal science'. This was simply because Popper forcefully articulated the ideal to which many scientists aspired without openly criticizing their failure to meet it in their practice. This discrepancy eventually opened the door to the 'social studies of science', whose scandalous reputation lies precisely in revealing the myriad ways in which scientists' words and deeds are at odds with each other.

Unfortunately, most science studies practitioners respond to their discovery by suggesting that Popper-style normative discourse be junked altogether in favour of modes of legitimation that enable the scientists to carry on with their day-to-day business with the least resistance. As for Adorno, his progeny in cultural studies have tended to fixate on his defence of 'difficult writing' as a form of reflexive resistance against hegemonic ideological structures that might co-opt the words of authoritative academics for their own purposes (as arguably happened in Popper's case). However, in practice, Adorno's strategy has led to a dissipation of the critical impulse, as the criticized hegemons often have not recognized themselves in the criticism — let alone understood the criticism sufficiently to feel motivated to respond to it.

The irony of Adorno's and Popper's fate can be seen by observing their points of agreement. In particular, both Adorno and Popper regarded philosophy and sociology as mutually reinforcing, not antagonistic, disciplines. In other words, one cannot adequately theorize about the aims and norms of inquiry without considering the institutional frameworks in which they might be realized. For this reason, I have found both Adorno and Popper worthy progenitors of my own project of social epistemology. Nevertheless, neither really engaged with the policy issues that emerge from this union of philosophy and sociology, especially as they pertain to the university as an institution whose critical character rests on ensuring that the mode of knowledge production in society does not simply imitate the mode of biological reproduction. If one had to identify a minimal social precondition for the sort of critical inquiry co-championed by Adorno and Popper, this would be it, as it provides a safeguard against the simple inter-generational transmission of lore and offices along family lines. In its long history, the university has relied on a wide variety of policies for injecting a critical perspective into the knowledge system, ranging from formal examinations to affirmative action legislation. Generally speaking, these policies have made it easier for people from socially and intellectually marginal perspectives to challenge dominant groups and beliefs. Perhaps these challenges have not come strong or fast enough, but the university is unique in the consistency with which it has provided them over the last millennium (Fuller 2003, Chapter 12).

Intellectual life has paid a heavy toll for the failure of the two great modern exponents of the Rationalist Left to offer a new legitimation for the university when it was needed in the 1960s. As a result, we currently live in a polarized epistemic universe defined by Habermas (the only person who materially benefited from the *Positivismusstreit*) and Jean-Francois Lyotard, whose famous *The Postmodern Condition* was widely read as sounding the death knell of the university as a unified and monopolistic site for knowledge production. (Lyotard 1983 was written shortly after the creation of several 'new universities' in France that served to dissipate academic power in the name of 'democratization'.) In Table 3, I portray our 'post-critical' condition. It is one in which what Kant originally called 'the conflict of the faculties' no longer seems to have a place, as the university has been reduced to either a pure transcendental idea unrelated to any actual institutional manifestation (Habermas) or a pure physical space in which various unrelated knowledge-based activities are transacted (Lyotard). The clearest sign of our 'post-criticality' is the increasing tendency to sever matters of research from those of teaching, so that the production of new knowledge is increasingly placed in more elite hands (through intellectual property legislation), while the curriculum is narrowly focused on putative job skills. The idea of 'general education' as a crucible for the incorporation of new knowledge into a curriculum that would equip all students for critically facing the future is fading into the distant past. The time is ripe for the remaining forces of the Rationalist Left to consolidate around a renewed justification for the university, so that the institutional framework needed for the free pursuit of critical inquiry may be assured.

Table 57.3   THE POST-CRITICAL NON-DISPUTE OF POSTMODERNITY

	ADORNO + POPPER	HABERMAS	LYOTARD
IMAGE OF SOCIETY	Multiple conflicting factors constraining collocated individuals	Maximum tolerable individual differences within common ideals	More or less transient associations of individuals
COURSE OF INQUIRY	Difference confrontation and resolution	Difference resolution by pre-empting confrontation	Difference proliferation without expecting resolution
ATTITUDE TOWARD INQUIRY	Critical (How it might be, but is not)	Transcendental (How it must be — even if it is not?)	Empirical (How it is — but as it should be?)
ROLE OF ACADEMIC DISCIPLINES	Disciplines interrogate each other	Disciplines contribute parts to the whole	Disciplines pursue divergent interests
SOCIAL ROLE OF THE UNIVERSITY	Social space where disciplinary differences are faced and resolved	Regulative ideal toward which disciplinary interests converge by their own means	Physical site for the pursuit of diverse interests but conceptually inert

Bibliography

Adorno, T. W., Albert, H., Dahrendorf, R., Habermas, J. & Popper, K. R. (1976). *The Positivist Dispute in German Sociology*. London: Heinemann.

Adorno, T. W. & Horkheimer, M. (1972). *The Dialectic of Enlightenment*. New York: Continuum.

Bergson, H. (1932). *Deux sources de la morale et de la religion*. 12th edition. Paris: Librairie Félix Alcan. English translation 1935. *Two Sources of Morality and Religion*. London Macmillan.

Feyerabend, P. K. (1979). *Science in a Free Society* London: New Left Books.

Fuller, S. W. (2000a). *The Governance of Science: Ideology and the Future of the Open Society*. Milton Keynes: Open University Press.

———— (2000b). *Thomas Kuhn: A Philosophical History for Our Times*. Chicago: University of Chicago Press.

———— (2002). *Knowledge Management Foundations*. Woburn MA: Butterworth-Heinemann.

———— (2003). *Kuhn versus Popper: The Struggle for the Soul of Science*. London: Icon Books.

Gadamer, H.-G. (1975). *Truth and Method*. New York: Seabury Press.

Gibbons, M., Limoges, C., Nowotny, H., Schwartzman, S., Scott, P., & Trow, M. (1994). *The New Production of Knowledge*. London: Sage.

Goodman, N. (1954). *Fact, Fiction, and Forecast*. Cambridge MA: Harvard University Press.

Habermas, J. (1971). *Knowledge and Human Interests*. Boston MA: Beacon Press.

Hacohen, M. H. (2000). *Karl Popper – The Formative Years, 1902-1945. Politics and Philosophy in Pre-war Vienna*. Cambridge & elsewhere: Cambridge University Press.

Jarvie, I. C. (2001). *The Republic of Science: The Emergence of Popper's Social View of Science, 1935-1945*. Amsterdam & Atlanta: Editions Rodopi B.V.

Lyotard, J.-F. (1983). *The Postmodern Condition*. Minneapolis MN: University of Minnesota Press, 1983.

Merton, R. K. (1973). *The Sociology of Science*. Chicago: University of Chicago Press.

Notturno, M. A. (1999). *Science and the Open Society*. Budapest: Central European University Press.

Popper, K. R. (1945). *The Open Society and Its Enemies*. London: George Routledge & Sons. 5th edition 1966. London: Routledge & Kegan Paul.

Quine, W. V. O. (1960). *Word and Object*. Cambridge MA: MIT Press.

Ringer, F. (1969). *The Decline of the German Mandarins*. Cambridge MA: Harvard University Press.

Shearmur, J. F. G. (1996). *The Political Thought of Karl Popper*. London: Routledge.

58

Popper and the Rationality Principle[*]

Maurice Lagueux

Though Karl Popper's short paper on the rationality principle may not be the most frequently discussed of all of his writings on epistemological matters, it is very probably the most radically criticized. The fact that this champion of falsifiability suggested in this text not to reject a principle that he emphatically declares false has always been a source of embarrassment for his disciples and has often been characterized by his adversaries as a rather shameful theoretical development. In the present paper, I should like to show that, in spite of this fact, Popper's views on rationality, while at moments somewhat awkwardly formulated, are much more sensible than it is usually acknowledged and that they might even be considered as one of his most interesting contributions, and surely as his most underestimated one.

1 The nature of the rationality principle

But let us first recall what these views are. While frequently referring to reason and to rationality, Popper devoted only a few pages to the analysis of the rationality *principle* as such. It is well known that his ideas on the matter reached the philosophical community through the 1967 publication in French of a short paper entitled 'La rationalité et le statut du principe de rationalité', whose English version, unpublished until the 1980s, is now included in the anthology *Popper Selections*.[1] Despite multiple criticisms of the views expressed in this paper, Popper never repudiated nor revisited it. However, in 1994, the year of his death, the text from which this paper on the rationality principle was derived was finally published under the editorship of M. A. Notturno in *The Myth of the Framework* (Popper 1994), with the title 'Models, Instruments and Truth: the Status of the Rationality Principle in the Social Sciences'. A footnote at the beginning of this text confirms the fact that the paper published in French was indeed an extract from this

[*]The author would like to thank Boudewijn de Bruin, Niall Mann, Robert Nadeau, Alex Sager, and an anonymous referee for their very useful comments. Financial assistance from the SSHRC (Ottawa) was also greatly appreciated.

[1]The Editors have drawn my attention to the fact that this text appeared first on pp. 357-365 of the anthology *A Pocket Popper*, published by Fontana in 1983. However, since this edition was withdrawn some years later, and now only *Popper Selections* exists, all references in the present paper are to this 1985 edition. The page numbering of the two editions is the same.

original text, the latter being the result of a lecture delivered at Harvard in
1963. Properly speaking, the French paper on the rationality principle was
not an extract from the original; it was rather a slightly extended rephrasing
of only those ideas concerning the principle of rationality found in the earlier
paper. Nonetheless, given that the earlier text presents some points slightly
differently, it may help to clarify the later text on the rationality principle.

A first point, one which generated considerable debate, concerns the very
nature of the rationality principle. Popper proposed his own version of this
principle. His basic formulation is the following: '[a]gents always act in a manner appropriate to the situation in which they find themselves' (Popper 1983,
p. 361). This formulation was roughly the same as in the original lecture, according to which the principle requires that 'the various persons or agents
involved act *adequately*, or *appropriately* — that is to say, in accordance with
the situation' (Popper 1994, Chapter 8, § 4). With this version of the rationality principle in mind, Popper has no trouble in claiming that such a principle
is clearly false and that, consequently, it is anything but a priori. Who would
deny that people frequently act in ways that are not appropriate to the situation? Popper proposes his famous example of the 'flustered driver' who,
by trying stupidly to park his car in evidently too small a space, *manifestly
does not act in a manner that is appropriate to the situation in which he finds
himself*. Many would even observe that such inadequate behaviour associated with neurosis and other forms of abnormal behaviour is far from being
rare among human beings. Nonetheless, Popper maintains that the rationality principle is still a 'good approximation' to what takes place in human
behaviour. He argues that cases of neurosis have indeed been explained by
Freud and other psychologists, precisely with the help of their own version of
the rationality principle. In such cases, however, the principle was presented
in a significantly different version since typical responses of neurotic people
are described as appropriate to the situation '*as they see it*' (Popper 1983,
p. 363). The important modification introduced with this new version of the
principle was underscored by critiques (for example, Nadeau 1993) that concluded that a principle thus construed can no longer be false and is clearly a
priori, in a manner similar to Ludwig von Mises's version of rationality principle. It is well known that the latter is a priori since it can allow one to present
as rational any action whatsoever, since actions can always be described as
appropriate responses to situations seen in one manner or the other (on this,
see Lagueux 1995). Was Popper careless enough to refer to an a priori version
of a principle that, only a few pages earlier, he emphatically claimed to be in
no way a priori?

In a footnote to one of the paragraphs added to the text of his earlier
lecture in order to answer certain objections, Popper acknowledges without
the least hesitation that he refers successively to two versions of the principle
and he even submits a third intermediate version according to which the
situation is said to be 'as the agent could (within the objective situation)
have seen it' (Popper 1994, Chapter 8, note 19; italics suppressed). However,

even if he were fully aware of the fact that the implications of the principle differ significantly according to the version adopted, Popper formally denies that any of his three versions makes the principle a priori. He rather claims that 'we sometimes act in a manner not adequate to the situation in any of the senses (1), (2) or (3)' (ibidem). Strictly speaking then, in whatever version it is formulated, the principle is false and in none of them is it a priori. According to Popper, even versions (2) and (3) are false since they are also falsified by the case of the flustered driver. The latter sees perfectly well that he cannot park his car in such a small space, but he is irritated to such a point that he makes desperate manœuvres in order to park it there anyway, manœuvres that, afterwards, require him to struggle to drive the car out of the cramped space into which it was needlessly squeezed. The driver behaves in a manner *that is inappropriate* to the situation *even as he himself sees it.* In contrast, the pedestrian who throws himself in the way of an oncoming cyclist in order to avoid being hit by a car acts in a way that is appropriate to the situation as he himself sees it. There is no doubt that if the pedestrian had a better view, he *could* have seen also the bicycle and thus have avoided both accidents; however, taking into consideration what he actually sees, according to version (2), his response to the situation is completely appropriate. But since it cannot be excluded that, in similar circumstances, another pedestrian who was as irritated as the flustered driver could, without any understandable reasons, choose to remain in the way of the car, the principle is false and not a priori. Thus, the claim that in *almost all* cases people behave in a rational way (understood in this sense) is based on empirical knowledge. Consequently, the rationality principle according to which people *always* behave in such a way is false (and, thus, not a priori), while approximately true.

But can we really say that the flustered driver acts as he does without reason? Are we certain of the fact that he does not see the situation in a way that renders his behaviour relatively appropriate? In a previous paper (Lagueux 1993), I argued that he may, for example, derive satisfaction from the fact that his conduct demonstrates to the surrounding population that a city in which it is impossible to park one's car is a city badly administered. On this basis, I concluded that the main shortcoming of Popper's thesis was that its psychological account of what might be going on in the mind of a flustered driver was insufficient and that this example, after all, was probably not the most convincing illustration of irrational behaviour. However, the search for a better example should unavoidably lead one to the conclusion that no such example can do the job, precisely because an arbitrarily imagined example can always be arbitrarily construed in such a way that it associates the behaviour involved with a relatively appropriate reason. Even psychologists who have experimentally challenged the rationality of human behaviour tend to invoke another form of rationality to explain their findings. For example, in a famous paper documenting the fact that people's decisions are frequently influenced illogically by the 'frame' in which the situation is presented, Amos Tversky and Daniel Kahneman explain that people are not 'necessarily irrational', since the incriminating behaviour can at least sometimes 'be justified by reference to the mental effort required to explore alternative frames and avoid potential inconsistencies' (Tversky and Kahneman 1981/1986, p. 138). This is consonant with Popper's view, according to which testing a theory is testing a theory as a whole, in such a way that it is always possible to conclude that any alleged refutation of rationality instead refutes only a theory consisting of *a model plus the rationality principle*. If this is true, modifying the model (for example, including in it the compulsion to denounce the city administration) may be sufficient to save the rationality principle. Clearly, for Popper, the rationality principle is false not by virtue of having been formally falsified, but because it would be extravagant to attribute rationality to any action of any agent unless doing this on an a priori basis, which is judged groundless. Therefore, the point is not to find a better example of irrationality but to decide at a more general level whether one is correct to claim a priori, as von Mises did, that all actions are rational simply because they are purposeful. Naturally, if one considers that an action is purposeful (and therefore rational) by definition, such a claim can be established a priori, but the resulting tautology can hardly be the basis of an empirical science.

For Popper, social sciences must be empirical sciences, but they must nonetheless be based on a rationality principle that stipulates that, in fact, human beings are *constituted* in such a way that they usually adapt their actions to what they see as their own interests. Considered in this fashion, this principle cannot be characterized as a priori. Let us try to illustrate why, with the help of a thought experiment. In order to eliminate any confusion between a priori reasoning and introspection (or internal experience), let us consider an inhabitant of Sirius who is capable of deduction and induction but unable to experience self-interest. Arriving on planet Earth, this newcomer would be unable to conclude through a priori reasoning that (a) human beings are constituted in such a way that, depending on *the way they see* their situation, they can evaluate what is called their self-interest; and that (b) they systematically tend to adapt their actions to what is required by that self-interest. At first glance, such newcomers from outer worlds might sooner think that human beings are absolutely irrational (or rather non-rational) organisms in a way similar to the way most plants and animals appear to us. However, through careful observation of the regularities in human behaviour, they could *arrive at the empirical conclusion* that this behaviour is goal-oriented and not mechanically commanded, and from this they could induce that human beings are rational. With still more careful observation, they could even observe that very often human beings *see their situation in an erratic way* and that, in these circumstances, their (still rational) behaviour is adapted accordingly. Occasionally, however, they would have no other choice but to acknowledge that human behaviour is such that it appears irremediably stupid. Given these conclusions, they could, if their aim were to understand human behaviour, adopt empirically a rationality principle even if experience has convinced them of the fact that this principle is approximately but not universally true. Such is the kind of principle that, according to Popper, is required by any model devised by social scientists.

If we grant Popper the empirical character of each version of his principle, we may raise the following question: how can Popper modify so freely the very meaning of a principle deemed to be so fundamental, in such a way that he can use simultaneously three versions of it? The answer must be looked for in his notion of model. According to Popper, in its very fabric, the model of an explanatory theory includes, in typified form, all initial conditions characterizing the situation in which the phenomenon to be explained takes place. This means that what the agent sees may or may not be considered as part of the objective situation that the model describes. Therefore, from a formal point of view, all three formulations of the principle are not as different as they appear, since they differ only in their adaptation to the variable extension of the knowledge that is included in the relevant model describing the situation. The first version supposes that the agent has true knowledge; what Popper calls the second version implies that the alleged knowledge is partially wrong; and the third version corresponds to an intermediate case. In all cases, the rationality principle claims that the agent will act in a way appropriate to the state of this knowledge. For Popper, the important point is that, regardless of whether or not this model includes the (possibly incorrect) way in which the agent sees the situation, the model cannot work by itself. It needs to be animated by something else, in the same way that a mechanical model explaining the movement of the planets has to be animated by 'Newton's universal laws of motion' (Popper 1983, p. 358). But, with almost all models implemented in social sciences, the animation is provided by the rationality principle. Thus, a model that includes only objective aspects of the situation needs to be animated by the basic version of the principle according to which 'agents always act in a manner appropriate to the situation in which they find themselves'. But if one includes also subjective aspects of the situation in one's model, more precisely if one includes in it a description of the way in which the agent sees the situation, then such a model needs to be animated by the version of the same principle according to which 'agents always act in a manner appropriate to the situation *as they see it*'. Since Popper is not obliged to decide to what extent the content of the model should be pursued, he is not obliged to decide which version of the rationality principle should be used, or, if one prefers, he is not obliged to decide to what kind of description of the situation this principle should correspond.

2 Why immunize the rationality principle?

For Popper, the important point is that an explanatory model in social sciences cannot work without the help of the rationality principle, whose content, while empirical, tends to be minimal to the point of being 'almost empty'. Since refinements in social sciences model making imply that models include more and more detailed pictures of situations, the rationality principle tends to be reduced to the simple idea that the agent actually agrees with what is clearly presented by the model as the appropriate thing to do. It is clear that for Popper the rationality principle as such need not include more than this, since all other physical and psychological aspects of the situation are preferably taken over in typified form by the model itself. In this context, it is not surprising that in both versions of his text, Popper claims that this minimal rationality principle 'has nothing to do with the assumption that men are rational in this sense — that they always adopt a rational attitude' (Popper 1983, p. 365). Since Popper takes the trouble to specify 'rational in this sense', it is legitimate to ask more precisely what sense is in question. Clearly, given that Popper associates 'this sense' with 'a rational attitude', the sense in question is one that he attributes to the notion of 'rationality as a personal attitude' in the paragraph preceding this last quotation: 'Rationality as a personal attitude is the attitude of readiness to correct one's beliefs. In its intellectually most highly developed form, it is the readiness to discuss one's beliefs critically, and to correct them in the light of critical discussions with other people.' (Popper ibidem), a view that is closely connected to his 'critical rationalism'. Thus, it is clear — and Popper does not seem to say anything else — that the rationality principle (stating that individuals act in a manner appropriate to their situation) 'has nothing to do' with this tendency to correct oneself by criticism which, for Popper, constitutes authentic rationality. Popper immediately emphasizes that, far from being as rich as this, the principle in question is only a 'minimum principle': 'it assumes no more than the adequacy of our actions to our problem situations as we see them' (ibidem) or, to put it in the terms that I used above, it assumes that the agent will agree with what is clearly presented by the model itself as the appropriate thing to do.

But, as we have seen, nothing can assure us that the agent will actually agree accordingly, even in such a situation; consequently, it is clearly false to maintain that agents will always choose to act in the appropriate fashion. At this point, the question to be raised is one that has so often been formulated as a decisive objection to Popper's view (for example, Hands, 1985): why does the champion of falsificationism refuse to reject a principle that he himself says is false? Given that Popper attributes to the rationality principle such a determinant role (from a methodological point of view), one could easily think that Popper's decision to immunize this principle against falsification is due to the fact that such a principle is nothing but a *methodological* principle somewhat similar to Popper's famous methodological principle, so convincingly defended in *The Logic of Scientific Discovery* (1959), that stipulates that, given equally successful hypotheses, a preference must be granted to those that are the most easily falsifiable. In the two cases, we should be dealing with a methodological postulate whose empirical testing would be absurd. But such an easy way out is not accepted by Popper who rejects it in the most unequivocal terms. When called to say whether the rationality principle is a 'methodological principle' or an 'empirical conjecture', his answer is that '[t]his second case is precisely the one that corresponds to my own view of the status of the rationality principle: I regard the principle of adequacy of action (that is the rationality principle) as an integral part of every, or nearly every, testable social theory' (Popper 1983, p. 361; see also Popper 1994, Chapter 8, § 12). He firmly maintains this point because he sees the rationality principle as an integral part of any empirical theory in social sciences, that is, as its animating part, just as the laws of motion are an integral part of Newton's astronomical theory. In contrast, a *methodological* principle *cannot be* a part of a scientific theory whose parts must be, according to him, empirical and hypothetical rather than a priori.

But if the rationality principle cannot be *itself* a methodological principle (or a methodological rule), the *decision* to immunize it can nonetheless be considered as based on a methodological principle. As Popper says, 'if a theory is tested, and found faulty, then we have always to decide which of its various constituent parts we shall make accountable for its failure' (Popper 1983, p. 362). The methodological decision has simply to be disentangled from the rationality principle itself since, in contrast with the latter, the former is not part of the empirical theory. Thus to remove any trace of contradiction from Popper's views on the rationality principle, it remains only to show that the methodological decision according to which the rationality principle (while being an empirical hypothesis) must be immunized against falsification is compatible with the methodological decision according to which preference must be granted to hypotheses that are the most easily falsifiable. However, presenting the decision to immunize the rationality principle as a methodological rule may look paradoxical since, according to Popper, the supreme rule 'says that the other rules of scientific procedure must be designed in such a way that they do not protect any statement in science against falsification' (Popper 1959, § 11). But the point is that, in Popper's mind, the principle of rationality is not protected against falsification by the decision to maintain it since, according to him, it is already falsified. Far from protecting scientific statements against falsification, this decision, according to Popper, allows us to falsify the other statements of the model, the only ones that are meaningfully falsifiable.

There is little doubt that it was in order to show that his methodological decisions were inspired by a consistent approach that, in a paragraph of fifteen lines, Popper expounded four arguments (Popper 1983, p. 362) that refer to the fact that the fundamental role of the rationality principle is to help us to learn more about the world. For Popper, falsifiability is nothing but a means to promote our understanding by making theories testable rather than arbitrary and ad hoc. But these arguments suggest that, for the sake of understanding, dismissing the rationality principle is not recommendable even if it is not universally true, since replacing it by a principle admitting irrationality would open the door to arbitrariness and adhocness and would make true understanding impossible. Indeed, if irrationality could be invoked in order to explain some social phenomena, any kind of irrational behaviour could be arbitrarily appealed to in an ad hoc fashion in the case of each unusual social phenomenon to be explained. In fact, serious social scientists have understood this point, and it is for this reason that almost all alternative theories proposed by them invoke one form or another of the rationality principle and exclude facile appeals to irrationality. For Popper this fact clearly illustrates that it is useless to reject the rationality principle if the goal of this rejection is to improve our understanding with the help of a better theory, since alternative theories worthy of consideration equally make use of the same principle. Moreover, according to Popper, falsifiability is an attractive idea because it makes possible testability and, consequently, better knowledge and better understanding. However, since different component parts of a theory cannot be falsified through the same test and since the theory to be tested is nothing but a model composed of a number of various elements to which an animating principle is added, when the test of a theory fails, one must choose between declaring false either one of the model's elements or the rationality principle that animates it. But, as Popper asks, what do we gain by blaming the rationality principle as such? We already know that it is false, or, at the very least, we know that it is not universally true. To observe, on the basis of various tests, that in some (relatively isolated) cases, it does not work, teaches us nothing that we did not already know. Nor would it provide us with information which could help us to improve our theory. In contrast, testing certain of the component parts of the model itself can be very instructive and very helpful if we want to modify our theory in order to improve it. It is in this fashion that we can improve our knowledge and our understanding. Popper seems to conclude that, given this situation, we lose nothing by maintaining a false principle whose rejection, in contrast, would leave us at a dead end. Consequently, if our goal is knowledge and understanding, maintaining a (false) principle that allows us to construct progressively more accurate explanatory models would appear to be a good decision.

3 The particularity of the rationality principle

These arguments were designed in order to justify the methodological decision not to treat the rationality principle in the same way as any other (declared false) part of a theory. However, even if they highlight some of the non-negligible advantages of immunizing the rationality principle, one might easily remain unconvinced by them since they do not reveal the particularity of the principle that justifies its treatment in such a way. There is little doubt that if Popper avoids particularizing this principle too much, it is because, according to him, it plays exactly the same animating role that animating principles, such as Newton's universal laws of motion, play in physicists' models. Indeed, before introducing the comparison between these two kinds of models, Popper says that 'it is important to realize the close similarity of explanations in the social sciences with explanations ... in the natural sciences' (Popper 1983, p. 358). However, notwithstanding this parallelism, it is clear that Popper would agree that it would not make sense to immunize in the same way Newton's laws of motion if ever they were declared to be false. More important, even if Newton's laws animate the planetary model referred to by Popper, they do not animate all or almost all of the models constructed by natural scientists, whereas, according to Popper himself, it would be difficult to conceive of a model in the social sciences that would not be animated by the rationality principle. Thus, one must admit that the rationality principle occupies a place in the social sciences without an exact equivalent in the natural sciences. Popper was too committed to the unity of science to give too much significance to this singular character of the social sciences and to characterize the rationality principle accordingly, but his 'situational analysis' theory draws sufficient attention to some specific features of these sciences. Even if, for these reasons, Popper does not seek to determine what accounts for the exceptional role played by the rationality principle, other theoreticians have understood that this principle occupies an exceptional place because it is a condition of intelligibility of any phenomenon that derives from human action. As was clearly seen, for example, by Austrian economists such as Menger, Mises, Hayek, and Lachmann, a social phenomenon is explained when it is reduced to the consequences (usually unwanted) of human actions that are intelligible. And human actions are intelligible — they can be understood — when they are deemed to be rational, when they are motivated by reasons, which is to say when they are appropriate responses to situations as seen by those who make them. Were an action declared irrational in the sense of not being motivated by any reason whatsoever, such an action would clearly be unintelligible. How, indeed, could one pretend to understand an action and at the same time to declare it irrational or to declare it a totally inappropriate response to the situation even as the agent sees it?

But maintaining this principle after acknowledging that it is not universally true is simply to claim, as Popper did, that, in spite of the fact that strictly irrational decisions occur, human actions are nonetheless normally understandable. It is to claim that human actions are normally intelligible, not because they can be subsumed under a universal law, but because they can be subsumed under the principle of rationality. Being subsumed under this principle means that they are intelligible because they are rational. Natural phenomena cannot be explained in such a fashion because they do not derive from intelligible human actions. While reluctant to admit that the social sciences could, for this reason, differ radically from the natural sciences, Popper clearly understood that the rejection of such a principle (for being not universally true) would lead to the rejection of the very possibility of understanding social phenomena.

For sure, one might prefer another type of science, which would not invoke notions like rationality and understanding. Accordingly, it seems that Popper's reluctance to push far enough the analysis of the specific character of the rationality principle is due to his own desire to see both the natural and the social sciences put on the same footing. However, while it is not strictly impossible that a science of social phenomena based on neurophysiological findings coupled with natural selection might be developed in the future without leaving any role for the rationality principle, almost all explanatory theories of social sciences developed up to now (or, at the very least, up to Popper's time) are based on this principle. Popper, who clearly understood this, managed to underscore as much as possible the parallelism between the natural sciences and this type of social science. To do this, he had first to depsychologize the rationality principle. Social sciences are based on understanding human actions, but this view should not, in his mind, be associated with either a Diltheyan *Verstehen* or a Collingwoodian knowledge of actions from inside. The tendency to do what looks appropriate, which is precisely what the rationality principle highlights, does not imply a kind of psychological introspection. It is for this reason that Popper reduced the rationality principle to a minimal principle requiring nothing more than an almost mechanical response to a situation. What allows Popper to say that such a mechanical response should be an appropriate one is not a psychological analysis of what is going on in the mind of the agent, but rather the fact that the situation is modelled in such a way that the model includes all the features that should normally bring the agent — of whom it is only required that he attend to his own interest — to react in the very way that the model itself presents as appropriate.

Thus, what is required of the rationality principle is simply the idea that the agent is not stupid enough to avoid responding in a way that, given the situation as he sees it, corresponds to his own interest. The rationality principle thus construed is really 'almost empty' as Popper says; in fact, it excludes only sheer stupidity. It is true that sheer stupidity exists in human behaviour — that we are convinced of this in the case of the flustered driver or on the basis of any other consideration, matters little — and it is for this reason that Popper says that the rationality principle is false; however, such stupidity is far from being prevalent among human beings, and it is for this reason that Popper characterizes the rationality principle as a 'good approximation' to the truth. Popper did not associate explicitly his minimal version of the rationality principle with the non-stupidity of most human beings, but most compelling explanations provided by economics, throughout its history, can be reduced to theories based on a rationality principle understood in this minimal fashion.

To take only one of my favourite examples, consider Turgot who, as early as 1766, argued that a 'current price' *has* to prevail in a market (and not simply *should* prevail, as earlier 'just price' theorists maintained): '...if one [of the wine sellers] is not willing to give more than *four pints* for *a bushel*, the Proprietor of the corn will not give him his corn, when he comes to learn that someone else will give him *six* or *eight pints* for the same bushel' (Turgot 1898, p. 29). Turgot's argument was clearly based on the fact that people are rational in the sense that they are not stupid. Who would be stupid enough to give one bushel of wheat in exchange for only four pints of wine when it is well known that other wine sellers would be happy to give six or eight pints for the same bushel? Construed in this way the rationality principle implicitly but clearly used by Turgot is as minimal as the one proposed by Popper. It is clear that such a principle is false since there are always people stupid enough to give something in exchange of four pints even when they know that they can get six or eight pints for the same thing (and this even when the model is conceived of in such a way that altruism is excluded), yet it remains an approximation good enough to be used by almost all explanatory theories of economics. It has been argued in Lagueux (2004) that almost all the explanatory theories of classical, Marxian, and Austrian economists are clearly based on such a principle, and that neoclassical theories are also based on it, even if these latter are usually modelled in such a way that it is strict maximization that is presented to non-stupid agents as the appropriate thing to do. In each of these cases, models must be animated by a minimal principle that says only that people are normally not stupid enough to refrain from doing what those models present as the appropriate thing to do. Since almost all economic theories and most of social science theories can be construed in this way, it would appear reasonable to conclude that Popper's highly criticized ideas on the rationality principle, far from being a shameful part of his work, are rather the result of a shrewd though somewhat sketchily exposed analysis of the state of social sciences.

Bibliography

Hands, W. (1985). 'Karl Popper and Economic Methodology, A New Look'. *Economics and Philosophy* **1**, pp. 83-99.

Lagueux, M. (1993). 'Popper and the Rationality Principle'. *Philosophy of the Social Sciences* **23**, pp. 468-480.

———— (1995). 'How Could One Be Irrational?' In M. Mathieu & R. S. Cohen, editors (1995), pp. 177-192. *Quebec Studies in the Philosophy of Science*, Book II. Dordrecht: Kluwer Academic Publishers.

———— (2004). 'The Forgotten Role of the Rationality Principle in Economics'. *Journal of Economic Methodology* **11**, pp. 31-51.

Nadeau R. (1993). 'Confuting Popper on the Rationality Principle'. *Philosophy of the Social Sciences* **23**, pp. 446-467.

Popper, K. R. (1959). *The Logic of Scientific Discovery*. London: Hutchinson. Expanded English translation of K. R. Popper (1935). *Logik der Forschung*. Vienna: Julius Springer Verlag.

———— (1967). 'La rationalité et le statut du principe de rationalité'. In E. M. Claassen, editor (1967), pp. 142-150. *Les fondements philosophiques des systèmes économiques. Textes de Jacques Rueff et essais rédigés en son honneur 23 août 1966*. Paris: Payot.

———— (1983). *A Pocket Popper*. London & Glasgow: Fontana Press. Now available as *Popper Selections*. Princeton NJ: Princeton University Press, 1985.

———— (1994). *The Myth of the Framework*. London: Routledge.

Turgot, A. R. J. (1898). *Reflections on the Formation and the Distribution of Riches*. Translated by W. J. Ashley. New York: Macmillan & Co.

Tversky, A. & Kahneman, D. (1981). 'The Framing of Decisions and the Psychology of Choice'. *Science* **211**, pp. 453-458. Reprinted in J. Elster, editor (1986), pp. 123-141. *Rational Choice*. New York: New York University Press.

59

Popper's Conception of the Rationality Principle in the Social Sciences[*]

Boudewijn de Bruin

In this paper I shall discuss and criticize Popper's conception of the rationality principle in the social sciences. First, I sum up Popper's outlook on the *role* of a principle of rationality in theorizing in the social sciences. Then, I closely and critically examine his view on the *status* of the principle of rationality concluding that the arguments in favour of Popper's view are quite weak. Finally, I contrast his standpoint with an alternative conception. This, I shall show, may help us understand better Popper's reasons for adopting his perspective on rationality.

1 Introduction

Popper's *kritizistische Methodenlehre* of trial and error applies to natural and social sciences alike. As a solution to some problem P_1 researchers develop a tentative theory TT_1. This theory is put to severe tests that may result in its refutation by pointing out errors. Such an elimination of errors EE leads to a new problem situation P_2 challenging the researchers to come up with a new tentative theory TT_2, and so on and so forth. But social and natural sciences not only share the *formal* aspects of scientific progress captured by this 'tetradic schema', they are also similar on a *substantial* level. A theory, roughly speaking, is a *model* together with a set of forces, principles, and laws that make it run and, to use Popper's term, 'animate' it. It is a pack of initial conditions together with universal laws.

The interrelations between models and animating forces in the social sciences are given by Popper's 'logic of the situation'. Roughly, to explain an action of a (social) agent the social scientist has to provide an analysis of the situation in which the agent acted. This is the model. The rationality principle animates this model by declaring that the agent acted adequately and rationally in the situation.

[*]I should like to thank Maurice Lagueux, Martin Stokhof, and two anonymous referees for their written comments on an earlier version of this paper. I should like to thank also Philippe Mongin for inspiring discussions of his paper on the principle of rationality and the unity of the social sciences.

Popper explained the details of this view in his 1963 lecture at Harvard, and to some extent also in *The Poverty of Historicism*.[1] Here follow some brief notes on model and animating force.

The *model*, that is the situation in which an agent is located, Popper characterizes by (a) the physical and social restrictions the possible actions of the agent are subject to, (b) the goals or aims of the agent, and (c) the knowledge and information the agent possesses. The crucial task for a social scientist in giving a situational analysis is to describe and characterize this situation. For Popper this amounts to a 'logical' analysis. The aim is not to give a 'psychological' description of the three components of a situation by, for instance, retrieving the goals an agent was consciously aware of, but rather to lay bare by logical analysis a whole scale of (possibly unconscious) goals that are relevant for the situation and determine it *objectively*.[2]

The *animating force*, that is the rationality principle, Popper describes as 'the assumption that the various persons or agents involved act adequately or appropriately — that is to say, in accordance with the situation' (1994, p. 169). This principle has to be interpreted 'logically' as well. It 'does not play the role of an empirical explanatory theory' (ibidem) because social theorists should 'pack [their] whole explanatory theory into an analysis of the situation — into the model' (ibidem).

2 Why Popper treated the rationality principle as unfalsifiable

Could an animating force that does not play an empirical role in a theory possibly make sense in the light of Popper's views on falsifiability? 'My views on the rationality principle', Popper writes in a section added later to the 1963 Harvard lecture, 'have been closely questioned' (ibidem, p. 177). His interlocutors were not satisfied with his description of the rationality principle as a non-empirical, metaphysical, or methodological principle rather than as an empirical hypothesis. What was his answer? First, modifying his original statement a little, he asserts that the rationality principle has, indeed, to be viewed as empirical. He regards it 'as an integral part of every, or nearly every, testable social theory' (ibidem). Second, he puts forward and defends the methodological rule that whenever social theories are falsified the rationality

---

[1]I am very grateful to David Miller for giving me access to copies of typescripts of various versions of Popper's paper, as well as for providing me with the following historical data. 'Models, Instruments, and Truth' is based on a lecture that Popper delivered at the Department of Economics at Harvard University on 26 February 1963. In 1963 and 1964 two sections were added. A small extract was circulated in the London School of Economics in 1967 and 1968. This English extract was translated into French and published as 'La rationalité et le statut du principe de rationalité' (1967). (The name of the translator is unknown.) A Spanish translation of the French translation appeared a year later. A revised version of the English extract was published in Popper (1983). An even further revised version then appeared under the title of 'Models, Instruments, and Truth', in Popper (1994). This is the version I shall quote from.

[2]The different definitions of 'situation' Popper introduces are examined in M. Lagueux, 'Popper and the Rationality Principle', this volume, Chapter 58. Cp. Jarvie (1998).

principle should *not* be blamed. It is a '*sound methodological policy* to decide not to make the rationality principle ... accountable' (ibidem, author's emphasis).

This, it seems to me, is a coherent answer to the question. Its plausibility, however, depends on the plausibility of the methodological rule Popper introduces. I shall discuss the arguments Popper gives in its favour, but before doing that I shall briefly discuss Popper's notion of methodological rule.

In *The Logic of Scientific Discovery* (1935/1959) Popper introduces a hierarchy of methodological rules. At the top of this hierarchy stands a 'supreme rule' guiding all other rules. Lower rules are accepted when they conform to higher rules. The hierarchy is not a deductive system; methodological rules are not deduced from other rules. Furthermore, they do not regulate the transformation of linguistic formulas as the rules of logic do. They are rather conventions comparable with the constitutive rules of chess. This means that accepting or rejecting a methodological rule is a human *decision*.

The supreme rule that lies at the top of Popper's system is prompted by the demarcation principle that identifies the empirical character of a system of their testability, that is, with their falsifiability. The supreme rule says that the other methodological rules 'must be designed in such a way that they do not protect any statement in science against falsification' (1935/1959, § 11). In other words, a methodological rule has to contribute to the testability of theories.

What are we to think of the rule not to give up the rationality principle? Immunizing the rationality principle against falsification, does that really add to the testability of social theories? Let us take a closer look at the arguments Popper gives for this methodological rule. I shall treat them relatively elaborately because I think that they form an important aspect of his views of rationality. There are five of them, and I shall comment upon them in passing.

(1) *Blaming the model for falsification of the theory teaches us more than blaming the rationality principle* (1994, p. 177). Popper suggests that learning that the rationality principle is false provides us with less insight than learning that the situational model is no good. Once we blame the model, we learn that something was wrong with the original sketch of the situation, and that to come up with a new tentative theory we have deepen our analysis of the agents' restrictions, knowledge, and goals.

The argument seems plausible, but only given that we adhere to the logic of situational analysis. For Popper does not compare social theories of *his* kind with those resulting from competing methodologies where the animating forces (but also the models) may very well be quite different.[3] Comparing an alternative social theory with one of Popper's kind, however, would mean comparing the alternative with the (Popperian) *combination* of model and animating force. In such a comparison a *separation* of the model and the rationality principle would not make sense.

---

[3] One example from many is Boudon (1990).

(2) *The model is better testable than the principle of rationality* (1994, p. 178). This is a rather unfortunate, and strictly speaking senseless, reformulation of the first point. Again, to test the principle of rationality you need the situational analysis. Ironically enough, fewer than ten lines below the statement of this argument Popper remarks that 'we must not forget that we can test the theory only as a whole' (ibidem).

(3) *The principle of rationality, though false, is sufficiently close to the truth* (ibidem). That is, an empirical refutation of a social theory (model plus principle) will generally be due to the model rather than to the principle: 'the main responsibility will normally attach to the model' (ibidem). Again this does not make sense by the book, since the principle of rationality is not refuted on its own but always together with a model. If, moreover, Popper means that social scientists hold the model liable in most of the cases, then that is nothing less and nothing more than the statement that social scientists normally follow the methodological rule he wishes to defend. That is, however, not a good argument since an argument should show us that the methodological rule is compatible with rules higher up in the hierarchy.

(4) *Giving up the principle of rationality leads to arbitrary model-building* (ibidem). It is clear though that giving up the principle of rationality means giving up situational logic. To see, then, whether the models become arbitrary we should need a comparison with other methodologies — with problems as before.

(5) *Most social theories share the principle of rationality* (ibidem). That means that theories that survive testing will include the principle of rationality most of the time. The point of this argument seems to be that the methodological rule is not very far-reaching in the sense that it rules out only a small fraction of contemporary social science. Again, though showing that the acceptance of the methodological rule will not lead to a universal reformulation of the social sciences, it does not make clear what is wrong with theories inspired by methodologies that are not based on the principle of rationality or assign a different role to it.

3 An alternative picture

The conclusion is that Popper's answer to his interlocutors' worries about the status of the rationality principle, although coherent, is not backed up by very plausible arguments. In the remainder of this paper, I shall examine the reasons Popper may have had to answer in this way. My strategy is to contrast Popper's position with a competing picture. I shall start with a short presentation of this alternative. Then, I shall lay bare the motivation behind Popper's own answer by showing that particular views — first, on *action*, second, on the *unity of the sciences*, and third, on the *falsifiability of rationality* — prevented him from choosing the alternative. I should emphasize that it is *not* my intention here to defend the contestant; it appears here only as part of an exegetical strategy.

To introduce the alternative view on the principle of rationality, I start with a brief recapitulation of Popper's conception of the principle of *causality*; that is, the assertion that every event can be causally explained or deductively predicted. Popper (1935/1959), §.12, mentions two interpretations of this statement. It is *tautological* if you mean only that a causal explanation can be constructed; it is *metaphysical* (that is, not falsifiable empirically) if it means that all events are ruled by laws. In Popper's philosophy the principle of causality obtains the form of a methodological rule. The rule says that one should always try to explain in causal terms and to search for laws (ibidem, § 78), and that one should try to leave nothing unexplained (ibidem, § 36). This rule is, of course, part of the hierarchy of methodological rules discussed before with the supreme rule of falsifiability on top. A bit lower we find, inspired by the *principle* of causality, the *rule* of causality; it imposes on science (natural as well as social!) the *formal* restriction to work in a deductive-nomological framework (ibidem, § 12). Much lower, inspired by the *principle* of rationality, we find the *rule* not to give up the rationality principle; it imposes restrictions on the *content* of social theories (to wit, that they all contain the rationality principle as the animating force).

The alternative outlook on the rationality principle that I wish to introduce as part of my exegetical strategy, now, *raises* the rule of rationality to the same level in the hierarchy as the rule of causality; it renders it a similarly *formal* restriction on theories. This alternative methodological rule says that one should always try to explain human behavior in terms of reasons. It is *not*, or at least not immediately, a restriction on the content of social theories.[4]

To show why Popper did not advocate this alternative formulation of the methodological rule, I shall conclude with a discussion of his ideas on action, on the unity of the sciences, and on the falsifiability of the rationality principle.

(1) *Action* — The tetradic schema of theoretical rationality as a process of trial and error (the conception of science as problem solving) just as well applies to the practical rationality of *actions*, or so Popper claims. Whereas in the theoretical case researchers develop a tentative theory as a solution to some (scientific) problem, in the practical case agents choose actions as solutions to (practical) problems. And where tentative theories have to be adequate, actions have to be adequate as well; that is, agents act rationally or adequately in the situation they face.

The analogy between theoretical and practical rationality, however, works well only for the first two steps of Popper's tetradic schema. Having put forward a tentative theory to some problem, the third step of error elimination has the researchers severely test their tentative theory. By pointing out errors such testing may result in falsification of the theory. What counts as a falsification? To avoid a *psychological* foundation of knowledge ('the doctrine that statements can be justified not only by statements but also by perceptual

---

[4]I am here indebted to Mongin (2002).

experience' (1935/1959, §25), Popper takes a falsification to be a clash between so-called 'basic statements' and the logical consequences of the theory;
not, that is, a clash between experience and the theory. To avoid *subjectivism*,
the researchers have to agree intersubjectively on the truth values of the basic
statements.

Whether a *theory* is an adequate answer to a problem depends, then, on
whether it clashes with sentences intersubjectively agreed on. Can we say
something similar for *actions*? I believe we cannot. Where a clash between a
theory and a basic statement is a simple and objective matter of logic, it is not
at all clear where to look for the analogues of clashing in the practical case; and
where to look for the analogue of intersubjectivity, and the analogue of basic
statements. A strict and literal application of the tetradic schema to practical
rationality in which adequacy of action is defined in terms of intersubjective
falsifiability does not make sense.

Falsification *in a broader sense* is to show that a proposed solution for a
problem is no good. An action would then be falsified (and hence inadequate)
if it did not solve the problem. But this less strict reading of the analogy does
not get us very far either. We cannot take it to be the case, for instance,
that an action solves a problem whenever the agent's goals are reached, as it
is quite possible that the problem situation can impose such restrictions on
the agent that he can make the achievement of his goals only more or less
probable (but not certain). And conversely, the very reaching of a goal does
not make the action performed an adequate solution to the problem because
the goal may have been reached *by accident*, or with the help of fate.

The conclusion is that the analogy between theoretical and practical rationality does not hold water. Whereas for theoretical rationality Popper uses
a clear and well-defined notion of adequacy in terms of intersubjective falsifiability, for practical rationality he does not provide us with more than a
primitive notion. Popper does not seem to be aware of this problem, and that
explains, I believe, why he does not choose the alternative rule of rationality
in terms of reasons.

A related sign of the problems of his views can be seen in his illustrations of human actions studied by sociologists, historians, or anthropologists.
Popper almost always uses examples of a rather *theoretical* character. He describes Galileo's allegedly irrational choice of a theory of tides that denies
any lunar influence as a choice that, given Galileo's knowledge and scientific
aims, was entirely rational. He describes the misconceptions about reality of
the 'madman' as a rational reply to situations that are in some sense rare
and pathological. He describes a general's acts of war as the rational result
of his 'limited experience, limited or overblown aims, limited or overexcited
imagination' (1994, p. 178). Certainly these cases are all examples of decisions that can be explained as a rational and adequate reply to a particular
problem situation; situations, however, in which the problem is to choose a
theory rather than an *action*. Certainly the three components of a situational

analysis (environmental restrictions, goals, information) can easily be given; Popper's examples, however, are no ordinary instances of agents acting. What these examples lack is a rather essential feature of human action: the wish to change the world in certain respects.

(2) *Unity of Science* — The rule of causality is the driving unifying force in Popper's system of science. It requires that all explanations fit the deductive-nomological pattern; and so it gives, if conscientiously followed, *formal* unity to scientific explanation. If we now replace Popper's methodological rule about the rationality principle by the alternative rule of rationality to explain human behaviour in terms of reasons, then this unity collapses. The rule of causality loses its hold on *social* theories; the explanation of human actions does not invoke universal laws any longer; the deductive-nomological approach is given up in favour of reasons; that is, the natural sciences bow down to causes, the social sciences to reasons. And this goes against Popper's aspirations of unity in the sciences.

Nevertheless, Popper seems to have been aware of the impossibility in the social sciences of taking literally his methodological recommendations to phrase social explanations in terms of universal laws and initial conditions. His method of situational analysis, his usage of 'typical' initial conditions (a deviation from the tenets of *The Logic of Scientific Discovery* that we have not emphasized much up to this point), is exactly intended to find an answer to this dilemma. For he writes, 'only in this way can we explain a social event', later adding between parentheses, 'only in this way because we never have sufficient laws and initial conditions at our disposal to explain it with their help' (1994, p. 168). Here Popper comes close to voiding the methodological rule of causality (to explain in a deductive-nomological manner) for the social sciences.

A reason for Popper, then, not to embrace the alternative view on practical rationality may have been that he would have had to give up the *formal* unity of the sciences embodied in the rule of causality. However, the alternative picture does not go against Popper's broader and unifying idea of science as an enterprise directed at 'understanding'. It is interesting to quote from the Chapter 4 of *Objective Knowledge* (1972). Expressing a kind of unity it nevertheless comes quite close to the alternative; that is, to positioning the rationality principle and the causality principle at the same level in the methodological hierarchy (1972, Chapter 4, § 11):

> As we understand men in virtue of some rationality of their thoughts and actions, so we may understand the laws of nature because of some kind of rationality or understandable necessity in them.

(3) *Rationality Falsified?* — Exalting the principle of causality to a method-ological rule, it might be argued, will be up against much fewer conceptual problems than lifting the rationality principle to such a rule. In the former case a tautological or metaphysical principle turns into a rule, whereas in the latter case an empirical (and allegedly falsified) statement is transformed into

a rule. And this, one might argue, works mischief; and that is why one should *not* opt for the alternative view on the rule of rationality.

However, Popper need not argue like this. Careful consideration of the supposed falsifications shows that the alternative rule of rationality is more true to the structure and the mechanism of social explanations, even from Popper's slant. He presents the following (basic?) situations as falsifications of the rationality principle: 'flustered drivers trying to get out of a traffic jam, or desperately trying to park their cars when there is hardly any parking space to be found, or not at all' (1994, p. 172). But without knowing the exact goals of the drivers we cannot say anything about their rationality. Without a situational analysis, that is, the rationality principle is not only, as Popper says, '*almost empty*', (ibidem, p. 169, author's emphasis) but also rather powerless. Returning to the earlier discussion, a theory — 'we must not forget' (ibidem, p. 178) — can be tested only as a whole.

Altogether it does not make sense to say that the rationality principle is falsified on its own; but that does not mean that it is *not* an empirical statement. However, there are good reasons to doubt whether the kind of principle of rationality that Popper discusses is really empirical at all. Without spelling out any details, one could as well phrase it as a metaphysical principle that all actions have reasons; and the resemblance of such a formulation to the metaphysical principle of causality (that is, that all events are ruled by laws) would *not* be accidental.

4 Conclusion

Phrasing practical rationality as a metaphysical principle has as an additional advantage that what Popper says in his first (of the five) arguments for his methodological rule makes sense for the alternative rule of rationality as well. Recall that he defended his rule never to give up the rationality principle in the face of falsifying evidence by stating that 'we learn more if we blame the situational model' (ibidem, p. 177) and that 'our model is far more interesting and informative' (p. 178) than the principle of rationality. A metaphysical reading of practical rationality makes this understandable as well. What we find interesting in an explanation of human actions, or what we find informative, is the specification of the goals and the knowledge of the agent, the physical and social restrictions he is subject to; that is, the *reasons* why the agent carried out the action. It is, indeed, much less interesting *that* the agent acted on reasons, *that* he was rational, *that* he acted adequately or rationally in the situation in which he found himself. An explanation of someone's action is, then, the same as reporting his reasons, his goals, his information, his restrictions, his misconceptions, and so on. Of course it can be very hard and troublesome to give reasons for an action — and sometimes one may be tempted to say that a person acted without reasons — but that is nothing more than the expression of one's own failure to explain the action.

Bibliography

Boudon, R. (1990). *La logique du social*. Paris: Hachette.

Jarvie, I. C. (1998). 'Situational Logic and its Reception'. *Philosophy of the Social Sciences* **28**, pp. 365-380.

Mongin, P. (2002). 'Le principe de rationalité et l'unité des sciences sociales'. *Revue Économique* **53**, pp. 301-323.

Popper, K. R. (1935). *Logik der Forschung*. Vienna: Julius Springer Verlag. English translation K. R. Popper (1959). *The Logic of Scientific Discovery*. London: Hutchinson.

—— (1957). *The Poverty of Historicism*. London: Routledge & Kegan Paul.

—— (1967). 'La rationalité et le statut du principe de rationalité'. In E. M. Claassen, editor (1967), pp. 142-150. *Les fondements philosophiques des systèmes économiques. Textes de Jacques Rueff et essais rédigés en son honneur 23 août 1966*. Paris: Payot.

—— (1972). *Objective Knowledge*. Oxford: Clarendon Press. 2nd edition 1979.

—— (1983). *A Pocket Popper*. London & Glasgow: Fontana/Collins. Now available only as *Popper Selections*. Princeton NJ: Princeton University Press, 1985.

—— (1994). *The Myth of the Framework*. London: Routledge.

60

Seven Decades of
Economic Methodology
A Popperian Perspective

Lawrence A. Boland

For many decades, much of the methodology writings by economists were directed at convincing others or maybe themselves that economics is a science like any other. To do so involved two key essentials: one was an understanding of what other sciences are like and the other was an understanding of what philosophers of science thought about the other sciences. Too often, economists were satisfied in obtaining only the latter and thus putting too much faith in philosophers. Things are worse today because we now have professional methodologists of economics. Like their predecessors, they rely too much on philosophers of science and understand little about what other scientists do. But unlike their predecessors, they know little about what economists do.

Philosophers of science in the first third of the twentieth century were standing on their heads trying to deal with Albert Einstein's revolution and the apparent collapse of the foundations of Newtonian physics. During most of the nineteenth century, philosophers of science were convinced that science had a solid inductivist foundation — that is, that the true theories of science were the result of careful observations followed by an expert application of inductive logic. But, had theories been developed this way, how could there have been room for the revolutionary ideas of Einstein? Was it not true that the laws of physics are immutable?

Before Newton's immutable laws of physics were put into question, almost everyone thought that finding true theories was the goal of every science. Moreover, almost everyone thought that scientific induction was the infallible method of doing this. Science was simply the organized application of the scientific method. But when it came to explaining the simple mechanics of magnetism such as the movement of a compass needle, Newton's mechanics fell short. And rather than give up the faith in an infallible scientific method, nineteenth-century philosophers of science chose to move the goal posts. Rather than aim for true theories of science, scientists were characterized as aiming for the 'best' theories. At least, it was thought, this would be an achievable goal.

Much of philosophy of science even today is concerned with the logic of choosing the best theories. In the 1930s, it was believed that scientific method was directed at choosing the theories that can logically be verified, that is, proven true with 'positive' observations made after the creation of the theory — the view that became known as logical positivism. According to this view, a scientific theory was distinguished from religion or other metaphysics on this basis alone.

Karl Popper entered the scene by challenging the view that the goal of science was to create a stable scientific atmosphere of agreement over what was considered the best theory available. Popper thought he was extending Einstein's view — which was that science is never stable but in a state of constant revolution. And Popper's reason for this was that science was an enterprise of coordinated criticism rather than coordinated agreement. Practising what he preached, Popper pounded his fists on the doors of the logical positivists in Vienna trying to convince them that they were going down the wrong path. Their path involved a logic of probabilities where the 'best' theory is the one that can be shown to be the most probable theory given the positive evidence made available by inductivist scientists. Popper argued that this would not be very interesting science and instead scientific theories are interesting because they appear at first to be the least probable explanations of positive evidence.

While Popper was being shunned by the philosophers of the day, an economics scholar, Terence Hutchison (1938), thought he would take up the challenge by arguing that what made scientific economic theories interesting was not that they are verifiable but that they were 'testable'. He specifically gave credit to Popper for this view. Unfortunately, Hutchison did not completely understand what Popper was saying. Moreover, Hutchison's view was pretty much ignored in economics. Instead, anyone writing on methodology at that time continued the logical positivist line that verifiability was the true test of a scientific theory.

In the 1960s there was much talk about testability in economics but none of this had to do with Hutchison's path-breaking view of methodology. Instead, the 1940s and 1950s were the battle ground for the movement to make economics a mathematical science. A main criticism of mathematical economics was that mathematics could provide only tautologies — which were claimed to be statements or theorems that are true by virtue of their logical form rather than their empirical content. More correctly, a tautology is a statement which does not depend on the definition of its non-logical words but only on its logical words such as 'and', 'or', 'is' and 'not'. Thus, a tautology is a statement that is true simply because one cannot conceive of a counter-example. For example, the statement 'I am here or I am not here' is true regardless of who 'I' am or where 'here' is.

At the time of Hutchison's launch of testability-directed methodology, Paul Samuelson was beginning to write his PhD thesis, which promoted the mathematical basis for all economic theory. And Samuelson directly confronted the critics by saying that his version of mathematical economics could not be dismissed as a bunch of tautologies because he would require economic theorems to be testable and thereby conceivably false. For Samuelson, a testable theorem is 'operationally meaningful' by which he merely meant that it must be 'refutable in principle'. To be refutable in principle, a theorem could not be a tautology.

Before Samuelson's thesis (1947) could be finished and published, economics came under attack during the 1940s by philosophically armed critics who demanded, as a matter of proper philosophy of science, that economic explanations must be based on verifiable assumptions. In response to this, Armen Alchian (1950), followed by Milton Friedman (1953), launched a counterattack directed at the logical positivist philosophy of science. Their counterview was that assumptions did not have to be verifiable or even true so long as they 'worked'. This had echoes of the old battle between Bishop Berkeley and the promoters of Newton's science. Supposedly, Berkeley's fear was that if people believed in the things that made up Newton's laws of physics, they would no longer see the need for religion to explain the universe. So Berkeley said he would allow for Newton's science so long as its laws were considered mere instruments with no empirically verifiable existence in the universe. That is, the laws of physics are mere useful figments of our imagination — useful intellectual instruments. Alchian and Friedman saw that it was easier to side with the Bishop and thereby avoid the philosophical turmoil that was beginning to rear its ugly head in the hands of the critics.

This then was the current flowing through the writings on methodology during the 1950s and early 1960s. Almost all of the debate was about Friedman's defence of instrumentalism, a doctrine that many view as dishonest or simply wrong headed. Those who wished to promote mathematical economics were dismayed by Friedman's instrumentalism and set about criticizing it on perceived logical grounds. For the most part, Samuelson simply made fun of Friedman, trying to eliminate him with ridicule. And it seemed to work for most of us, and in particular, for those of us trained to be mathematical economists.

In the early 1960s, while Samuelson was putting down Friedman in the annual meetings of the American Economic Association (for example, Samuelson 1963), Richard Lipsey and Chris Archibald, to use the words of the latter, were 'building bombs in the basement' at the London School of Economics. They were under the tutelage of one of Karl Popper's students, Joseph Agassi (see Klappholz & Agassi 1959 and Agassi 1971). At first they thought they would build a new empirically based economics using Popper's views of the philosophy of science. Like Hutchison before them, they did not quite understand what they were being told. They thought that economics could be made empirical (as opposed to mathematically tautological) by promoting an econometric approach that stressed the need for 'falsifiable' research. Their bomb-making yielded only one significant work, namely, the first edition of Lipsey's famous textbook (1963), where Popper's view was openly promoted. Their project was soon dropped because they found that falsifying econometric propositions was not very easy and sometimes impossible. Popper's view played no role in the second edition (1966) and subsequent editions, and thus was soon forgotten. And, both Lipsey and Archibald jumped on the bandwagon of the critics of Popper by promoting what Popper called conventionalism. Conventionalism is the defeatist alternative to the inductivism that dominated late nineteenth-century philosophy of science. In the updated version of conventionalism, falsifiability rather than verifiability was now to be the watchword of science. And when economists of the 1970s and 1980s talked about the need for testability and falsifiability of their models and theorems, they were implicitly talking about Samuelson's methodological pronouncement and not Lipsey's weak moment at the beginning of his first edition.

In fact, during the late 1960s and all of the 1970s, hardly anything was said about methodology. And I can testify that it was very difficult to get journal editors even to consider publishing methodology, and thus very little was published. The only consistent exception was the last chapter of the various editions of Mark Blaug's history of thought textbook. As early as 1968 Blaug was promoting falsifiability as a test of true science — but he seemed to be unaware of Popper until the mid-1970s. Unfortunately, Blaug (1968) made the same mistake as Lipsey and Archibald by thinking Popper was promoting falsifiability as the essence of science. So, Blaug began complaining that economists talk about falsifiability but never practise it. He seems never to have recognized that economists were never trying to fulfil some sort of Popperian methodology but were instead simply invoking testability and falsifiability as a conventionalist criterion to choose the best model or theorem in the way recommended by Samuelson — that is, in a way that insulated mathematical economics from the charge of being a collection of tautologies.

Blaug and his followers were misled mostly by Imre Lakatos who, in a self-promoting way, tried to claim the mantle of Popper even before Popper died. Lakatos did not know much about science but he did know a lot about mathematics. As a result, Lakatos tried to formalize methodology with what he called 'the methodology of scientific research programmes' (I think he was using terminology he learnt from Agassi). It is not clear that Lakatos understood Popper's reasons for talking about falsifiability — namely, as a sufficient but not necessary condition for criticism. Popper called his approach to scientific explanation 'critical rationalism'. Lakatos misled economists also by his twisting Popper's view to overemphasize its growth of knowledge implications. This was unfortunate because such emphasis encouraged historians of economics to follow Blaug's lead and start talking about methodology only in terms of 'progress' and 'progressive' research strategies that Lakatos promoted. In all of this, Popper was maligned and Lakatos praised.

Blaug chose to spin off his final chapter to make a freestanding methodology book in 1980. The obvious success of this book (Blaug 1980) challenged the reluctance of other publishers. There soon was a mad scramble to find authors to write books on economic methodology. The editor for one publisher, George Allen & Unwin, took the first step by commissioning me to write my

1982 book and simultaneously by agreeing to publish Bruce Caldwell's PhD thesis (1982). The following two decades have witnessed a very active development of a separate subdiscipline of economic methodology with now two well-established journals backed by two major publishers. Unfortunately, until quite recently, almost all of the publications in these two decades have tried to turn the clock back to the 1930s problems and questions that continue to interest philosophers rather than address the methodological issues that are of interest to mainstream economists.

Methodology as a separate subdiscipline of mainstream economics has shown the developmental signs of youth and adolescence. It would still be floundering in the basement had it not been for the efforts of two leaders of the History of Economics Society, Warren Samuels and Mark Perlman. Together, they encouraged historians of economic thought to make room in their annual meetings for sessions explicitly on methodology. Critics might easily say that this was a big mistake to tie one's dinghy to a sinking ship. When I was a PhD student in the 1960s, history of thought was a required course but over the last two decades, it has been difficult to find a history of thought course — let alone a required course — in any major economics programme. Nevertheless, methodology has found a viable place at least in the published literature if not the curricula.

Over the last two decades there have developed at least four camps. The biggest is made up of those methodologists who approach the subject with the interests of the historian of science. This camp spent most of the 1980s exploring how they might apply their understanding of Lakatos to the history of economic thought. As a consequence, there are many articles about 'appraisal' of economic theories and methods. And thus there is much discussion of negative or positive 'heuristics', 'hard cores', 'protective belts' and 'novel facts'. For the most part, this kind of discussion, particularly that concerning the 'hard cores' of research programs, was nothing more than a replacement for the 1970s fascination with Thomas Kuhn's 'paradigms'. All of this Lakatos-inspired methodology literature has at best been a waste of time. At worst, it became a stalking horse for critics of Karl Popper's view of science. Unfortunately, Lakatos did not understand Popper but, nevertheless, these critics were thrilled to have the Lakatos-created cartoon-character of Popper to bash away at. Of particular concern was the identification of Popper's view with so-called 'falsificationism'. Lakatos was responsible for this characterization of Popper and it is a false characterization that continues to be promoted in history of economic thought circles by Blaug and his followers — despite Popper's explicit denial of such a characterization (1983, pp. xxxi-xxxv; for more about distinguishing 'falsificationism' from Popper's 'critical rationalism' in economic methodology, see Boland 1994).

The second camp is the fastest growing but the least serious. It began with a few methodologists who became bored with the grinding that goes on in the Lakatos-inspired methodology literature. To overcome the boredom there was an eagerness to create and pursue buzz-words and fads. In the mid-1980s,

the fads were concerned with finding an alternative philosopher of science one
could quote to create and demonstrate an independence from the 'old' views.
In the late 1980s, the fad was so-called 'recovering practice' which supposedly
was directed at understanding how economists practise their trade rather
than how they should practise it. But this too became boring. To overcome
this, other methodologists subsequently tried to get everyone interested in the
fad of deciding between whether the practice of economics is concerned with
'realism' or is just a 'social construction' and thus relativist. More recently
the fad has been about examining whether or not models are 'mediators',
whatever that means. This too is beginning to get boring. It is difficult to
take seriously the frequent gathering around the latest fads in order to hold
conferences about them (see further Boland 1995). It may make all the eager
conference participants feel as if they are doing something — something 'new'
— but it is hard to take seriously any study of methodology that takes a back
seat to the immediate social needs of conference participants.

The third camp is driven by the interest of analytical philosophers who still
worry about the problems and questions raised in the 1930s. And they are
still licking the wounds inflicted by Popper. Their main hope is to eliminate
Popper from the scene. But the main problem with this camp is that none
of them has anything more than an elementary understanding of mainstream
economics. While other philosophers are thrilled with each publication from
this camp, mainstream economists ignore them completely. After all, it is the
concerns of this philosophy camp that Friedman's methodology intentionally
addressed and provided economists with a reason to ignore the philosophers
of the 1930s. Today, it is McCloskey's (1983) emphasis on rhetoric that has
replaced Friedman, but the message and purpose are the same, namely, to
give reason to ignore this philosophical camp. McCloskey's main argument
is that the philosophical camp is concerned only with 'big-M methodology'
whereas ordinary economists are concerned with 'small-m methodology'.

The fourth camp is very small, namely me and a couple of my students
(for example, Wong 1978/2006) — although there are signs that it may be
growing. This fourth camp is concerned mostly, maybe exclusively, with small-
m methodology from a real Popperian perspective. Popper enters the scene
by our viewing every social event, including scientific decisions, as problem-
solving ploys. The activity of this fourth group is sometimes criticized for
being 'always the same' but such criticism may merely reflect a concern for big-
M methodology by methodologists who do not understand the ever-changing
practice of economics and economic model builders that is the primary domain
of the small-m methodologist.

My interest in methodology from the beginning was in examining the reasons why economic model builders assume what they assume. I wrote my
PhD thesis to examine critically the testability allowed by certain common
assumptions of the day. If anyone is interested in what I found, they can
check Chapters 2 and 3 of my 1989 book. What I showed was that almost
all but the simplest Keynesian models are untestable as they would require

more data than is practical or possible. A simple Keynesian model with three endogenous variables, one exogenous variable, and six exogenous coefficients would take almost 500 observations to construct a logically sufficient refutation. And, with one of my senior advisor's simple macro models with just six endogenous variables, one exogenous variable and seven exogenous coefficients it would take over 24000 observations. And worse, any model with a Cobb-Douglas production function might take over 475000 observations. For those model builders who really think they are saying something significant by claiming their models are testable, I think it shows what I said before. Testability is sought only to avoid tautologies and has nothing to do with whatever Lakatos thought Popper said about falsifiability.

What Popper did say was that if you think observations matter, as a matter of logic, only observations that might be used to falsify a theory can be decisive. Confirming observations can never be decisive except in trivial situations. Testing by attempting to falsify someone's theory or explanation is just one of many types of criticism. And it is criticism, or more specifically a critical attitude, that is the hallmark of science. It is not empirical falsifiability as both friends and foes of Popper seem to think he was saying.

I have been practising a small-m approach to methodology for about forty years (for example, Boland 1968, 1970, 1971, 1982, 1986, 1989, 1992, 1997, 2003). Such small-m methodology does not interest philosophers and that is understandable of course. But it does interest economists. Moreover, I was pleasantly surprised at the HES meetings in Vancouver a couple years ago when even the methodologists started talking about the methodology of economic model building and stopped talking about topics such as 'realism', 'progress', 'falsificationism', and similar things that philosophers like to talk about. Today it is becoming clear that methodologists can make a contribution to mainstream economics by helping to sort out and criticize the usual assumptions concerning an economic agent's knowledge and learning. To do this, methodologists will have to give up the creation and pursuit of methodological fads and learn more about modern economic theory so that they can address the needs of practising economists. For example, methodologists should surely be able to help the mainstream economist to realize that the time has come for him or her to stop assuming that induction is a reliable process of learning. To assume that it is reliable is, after all, to assume a theory of learning that is almost 400 years old and one that was refuted over 200 years ago.

It might seem strange, but as a practising Popperian I think it is time for methodologists to stop talking about Popper. It is all right for them to criticize Popper, but this is something for philosophers to worry about. Today, there surely are more important things for economic methodologists to do — particularly if they are willing to address the needs of the practising economist.

Bibliography

Alchian, A. (1950). 'Uncertainty, Evolution and Economic Theory'. *Journal of Political Economy* **58**, pp. 211-221.

Archibald, G. (1961). 'Chamberlin versus Chicago'. *Review of Economic Studies* **29**, pp. 1-28.

Agassi, J. (1971). 'Tautology and Testability in Economics'. *Philosophy of the Social Sciences* **1**, pp. 49-63.

Blaug, M. (1968). *Economic Theory in Retrospect*. 2nd edition. Homewood: Irwin. 3rd edition 1978. Cambridge: Cambridge University Press.

——— (1980). *The Methodology of Economics*. Cambridge: Cambridge University Press.

Boland, L. A. (1966). 'On the Methodology of Economic Model Building. PhD dissertation, University of Illinois.

——— (1968). 'The Identification Problem and the Validity of Economic Models'. *South African Journal of Economics* **36**, pp. 236-240.

——— (1970). 'Conventionalism and Economic Theory'. *Philosophy of Science* **37**, pp. 239-248.

——— (1971). 'Methodology as an Exercise in Economic Analysis'. *Philosophy of Science* **38**, pp. 105-117.

——— (1982). *The Foundations of Economic Method*. London: George Allen & Unwin. 2nd edition, Boland (2003).

——— (1986). *Methodology for a New Microeconomics. The Critical Foundations*. London: Allen & Unwin.

——— (1989). *The Methodology of Economic Model Building: Methodology after Samuelson*. London: Routledge.

——— (1992). *The Principles of Economics: Some Lies My Teachers Told Me*. London: Routledge.

——— (1994). 'Scientific Thinking Without Scientific Method: Two Views of Popper'. In R. Backhouse, editor (1994), pp. 154-72. *New Directions in Economic Methodology*. London: Routledge.

——— (1995). 'Style vs. Substance in Economic Methodology'. In I. C. Jarvie & N. Laor, editors (1995), pp. 115-128. *Critical Rationalism, the Social Sciences and the Humanities*. Dordrecht & Boston MA: Kluwer Academic Publishers.

——— (1997). *Critical Economic Methodology: A Personal Odyssey*. London: Routledge.

——— (2003). *The Foundations of Economic Method: A Popperian Perspective*. 2nd edition. London: Routledge.

Caldwell, B. J. (1982). *Beyond Positivism*. London: George Allen & Unwin.

Friedman, M. (1953). 'Methodology of Positive Economics'. In M. Friedman (1953), pp. 3-43. *Essays in Positive Economics*. Chicago: University of Chicago Press.

Hutchison, T. (1938). *The Significance and Basic Postulates of Economic Theory*. London: Macmillan.

Klappholz, K. & Agassi, J. (1959). 'Methodological Prescriptions in Economics'. *Economica* NS **26**, pp. 60-74.

Lipsey, R. (1963). *An Introduction to Positive Economics*. London: Weidenfeld & Nicolson.

―――― (1966). *An Introduction to Positive Economics*. 2nd edition. London: Weidenfeld & Nicolson.

McCloskey, D. (1983). 'The Rhetoric of Economics'. *Journal of Economic Literature* **21**, pp. 481-517.

Popper, K. R. (1983). *Realism and the Aim of Science*. London: Hutchinson.

Samuelson, P. (1947). *Foundations of Economic Analysis*. Cambridge MA: Harvard University Press.

―――― (1963). 'Problems of Methodology: Discussion'. *American Economic Review, Proceedings* **53**, pp. 231-236.

Wong, S. (1978). *The Foundations of Paul Samuelson's Revealed Preference Theory*. London: Routledge & Kegan Paul. 2nd edition 2006.

61

Popper and Marx as *Frères Ennemis**

Allan Megill

Popper's negative relation toward Marx, and more especially toward Marxism, is about as well known as anything in his work and career. Popper and Marx diverged on many important issues, yet there is also a certain affinity between them, obscured by two factors. First, following the editor of Popper (1983), we can usefully see Popper's concerns as falling under the four general headings of theory of knowledge, philosophy of science, metaphysics, and social philosophy. Marx was not concerned with the first three of these topics, which makes it rather hard to cast about for similarities. Second, although on occasion Popper wrote admiringly of Marx — referring, for example, to Marx's 'honest attempt to apply rational methods to the most urgent problems of social life' (Popper 1945, Chapter 13, text to note 2), Popper's overall concern with attacking Marxism left in its wake the strong sense that Marx and Popper, although not quite so antithetical as Hegel and Popper, were antithetical enough. This impression is misleading, for Marx and Popper are actually much closer in their way of thinking than appears at first glance. In showing how this is so, I shall first clarify and assess Popper's objections to Marxism, and then I shall turn to what Popper and Marx, in spite of everything, have in common.

Popper offered two main criticisms of Marxism, and by extension of Marx himself. These criticisms were overwhelmingly directed at the doctrinaire or — to use Popper's favoured term — 'vulgar' Marxism that was ascendant in the first half of the twentieth century. In the present paper I am primarily interested in their applicability to the original Marx — who, like Popper, was a serious philosopher, and who never quite abandoned his early philosophical commitments.[1] First, Popper criticized Marxism on what can be called 'simple' methodological grounds. Popper claimed that like the psychoanalytic theories of Freud, Adler, and Jung, Marxism failed to subject its propositions to testing — failed to ask the 'falsification' question, namely, 'Under what conditions would I admit that my theory is untenable?' (I here use the falsification criterion as Popper formulates it in *Unended Quest*, 1974/1976,

---

*My thanks to Phillip Honenberger for his help with this article, and to Malachi Hacohen for expert advice and warnings.

[1]For a reading of this Marx, see Megill (2002).

§ 9).[2] One needs to be attentive to what Popper was actually saying when he criticized Marxism on this score. In *Unended Quest* Popper holds that psycho-analytic theories — which he grouped with '(sufficiently vague) astrological lore' (ibidem) — are not falsifiable (properly testable) at all. But in Popper's view 'Marx's theory' was indeed falsifiable — that is, it was susceptible to the setting up of tests which, if failed, would require rejection of the theory. Clearly, Popper's opinion of Marxism — at least in so far as 'Marxism' meant 'Marx's theory' — was less negative than his opinion of the psychoanalytic theory of Freud and his followers.

Popper contends in *Unended Quest* that the problem with Marxism was not that 'Marx's theory' was unfalsifiable, but rather that it had actually been falsified — for it had been 'refuted by events that occurred during the Russian Revolution' (ibidem). Marx had held that revolutionary changes start at the economic base: as Popper characterizes the position, 'means of production change first, then social conditions of production, then political power, and ultimately ideological beliefs, which change last'. According to Popper, in the Russian Revolution changes had occurred in a quite different way: political power changed first, which altered the ideology, which in turn led to a change from the top of the means of production and the social conditions of produc-tion. In Popper's view, Marxism's adherents had evaded this actual refutation of Marx's theory by reinterpreting it, 'transforming it into the vulgar-Marxist (or socioanalytic) theory which tells us that the "economic motive" and the class struggle pervade social life' (ibidem). Popper is correct in claiming that many aspects of Marx's theory are capable of generating testable proposi-tions, and he is equally correct in noting how frequently such falsification was ignored by subsequent *marxisant* intellectuals.

Popper's 'simple' methodological critique of Marxism has some affinities with what was perhaps the pre-eminent earlier critique, offered by the Austr-ian economist, bureaucrat, and sometime finance minister, Eugen von Böhm-Bawerk, in his 1896 study, *Karl Marx and the Close of His System*. Böhm-Bawerk, an exponent of the new subjective or marginal utility theory of value, found Marx's reasoning in *Capital* to be 'full of the most obvious faults of logic and method which deprive it of all cogency', and shared with Popper a neg-ative attitude to what he saw as Marx's 'purely logical proof ... dialectical deduction' (Böhm-Bawerk 1896, pp. 66 and 68). But whereas Böhm-Bawerk focused on Marx's theory of capitalism, Popper focused on something much broader — Marxism as a *Weltanschauung*. In short, he directed his critique at what he took to be Marx's conception of society and history generally, fo-cusing his attention on Marx's claims concerning social causation as laid out in 'the materialist conception of history'. (The most lapidary statement of the

[2]The brevity of *Unended Quest* makes it a useful touchstone. Popper's objections to Marx and Marxism are of course laid out in much greater detail in *The Open Society and Its Enemies*, *The Poverty of Historicism*, and *Conjectures and Refutations* (especially in the essays 'What is Dialectic?' and 'Prediction and Prophecy in the Social Sciences'). See Popper (1945), (1957), and (1963), Chapters 15f.

so-called materialist conception of history [also known as 'historical materi-alism'] is to be found in the Preface to Marx's 1859 work, *A Contribution to the Critique of Political Economy* (Marx & Engels 1978, pp. 4f.).)

Popper and his contemporaries saw the broad generalizations that made up the materialist conception of history as central to Marxism (they thought also, following Engels of the *Anti-Dühring* (1877-1878), that Marxism involved a dialectical materialism that was based in natural science). We now know, of course, that Marx was much less preoccupied by the materialist conception of history than people once thought. Terrell Carver has noted that Marx laid little emphasis on the 'propositional generalisations' of the 1859 preface. However, as Carver also emphasizes, Engels read Marx's generalizations not as a mere 'guiding thread' for his studies but as 'scientific laws, or law-like tendencies'; and Engels's reading had an immense impact both on subsequent Marxists and on anti-Marxists (Carver 1996, pp. xivf.). Engels, not Marx, invented the terms 'materialist conception of history' and 'historical materi-alism'. As for the term 'dialectical materialism', it was first used by Plekhanov in 1891 and then by Lenin in 1894: it appears nowhere in the Marx-Engels corpus (Megill 2002, p. 330, note 2; Jordan 1967, p. 3). Popper's attribution to Marx of a generalized 'sociological determinism' and 'economic historicism' (titles of Chapters 13 and 15 of 1945) is hardly tenable today. Other mat-ters — most notably, the structure of the modern (bourgeois) economy and revolutionary tactics and strategy — were far more on Marx's mind.

To the degree that Popper assumes that the materialist conception of his-tory had the same weighty significance for Marx that it had for the adherents of doctrinaire Marxism — and he does appear to make this assumption — , his 'simple' methodological critique of Marx was somewhat misdirected. How-ever, it was not *misconceived*. First, Popper himself acknowledged, in a note near the end of Chapter 17 of *The Open Society* (1945), that 'In fairness to Marx, we must say that he did not always take his own system too seri-ously, and that he was quite prepared to deviate a little from his fundamental scheme; he considered it as a point of view ... rather than as a system of dogmas' (Popper 1945, Chapter 17, note 28; note 30 in later editions). Here, as at many other places in Popper's writing, a sense of admiration for Marx shines through. Second, there *was* a dogmatism in Marx, although it makes more sense to see Marx's dogmatism as connecting with his analysis of capi-talism than with his few articulations of the materialist conception of history. Marx's overwhelming focus was on the analysis and critique of capitalism, not on articulating a general theory of society and history. But Popper's mis-conception about where the weight of Marx's own theoretical project lay in no way undermines his 'simple' methodological critique. Marx was a serious student of the mid-nineteenth-century capitalist economy, but he came to this study with a predetermined conclusion that he never abandoned, namely, that the current system is doomed to collapse as a result of irremediable internal contradictions. He arrived at this characteristically left-Hegelian conclusion late in 1843, before his serious economic studies. (The key text is Marx's

'Contribution to the Critique of Hegel's *Philosophy of Right*: Introduction';
Marx & Engels 1978, pp. 53-65.)

It says something about Marx's underlying intellectual integrity that, as
far as we can tell, he never deceived himself into thinking that he had *succeeded* in showing how capitalism must collapse. After all, there is a reason
why he never got beyond Volume 1 of *Capital* (Engels cobbled together after
Marx's death the so-called Volumes 2 and 3 of *Capital* out of Marx's massive
economic manuscripts). Why then did Marx pursue his analysis of capitalism
for so long, in spite of his difficulty in bringing the ship home? One answer
is psychological: Marx *wanted* capitalism to collapse, and he kept looking for
what he had not yet been able to find. But Marx's persistence in this search
also had a lot to do with his method in *Capital*. The proper function of method
is to keep us from error. Böhm-Bawerk was right: the method that Marx deployed in *Capital*, far from protecting him from error, kept him entangled in
it. It was a method that focused on the search for abstract essences — and
ended up insulating the claims made from any sort of immediate disconfirma-
tion.[3] And Popper likewise was right, although the basis for his criticism was
not a detailed reading of *Capital* but only an attentiveness to what Marxists
in his own time were saying.

Popper's second objection to Marxism is a *complex* methodological objection. In essence, Popper's objection here is that Marxism attempts to engage
in historical prophecy (Popper also attributed this fault to Marx himself; for
example, in 1945, Chapter 13). The claim that Marxism engages in historical
prophecy may not sound like a methodological objection, but it is. Popper
explicitly names it as such, linking it with the methodologically erroneous positions that he calls 'historicism' and 'holism'. In *The Poverty of Historicism*
Popper characterizes 'historicism' as a 'doctrine', or 'doctrines', of method,
and in *The Open Society* he groups the first five chapters attacking Marxism
under the section heading 'Marx's Method' (Popper 1957, Introduction and
§ 18; Popper 1945, Chapters 13-17).

What exactly does Popper mean by 'historicism'? In part, as just noted,
Popper holds that it is a method — a *poor* method. It also seems to be a view
as to how the world actually operates, not just a method. But what is the content of this view? Maurice Mandelbaum suggests that Popper conflates under
the single name *historicism* two beliefs that 'are in principle separate'. One
of these is belief in 'the possibility of predicting future events in history'. The
other is belief in the existence of 'rhythms, patterns, or laws that underlie the
evolution of history', such that history *must* pass through a certain sequence
of historical stages, or *must* eventuate in a particular, predictable outcome.
As Mandelbaum points out, in *The Poverty of Historicism* Popper cites the
prediction of a typhoon as an illustration of 'historical prophecy' (Popper

---

[3]Some sense of the flavour of Marx's method can be readily got from a section of Marx's
raw-draft manuscript, the so-called *Grundrisse* (1857-1858), which Marx's editors have
entitled 'The Method of Political Economy' (Marx & Engels 1978, pp. 236-244). The *Grundrisse* was Marx's first attempt to pull together what eventually became *Capital*, Volume 1.

1957, §15). One could substitute for the typhoon other examples having a more historical cast, such as predicting an outbreak of war, the collapse of a regime, the emergence of an ecological crisis, and so on. Such 'historical prophecy', Mandelbaum rightly suggests, is not the same as 'a belief that there are rhythms, patterns, or laws that underlie the evolution of history'. The difference is between predicting particular future events, and holding that irreducible laws of historical development exist and can be discovered by human beings (Mandelbaum 1971, pp. 391f., note 44; for Popper's reference to rhythms, patterns, and laws, see Popper 1957, Introduction).

The distinction between (a) prediction and (b) prediction on the basis of an assumed knowledge of the direction in which history is moving is clearly important. However, contra Mandelbaum, it seems clear from what Popper says in the Introduction to *The Poverty of Historicism* that, by 'historicism', he means only (b) and not (a). I believe that Mandelbaum fell into his mistaken claim about Popper through a faulty inference from the fact that Popper claimed that Marx, and also John Stuart Mill, were historicists. To take the simpler case first: in *The Poverty of Historicism* Popper equates Mill's position on social prediction with that of Auguste Comte, whose 'law of the three stages' indeed purported to be a developmental historical law (Popper 1957, §22, note 3). But while Popper is able to find indications that John Stuart Mill believed in the possibility of making reliable predictions about the future, there is no evidence, as Mandelbaum rightly notes, that Mill believed in laws of historical development. Mandelbaum is mistaken only in thinking that Popper made this mistake because he 'conflated prediction with laws of development' (Mandelbaum 1971, pp. 391f., note 44). On the contrary, Popper's error was empirical and not conceptual: he simply got Mill wrong.

The same is true of Popper's claim that Marx was a historicist — that is, Popper makes an empirical error here also, not a conceptual one. To be sure, Engels, who was a good journalist but a bad philosopher, *was* a historicist. For example, in his posthumously published *Dialectics of Nature* Engels claimed to have discovered 'dialectical laws . . . just as valid for motion in nature and human history as for the motion of thought' (quoted by Jordan 1967, p. 109). There is nothing even remotely like such a view in Marx — but Marx *was* committed to the possibility of certain kinds of prediction. As he wrote in the preface to the first edition of *Capital* (1867), it was his aim in that work to lay out 'the law of economic motion of modern society' (Marx & Engels 1978, p. 297). In the context of Marx's time, a law of motion was clearly a Newtonian law explaining the workings of a particular system, not a law of development necessitating a movement from one system to another. Marx wanted to believe that the laws of capitalism will necessitate capitalism's collapse. This is not the same as holding that the collapse of capitalism is mandated by laws governing the historical process in general. In sum, to the extent that Popper's second objection to Marxism is that it is historicist, the objection does not stand up, at least if, by 'Marxism', we mean 'Marx's own views on society and history'.

Popper's 'complex' methodological objection to Marxism has another, variant form, according to which the problem with Marxism is its 'holism'.[4] Holism and 'historicism' are closely related, given that laws of historical development purport to indicate how history *as a whole* is destined to move. To be able to say how history as a whole is destined to move, one needs to exclude the possibility that *particular* historical entities can have an independently determinative role in the historical process. If Marat can substantially change the course of the French Revolution by having a good breakfast in the morning, in consequence delivering a surprisingly forceful speech against the Girondists later that day, thus setting in motion the events that led to the Terror, laws of historical development cannot hold with respect to the Revolution. More abstractly put: if a historical individual is able to have a real impact on history, there can be no laws of historical development. Accordingly, historicism requires holism. That is, it requires that one regard only the social order *itself*, rather than particular components of it or relations within it, as historically relevant. Popper considers this view an indefensible obfuscation.

Was Marx a holist? Holism is in part an ontological position, and, as noted at the beginning of this paper, Marx was not concerned with that kind of (deeply philosophical) issue. So it is not surprising that some unclarity surrounds the question of Marx's alleged holism. While I cannot discuss the matter in detail here (instead, see Megill 2002, pp. 212-226 and Shiell 1987), I can at least lay out the gist, which is that insofar as Marx had a position on the subject, he has to be characterized as an ontological individualist and not an ontological holist. Consider his assertion in a letter written to a Russian correspondent, P. V. Annenkov, dated 28 December 1846, to the effect that 'the social history of men is never anything but the history of their individual development ...' (Marx & Engels 1978, p. 137). Marx's claim here is that human history is simply what human beings, all added up together, do. This is individualism, not holism. There is no evidence that Marx ever diverged from this position.

To be sure, the matter is not so simple, for Marx also shows holist tendencies. I have elsewhere characterized Marx as an individualist in his (implicit) ontological assumptions, while also being to some significant degree a holist in matters of method (Megill 2002, pp. 212-217). Marx's holist side seems to have two main roots. One was his absolute hatred of the existing capitalist order. Marx was not at all satisfied with the thought that the world can be adequately improved by changing *individual aspects* of capitalism — that is,

---

[4]I focus in this brief paper on Popper's attack on what is often called 'methodological holism' (although its underlying assumptions are often ontological and not just methodological). Holism of this sort can be defined in several ways, but perhaps it is best seen as the view that in order to understand something — whether a particular object, or the social order, or history — one must understand it *as a whole*, and not just by trying to grasp the particular parts and relations of which it is constituted. For Popper's own discussion of holism, by far the most important reference is Popper 1957, §§ 22-24; see also Hacohen (2000), Chapter 10, especially pp. 464-466, 482-484.

he was not a reformist. On the contrary, he wanted to hold that capitalism *as a whole* must be overcome — in short, he was a revolutionary (note that the reformist/revolutionary distinction does not equate to the distinction between nonviolent change and violent change). In part because of this strongly negative orientation toward the existing order, Marx contended again and again that *capitalism itself* — and not specific bad things occurring *within* capitalism — is the problem. Second, Marx never actually worked out in detail his explanation as to why capitalism is doomed to failure, as he held it was. In the absence of a specific explanation why capitalism is doomed, it sometimes looks as though Marx is trying to say that its failure is connected to capitalism *as a whole*. I have called this apparent position 'the holism of explanatory failure' (ibidem).

In sum, Popper's objection to Marx's alleged holism has some merit, although it would be better to see Marx's *real* failing as lying not in a commitment to holism but rather in his unwillingness to give up a long-held view — namely, that capitalism *must* collapse — in the face of his inability to show how this would happen. In other words, at this point Popper's 'complex' methodological objection to Marx reduces to the simple objection that he had failed to confront with adequate directness the possibility that his theory was wrong.

So far, we have seen Popper and Marx in more or less direct confrontation with each other. But the confrontation masks, I have suggested, an underappreciated affinity: Marx and Popper are in some sense *frères ennemis*, brothers under the skin. For all their differences, they share a commitment to science and to certainty, or rather (to cover Popper's case) to science and to an *ideal* of certainty. (Admittedly, for Popper scientific knowledge is 'certain' only in 'an extraordinarily highly qualified sense' — that is, it is 'much better tested than many theories which [in everyday life] we constantly trust our lives to', such as that the floor we are standing on will not collapse (Popper 1972, Chapter 2, § 22).) We might refer to this set of shared commitments as constituting a *rationalism* that Marx and Popper have in common. If so, where Marx was the Enlightenment's sunniest heir and most confident champion, Popper is a *disabused* adherent of reason (which is why some commentators, most notoriously David Stove 1982, see him as reason's betrayer). On the one hand, Marx is supremely confident in the power of science to arrive at *the* truth about the world; on the other, Popper holds that even science is fallible. In the face of this central epistemological difference, other differences appear as relatively minor. Congruent with Marx's epistemological confidence is the tendency of his method (at least, the method deployed in *Capital*) to give error too many places to hide. Congruent with Popper's disabused attitude is his deep interest in 'meta' subjects — theory of knowledge, philosophy of science, metaphysics — that did not concern Marx at all. Likewise, Popper's preoccupation with demarcating the boundary between science and non-science is the concern of someone worried about how rationality will be preserved in the face of irrationality.

But their common commitment to science remains, linking the rationalist and the critical rationalist. By 'science', I mean both a body of claims and a set of practices. Marx and Popper would agree that scientific claims are generated by systematic thought and investigation and that they have a universal form within their intended range. They would agree also that these claims are universally authoritative, in the sense that any and all rational persons can in principle come to see that they are 'true' — even if 'true' means only 'not yet having been falsified'. (Of course, Popper takes scientific claims to be only temporarily authoritative, since they can be tested and found wanting at any time, and indeed it is our duty always to remain critical.) As for Marx, he pretty much ignores the possibility of any sudden, near-term falsification of scientific claims that have already been proved in practice, although he certainly holds that scientific claims can be superseded. Thus in the Postface to the 1873 edition of *Capital* Marx refers to the 'lively scientific activity' that had taken place in the field of political economy in Britain, yet he also holds that this 'scientific bourgeois economics' had a deeply inadequate view of the developing capitalist economy (Marx 1867/1977, pp. 96-98).

As devotees of science, Marx and Popper held many things in common — most notably, commitment to the possibility of a better world, a deep conviction that it is important to work for a better world, and an equally deep conviction that science and technology (or, in Popper's case, 'social engineering') offer crucial means for such improvement. Although Popper would have been surprised to learn it, this common orientation is perhaps best manifested in Popper's and Marx's views on history. I am thinking first of the later Popper's speculations on 'evolutionary epistemology' and the 'third world'. In these reflections Popper sees the 'third world' of objective knowledge emerging as *'the unplanned product of human actions'* carried out over time (Popper 1972, Chapter 2, § 16; Chapter 4, § 4; Chapter 7, § 1, and elsewhere). But Marx *also* has the notion that historical development is a matter of the improvement, by way of confrontation with the real world, of human knowledge: in this aspect of Marx's work, *history* takes on the guise of a universalized *history of science* (Megill 2002, pp. 192-210). This is most visible in the second thesis on Feuerbach, where Marx asserts that 'Man must prove the truth, that is, the reality and power, the this-sidedness of his thinking in practice' (Marx & Engels 1978, p. 144). Along a similar line, Marx & Engels's collaborative 'The German Ideology' is, in one of its aspects, a history of how human beings, who have to satisfy their needs in the face of a recalcitrant nature, come to confront nature, and then society, *more and more intelligently*. This is certainly a view to which Popper would have resonated had he been able to discern it. But of course the Marxian conception of history to which I am alluding was much covered over, not only by the misinterpretations of subsequent writers, beginning with Engels, but also by Marx's own overwhelming preoccupation with a social order — 'modern society' — within which, in his view, knowledge had become estranged from human beings and had turned into an external force oppressing them.

It remains only to suggest something of the limitations of the cognitivist view of history and society that Marx and Popper share. Popper and Marx are true intellectuals, a fact that is both a strength and weakness. It is hard to imagine anyone pursuing more tenaciously the particular problems that they found compelling. At the same time they both have a degree of insensitivity to aspects of the world that do not lend themselves as readily as they would have hoped to solutions of a scientific and technological character. Consider Marx, who in his 'Critical Marginal Notes on "The King of Prussia and Social Reform" ', *The Communist Manifesto*, *The Civil War in France*, and his 'conspectus' on Bakunin's *Statism and Anarchy*, insisted that the future socialist order would be completely nonpolitical (Megill 2002, pp. 57f.). Presumably politics would not be necessary because human beings, now freed from class conflict and guided by scientific and technical knowledge, would readily agree as to what the social order requires at any given moment.

Unlike Marx, Popper certainly never suggests that politics is something that will be superseded. But he does have a quite thin and distanced view of what politics involves. A heavily struck note is his conviction that political authority is a dangerous thing and that there need to be ways of restricting it. In Volume I of *The Open Society* he contends that Plato's question, *Who should rule?* ought to be replaced by the more important question, *How can we so organize political institutions that bad or incompetent rulers can be prevented from doing too much damage?*, while in Volume II he says that the most important question is 'how can we tame them?' (Popper 1945, Chapter 7, § I; Chapter 17, § VIII). This is fair enough, but we get little more from Popper than this claim that our governors ought to be subject to recall, and the further point that fallibilism requires that we be non-dogmatic in political matters. In fact, what Popper really seems to favour is 'social engineering'. It is of course a 'piecemeal' social engineering, in contrast to the global social engineering of Soviet Marxism in the 1930s. But it is engineering nonetheless. One is tempted to see Popper as still under the thrall of the Vienna of 1895-1914, where one constantly noticed the marvellous engineering deployed by the Austro-Hungarian monarchy in reconstructing the imperial city. Yet at the same time the popular politics of the city put an anti-Semitic rabble-rouser into the mayoral seat and the politics of the monarchy led to a disastrous war that destroyed what assimilated Jews in Popper's situation would forever look back to, through a nostalgic haze, as a (potentially) cosmopolitan multinational empire (see Hacohen 1999).

The ability to dismiss one's 'rulers' is indeed important, but politics is also a matter of continual compromises, haggling, bargains, and trades that have a more than merely periodic role to play, and that bear little resemblance to scientific-technical-bureaucratic engineering. What Popper sometimes refers to as 'sentiments' — commitments, allegiances, preferences, faiths, and the like — seem to be essential features of all political relations among human beings (1945, Chapter 13, note 1). In *The Poverty of Historicism* Popper sees his beloved 'piecemeal technologist or engineer' as wishing 'to apply something like scientific method in politics' (1957, § 24). But Popper ought to have noted the high degree to which politics addresses issues that are not amenable to 'scientific method'. In politics it is not just a matter of building a new highway, but of deciding through whose neighbourhood it should run or whether it should be built at all. Attempts to make social engineering substitute for political deliberation and compromise seem likely to lead to an impairment of politics (and also of the effectiveness of those politicians foolish enough to appeal to the authority of social engineering). More distressingly, if the social engineers are armed, there may be a temptation to manufacture agreement by eliminating those who fail to recognize the rightness of their prescriptions. This was of course one aspect of the corrupted Stalinist variant of Marxism that so horrified Popper.

For better or worse, identities and commitments rooted in places other than scientific rationality seem unavoidable in the social and political order. Admirably committed to fallibilism, the Popperian (more than the Marxist) ought to be able to anticipate the continued influence of political forces that elude our understanding (such as ethnic identity or religious commitment). These things, so long as they exist, will hardly be susceptible to engineering. Politics does not *necessarily* revolve around such realities, but even if they were not a factor, other 'non-rational' commitments and allegiances likely would be. In fact, the existence of such realities suggests that it is a mistake to think of rationality in terms of the universal generalizations of the natural scientist or engineer. The philosopher Louis Mink once suggested that we need to get beyond the simple opposition between a powerful theoretical/nomothetic science and a weak, 'merely descriptive' idiographic science, and to think also of narrative and categoreal 'modes of comprehension'. A mode of understanding that such philosophers as Windelband, Popper, and Hempel saw as tied to *mere* particulars is actually, Mink showed, tied up with the human attempt to 'configure' human experience into unifying narratives. For its part, 'categoreal' understanding is a matter of articulating conceptual frameworks in terms of which particulars can be seen to make yet another kind of sense — a sense that has to do with seeing objects as examples of the same larger *category* or *genre* of object (Mink 1998).

Identities and narratives are central to the operation of political orders. In modernity, identities and narratives are always up for grabs: it is a matter of competition among different categoreal (identity) and configurational (narrative) understandings of the world. Marx expected that the elimination of class conflict would enable human beings to rise above *all* kinds of division, since he saw ethnic and religious division as non-essential, and Popper always longed for the Central European cosmopolitanism that he associated with the idea of a reformed Habsburg Monarchy (Hacohen 1999). These were dreams dreamt by two honest heirs of the Enlightenment who would perhaps be surprised to find themselves in the same boat. Both thinkers stimulate us, by the tenacity of their thinking, to think about the world in new ways. Both offer ideal models that can attract us in various ways.

They are models marked by the rationalism of both thinkers. Marx's rationalism is most noticeable in his insistence that the anarchic and unpredictable market will have no place in socialism (Megill 2002). Popper recognized and feared the power of emotions and 'irrational' identity politics and adamantly refused to concede any grounds; his main drive was to rationalize. However, there is no reason to fixate *literally* on models articulated by thinkers whose projects are now history. Marx's critique of the 'bourgeois mode of production' is surely more valuable than his mid-nineteenth-century image of what the future liberated society should look like. Popper's image of the future is closer to something one would want to bring into being, but here it would be a matter of laying less emphasis than Popper does on a 'demarcation' of rational from irrational, while emphasizing (in a Popperian spirit) the conjectural and fallible character of our proposals for the future, as well as the need for deliberation and conversation that would aim for something less hard-edged than 'refutation'.

Bibliography

von Böhm-Bawerk, E. (1896). 'Karl Marx and the Close of His System'. In P. M. Sweezy, editor (1949), pp. 1-118. *'Karl Marx and the Close of His System', by E. von Böhm-Bawerk, and 'Böhm-Bawerk's Criticism of Marx', by R. Hilferding.* New York: Augustus M. Kelley.

Carver, T. (1983). *Marx & Engels: The Intellectual Relationship.* Bloomington IN: Indiana University Press.

———, editor & translator (1996). *Karl Marx. Later Political Writings.* Cambridge: Cambridge University Press.

Engels, F. (1877-1878). *Anti-Dühring: Herr Eugen Dühring's Revolution in Science.* In K. Marx & F. Engels (2004), pp. 1-309. *Collected Works.* Volume 25.

Hacohen, M. H. (1999). 'Dilemmas of Cosmopolitanism: Karl Popper, Jewish Identity, and "Central European Culture"'. *Journal of Modern History* **71**, pp. 105-149.

——— (2000). *Karl Popper – The Formative Years, 1902-1945. Politics and Philosophy in Pre-war Vienna.* Cambridge & elsewhere: Cambridge University Press.

Jordan, Z. A (1967). *The Evolution of Dialectical Materialism: A Philosophical and Sociological Analysis.* London: Macmillan.

Mandelbaum, M. (1971). *History, Man, and Reason: A Study in Nineteenth-Century Thought.* Baltimore MD: Johns Hopkins University Press.

Marx, K. (1867). *Capital: A Critique of Political Economy*, Volume 1. English translation by B. Fowkes, 1977. New York, Vintage Books.

Marx, K. & Engels, F. (1978). *The Marx-Engels Reader.* 2nd edition. Edited by Robert C. Tucker. New York: Norton.

Megill, A. (2002). *Karl Marx: The Burden of Reason (Why Marx Rejected Politics and the Market).* Lanham MD: Rowman & Littlefield.

Mink, L. O. (1998). 'History and Fiction as Modes of Comprehension'. In B. Fay, P. Pomper, & R. T. Vann, editors (1998), pp. 121-136. *History and Theory: Contemporary Readings.* Malden MA: Blackwell.

Popper, K. R. (1945). *The Open Society and Its Enemies.* London: George Routledge & Sons. 5th edition 1966. London: Routledge & Kegan Paul.

——— (1957). *The Poverty of Historicism.* London: Routledge & Kegan Paul.

——— (1963). *Conjectures and Refutations: The Growth of Scientific Knowledge.* London: Routledge & Kegan Paul. 5th edition 1989.

——— (1972). *Objective Knowledge.* Oxford: Clarendon Press. 2nd edition 1979.

——— (1974).'Intellectual Autobiography'. In P. A. Schilpp, editor (1974), pp. 1-181. *The Philosophy of Karl Popper.* La Salle IL: Open Court. Reprinted as *Unended Quest* (1976). London & Glasgow: Fontana/Collins.

—— (1983). *A Pocket Popper*. London & Glasgow: Fontana/Collins. 2nd edition (1985). *Popper Selections*. Princeton NJ: Princeton University Press.

Shiell, T. (1987). 'On Marx's Holism'. *History of Philosophy Quarterly* **4**, pp. 235-246.

Stove, D. C. (1982). *Popper and After: Four Modern Irrationalists*. Oxford: Pergamon Press.

62

Popper's Conception of History Seen from the Kantian Tradition

Shijun Tong

Among three arguments given by Kant for the hope of human progress towards perpetual peace and a cosmopolitan civil society, the one that emphasizes the moral significance of this hope itself would seem to many people now to be more unrealistic than ever before. According to my understanding, however, it is just this argument that was regarded by Popper as the most important one. This article discusses Popper's conception of history from this perspective, and compares it with Habermas's version of 'critical rationalism', which develops Kant's moral argument in a different way.

1 Kant as a philosopher of history: Three arguments for historical progress

The first argument that Kant gives for his idea of historical progress towards perpetual peace and the cosmopolitan civil society (here I put aside the difference between these two goals of progress and focus on the idea of progress) may be called 'the argument of not being impossible'. The idea of human progress is justified, according to Kant, not because it will be realized at any rate, but because it involves nothing that is impossible (Kant 1970/1991, p. 88):

> since the human race is constantly progressing in cultural matters (in keeping with its natural purpose), it is also engaged in progressive improvement in relation to the moral end of its existence. This progress may at times be *interrupted* but never *broken off*. I do not need to prove this assumption; it is up to the adversary to provide his case.

Here Kant is making an assumption concerning 'possibility'. From the logical point of view, an assumption concerning 'possibility' is a very weak one, whereas its negation (that is, the assumption that it is not the case that progress is possible) is a very strong one. The burden of proof, therefore, is on the party who holds the stronger assumption. Kant, as a moral philosopher, is satisfied with the task of showing that moral aims such as human progress are not impossible, since 'so long as it is not demonstrably impossible to fulfill them, [they] amount to duties' (ibidem, p. 89).

The second argument given by Kant for the idea of human progress may be called 'the argument of a plan of nature'. According to Kant the philosopher of history, human progress is not only a result of the functioning of what is good in human nature, but also something that is realized by means of what is bad in human nature (ibidem, p. 44):

> The means which nature employs to bring about the development of innate capacities is that of antagonism within society, in so far as this antagonism becomes in the long run the cause of a law-governed social order.

Man has an inclination to live in society, on the one hand, and has a tendency to live as an individual or to isolate himself, on the other. He then encounters resistance all around, but it is (ibidem, pp. 44f.)

> this very resistance which awakens all man's powers and induces him to overcome his tendency to laziness. Through the desire for honor, power, or property, it drives him to seek status among his fellows, whom he cannot *bear* yet cannot *bear to leave*. Then the first true steps are taken from barbarism to culture, which in fact consists in the social worthiness of man. All man's talents are now gradually developed, his taste cultivated, and by a continued process of enlightenment, a beginning is made towards establishing a way of thinking which can with time transform the primitive natural capacity for moral discrimination into definite practical principles; and thus *pathologically* enforced social union is transformed into a *moral* whole.

It is in this sense that Kant says '(t)he history of the human race as a whole can be regarded as the realization of a hidden plan of nature ...' (ibidem, p. 50).

The third argument Kant advances for human progress may be called 'the argument of man's moral duty'. The major reason why we can have the idea of human progress towards cosmopolitan civil society and perpetual peace, according to Kant, is that this idea itself has great practical impact upon history. In 'The Contest of Faculties' (1970/1991, pp. 176-190; cp. p. 177) Kant says that the Jewish prophets in the past, and the contemporary politicians who claim that one must take men as they are, and theologians who prophesy the complete decline of religion and the imminent appearance of the Antichrist, are actually helping realize what they have prophesied. This is to talk about the self-fulfilling function of social predictions in a negative way: those negative predictions which say that history will degenerate will influence history in such a way that something verifying these predictions will come about as predicted. From the same consideration, in the 'Idea for a Universal History with a Cosmopolitan Purpose' (1970/1991, pp. 41-53) Kant says that human progress, the chiliastic expectation of philosophy, is by no means a mere illusion, because although it cannot be derived from experience, it can nevertheless have influence on empirical processes. A great many empirical facts have shown that this kind of progress is possible, human efforts can help realize this possibility, and these efforts are in turn related to man's understanding of history: '...human nature is such that it cannot be indifferent even to the most remote epoch which may eventually affect our species, so long as this epoch can be expected with certainty' (ibidem, p. 50). Therefore Kant argues that this understanding of history 'must be regarded as possible and even as capable of furthering the purpose of nature itself' (ibidem, p. 51). Kant's position, I think, can be summarized as follows: Although human progress as a whole has no certain guarantee, we have a moral duty to work for it; or, to be more exact, just because human progress towards perpetual peace has no certain guarantee, we have a stronger duty to advance it. We can even say that we not only have the duty to advance human progress, but also have the duty to believe in progress, to have hope for progress, and to expect wholeheartedly that perpetual peace and a cosmopolitan society will come eventually. This is not a mere idea concerning the future that lies limitlessly far ahead, but an idea that has direct impact upon what we are doing and what we are choosing here and now.

2 Popper as a neo-Kantian: Our moral responsibility for human history

Of the three arguments described above, the last one seems to be more pertinent to the post-'9/11' world. The terrorist attacks exposed in a clear way how fragile our civilization is, and to what degree our society is a 'risk society'. In our times, modern science has already peeped into human genes, a small group of terrorists have mastered and are ready to make use of weapons of mass destruction, and a small number of nuclear powers have so many nuclear warheads in their hands that all life on earth could be wiped out many times. The most dangerous risk in this situation is a full-fledged clash of different 'civilizations'. Whether or not we will have a full-fledged clash of civilizations, which will almost certainly mean a large-scale retrogression, if not a total elimination, of human civilization, depends, to a great degree, on whether we think we are heading for it, or whether we think we have already entered an epoch like that. The reason is that description and prediction of social phenomena, as Karl Popper analyses them, are different from those of natural phenomena in that they belong to the same category as their own objects, and can therefore play a role in the functioning of these objects.

It is for this reason that I think Kant's idea of perpetual peace, and his ideal of a cosmopolitan civil society, though looking paler than ever before, are much more urgently needed than any pessimistic description and prediction of our world that we can read every day in newspapers and magazines. Without this positive image of 'perpetual peace', another image of 'perpetual peace', or 'the picture of a graveyard', as Kant writes at the beginning of his famous essay, will prevail: it will very possibly not only symbolize the destiny of those who were buried in the debris of the World Trade Center in New York, but also become the destiny of the whole species called homo sapiens.

In reasoning in the above way, I was basically following Karl Popper's idea. Popper, in my view, also prefers Kant's third argument for human progress.

The first two of Kant's arguments for human progress would seem to Popper either too weak or too strong. The 'argument of not being impossible' is too weak according to Popper's standard in that merely saying that something is possible amounts almost to saying nothing of it, because the same can be said of so many other things, many of which are in sharp conflict with one another. In Popper's view, what science tells us is more what is impossible than what is possible, and social action — what he calls 'piecemeal social engineering' — is underwritten only by scientific knowledge that tells us 'what kind of things can never happen'.

If the 'argument of not being impossible' is problematic for having said too little, then the 'argument of the plan of nature' is problematic for having said too much. Kant thinks that the problem of setting up a constitutional state can be solved even by a nation of devils, so long as they possess understanding; he also says that selfish considerations of different nations will lead them to the conclusion that a cosmopolitan civil society is a better choice than wars among them. The assumption underlying these considerations is that people, in the worst case, strive for their selfish interests. This assumption, however, does not appear to be defensible when we are dealing with a group of people whose activities are basically not motivated by utilitarian considerations, and when a small number of people can bring irremediable damages to all parties concerned. Kant's idea of the 'plan of nature', which is apparently similar to Adam Smith's idea of the 'invisible hand', was later developed by Hegel into his thesis of 'the cunning of Reason'. Popper regards Hegel's philosophy of history based on this thesis as a typical case of what he calls 'historicism' and 'essentialism', and regards the former as an enemy of what he calls 'the open society'. Human history, according to Popper, does not have any predetermined goal, but involves innumerable possibilities. If to say that history has a meaning is to imply that this meaning is derived from a goal or aim of history, then Popper refuses to accept that history has any meaning (Popper 1945, Chapter 25).

But this does not mean that Popper denies history any chance of having a meaning. Here Popper refers to Kant — in my view, Popper fully endorses Kant's third argument for human progress as mentioned above. He says (ibidem, Chapter 25, § IV):

> the only rational as well as the only Christian attitude even towards the history of freedom is that we are ourselves responsible for it, in the same sense in which we are responsible for what we make of our lives, and that only our conscience can judge us and not our worldly success.

In other words (ibidem): 'Although history has no ends, we can impose these ends of ours upon it; and *although history has no meaning, we can give it a meaning.*' Like Kant, Popper also thinks that this task, hope, or obligation can have practical consequences in history. A lesson we can learn from history, according to Popper, is that it is not altogether useless to give history an ethical meaning, or try to call ourselves cautious moral reformers. On the contrary, we will never understand history if we underestimate the historical force of ethical aims. It is true that these aims often lead to terrible results unexpected by their designers. But in some respects, we are now closer than any preceding generation to the aim and ideal of the American Revolution or the Enlightenment represented by Kant. Of special importance, in Popper's view, are the idea of emancipation through knowledge, the idea of a pluralist or open society, and the idea of ending the formidable history of wars by establishing perpetual peace; though all being remote ideals, these ideals have already become the aim and hope of almost everybody (Popper 1992, Chapter 10).

On the one hand, history is said to have no meaning in itself; on the other hand, we are said to be able to give history a certain meaning. Holding these two positions at the same time, Popper admits, presupposes a dichotomy between facts and values that can be dated back to Hume: 'Facts as such have no meaning; they can gain it only through our decisions'(Popper 1945, Chapter 23, § IV). Historicism is, in Popper's view, one of the efforts to overcome this dualism, and its root lies in the fact that it dares not admit that we shoulder ultimate responsibility even for the standards we choose for ourselves.

To say that all decisions should be made by ourselves is not to say that we have to make our decisions in a vacuum: Popper wants neither to be a nihilist who says 'nothing matters' nor to be a relativist who says 'anything goes'. That is why he resorts to the force of traditions, especially the force of the liberal tradition, with his critical rationalism as its theoretical explication: though not a 'rational' foundation for deciding to develop an equal and just society, it has provided us with a set of values and ideals that no other traditions seem to have given us to the same degree, and it has provided us with a framework within which different people can discuss their ideas, and can work out their differences.

It should be noted that in some passages Popper seems to emphasize the importance of the tradition of critical rationalism not so much for its endorsing the values of non-violence, freedom, justice, and the like (since these values are claimed to be endorsed even by their most dangerous enemies) as for its endorsing the method of critical discussion of what are the most efficient ways to realize these values, since most disasters in human history result from people's ignorance of the relation between what they are doing and what they are supposed to be searching for.

3 Habermas as a 'critical rationalist': Communicative reason between fact and norm

When Popper talks about tradition or traditions, he has in his mind mainly Western or European traditions. As a non-European reader of his works, I want to know whether it is possible to have an argument for human progress that is not only beyond the 'logical possibility argument', which is too weak, and the 'historical necessity argument', which is too strong, but also supported by something broader and deeper than a particular tradition or 'moral framework' in Popper's words. On this point, we can probably get some help from Jürgen Habermas, who is both a 'critical rationalist' in his own way and an opponent of Popper's presumptive 'positivism' and 'decisionism'.

Like Popper, Habermas admits that it is important to make a distinction between facts and values. But it is one thing to say that there are conceptual distinctions between facts and values, and another thing to say that no middle term can be found to bind them together. In Habermas, to look for this middle term is to look for something hard and beyond people's irrational decision in particular situations. Habermas resorts to something similar to what Kant calls 'the facts of reason', that is, 'communicative reason' that exists in the form of presuppositions for everyday linguistic communicative actions. These presuppositions are neither something purely constitutive (facts), nor something purely regulative (norms). No communicative action is possible without them, but nowhere are they fully realized, since actual communicative actions are more or less coerced and distorted. And even though actual communicative actions are more or less coerced and distorted, they are judged to be so only because those presuppositions are applied as criteria. We may call this idea an 'argument of pragmatic indispensability' for human progress, which seems to be different from all of Kant's three arguments, but keeps an important connection with Kant's 'argument of man's moral duty'.

The key concept in this argument is 'communicative reason', and this concept plays a role in Habermas's critical theory similar to the role that the concept of 'practical reason' plays in Kant's transcendental philosophy. There are some interesting correlates and differences between these two concepts.

On the one hand, like 'practical reason', 'communicative reason' is also directly related to human practices, but the agent of 'communicative reason' is intersubjective communication among different subjects, while the agent of 'practical reason' is either the individuals as the subject at the micro level or the group (nation-society) as the subject at the macro level. Inscribed in the linguistic telos of mutual understanding and forming an ensemble of conditions that both enable and limit, 'communicative rationality is expressed in a decentered complex of pervasive, transcendentally enabling structural conditions, but it is not a subjective capacity that would tell actors what they *ought* to do' (Habermas 1996, pp. 3f.).

On the other hand, like 'practical reason', 'communicative reason' has a normative significance for human activities, but this normative significance is much weaker than in the case of 'practical reason'. Not being an immediate source of rules of action, communicative reason 'has a normative content only insofar as the communicatively acting individuals must commit themselves to pragmatic presuppositions of a counterfactual sort' (ibidem, p. 4).

On the basis of the idea of communicative reason, therefore, Habermas's 'argument of pragmatic indispensability' can be seen as a discourse-theoretical version of Kant's 'argument of human beings' moral duty'. Like Popper, Habermas would not have liked the 'argument of logical possibility', since he thinks it important to appropriate arguments and materials from various fields so as to give our moral ideas stronger supports. Nor would he have liked the 'argument of historical necessity', since in his view the future of human history is to a large degree still to be decided by each of the coming generations. These two sides of Habermas's thinking are combined in his understanding of the term 'developmental logic': a fixed (though fallible) sequence of developmental stages both in personal development and societal development, at each of which there is a limited set of alternatives. On the basis of his theory of communicative action, Habermas develops his theory of socialization and modernization not as theories of inevitable tendencies and necessary laws, but as theories of possibilities and preconditions for realizing these possibilities. From this we can understand why, in an interview made during his 2001 visit to China, where he was asked whether he was a pessimist or not, Habermas replied: 'Theoretically I am a pessimist; but practically, as a good Kantian, I have to act like an optimist' (Habermas 2002). While there is no theoretical reason to give us objective guarantees for realizing our hope for a better society (pessimism in theory), we should nevertheless on no account give up this hope (optimism in practice). Like Popper, Habermas can also be called a cautious optimist. Both derive their cautiousness from their rejection of historical determinism, but while Popper bases his optimism more on the force of a particular tradition and the human capability of cognitive learning (with regard to the best means to reach good goals), Habermas bases his optimism more on the force of a universal potential of rationalization and the human capability of normative learning (with regard to what is 'right' to all and what is 'good' to us). This is obviously a result of Habermas's disagreement with Popper's decisionistic view of culture and positivistic conception of rationality. Both of these views can be seen clearly even when Popper was defending himself against the accusation of 'positivism' made by Habermas and others: 'And it is a fact that my *social theory* (which favours gradual and piecemeal reform, reform controlled by a critical comparison between expected and achieved results) contrasts with my *theory of method*, which happens to be a theory of scientific and intellectual revolution' (Popper 1994, Chapter 3, §I). Popper does not seem to be interested in the problem of whether it is necessary or even possible to have any *rational* deliberation and discussion over the *aim* and *motivation* of reform.

Bibliography

Habermas, J. (1996). *Between Facts and Norms: Contributions to a Discourse Theory of Law and Democracy*. Cambridge MA: MIT Press.

———— (2002). 'China: Schmerzen der Gesellschaft'. *Die Zeit*, 20, 2002.

Kant, I. (1970). *Political Writings*. Edited with an introduction and notes by H. S. Reiss. 2nd edition 1991. Cambridge & elsewhere: Cambridge University Press.

Popper, K. R. (1945). *The Open Society and Its Enemies*. London: George Routledge & Sons. 5th edition 1966. London: Routledge & Kegan Paul.

———— (1992). *In Search of a Better World: Lectures and Essays from Thirty Years*. London: Routledge.

———— (1994). *The Myth of the Framework: In Defence of Science and Rationality*. London: Routledge.

63

Rationality and Other Cultures

Kei Yoshida

1 Introduction

Human beings act in order to solve problems or to attain purposes, according
to their environments and situations. In other words, some human actions are
intended as solutions to problems. In this sense, these actions can be called
rational: they are goal-directed activities.

There are, however, some actions for which we can discern no goal and
so seem to be irrational, especially in other cultures. Here, we are faced
with an important problem: how should we describe and explain these 'irrational' activities? If those who accept more or less scientific or Western
thinking criticize or judge these activities, then it seems that they superim-
pose their views on others and judge that others are inferior in being less
critical. Peter Winch claims that we should not criticize or judge other cultures or world views because they have their own rationalities and that these
may not include self-criticism. According to Winch, criticism simply shows our
ethnocentrism. In his book, *The Idea of a Social Science and Its Relation to
Philosophy* (1958; ISS, hereafter), and his paper, 'Understanding a Primitive
Society' (1964; UPS, hereafter), Winch claims that each culture has its own
rationality which is entitled to be understood internally, not externally. This
approach to rationality and understanding other cultures seems, however, to
lead towards relativism. The reason for this is that Winch rejects rationality independent of context or language. Jarvie & Agassi avoid relativism by
opting for rationality as a matter of degree rather than different rationalities.
By contrasting Winch's view with Jarvie & Agassi's, I shall develop a better model of rationality and cross-cultural communication between different
cultures.

2 A Winchian model of rationality

First, we shall take a look at a Winchian model of rationality. In order to do
so, we need to analyse Winch's views of reality and language since they are
closely related to his argument for the claim of different rationalities.[1]

---

[1] As to other issues — such as whether Winch fairly understands Evans-Pritchard's
anthropological methods, and whether Winch knows Zande culture better than does Evans-
Pritchard, a field-work anthropologist — see B. D. Lerner's works (1995a, 1995b, and 2001).

Winch argues that our languages — such as scientific and religious ones — influence our understanding of reality. On Winch's account, the reality represented by a scientific language is not necessarily the same as that by a religious one.[2] Winch claims as follows (UPS, p. 309; emphasis in original):

> What is real and what is unreal shows itself *in* the sense that language has. Further, both the distinction between the real and the unreal and the concept of agreement with reality themselves belong to our language. ... If then we wish to understand the significance of these concepts, we must examine the use they actually do have — *in* the language.

In short, our understanding of reality depends on contexts, namely, particular languages. That is, in investigating other cultures, an anthropologist needs to understand contexts or languages where concepts and ideas are discussed and used. Moreover, we cannot understand even part of the contexts or languages without understanding the whole (ISS, p. 107; emphasis in original).

> But ideas cannot be torn out of their context in that way; the relation between idea and context is an *internal* one. The idea gets its sense from the role it plays in the system. It is nonsensical to take several systems of ideas, find an element in each which can be expressed in the same verbal form, and then claim to have discovered an idea which is common to all the systems. This would be like observing that both the Aristotelian and Galilean systems of mechanics use a notion of force, and concluding that they therefore make use of the same notion.

That is, Winch claims that without a proper understanding of the whole, we can never understand the ideas in a particular culture. Here is a reason some scholars regard Winch as an idealist (Gellner 1968; Williamson 1989). Yet, if a context or language defines a view of reality in a culture or society, discussing the 'agreement with reality' almost does not make sense. Even if something is in agreement with reality, it can be described only within a particular language, say, a scientific language. Hence Winch casts doubt on the notion of objective reality; however, it does not follow that he rejects it. Rather, he admits that the idea of the 'agreement with reality' is important (UPS, p. 309). What Winch means is that 'discussion about it [objective reality] takes place within a universe of discourse, but discussion about measuring the success of the universe of discourse in capturing objective reality cannot take place within that universe of discourse' (Jarvie 1972, p. 45). In short, Winch means that the criterion of objective reality is within a context or language investigated, not outside of it. Moreover, even if we attempt to discuss objective reality, it must be done within a particular context or language. That is, we cannot go outside that context or language. Hence we cannot appeal to criteria that are independent of particular contexts or languages. Or we can say

[2]This means that a culture has many languages for describing different aspects of the life in it. Yet Winch seems to think that the Azande do not have a scientific language or one similar to it. So he rejects discussion about Zande magic from a scientific point of view and does not propose any Zande counterpart of science.

as follows: even if there are objective reality and some criteria, how can we know and describe them without employing particular contexts or languages such as a scientific or religious one? This is a highly sceptical question about the existence of objective reality and criteria. Winch's answer is negative. In his view, we cannot describe objective reality independently of our language.

So far, we have discussed Winch's view of reality and of language. We can easily discern that this view is closely related to his discussion about rationality and other cultures. In Winch's view, the judgment of whether acts in a 'primitive' society are rational must be made within a language of the society in question, following the internal criteria that those people are currently using. It is a mistake to judge the activities in some other culture from our point of view. In Winch's view, Zande magic is a wholly different conceptual enterprise from Western science. Hence we cannot use the criteria of Western science to evaluate whether or not Zande magic is rational. That is, our criteria are meaningful only to us, but not to them (UPS, pp. 316f.; emphasis in original).[3]

> Something can appear rational to someone only in terms of *his* understanding of what is and is not rational. If *our* concept of rationality is a different one from his, then it makes no sense to say that anything either does or does not appear rational to *him* in *our* sense. ... If then, in the explanation, we say that in fact those criteria *are* rational, we must be using the word '*rational*' in *our* sense. For this explanation would require that we had previously carried out an independent investigation into the actual rationality or otherwise of those criteria, and we could do this only in terms of an understood concept of rationality — *our* understood concept of rationality.

Judging from Winch's argument, we cannot but conclude that he denies the possibility of universal trans-cultural judgment. In Winch's view, in order to make a trans-cultural judgment, we must have criteria that exist independently of our language. Yet Winch would claim that we cannot have such criteria. For Winch, criteria and a language to which they belong are not separable. That is, these criteria are dependent upon a context or language. If we cannot have such context-independent criteria, we must use our own criteria, which are inevitably connected with our particular language. If this is the case, our judgment of other cultures is simply the reflection of our world view, not a transcultural one, in that our language defines our world view. From a Winchian (or interpretivist) point of view, however, this is ethnocentrism. Hence a Winchian interpretivist would claim as follows: in order to investigate other cultures or their aspects, we must abandon the idea of explaining and judging them externally. Rather, we need to understand other cultures internally. Each culture has its own rationality. Without internal understanding of

---

[3] Or we could argue that the Azande do not have a concept of rationality at all. Yet Winch would not say so. Winch's main point is that different cultures have different rationalities. Hence Winch would say that the position described above is quite ethnocentric. I am grateful to Prof. I. C. Jarvie for drawing my attention to this point.

their rationality, we can never investigate other cultures. If we try to invest-igate Zande magic from a scientific point of view, it means that we miss some important aspects of it. Zande magic is quite different from Western science. It *expresses* the Zande form of life.

3 Towards a pluralistic model of rationality

We have so far analysed Winch's view of rationality. His view has many prob-lems. Because of them, Winch falls into relativism — even if he denies it. In this section, I shall discuss Jarvie & Agassi's view of rationality as an alter-native to Winch's and stress the importance of a critical attitude by referring to Popper's paper, 'Towards a Rational Theory of Tradition' (1949). I shall show this to be a better model of rationality for explaining other cultures.[4]

In a series of joint papers, Jarvie & Agassi have relativized the criteria of rationality and argued that rationality is better seen as a matter of de-gree (Jarvie & Agassi 1967, 1973, 1979, 1980, and 1996; also see Agassi 1977 and Jarvie 2005). In their view, no one is completely rational or irrational. If there is a difference between Western science and Zande magic, it is not the difference between rational and irrational, but the difference between more rational and less rational. To clarify this, Jarvie & Agassi distinguish three levels of rationality: rationality 1, 2, and 3. Rationality 1 is 'the goal-directed action of an agent with given aims and circumstances, where among his cir-cumstances we included his knowledge and opinions' (Jarvie & Agassi 1979, pp. 353f.). Jarvie & Agassi refer to magical incantation for the treatment of illness, to blood-letting, and to the routine use of antibiotics, as examples of this level. In short, rationality 1 is that of goal-directed action in order to solve problems. Many actions can be called 'rational' on this level, if they are goal-directed. It seems to me that not only human beings, but also animals can act in order to solve problems. For instance, think about apes washing muddy potatoes. This shows that even apes display some rationality as they solve their problem, namely, to make muddy potatoes edible — although apes seem to lack the next levels of rationality. It does not make sense to draw a line between different cultures if we cannot even differentiate between human beings and apes. In this sense, not only we, but also the Azande, are rational on the level of rationality 1.

Yet there are other levels of rationality: rationality 2 and 3. According to Jarvie & Agassi, rationality 2 adds 'the element of rational thinking or thinking which obeys some set of explicit rules, a level which is not found in magic in general, though it is sometimes given to specific details of magical thinking within the magical thought-system' (1979, p. 354). The problem of rationality 2 is that it does not allow members to criticize their own system, although it has some elements of rational thinking. Following Frazer, Jarvie & Agassi claim that 'magic in general is pseudo-rational' because it lacks

---

[4] Jarvie (1970) has already criticized Winch from a critical rationalist point of view. My criticism of Winch is strongly influenced by Jarvie's.

articulate4 standards of rational thinking (ibidem). That is, magic is rational in that it tries to solve problems and has some standard or rule of rational thinking; however, it is not critical. It does not permit the criticism of its own system. To introduce this, Jarvie & Agassi distinguish another level of rationality: rationality 3. Jarvie & Agassi argue that '[t]he third level of rationality [rationality 3] we proposed to isolate was that of goal-directed action (rationality 1) subject to thinking that conforms to not just some rule or standard of rational thinking (rationality 2), but the best available rules for, the highest standards of, rational thinking (rationality 3)' (ibidem). By 'the best available rules for, or the highest standards of, rational thinking', what Jarvie & Agassi mean is this: in order for us to be highly rational, we must be critical of not only other ideas or systems, but also *our* own thinking; that is to say, we must be self-critical. Otherwise our thinking does not satisfy the highest standards of rational thinking. Hence it is not highly rational. In fact, it is fairly easy for us to criticize other ideas and systems, which are different from ours. Yet, in order to be highly rational, we must expose our own views to severe criticism, first of all. In this sense, Jarvie & Agassi think that 'Frazer was not as rational as he could have been, because he was uncritical of his own scientific philosophy and evolutionism while offering and justifying his judgements on magic' (ibidem). That is, for Jarvie & Agassi, not only magic in general, but also other systems of thought are not highly rational, if they do not satisfy the highest standards of rational thinking, that is, critical thinking.

Having summarized Jarvie & Agassi's view of rationality we can turn to their explanation of why science is more rational than magic. Magic is rational in that it is goal-directed and has, sometimes, some elements of rational thinking; however, it does not allow the criticism of its own system and thus promote mutual criticism. Contrary to this, science recommends self- and mutual criticism among competing schools. Without criticism, science could have never been developed as such. For instance, if Einstein had followed Newtonian mechanics dogmatically, he could have never developed his special and general theories of relativity. In this sense, criticism or a critical attitude is the core of science. Certainly, even science cannot be completely critical, namely, rational, if we think about the emergence and existence of normal science. As Kuhn points out, scientists sometimes stick to their paradigm or received/pet theory. However, they can be criticized by other or future scientists who do not support the paradigm in question. In this sense, science is more rational than magic or other systems of thought, for example, metaphysics or theology, in that it permits the criticism of its own system or mutual criticism among schools. The reason we rate science more rational than magic is that science allows mutual criticism. Some may think that our argument is based on the belief that scientific knowledge is more certain than magic. This is not the case. According to Popper, scientific theories must be, in principle, falsifiable. If not falsifiable, they are not empirical science. Hence scientific knowledge is not certain at all, no more than magic is. In a sense, there is no difference between science and magic, as to certainty.

As argued above, the reason we rate science more rational than magic is
not that science is more certain than magic, but that science is more criticiz-
able than magic. In order to clarify this point, Popper's argument is helpful.
According to Popper, science has the second-order tradition of criticizing a
myth. In his paper, 'Towards a Rational Theory of Tradition', Popper differentiates between science and myth as follows (1949, p. 44):

> My thesis is that what we call 'science' is differentiated from the older myths
> not by being something distinct from a myth, but by being accompanied by a
> second-order tradition — that of critically discussing the myth.

That is, science is also a myth, in a sense. What differentiates science from
other myths is that the former has the tradition of critical discussion, but the
latter do not. Popper writes (ibidem, p. 45):

> But why are they different? Because if one adopts this critical attitude then
> one's myths do become different. They change; and they change in a direction
> towards giving a better and better account of the world — of the various things
> which we can observe.

I think that Popper's point is not mistaken, given that the origin of science is
Greek cosmology. From a present scientific point of view, Greek cosmology is
not science at all. Perhaps, one of the main reasons Greek cosmology became
science is that Greek philosophers recommended critical discussion about different ideas. Through critical discussion, Greek cosmology could change and
improve, hence, develop as science. This is the crucial difference between science and myth or magic. If Zande magic had the second-order tradition of
critical discussion, it could have developed and become another type of knowledge, which might have been different from Western science. However, it did
not have such a tradition. Hence it could not change rationally, compared
with Greek cosmology as a precursor of science. Jarvie & Agassi claim that
'[n]ot magic, but the uncritical attitude to ideas embedded in the social institutions of magic-oriented groups is what inhibits the jump to universalist
science: members are doing their top rational best as long as they have no
science' (1996, p. 469). That is, the difference between science and myth is not
based on these systems of thought themselves, but on people's attitudes towards their traditions and on the institutional character (or the second-order
tradition) that enables them to be critical of their own systems.

So far, we have discussed the importance of criticism or the critical attitude. However, what do we mean by criticism? It seems to be generally
believed that the term 'criticism' has a negative connotation, namely, that it
is something to be avoided (or at least regretted). A Winchian interpretivist
would claim that if we criticize other cultures, we simply expose our ethnocentrism. Yet criticism need not mean blame, condemnation, or anything like
that. Criticism need not be a personal attack. Rather, the reason we take criticism positively and seriously is that it prompts us to reconsider and improve
our pet views. When we criticize other cultures or their aspects, it need not

be done in order to devalue them, but to open the way to their improvement. Some may think that this is arrogant or ethnocentric. Yet criticism is not one-sided. If people living in other cultures do not agree with our criticism of their cultures, they can counter-criticize.

In investigating seriously other cultures or their aspects, we cannot but presuppose our own subjective biases or expectations *as a matter of fact.* That is, our explanation of other cultures is vitiated by our subjective biases or expectations. Yet, by trying to articulate and criticize our biases, we can sometimes reconsider and modify them. Hence we may be able to give better explanations of other cultures than they do of themselves. Of course, these better explanations are also fallible. So, they will need to be criticized in turn. This activity of criticism is, in principle, endless. Even if we choose to stop criticizing, that does not mean that our explanation is certain or perfect. We just stop it tentatively. If we are in doubt, we may want to continue criticizing. In short, the reason we stress the importance of criticism is that we admit the fallibility of our explanation. By severe criticism, we are trying to articulate and improve our view. In order to do so, we need not only self-criticism, but also criticism from others. The reason for this is that others may teach us something that we miss or ignore. By facing different cultures, we have a chance to think about our outlook and to learn something from theirs. By encountering us, people living in other cultures also have an opportunity to consider their own tradition.[5] I think that here is a possibility of a pluralism that Popper pioneered. It is easy to regard different cultures or aspects of them as irrational and declare the superiority of the Western notion of rationality over others or vice versa. This must be rejected. Yet it is also easy to claim that different cultures have different rationalities. A Winchian relativist would say that this is the only way to tolerance. Yet claiming so seems to mean keeping the door closed to different cultures and peoples and their potential criticisms of us. Certainly, it is difficult to admit and to accept different cultures, customs, and people. I would not deny it. In some cases, they can be a threat to us in that they are different from us and ours and we do not know them well. We will feel at ease if we keep the door closed. However, openness to the others and their criticism is a key to pluralism. Being open to others may require us to reconsider and revise our pet views. This may be bitter, mentally. Yet our aim is not to protect our biased views, but to

---

[5]To clarify my claim, I should like to mention my own experience as a Japanese living in the English-speaking world. Some people living in the English-speaking world do not know Japan and its culture well. Or sometimes they have stereotyped views, which can be represented by Fujiyama, geisha, Kabuki, samurai, etc. So, I need to explain critically how these stereotyped views are misunderstandings or partial pictures of Japan. By doing so, I give these people an opportunity to reconsider and modify their views of Japan. But, this is not one-sided in that I cannot but reflect on Japan, its culture, and my own origin when I explain Japan and its culture to them. In other words, these people give me an opportunity to take a look at and think about my own culture and tradition from a different perspective. The same thing would hold true for people to whom I talk in that they learn a different culture or its aspects. I am thankful to one of the anonymous referees for the request that I should provide more concrete illustrations of my contention.

change and improve them by mutual criticism. If, by mutual criticism, we can reconsider and improve our views and we may contribute to the improvement and modification of others' views, why must we be afraid of facing different cultures and people?

4 Conclusion

We have discussed the problem of rationality and other cultures. It seems to me that the so-called 'rationality debate' is an attempt at self-criticism by Western thinking. By facing different cultures, Westerners had (and still have) a chance to consider their own ethnocentrism. Even if their consideration is not perfect, their view could and can change by critical discussion. It shows the strength of Western scientific thinking, although this does not justify Western science, of course. Is it possible for people in other cultures to change, reconsider or criticize their own views? Did they take the Western tradition seriously and critically? I think that this is a very important problem in thinking about cross-cultural communication. From a Western point of view, the problem was how Westerners can and should explain (or understand) different cultures; however, from a non-Western point of view, the problem is not only how non-Westerners can and should be explained (or understood), but also what they think about Western science and its tradition. The West brought the scientific tradition to the non-Western world. The strength of non-Western thinking is dependent upon how non-Westerners take a stance towards Western scientific tradition. This does not mean that non-Westerners must reject the Western scientific tradition. Yet, in order to be highly rational, critical, they must not accept Western thinking uncritically. Hence non-Westerners need to reject two extremes: the emotional or political rejection of Western thinking and the uncritical acceptance of it. I should like to finish my paper with the following quotation (Popper 1949, p. 45). ' "I hand it on to you, but tell me what you think about it. Think it over. Perhaps you can give us a different story." ' On Popper's account, this text is a hidden attachment, of a second-order character, to the scientific tradition. What non-Westerners must do is to think about this scientific tradition.

Bibliography

Agassi, J. (1977). *Towards a Rational Philosophical Anthropology*. The Hague: Martinus Nijhoff.

Gellner, E. (1968). 'The New Idealism: Cause and Meaning in the Social Sciences'. In I. Lakatos & A. E. Musgrave, editors (1968), pp. 377-406, 426-432. *Problems in the Philosophy of Science*. Amsterdam: North-Holland Publishing Company.

Jarvie, I. C. (1970). 'Understanding and Explanation in Sociology and Social Anthropology'. In R. Borger & F. Cioffi, editors (1970), pp. 231-248, 260-269. *Explanation in the Behavioural Sciences*. Cambridge & elsewhere: Cambridge University Press.

———— (1972). *Concepts and Society*. London & Boston MA: Routledge & Kegan Paul.

———— (2005). 'Workshop Rationality, Dogmatism, and Models of the Mind'. In D. M. Johnson & C. Erneling, editors, pp. 471-486. *The Mind as a Scientific Object: Between Brain and Culture*. Oxford: Oxford University Press.

Jarvie, I. C. & Agassi, J. (1967). 'The Problem of the Rationality of Magic'. *British Journal of Sociology* **18**, pp. 55-74.

———— (1973). 'Magic and Rationality Again'. *British Journal of Sociology* **24**, pp. 236-245.

———— (1979). 'The Rationality of Dogmatism'. In T. Geraets, editor (1979), pp. 353-362. *Rationality Today*. Ottawa: University of Ottawa Press.

———— (1980). 'The Rationality of Irrationalism'. *Metaphilosophy* **11**, pp. 127-133.

———— (1996). 'Rationality'. In A. Barnard & J. Spencer, editors (1996), pp. 467-470. *Encyclopedia of Social and Cultural Anthropology*. London: Routledge.

Lerner, B. D. (1995a). 'Understanding a (Secular) Primitive Society'. *Religious Studies* **30**, pp. 303-309.

———— (1995b). 'Winch and Instrumental Pluralism'. *Philosophy of the Social Sciences* **25**, pp. 180-191.

———— (2001). *Rules, Magic, and Instrumental Reason: A Critical Interpretation of Peter Winch's Philosophy of the Social Sciences*. London: Routledge.

Popper, K. R. (1949). 'Towards a Rational Theory of Tradition'. In F. Watts, editor (1949), pp. 36-55. *The Rationalist Annual 1949*. London: Watts and Co. Reprinted as Chapter 4 of K. R. Popper (1963). *Conjectures and Refutations. The Growth of Scientific Knowledge*. London: Routledge & Kegan Paul. 5th edition 1989. London: Routledge.

Williamson, C. (1989). 'Witchcraft and Winchcraft'. *Philosophy of the Social Sciences* **19**, pp. 445-460.

Winch, P. (1958). *The Idea of a Social Science and Its Relation to Philosophy*. London & New York: Routledge & Kegan Paul.

———— (1964). 'Understanding a Primitive Society'. *American Philosophical Quarterly* **1**, pp. 307-324.

64

How to Avoid Giving Unwanted Answers to Unasked Questions
Realizing Karl Popper's Educational Dream[*]

Joanna Swann

1 Introduction

In keeping with the aspirations expressed in Karl Popper's educational dream
(Popper 1974/1976, §9), I propose that we should try to create schools in
which students learn without boredom, in which they are stimulated to pose
and discuss problems; schools 'in which no unwanted answers to unasked questions have to be listened to' (ibidem), and in which studying is not undertaken
simply to pass examinations. This set of aspirations may not be fully realizable, but each aspiration is nonetheless important as a standard at which to
aim. My only quibble with Popper's formulation is that it neglects the idea
that students need to engage in practical trial and error-elimination, rather
than merely participate in discussion.

The crux of my argument in this paper is that the standards expressed in
Popper's dream can be most effectively pursued through the development of
student-initiated curricula. The argument, influenced in particular by Popper
(1972/1979 and 1974/1976) and the educational theory of Tyrrell Burgess
(1977), is rooted in Popper's evolutionary epistemology. One of Popper's sem-
inal, though largely unrecognized, achievements is his well-argued challenge to
the commonly held view that some learning takes place through the transfer
of ideas from without the organism, by instruction from the environment. Following Popper, one can argue that learning does not take place in situations
where the organism's expectations remain unchallenged. Although learning
takes many forms, invariably it is a creative process, provoked by the discovery (conscious or unconscious) of error or specific limitation (Swann 2003b).

Authors have construed in various ways the implications of Popper's phil-
osophy for education. The Popperian approach to education developed by
Burgess and myself is more structured than that of, for example, Henry
Perkinson (1993), though the underlying social values are similar. Perkinson's

*I am grateful to Richard Bailey, Tyrrell Burgess, John Halliday, Brian Marley, Dylan
Wiliam and two anonymous referees for feedback on one or more earlier versions of this
paper.

epistemology is similarly evolutionary and non-inductivist (1971, 1984). These approaches can be contrasted with conservative interpretations of Popper, in which greater emphasis is placed on the value of tradition; see, for example, Richard Bailey (2000). Interesting though it may be to reflect on the various educational theories for which Popper's writings have provided the stimulus, this paper does not discuss the work of Perkinson, Bailey, and others (the contributors to Zecha 1999, for example).

2 Teaching

Significant aspects of what we learn, especially when we are children, are a consequence of being taught. But, of course, often we do not learn what our teachers wish us to learn, and invariably we learn things other than or additional to what they intend. Nevertheless, if we were not taught by our parents, other family members, our peers and, on a more formal basis, teachers in school, we, our relationships, and our society would be very different. This is not to deny the importance of untutored learning; but such learning will not on its own enable a child to become a functionally proficient member of human society, someone who, for example, engages fully with the world of objectified knowledge. Even autodidacts will have benefited from some teaching.

But what, if anything, must be taught? And how, in general, can teachers promote learning? Popper provided an answer to the first question in his intellectual autobiography. Of reading, 'riting and 'rithmetic — the so-called 3Rs — he wrote (1974/1976, § 3): 'They are, I think, the only essentials a child has to be taught; and some children do not even need to be taught in order to learn these. Everything else is atmosphere, and learning through reading and thinking.' I agree with Popper that some children, a few, learn the 3Rs with little or no obvious teaching, but in this quotation he undervalued the importance of learning through conversation. Perhaps his jaded view of the schooling he received (ibidem, § 8), and his intellectual precociousness, led him to downplay the value of teaching. His educational dream, by contrast, offers a more optimistic view of what schools can become.

The outcomes of schooling are disappointing, not least because schools are expected to serve many purposes, some of which conflict with the promotion of learning. In particular, schools are instrumental in the process of social selection that influences post-school opportunities, wealth, and status. This process conflicts with the provision of a learning service in that it penalizes failure and damages confidence; often it discourages learning. But rather than dismiss teaching as a limiting and potentially harmful activity, I propose that we strive to create schools in which the promotion of learning is the overriding aim. Below, drawing on a Popperian analysis of learning, I propose 13 theses for the conduct of teaching. The ideas embedded in some of the theses are also relevant to the teacher as learner, and to how education institutions can support the learning of teachers in the context of teacher education and provision for continuing professional development. In the following section of the paper I outline an approach to the curriculum in which the teaching implications of the 13 theses may be realized.

First thesis: There is no learning without autonomous activity on the part of the learner. The most important factor in learning is the freedom to explore (see the gondola kitten experiment of Held & Hein 1963, discussed in Popper & Eccles 1977 and in Swann 1999c). The teacher should try not to restrict the student's autonomous activity, unless such activity is detrimental to the well-being of the student and/or other persons. In most schools the freedom to act autonomously is significantly curtailed. If students are to learn more, then teaching must be organized to allow greater opportunity for autonomous activity.

Second thesis: A fully autonomous learner is not dependent on others for the what, when, why, and how of her learning, yet is able and willing to interact with other people and draw on other resources in order to learn.

To this end, students should be encouraged to: exercise initiative (in the form of self-initiated and self-regulated trial and error-elimination); develop self-awareness; become skilled and knowledgeable with regard to methods and processes associated with learning; assume responsibility for their actions and their outcomes; develop descriptive and argumentative language, and good social and communication skills. A degree of meta-learning — for example, learning about the significance of the discovery of error — is part of this process. So too is the development of literacy and numeracy (see the earlier quotation from Popper regarding the 3Rs).

Third thesis: Desire is crucial to learning — it stimulates the will to act. The teacher should strive to recognize and work with the student's desires, specifically what the student wants to become able to do, become better at, and learn more about. The teacher may decide to stop the student from acting on specific desires when the outcome is judged to be unacceptable, and she may challenge the student to modify her desires; but, whenever possible, the inhibition of desire should be avoided.

Fourth thesis: There is no learning without the discovery of error or specific limitation. The strategy of deliberately seeking out errors and specific limitations in assumptions, policies, and practices is the principal means by which learning can be accelerated. When we recognize our mistakes and limitations, we are better placed to eliminate the former and reduce the latter. Teachers should help students to do this as quickly as possible (see Popper 1972, Chapter 6, § XXI).

The identification of error is, of course, a conjectural issue — people can be mistaken about what is false, in the same way that they can be mistaken about what is true.

Fifth thesis: The teacher must provide a safe place in which to learn, where the discovery of error or limitation is not penalized *per se*. Rules and sanctions may be necessary to discourage and prevent behaviour that is undesirable because, for example, it inhibits the learning of other students; but the purpose of any sanction should be to maintain the efficacy of the learning environment rather than to punish the student.

In many schools, teachers are expected to produce students who give 'the right answers' and perform tasks according to narrowly conceived standards. In these circumstances, teachers will be more inclined to penalize failure of understanding, failure to give the prescribed answer, failure to agree, failure to conform.

In general, if we expect the discovery of error and limitation to incur a penalty, we are likely to try to avoid errors and limitations being discovered: we do less, we learn less. The worst case scenario is that this becomes habitual.

Sixth thesis: Before helping the student to discover and respond to errors and specific limitations in the ideas the student brings to the learning environment, the teacher may first have to foster the student's self-confidence (Burgess 1977, p. 160). Learning entails a willingness to try, and willingness to try involves the risk of failure. A confident student generally expects something good to obtain from situations that are not found to be entirely successful, and does not abandon hope when errors and specific limitations are discovered.

Seventh thesis: Criticism facilitates the discovery of error; it is central to the business of teaching. The teacher should create situations in which a student's assumptions about herself, the world and her place in it, are revealed and then challenged. Given that learning cannot take place without some form of criticism, there will be situations in which inadequate criticism is a significant impediment to learning. Most people receive a great deal of criticism during the course of their schooling, but often it fails to address the assumptions that have the greatest influence on the way they interact with the world. Where there is a prescribed curriculum of knowledge and skills to be taught, much of the criticism focuses on the student's interactions (or lack of interaction) with its content. A prescribed curriculum often disregards erroneous ideas that students bring to the classroom; these ideas, by being ignored, are allowed to continue unchallenged.

But criticism can sap confidence and inhibit learning. This is true even when the criticism is valid and the student recognizes that this is so. In general, most people require some acknowledgement of the positive features of their endeavours before they can cope with errors or specific limitations. Teachers should therefore be mindful of the importance of confidence, and not routinely express criticisms as soon as errors and limitations are revealed. Decisions about when and how to criticize are a matter of professional judgement.

Eighth thesis: Teaching that is successful in promoting learning on anything other than an ad hoc basis requires the teacher to initiate and maintain educational relationships with her students, and to encourage them to develop such relationships with each other and with other people. Effective educational relationships are based on trust and mutual understanding; they promote student confidence and enable the student to cope with and benefit from criticism. Such relationships can challenge without being coercive or manipulative. They involve the teacher in, among other things, listening, the development of empathy, appropriate boundary setting, and — where there is more than one student — the practice of equity.

Ninth thesis: Although one of the teacher's principal tasks is to challenge students, she should strive to avoid offering unwanted answers to unasked questions. Of course, there will be some things the teacher wishes her students to learn (safety procedures, for example) and be able to do (such as read), and there is clearly a role for teachers in terms of stimulating students to consider ideas beyond their previous experience. But when a teacher introduces ideas and activities that are not a direct response to a student's expressed interests, or cannot be related in the student's mind to something that she perceives to be important, then the student may become bored or confused. In addition, time spent on unwanted answers to unasked questions allows less time for the teacher and student to focus on the student's expectations and aspirations (see third, sixth, and twelfth theses).

Students will interpret what they are told or shown in the light of their expectations. Given that learning by instruction from the environment does not take place, the teacher's efforts to convey a particular idea will invariably be problematic and often prove unsuccessful.

Tenth thesis: The teacher must be prepared to embrace non-authoritarian values. Such values are consistent with the idea that there are no firm grounds for knowledge, no absolute authorities when it comes to making judgements about what is true, valid, and good. Such values are also consistent with the idea that we cannot control what another person learns. The teacher should not underestimate the difficulty of this task; authoritarianism is deeply embedded in the organization and structure of formal education (for discussion, see Perkinson 1971).

Authoritarian approaches to education have 'a common view of the learner's relationship to the teacher: it is one of dependence' (Meighan 1981, p. 183; 2003, p. 214). When we encourage students to depend on us for any aspect of their learning, we discourage them from criticizing our ideas and practices, and we may deny them the opportunity to make decisions for themselves. Opportunities for learning are thereby limited. In order to maximize learning, students should be encouraged to criticize potentially any aspect of the world in which they find themselves — no person, idea, or institution should be above criticism.

Eleventh thesis: Teachers should try to avoid being seduced by 'the myth of the subject' (Popper 1983, p. 5). The discrediting of the idea of secure knowledge, and the realization that learning is a trial-and-error process, undermines the epistemological basis for organizing teaching and learning according to academic or school subjects. In general, subject-based teaching is an administrative convenience; it bears little relationship to the ways in which knowledge is construed and utilized in life outside school, and it is often an impediment to the development of curricula focused on students' learning problems (see next thesis).

Twelfth thesis: The teacher should, as much as possible, organize the curriculum on the basis of the students' learning problems. Logically speaking, we are best advised to concentrate on those aspects of learning that we know, or anticipate, to be problematic; these can be formulated as learning problems. (See next section of the paper.)

Thirteenth thesis: The teacher is advised to adopt a problem-based methodology as a means of pursuing improvement in learning in her classroom (or other learning environment). Among other things, this involves the teacher in reflecting on the present state of affairs, on what is right with it and thus worth defending, and what is wrong and ripe for change. It also involves being alert to the potential for unintended and undesirable consequences when new policies and practices are introduced.

Methodological steps that the teacher might work through (either alone or in collaboration with colleagues) have been set out in various publications (including Swann 2003b). The rationale for the adoption of a problem-based approach to planning and evaluation, in contrast to the use of objectives or targets, is provided in Swann (1999a).

3 Student-initiated curricula

Adopting a largely non-interventionist approach to the curriculum is one way for schools to avoid situations in which students are offered unwanted answers to unasked questions. This approach may work well with students already able to operate as autonomous learners in a range of problem areas. Such students would also require effective social and political skills for working with their peers and others. But for the majority of students — those who, in order to progress, require encouragement, support, or challenge with regard to at least some of their learning — the adoption by their teachers of a largely non-interventionist approach would represent an abdication of responsibility.

So how can schools and teachers best organize the curriculum with a view to promoting learning? My answer, in accordance with the twelfth thesis above (and compatibly with the other theses), is: by the development of student-initiated curricula, that is, curricula that address students' learning problems — formulated by the students, with the help of their teacher(s). Below is a seven-stage procedure for developing student-initiated curricula. The first version of the procedure was created in the context of my doctoral research programme (Swann 1988), for which Tyrrell Burgess was one of my supervisors. (A later version was published in Swann 1999b.) The programme, which ran from 1981 to 1988, involved both the study of Popper's philosophy and action research that focused on teaching and learning in my primary school classroom (working with students aged 7 to 11 years). When devising the seven-stage procedure, I drew on my understanding of institutional structures and practices developed at the School for Independent Study at North East London Polytechnic (now the University of East London). Burgess was the School's founding Head, and the School's institutional structures and processes were to a significant extent influenced by his interpretation of Popper's epistemology.

The procedure is designed for teachers working with a group or class, but can be used in any teacher–student relationship. It could be adopted when planning an entire formal curriculum, or parts thereof. Given the particular focus of this paper, I elaborate on Stage 1, the stage at which the students are responsible for initiating curriculum content.

Stage 1: The teacher sets out to help students formulate their learning problems.

In practice, the most effective procedure, especially with young children, may be for the teacher to ask the students to think about 'what they are good at, what they can do' — to encourage a sense of achievement — and after this to consider 'what they would like to become better at, what they would like to know more about'. Only after working with the problem-based approach for a period of time may a student decide, for example, that her principal learning problem is one of 'how to become a reader'. Note that students may focus on problems that we, as teachers, consider to be peripheral, but which nonetheless will lead to more profound learning. For example, a child may spend several weeks studying dinosaurs, and in the process greatly improve her ability to read and write.

Perhaps the most important feature of Stage 1 is that the teacher must recognize that she cannot control what the student's learning problems will be. The teacher's problem and the student's problem are always different, though they may share an understanding of a problem situation. The adoption of student-initiated curricula does not rule out a two-way exchange between teacher and student; it is not inconsistent with a sharing of interests and problem contexts. What is wrong with most institutional education is that students never get to make decisions about the content of their formal learning. What they learn most strongly is to do the bidding of others; that their initiative is not welcomed; that they can make choices (if they are fortunate) but not exercise preference; and that they will be undervalued or penalized if they fail to meet the narrowly conceived expectations of both teacher and school. But if students are not permitted to formulate and develop their own programmes of learning, few will become fully autonomous learners. Without the habit of initiating curricula, students mostly learn dependency (though a few learn rebellion).

Helping students to formulate learning problems is rarely unproblematic. Mostly, students do not formulate learning problems because (a) they are not given the opportunity, (b) when they are asked a question about what they wish to learn they interpret this as a 'test', whereby they have to work out what the teacher wants them to say or do, and (c) the formulation of the most significant learning problems is often accompanied by feelings of discomfort.

Stage 1 usually requires the teacher to find ways of removing factors which impede students from formulating their learning problems. This involves skill as well as understanding. In addition, although in my own primary school

teaching I organized much of the week on the basis of student-initiated curricula, I taught specific (often short) lessons, mainly on aspects of mathematics, also on reading and writing (see second thesis). I also organized regular sessions of whole class games and other activities designed to encourage
personal and social development. This was necessary because many students
lacked confidence (see sixth thesis) and were unused (outside of school) to
collaborative endeavour (see eighth thesis). Using student-initiated curricula
does not necessitate a complete absence of teacher-initiated work, but for the
approach to be effective, commitment and sustained effort are required.

Stage 2: At the second stage, the teacher identifies which of the students'
learning problems can be addressed within the specific learning environment
with the help of the teacher, other teachers and students, and by using existing resources, or by involving individuals and agencies external to the learning environment. Students may formulate learning problems for which the
teacher/school can be of little or no help; but some ideas which at first seem
impractical or even impossible may be addressed in a modified form.

Stage 3: Some of the students' learning aspirations may be inappropriate
or incapable of being addressed by the teacher(s) and the institution. A student may wish to pursue learning that is morally unacceptable, or not feasible
in terms of resources. When a student's learning proposal is rejected, the
arguments underlying this decision should be made clear.

Many judgements with regard to the curriculum involve values extrinsic
to the general question of what promotes and what inhibits learning. What
counts as morally unacceptable, for example, involves judgements of this kind.
But, as a general principle, the problems that are the focus of the curriculum should be negotiated between the teacher and students, and as far as
possible the curriculum should be based on student preference. This does not
prevent the teacher from making suggestions, or prevent her from asserting
the importance of some things rather than others, or stop her from vetoing
the students' proposals (though one would expect there to be good reason for
her doing so).

Stage 4: The teacher's next task is to help students plan their learning,
paying attention to: their skills, talents and achievements; available resources
and expertise; their learning problems; time available; critical evaluation (by
helping students to state what would count as a failure of their educational
plans). Explicit attention to what happens when learning takes place may
form part of the discussion. (At the School for Independent Study, the learning
plans of undergraduate students were subject to formal validation.)

Stage 5: The teacher supports students in the fulfilment of their plans,
offering, where appropriate, encouragement, additional resources (when available) and critical discussion.

Stage 6: The teacher critically discusses with students the scope of their
learning problems and proposed solutions after they have been worked on, considering to what extent the formulated problems were well-conceived, whether
better problems could have been formulated, and what factors (if any) can

be identified to improve future problem formulation. In my experience, this is the most difficult step to apply satisfactorily. It might best be left until after the following stage, to allow time for reflection.

Stage 7: The teacher helps students to compile a record of their learning. The record will include a statement of the initial learning problems; it will show where trial solutions were found to be successful, where they failed and what was learnt from the experience. It will also include an outline of learning problems that have developed from the work undertaken. (At the School for Independent Study, student attainment was formally examined and accredited at this stage.)

4 Conclusion

Many educationists take the view that the principal purpose of education is to transmit and develop existing traditions of public knowledge, maintaining coherence and stability within social structures. They regard the development of public knowledge, rather than the development of the individual, as the primary aim of education. In contrast, the approach to student-initiated curricula that I have outlined treats education not as a contract between teacher and society, but as one between teacher and student (with the implication of long-term social benefit). Of educationists who dismiss the use of student-initiated curricula, because they lay greater stress on engaging students with the aspects of public knowledge that the teacher or other educational experts or policymakers judge to be worthwhile, I ask:

- How does the process you advocate address (in particular, challenge) the assumptions that influence the students' everyday lives?

- How does it help the students to deal with their learning problems (what they want to learn but are having difficulty learning)?

- How does it foster learner autonomy, particularly with regard to what is learnt?

Whatever one considers the purpose of education to be, one should not lose sight of the idea that learning is fundamentally an individual activity, critical, creative and open-ended. Of course, there will always be some things we want people to learn. Even so, the commonly accepted model of teacher–student interaction in which the student is thought to be able to receive ideas transmitted by the teacher, fails to take account of Popper's critique of induction and the challenge to educational orthodoxy that evolutionary epistemology presents. If we are intent, for whatever reason, on teaching things in which students have no initial interest, the Popper-influenced idea of creating with the students a 'speculative reconstruction of the objective problem situation in which the facts/theories/ideas being taught originally emerged' (anonymous referee) is to be valued, and is preferable to the idea that teaching is a matter of delivering to students a largely uncontentious body of facts. But such an approach still begs answers to the questions bulleted above.

The development of student-initiated curricula is, I suggest, our most effective means for pursuing, as a regulative ideal, the realization of Popper's educational dream. It makes sense to approach teaching with the intention of starting, as much as possible, with the expectations, preferences, and aspirations that the student brings to the classroom or other learning environment. There are no rigorous scientific studies that effectively cast doubt on such a practice (Swann 2003a). The use of student-initiated curricula at the School for Independent Study, and in my practice as a primary school teacher, did not lead to a narrowing of the curriculum, or a general failure to acquire basic skills. Indeed, the opposite seemed to be the case. And the formal programmes of learning that students developed, though different from those that teachers and external curriculum developers might have conceived on their behalf, were not foolish or inappropriate.

Student-initiated curricula of the kind described in this paper are entirely consistent with Popper's educational dream, his evolutionary epistemology, and the strand of anti-authoritarian argument that runs through his philosophy.

Bibliography

Bailey, R. (2000). *Education in the Open Society – Karl Popper and Schooling.* Aldershot: Ashgate.

Burgess, T. (1977). *Education after School.* London: Victor Gollancz.

Held, R. & Hein, A. (1963). 'Movement-produced Stimulation in the Development of Visually Guided Behaviour'. *Journal of Comparative and Physiological Psychology* **56**, pp. 872-876.

Meighan, R. (1981). *A Sociology of Educating.* New York: Holt, Rinehart and Winston. 4th edition 2003, with I. Siraj-Blatchford. London: Continuum.

Perkinson, H. J. (1971). *The Possibilities of Error: An Approach to Education.* New York: David McKay.

———— (1984). *Learning from our Mistakes: A Reinterpretation of Twentieth-Century Educational Thought.* Westport CT: Greenwood Press.

———— (1993). *Teachers Without Goals, Students Without Purposes.* New York: McGraw-Hill.

Popper, K. R. (1972). *Objective Knowledge.* Oxford: Oxford University Press. 2nd edition 1979.

———— (1974). 'Intellectual Autobiography'. In P. A. Schilpp, editor (1974), pp. 1-181. *The Philosophy of Karl Popper.* La Salle IL: Open Court. Reprinted as *Unended Quest* (1976). London & Glasgow: Fontana/Collins.

———— (1983). *Realism and the Aim of Science.* London: Hutchinson.

Popper, K. R. & Eccles, J. C. (1977). *The Self and Its Brain: An Argument for Interactionism.* Berlin & elsewhere: Springer International.

Swann, J. (1988). *How Can Classroom Practice Be Improved?: An Investigation of the Logic of Learning in Classroom Practice.* London: Council for National Academic Awards. Unpublished PhD thesis.

———— (1999a). 'Making Better Plans: Problem-based Versus Objectives-based Planning'. In Swann & Pratt (1999), pp. 53-66.

———— (1999b). 'The Logic-of-learning Approach to Teaching: A Testable Theory'. In Swann & Pratt (1999), pp. 109-120.

———— (1999c). 'What Happens When Learning Takes Place?'. *Interchange* **30**, pp. 257-282.

———— (2003a). 'How Science Can Contribute to the Improvement of Educational Practice'. *Oxford Review of Education* **29**, pp. 253-268.

———— (2003b). 'A Popperian Approach to Research on Learning and Method'. In J. Swann and J. Pratt, editors (2003), pp. 11-34. *Educational Research in Practice: Making Sense of Methodology.* London: Continuum.

Swann, J. & Pratt, J., editors (1999). *Improving Education: Realist Approaches to Method and Research.* London: Cassell.

Zecha, G., editor (1999). *Critical Rationalism and Educational Discourse.* Amsterdam: Editions Rodopi B.V.

Index

3Rs 262f.

a priori, apriorism 131–134, 187,
    198–200, 203
absolute validity 33
action, explanation of 209, 212–215
actuality 98f., 101–103
adaptation 131, 133, 135, 138,
    156, 160; *see also* darwinism;
    evolution; natural selection
Adler, A. 229
Adorno, T. W. vii, 166f.,
    169–173, 175f., 178, 181–183,
    186, 190–195
Agassi, J. 221f., 251, 254–256
Albert, H. ix, 58, 61, 63,
    166–176, 191
Alchian, A. 221
amoeba 132, 138, 140
animating force 209–211, 213
animating principle 203f.; *see*
    also models; rationality
    principle
anisotropy 63–65, 72
Annenkov, P. V. 234
Archibald, C. 221f.
Aristotle 98
    Aristotelianism 145f., 148–151
Arntzenius, F. 62
arrow of time 57, 63–65, 67f.,
    71–73
asymmetry 71f., 75
    causal 80–82
    cosmological 77
    thermodynamic 77, 79, 81
    wave 77–80, 82
authoritarianism 265, 270
autonomy 38–42, 263, 266, 269
    of sociology 166

Bacon, R. 183
Bächtold, M. xi
Bailer-Jones, D. M. xi
Bailey, R. 261f.
Barkow, J. H. 131
Bauplan 147f.
Bayes, K. 143
Bayesian decision theory 159
Bayle, P. 187
de Beer, G. 150f.
Beisbart, C. 57
belief 110, 159, 190; *see also*
    confidence; knowledge;
    probability
Bergson, H. 102, 189
Berkeley, G. 221
Bertrand's paradoxes 111
betting quotients 110
binding problem 131, 134f.
biology 123f.; *see also*
    adaptation; darwinism;
    evolution; natural selection
Birkhoff, G. 49–54
Black, M. 86
Blaug, M. 222f.
von Böhm-Bawerk, E. 230, 232
Bogen, J. 74
Boham, J. 143
Bohr, N. 90f.
Boland, L. A. xi, 224f.
Boltzmann, L. 75
Boniolo, G. 86, 93
Boole, G.
    Boolean algebra 7-11, 50f.
    see also Stone
Boudon, R. 211
Bransden, B. H. 90
Brink, C. 13
de Bruin, B. xi, 197

inferential definition 18, 24–27,
    30, 34
instrumentalism 85f., 88,
    101–103, 169–173, 221
intersubjectivity 39, 103, 214, 248
introspection 200, 206
intuition 39, 41–44
irrationality 199f., 203–206, 251,
    254, 257
irreversibility 57–62, 64, 68,
    71–75; *see also* asymmetry

James, I. M. 4
Japan 257
Jarvie, I. C. xv, 181, 210, 251–256
Jauch, J. M. 49
Jensen, H. D. 92
Joachain, C. J. 90
Johansson, I. 28
Johnstone, P. 9, 11
Jordan, Z. A. 231, 233
Jung, C. G. 229

Kahneman, D. 199f.
Kant, I.
    and epistemology 143, 187f.
    and Newtonian mechanics 88
    and philosophy of history
        243–49
    and science 174
    apriorism 39
    cosmopolitan purpose 244
    neo-Kantianism 182f., 193f.
    transcendental idealism 133,
        144
    universal history 244
Kaufman, T. 151
Kepler, J. 87f.
Kiefer, C. 57
Kittel, C. 89
Klappholz, K. 221
Kleene, S. C. 26
Knight, W. D. 89
knowledge 123, 125–128,
    131–139, 155f., 158–160, 262,
    264f., 269

sociology of 166
    see also belief; epistemology;
        pragmatism
König, H. ix
Koslow, A. 17–27, 31f.
Koyré, A. 149
Kraus, S. 32
Kuhn, T. S. 132
    on dogmatism 184, 255
    normal science 189, 193
    sociological approach to
        knowledge 144
    successor of logical positivism
        184
Kuipers, T. A. F. 10
Kyburg, Jr, H. E. 115

Lachmann, L. 205
Lagueux, M. xii, 198f., 207, 209f.
Lakatos, I. 132
    influence on philosophy of
        economics 222f., 225
    on crucial experiments 185
    on unfalsifiability 43, 145
    philosophy of mathematics 37f.
    successor of logical positivism
        184
Lam, V. 57
Lamarck, J.-B. 145, 147
Landau, L. 89
language 251–253, 263
Laplace, P.-S. 88
lattices 49, 51–54
law of excluded middle 50f.
law of large numbers 106
learning 261–270
Lehmann, D. 32
Leibniz, G. W. 187
Lejewski, C. 17
Lenin, V. I. 231
Lerner, B. D. 251
Le Verrier, U. J. 88
Lewis, D. K. 63, 105, 110
life 123–128
Lifshitz, E. 89
limiting cases 86

Lightning Source UK Ltd.
Milton Keynes UK
UKOW01f1328120717
305173UK00005B/523/P